Decoding Success: Indian Business Management Case Studies

OrangeBooks Publication

1st Floor, Rajhans Arcade, Mall Road, Kohka, Bhilai, Chhattisgarh - 490020

Website:**www.orangebooks.in**

© Copyright, 2024, Author with author Dr Girish Kelkar and Dr Abhay Kulkarni, Chief Editor and Director IICMR Institute

All rights reserved. No part of this book may be reproduced, stored in a retrieval system, or transmitted, in any form by any means, electronic, mechanical, magnetic, optical, chemical, manual, photocopying, recording or otherwise, without the prior written consent of its Chief Editor.

First Edition, 23rd March 2024

DECODING SUCCESS
INDIAN BUSINESS
MANAGEMENT CASE STUDIES

DR GIRISH KELKAR
CHIEF EDITOR: DR ABHAY KULKARNI

OrangeBooks Publication
www.orangebooks.in

Acknowledgement

In extending our deepest appreciation, we express our sincere gratitude to Dr Girish Kelkar and his family, whose groundbreaking work served as the cornerstone for developing this case study. Dr Girish Kelkar's unwavering dedication to the pursuit of knowledge and his commitment to enhancing the understanding of aspiring managers and industry experts in the field have been commendable.

The depth and quality of the material woven into this case study are a direct reflection of our steadfast dedication to advancing the discourse within the industry, a commitment inspired by Dr Girish Kelkar's invaluable contributions. We are privileged to have had the opportunity to build upon his scholarly foundation, and we wholeheartedly acknowledge the profound impact of his work on the domain of management studies.

Dr Girish Kelkar's mentorship and scholarly endeavours have undeniably enriched the intellectual landscape for those navigating the intricate terrain of industry practice. Though he is no longer with us, his legacy lives on through this work, serving as a testament to his enduring influence on the field. We have experience during his live session and PMI interaction during his endeavour in the MBA Department at IICMR Institute.

We express our gratitude to the editorial board members, namely Dr Sudhir Hasamnis, Dr Sh We express our gratitude to the editorial board members, namely Dr Sudhir Hasamnis, Dr Shailesh Kasande, and Dr Manisha Kulkarni, for their dedicated efforts in reviewing and enhancing the quality of the cases. We sincerely appreciate the Drishti case centre coordinators, Dr Jayasri Murali, and Dr Sarita Samson, for their tireless contributions. Special thanks are extended to Ms Puja Gawande for her meticulous collation and formatting of the cases. We extend our gratitude to the MBA community at IICMR for their collaborative efforts and invaluable contributions to this project In loving memory of Dr Girish Kelkar.

Preface

We extend our sincere gratitude to Dr Girish Kelkar, a visionary scholar whose insightful real cases have paved the way for the development of this case study. Dr Girish Kelkar's unwavering dedication to the pursuit of knowledge and his commitment to enhancing the understanding of both aspiring managers and seasoned industry experts in the field of Project Management has been truly commendable and significant.

In the pages that follow, readers will find an exploration of management intricacies inspired by the profound insights and exhaustive research encapsulated in Dr Girish Kelkar's original work. His tireless efforts and scholarly contributions have left an indelible mark on the academic landscape, setting a high standard for rigorous inquiry, intellectual rigour and industry practices for achieving business excellence.

This case study represents our collective commitment to advancing the discourse within the industry. We have endeavoured to uphold the highest standards of academic excellence, drawing extensively from Dr Girish Kelkar's thesis to illuminate key aspects of management studies. The material presented here is a testament to the depth and quality of his foundational research, which serves as the bedrock upon which this work stands.

The MBA Department at IICMR Institute acknowledges with gratitude the privilege of building upon Dr Girish Kelkar's scholarly foundation. His mentorship has been invaluable, and his endeavours have undoubtedly enriched the knowledge base for those navigating the complex landscape of industry practices of product and service industries. As IICMR embark on this journey through the intricacies of management scenarios, we invite readers to appreciate the legacy of Dr Girish Kelkar's contributions and join us in the collective pursuit of advancing management scholarship.

This case study serves as a bridge between theory and practice, fostering a deeper understanding of the challenges and opportunities that lie ahead in the dynamic domain. of management. This book is a treasure of best practices in the management discipline to achieve the next best practices to be developed in the arena of AIML & technology transformation. I am sure that professional readers after going through these case studies will be nourished with full of knowledge and thoughts.

Director IICMR Institute

Dr Abhay Kulkarni

Dedication Note

In the world of case studies, Dr Girish Kelkar stands as a luminary, and it is with great honour and enthusiasm that we present this collection of 30 meticulously documented case studies. These cases are a testament to Dr Girish Kelkar's dedication to the field and his unwavering commitment to advancing knowledge in project management.

This compilation is not merely a collection of cases; it is a gold mine of insights and learning opportunities generously shared with the academic and professional community. Dr Girish Kelkar's astute observations, analytical prowess, and depth of understanding have given birth to a resource that is invaluable for students and practitioners alike.

While these case studies bear the imprint of Dr Girish Kelkar's expertise, it is important to acknowledge the collaborative effort that has gone into refining and editing them. This book represents a synergy of minds, where the rich content provided by Dr Girish Kelkar has been meticulously curated and enhanced to ensure accessibility and relevance for a diverse audience.

We believe that this compilation will serve as a cornerstone for those in pursuit of knowledge in project management. Postgraduate and Undergraduate Management students, as well as individuals in management roles, will find these cases to be not only instructive but also illuminating in the application of theoretical concepts to real-world business scenarios.

As we release this treasure trove of case studies to the world, in his memory, we express our deepest gratitude to the late Dr Girish Kelkar for his intellectual generosity and commendable contributions to the academic and professional community. We were enriched by his contribution to IICMR while addressing Staff and Students during various flagship programmes and IICMR is privileged to convert his work in the form of case studies. May this collection inspire a new wave of insights, discussions, and advancements in the dynamic field of project management for the product and service industry. We also extend our sincere thanks to his family for handing over this treasure to us.

With profound gratitude,
Dr Abhay Kulkarni
Director, IICMR

A Special Tribute to Literary Endeavours

Some books seem to write themselves; this one most assuredly did not. Fortunately, others lent their shoulders to the task of pushing this boulder up the hill - Michael Hammer in the Acknowledgements of his book 'Agenda'.

The same thing happened with the book "Decoding Success: Indian Business Management Case Studies."

My husband, Dr Girish Kelkar, who had a long career in Engineering and Software and was working as a Management consultant with many MSMEs, was also a Project Management expert and trainer. He registered for Doctorate at the age of 63 years and completed it in 5 years. His thesis was on Project Management, 'Critical Success Factors for Projects - Indian Perspective' and he had deeply studied and presented about 30 cases in industrial and social sectors in his thesis. He wanted to publish a book on these case studies and was working on it till the end. Unfortunately, he could not complete it.

To fulfil Girish's wish to publish such a book of case studies, I approached Dr Abhay Kulkarni, Director IICMR, who was a friend and admirer of Girish. Girish used to visit IICMR frequently and was associated with the institute for their management education programmes. Dr Kulkarni agreed to take up the task of completing the Case studies book with the help of his faculty members and associates.

I am grateful to Mr Vijay Ghate, Girish's close friend and collaborator on his book, for his help and guidance in ensuring the right content and compliance of technical matters in the text.

I also want to express my sincere gratitude towards Dr Abhay Kulkarni and IICMR for all their cooperation and efforts. I would like to thank Dr Abhay Kulkarni, Director, IICMR, Dr Manisha Kulkarni, HOD, MBA @IICMR, Dr Sudhir Hasamnis, Associated Faculty, MBA@IICMR, Dr Jayasri Murali and Dr Sarita Samson, Drishti Case Centre Coordinators, Ms Puja Gavande, Assistant Professor, for their valuable contribution for completion of the book. I also thank all Faculty members at IICMR for supporting this cause.

I hope this book will be a great help for students not only in Project Management but overall understanding of business and governance.

Thanks,

Aparna Kelkar

About the Author

Dr Girish Kelkar was a Senior Management professional with 48 years of experience in the management of high technology companies including several software technology companies. He worked with members of the Board of Directors of several IT companies over the last 20 years. He was the founder Chairman of 'V3C3E3 Consultants Pvt Ltd' leading a group of hand-picked professionals.

Initially, he worked as a senior professional for Business and Engineering Applications in India and travelled across the world to set up various international operations. He directed software development projects in India, Nigeria, the UK and the USA. A man with multi-faceted experience and has worked with many MNCs & Indian Organizations (Alfa Laval AB Sweden, Satt-Control AB Sweden, Onward Technology Group India, Magic Software Enterprises Inc Israel (India & Nigeria), ALS Group Detroit USA, Core Objects Inc. USA, Jopasana Software & Systems Ltd. India, cMAT Software Group India).

Dr Girish did his Mechanical Engineering from the COEP, University of Pune and his post-graduate degree from the National Institute of Training in Industrial Engineering (NITIE). He was awarded 'The Fellowship of NITIE (PhD)-The topic for the PhD program is 'Critical Success Factors for Projects-Indian perspective'. Girish is a student of 'Jnana Prabodhini Prashala' and a member of Mensa International. He has published many professional articles and poems. He received many prestigious National and International awards for his professional contributions.

He served as a visiting faculty member at many institutions in India, Nigeria, the Middle East, South East and Canada. Girish was the past President of PMI Pune Deccan India Chapter (International Award-winning chapter for 2010) from 2008 to 2012 and won the 'Best Component Leadership Award for his professional contribution.

About the Book

Welcome to a comprehensive exploration of Indian management practices through a collection of 30 enlightening case studies. This book delves into the dynamic world of business in India, offering valuable insights and practical wisdom derived from the meticulous research work of Dr Girish Kelkar. These case studies show many different situations in Indian businesses. They help us understand the problems and successes in the Indian business world clearly and colourfully.

Dr Girish Kelkar, a distinguished scholar and researcher, has dedicated years to studying the intricacies of Indian management practices. His profound understanding of the subject is reflected in the depth and relevance of each case study presented in this compilation. Dr Kelkar's work lays the foundation for an insightful exploration of the diverse facets of management in the Indian context.

The torchbearer of this invaluable knowledge, the MBA faculty of IICMR Institute,, has taken Dr Girish Kelkar's research work to new heights. Through rigorous exploration, meticulous editing, and thoughtful presentation, the faculty has enhanced the accessibility of these case studies. Their collective expertise ensures that the content resonates with both students and professionals seeking to understand and navigate the complexities of Indian business management.

The book encompasses 30 management business case studies that span a wide spectrum of industries, providing a holistic view of the Indian business landscape. Each case study is rooted in real-world scenarios, offering practical insights that bridge the gap between theory and application. The book goes beyond surface-level analysis, offering strategic perspectives that enable readers to grasp the nuances of decision-making in the Indian business environment. for product as well as service industry from a project management perspective. Derived from Dr Girish Kelkar's research work and further refined by the MBA faculty of IICMR Institute, the book imparts practical wisdom that is directly applicable in today's dynamic business world.

This book is not just a compilation of case studies; it is a journey into the heart of Indian business management. Whether you are a student aspiring to understand the intricacies of the field or a seasoned professional seeking to navigate the nuances of Indian business, this collection will prove to be an invaluable resource. Prepare to embark on a learning experience that combines academic rigour with real-world relevance, guided by the expertise of Dr Girish Kelkar and the dedicated MBA faculty of IICMR Institute.

Content

Part 1
Case Studies

1. Case No 1: Pioneering Digital Horizons: Establishing a Joint Venture for ERP Solutions in Nigeria 2

2. Case No 2: Symphony of Success: A Technological Marvel Unveiled at the Presidential Inauguration International Sports Event Project 13

3. Case No 3: A Triumph of Leadership and Expertise in Project Management: Navigating Complex Challenges in Airlines Solutions 23

4. Case No 4: Strategic Transcendence: Pioneering an Independent Composite Material Company in India 43

5. Case No 5: Strategic Collaboration and Market Penetration: The Journey of a New Unit in Process Control Industries 55

6. Case No 6: The Uncharted Path: Unravelling the Complex Tale of APC_Avanti's Project Journey. 66

7. Case No 7: Building a New Frontier: Analytical Software Development in Bio-Science. 78

8. Case No 8: Revolutionizing Banking: A Tale of Total Branch Automation Project 94

9. Case No 9: Transformation of Concept to Industry Standard: The Unveiling of Optessa and its Global Impact on Manufacturing. 109

10. Case No 10: Mining the Challenges: A Comprehensive Analysis of a Mega EPC Project in the Indian Power Generation Sector 122

11. Case No 11: Riding the Wave of Technological Evolution: A Case Study on the Development of a Novel Banking Application 135

12. Case No 12: Project Phoenix: The Rise, Fall, and Lessons from AmanK's Chemical Chronicle 148

13. Case No 13: Master Plan for Sustainable Development: Holistic Approach to Water Management, Agriculture, Health and Education 156

14. Case No 14: Rebuilding Lives and Villages - A Tale of Rehabilitation and Transformation After the 1994 Marathwada Earthquake 170

15. Case No 15: Innovation Amidst Challenges: A Deep Dive into the Implementation of a Cutting-Edge Telecom Project in India 184

Part 2

Case Studies

16. Case No 16: Setting up a new greenfield project to design and manufacture Auto Components for OEMs 197

17. Case No 17: Setting up a new NGO to provide requisite support to handle difficulties of Destitute Women / Girl Children and Orphans 210

18. Case No 18: Building Rajiv Gandhi Setu - Bandra Worli Bridge - one of the unique and prestigious bridges in Mumbai - a long-awaited solution to traffic congestion in the Mega City innovative concept that has now become a role model in the country 227

19. Case No 19: Setting up a new Township for over 120,000 common citizens and over 50,000 visitors daily based on an innovative concept that has now become a role model in the country 250

20. Case No 20: Development of a specialized software platform for 'Metallographic Inspection' (With the help from a foreign customer) for the first time in the world in a new startup software unit 270

21. Case No 21: NM- Development of a specialized / customized IT platform for the National Stock Exchange (NSE) to ensure higher latency for the exchange (that is crucial for the efficient working of the National Stock Exchange (NSE)) for the first time in India. 283

22. Case No 22: Setting up new Steel Melting and Rolling shop for a 'Large Indian' Corporate Group in an economically backward area in Western India. 300

23. Case No 23: Case of up new Multi-Specialty Hospital set up by an NGO which was formed by young medical professionals at an early age to provide 'affordable medical services for the society at large, especially for the economically backward classes of society. 315

24. Case No 24: KGSN- Development of an innovative, comprehensive HR Database for the HR department of an Oil & Gas Industry interfacing with the existing ERP System in the Organization 335

25. Case No 25: Setting up a new railway track of strategic importance in Jammu & Kashmir for the Government of India in difficult terrain and an aggressive environment 347

26. Case No 26: Setting up of manufacturing unit for production of Decanters in India for global requirements 369

27. Case No 27: Setting up of a new greenfield project for the design and manufacture of 'Sports garments' set by a team of young highly qualified engineers 381

28. Case No 28: Case of setting up 'Food Products' startup unit in an economically backward area of Maharashtra as a startup initiative by an existing corporate organization 393

29. Case No 29: Development of an innovative, comprehensive Communication for the new International Airport of Pride 406

30. Case No 30: Case of setting up 'The Khandsary Sugar Project in an economically backward area of Maharashtra as a startup initiative by Renowned NGO 422

Part 1
Case Studies

Case No 1: Pioneering Digital Horizons: Establishing a Joint Venture for ERP Solutions in Nigeria

Dr Jayasri Murali, Mr Harshal Patil

Associate Professor, MBA@IICMR, Pune, Assistant Professor, MBA@IICMR, Pune

Acknowledgements:

We extend our sincere gratitude to Dr Girish Kelkar, whose insightful thesis laid the foundation for the creation of this case study. Dr Kelkar's untiring efforts in the pursuit of knowledge and commitment to enriching the understanding of aspiring managers and industry experts practicing in the field have been truly commendable. Our dedication to advancing the discourse within the industry is reflected in the depth and quality of the material drawn from his thesis. We are privileged to have had the opportunity to build upon his work, and we acknowledge his invaluable contribution to the realm of management studies. His mentorship and scholarly endeavours have undoubtedly benefited those navigating the complex landscape of industry practices.

Abstract:

This case study encapsulates a transformative journey undertaken by an Indian software development house. With a turnover exceeding 25 crores and a workforce surpassing 200, the organization ventured into the vibrant Nigerian market, recognizing the need for a local touch and establishing a Joint Venture (JV). Guided by a seasoned Project Manager, the JV encountered multifaceted challenges, from cultural disparities to security threats during daily commutes. However, innovation thrived amidst adversity, with the team securing a substantial contract from Chevron Nigeria, leading to the conceptualization and development of a cutting-edge Human Resource Database.

The venture emphasized inclusive growth by integrating Nigerian professionals into the team, bridging cultural divides and contributing significantly to the venture's success. Beyond the oil and gas sector, the JV's success extended to prominent players in the banking, insurance, and government sectors. The project's success was anchored in well-defined scopes, unwavering customer commitment, stellar project management, and effective risk mitigation. The legacy of this triumphant journey led to the establishment of similar ventures in other countries, further solidifying the parent organization's global footprint and showcasing the transformative power of technology in emerging markets.

1. Introduction:

A software development company, boasting a turnover exceeding 25 crores and a team exceeding 200 employees, opted to explore new business horizons in African countries, particularly Nigeria. With a seven-year track record of developing systems and modules for various Indian organizations, the company possessed the necessary skills and resources for this endeavour. Nigeria, rich in natural resources such as oil and gas, had witnessed substantial economic and industrial growth. Featuring multinational Oil & Gas companies, numerous banks, and large industrial units, the country required enhanced infrastructure for telecommunications and business software applications. This created a promising opportunity for establishing a new software development organization in Nigeria.

In due course, a basic feasibility report was crafted to delineate the requirements for setting up a new unit in Nigeria. A critical condition for establishing a unit in the country was the necessity of a local partner, mandating the establishment of a Joint Venture. Fortunately, an organization in Nigeria sought an international partner for a software unit, leading to discussions and negotiations with the Indian team. After deliberations, it was decided to proceed with the Joint Venture, and the individual leading the team in negotiating the deal became the Project Manager.

The Project Manager, aged around 48, was renowned in the industry as a competent and quality-conscious software professional. Having previously served as the Executive Director (Founder Director) in the current organization, he had extensive experience in handling international assignments and had gained the confidence of the Board Members. Following the contract signing, the management formally announced the project initiation, overcoming the initial challenges posed by the laid-back attitude of Nigerian Industry leaders. Over the years, Nigeria has continued to attract many Indian software companies.

The Joint Venture (JV) in Nigeria faced numerous challenges during this phase. The Nigerian partners in the JV lacked prior experience in managing software applications. Although there was available space, there was a lack of infrastructure for servers, networking components, computers, required software, and skilled professionals like programmers, business analysts, and system designers. Consequently, the Indian team took on the responsibility of establishing operations from the ground up. The JV partners in Nigeria offered essential support and funding for this new setup.

Moreover, working in Nigeria posed its own set of challenges for expatriates, requiring adaptation to unique social aspects. Despite these challenges, the JV partners in Nigeria actively supported and assisted visiting professionals, ensuring a reasonable work-life balance.

Unfortunately, the team faced security threats, with team members' cars being attacked over 10 times during their commute in the initial 5 years. The situation intensified in the third year when the Nigerian Managing Director of the company was tragically shot dead during travel outside his hometown. This presented a significant challenge for the Indian team, requiring them to comprehend and navigate these difficult circumstances.

Furthermore, there were ongoing tensions between the local and Indian team members right from the start. This was primarily due to cultural differences, varying levels of education, and distinct work approaches. While Indian team members were willing to work on Saturdays and Sundays, it was not feasible for their local counterparts. Additionally, the Indians received higher compensation due to their qualifications, training, and experience, causing dissatisfaction among the local team and leading to occasional confrontations.

On the business front, the JV partners had adept sales managers who swiftly uncovered various opportunities in the Nigerian market. Business operations in Nigeria followed a unique approach, emphasizing one-on-one relationships between salespersons and customers. An important client in this venture was Chevron Nigeria, open to testing a new application using the RAD (Rapid Application Development) tool. The Project Manager and three Indian developers dedicated day and night efforts to create a Proof of Concept (POC) for Chevron Nigeria, earning high praise from the customer. After extensive negotiations, Chevron Nigeria placed a substantial order of 1.2 Million USD for the complete development of a comprehensive Human Resource Database, spanning 18 months. This achievement was celebrated as the "Best Project of the Year" by Chevron HQ in the USA, acknowledging the dedication and success of the Project Manager and the entire team.

This victory significantly boosted the project team's morale, fostering high motivation among its members. Simultaneously, additional team members from India were incorporated to strengthen the project. However, it became evident that relying solely on the Indian contingent was not sustainable. Consequently, the Project Manager decided to bring in local members from the university as trainees, with six individuals joining the team. As raw resources, they required comprehensive training in concepts and hands-on development practices using the new RAD platform. This strategy proved effective and earned appreciation from local customers. Over time, the team comprised 17 members from local sources and 11 from India. Notably, some local professionals excelled over the next two years, significantly contributing to the new unit's growth alongside their Indian counterparts.

The team secured numerous orders from prominent organizations such as Shell, NAOC, Texaco, Total, and others in the Oil & Gas industry. Additionally, prestigious orders were received from leading banks and insurance companies in Nigeria, as well as from government organizations and local bodies, recognizing the JV's innovative technology platform.

In the following years, the newly formed JV experienced substantial growth, achieving a turnover of approximately 3.2 Million USD by the end of the fifth year. This success, despite various challenges faced by the team on personal and organizational levels, was highly appreciated by all stakeholders. The team effectively capitalized on the presented opportunity, navigating through the lack of matured systems platforms and grappling with domain knowledge from diverse industry-based applications. Undoubtedly, this project posed significant challenges for the team.

2. Objectives and Milestones in the Nigerian Joint Venture:

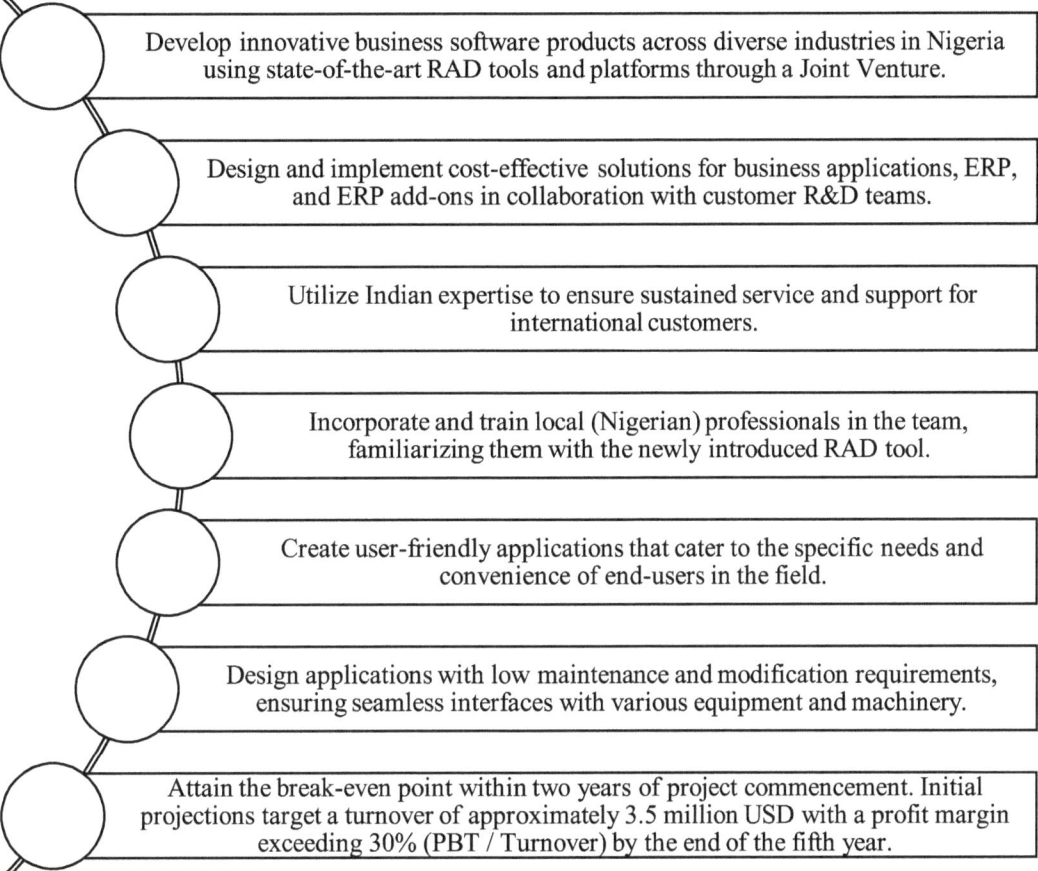

- Develop innovative business software products across diverse industries in Nigeria using state-of-the-art RAD tools and platforms through a Joint Venture.
- Design and implement cost-effective solutions for business applications, ERP, and ERP add-ons in collaboration with customer R&D teams.
- Utilize Indian expertise to ensure sustained service and support for international customers.
- Incorporate and train local (Nigerian) professionals in the team, familiarizing them with the newly introduced RAD tool.
- Create user-friendly applications that cater to the specific needs and convenience of end-users in the field.
- Design applications with low maintenance and modification requirements, ensuring seamless interfaces with various equipment and machinery.
- Attain the break-even point within two years of project commencement. Initial projections target a turnover of approximately 3.5 million USD with a profit margin exceeding 30% (PBT / Turnover) by the end of the fifth year.

Figure 1.1: Objectives and Milestones in the Nigerian Joint Venture

3. Project Challenges:

Operational and Infrastructural Hurdles	Cultural and Social Dynamics	Security and Safety Concerns:	Human Resource Management	Market and Technology Dynamics
• Inexperienced Local Partners: • Infrastructure Deficiency	• Cultural Adaptation • Tensions Between Teams	• Security Threats • Incident of Violence	• Dependence on Indian Contingent • Local Resource Integration	• Market-Specific Operations • Technology Implementation

Figure 1.2: Project Challenges

Inexperienced Local Partners: The Nigerian joint venture lacked prior experience in managing software application activities, necessitating substantial support and guidance from the Indian team.

Infrastructure Deficiency: Nigeria presented challenges with inadequate infrastructure, including servers, networking components, computers, and essential software, requiring the Indian arm to establish operations from the ground up.

Cultural Adaptation: Working in Nigeria posed cultural challenges for expatriates, demanding adjustments to unique social aspects and potential tensions between local and Indian team members.

Tensions Between Teams: Ongoing cultural and work style differences causing tensions between local and Indian team members. As the project progressed, the challenge of expanding the team to meet growing project demands and ensure continued success arose.

Security Threats: The team faced security risks, with team members cars being attacked over ten times during their commute and the tragic incident of the Nigerian Managing Director being shot dead during travel.

Incident of Violence: Tragic shooting incident involving the Nigerian Managing Director during travel.

Cultural and Work Style Differences: Differences in work culture, education levels, and work approaches between local and Indian team members led to ongoing tensions and occasional confrontations.

Dependence on Indian Contingent: Relying solely on the Indian team was deemed imprudent over time, leading to the decision to incorporate and train local members from Nigerian universities.

Training Local Resources: Inducting local members as trainees required thorough training in concepts and hands-on development practices on the new RAD platform.

Market-Specific Operations: The Nigerian market operated uniquely, emphasizing one-on-one relationships between salespersons and customers, demanding an understanding of and adaptation to this approach.

Technology Implementation: The team had to grapple with implementing technology in an environment where matured systems platforms were lacking, and diverse industry-based applications required domain knowledge.

These challenges, though formidable, were navigated successfully, contributing to the ultimate success of the joint venture in Nigeria.

4. Diamond Analysis of the Project Complexity:

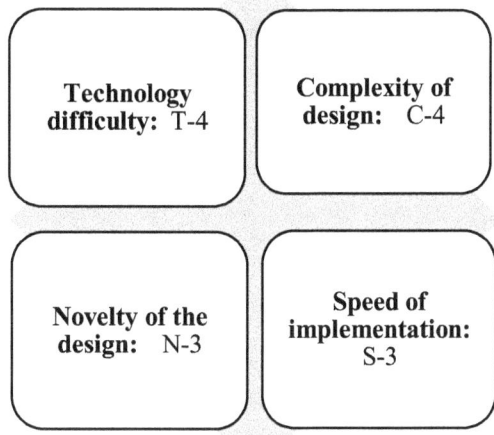

Figure 1.3: Diamond Analysis of the Project Complexity

5. "Project Overview":

The project, with a budget of USD 1.2 million over 5 years, aimed at establishing a new Joint Venture in Nigeria for developing Business Applications/ERP modules. The team composition included 10 members in the Head Office/QA/QC Group and 3 on-site members, peaking at around 40 members. Facing ambitious timelines, the project held the crucial objective of achieving a turnover exceeding USD 3.5 million. Challenges included training Nigerian employees unfamiliar with the RAD tool and a high-risk factor due to the new technology's untested nature. With no specific role for suppliers, logistics and clearances presented challenges, but the multi-location team coordination was manageable. Senior management provided excellent support, and customers, although initially sceptical about Indian software capabilities, became strong supporters. The competent Project Manager played a pivotal role, especially during challenging moments, showcasing adept leadership skills.

6. Key players in the team:

Figure: 1.4 Key Players in the team

Positive Aspects in the Project Ecosystem:

On the brighter side, the project environment exhibited numerous positive factors:

i. **Senior Management and Foreign Partners Support:** The project benefited from unwavering support from both senior management and foreign partners.

ii. **Focused and Detailed Planning:** The team maintained a high level of focus and diligently followed a detailed implementation plan in collaboration with customer personnel.

iii. **Effective Communication:** Continuous dialogue between the Customer Project Manager, local Project Manager, and the team facilitated swift issue resolution, ensuring the timely completion of the project. Regular monthly or quarterly project meetings attended by senior managers from both sides promoted proactive decision-making.

iv. **Harmonious Team Dynamics:** A harmonious team environment laid the foundation for a quality and undisturbed work atmosphere, contributing significantly to the project's success.

v. **Pre-dispatch Inspections:** Rigorous pre-dispatch inspections involving both local and customer QA/QC teams streamlined on-site software implementation, minimizing delays and waiting periods.

vi. **Decision-making Freedom:** The team enjoyed full freedom for decision-making and committing expenses in alignment with the Project Manager's decisions, fostering a smooth working process for the entire team.

7. Success Factors for Diverse Stakeholders:

Organizational Aspirations:

Punctual and High-Quality Project Delivery: Achieving project completion within the designated timeline while upholding quality standards.

Adherence to Stringent Industry Norms: Conforming to the rigorous standards set for the oil & gas and banking sectors.

Profitability Attainment: Realizing the projected profitability for the project.

Exemplary Application Development: Creating the application as a benchmark project for potential future business ventures.

Repeat Business Acquisition: Securing additional orders from the same customer.

Customer/User Anticipations:

Timely Delivery and Efficient Implementation: Ensuring the project is delivered on schedule and implemented seamlessly.

ROI Achievement: Attaining the committed Return on Investment (ROI) from the project.

Robust Support and Handholding: Providing steadfast support and guidance during the implementation phase.

Quality Documentation: Supplying top-notch documentation and expediting the process for add-on module development.

Team Members' Contentment:

Ensured Team Satisfaction: Guaranteeing the contentment of the project team members.

Skill and Domain Expertise Development: Fostering the acquisition of new skills and domain expertise to support the team's future growth.

8. Post-Completion Insights: Project Success Factors Identified by the Team:

Reflecting on the project's conclusion, discussions with the team members and the Project Manager highlighted critical success factors (CSFs) that, in retrospect, would have been instrumental. While these factors were not explicitly considered at the project's initiation, they proved invaluable for the team:

Clarity of Task and Scope: Emphasizing the importance of a clear understanding of tasks, scope, and specifications.

Customer Team Commitment: Recognizing the significance of unwavering commitment and active participation from customer teams throughout the project life cycle.

Senior Management Support: Acknowledging the need for complete support from senior management, granting necessary freedom for decisive actions.

Competent Project Manager and Trustworthy Team: Valuing the competence of the Project Manager and the trustworthiness of the entire team.

Alert Risk Management: Appreciating the role of alert risk management, especially concerning timelines, design, and changes during Proof of Concept (POC) and User Acceptance Testing (UAT).

Controlled Project Progress: Recognizing the importance of maintaining control over project progress through impeccable communication and coordination.

PMO Personnel Support: Appreciating the excellent support provided by Project Management Office (PMO) personnel in ruthlessly tracking issues and resolving them promptly.

QA/QC and Process Control Support: Valuing the strong support from Quality Assurance (QA), Quality Control (QC) teams, and process control engineers, attributable to robust processes in the parent organization.

Exceptional Teamwork and Task Force Support: Highlighting the exceptional teamwork and unwavering support from task force members.

Legal and Administrative Support: Recognizing the importance of good support from Legal Experts and Administrative teams.

Project Environment Impact Awareness: Acknowledging the significance of understanding the impact of project environments, encompassing social, geo-political, cultural, and local political factors, on both the project and team members.

Questions:

1. How did the Project Manager navigate and address the cultural differences between the Indian team and the local team members in Nigeria, especially considering variations in work approaches, work hours, and cultural nuances?

2. Considering the security challenges faced by the team in Nigeria, particularly the attacks on team members' cars and the unfortunate incident involving the Managing Director, how did the Project Manager ensure the safety and well-being of the team while maintaining project momentum?

3. Considering the challenges related to the scarcity of domain experts and the unfamiliarity of the Nigerian team with the RAD tool, how did the Project Manager strategize and execute training programs to bridge the skill gap and ensure effective collaboration between Indian and Nigerian team members?

Teaching note

Case No 1: "Pioneering Digital Horizons: Establishing a Joint Venture for ERP Solutions in Nigeria".

I. Case Overview

The case explores the challenges and triumphs of an Indian software development company's journey into the Nigerian market through a Joint Venture (JV). The focus is on the Project Manager's role in navigating cultural differences, security threats, and skill gaps to establish a successful venture.

II. Learning Objectives

- Understand the complexities of cross-cultural project management.
- Analyze strategies for addressing security challenges in a foreign business environment.
- Explore methods to bridge skill gaps and foster collaboration in a diverse team.

III. Pre-Class Preparation

- Students to review the case study and identify key challenges faced by the JV.
- Research on Nigeria's business environment, cultural nuances, and security concerns.

IV. In-Class Discussion

a. Cultural Differences and Team Dynamics

- Explore how cultural disparities impacted work approaches, work hours, and team dynamics.
- Discuss the Project Manager's strategies to bridge cultural divides and foster a harmonious team environment.
- Encourage students to propose alternative approaches to address cultural challenges.

b. Security Challenges

- Analyze the security threats faced by the team, including attacks on team members' cars and the tragic incident involving the Managing Director.
- Discuss the Project Manager's actions to ensure the team's safety while maintaining project momentum.
- Explore the role of local partnerships and government liaisons in managing security concerns.

c. Skill Gap and Training Programs

- Examine the challenges related to the scarcity of domain experts and the unfamiliarity of the Nigerian team with the RAD tool.
- Discuss the Project Manager's training strategies to bridge the skill gap and integrate local team members effectively.
- Explore alternative training approaches and their potential impact on project success.

V. Post-Class Reflection

- Discuss the success factors highlighted by the team post-completion.
- Reflect on the critical success factors (CSFs) identified, emphasizing their importance in project management.
- Encourage students to relate the case to real-world scenarios and propose recommendations for future international ventures.

VI. Assessment

- Individual or group assignments on proposing strategies for effective cross-cultural communication.
- Case analysis papers discussing alternative approaches to address security challenges.
- Presentation on designing comprehensive training programs for diverse teams.

VII. Additional Resources

- Relevant articles, books, or videos on cross-cultural project management.
- Case studies on successful international joint ventures in challenging environments.
- Guest speakers with experience in international business operations.

VIII. Conclusion

The case provides a rich learning experience, offering insights into the complexities of international business ventures. It encourages students to think critically, propose solutions, and apply theoretical concepts to real-world challenges.

Case No. 2: Symphony of Success: A Technological Marvel Unveiled at the Presidential Inauguration International Sports Event Project

Dr Jayasri Murali, Mrs Dipti Bajpai

Associate Professor, IICMR, Pune, Assistant Professor, IICMR, Pune

Acknowledgements:

We extend our sincere gratitude to Dr Girish Kelkar, whose insightful thesis laid the foundation for the creation of this case study. Dr Kelkar's untiring efforts in the pursuit of knowledge and commitment to enriching the understanding of aspiring managers and industry experts practicing in the field have been truly commendable. Our dedication to advancing the discourse within the industry is reflected in the depth and quality of the material drawn from his thesis. We are privileged to have had the opportunity to build upon his work, and we acknowledge his invaluable contribution to the realm of management studies. His mentorship and scholarly endeavours have undoubtedly benefited those navigating the complex landscape of industry practice.

Abstract:

In the realm of cutting-edge endeavours spearheaded by an Indian division of a global technology powerhouse, an innovative project took shape. Tasked with orchestrating the audio landscape for the inauguration of an international sports event by the President, the mission was to craft a state-of-the-art Public Address and Sound Reinforcement System. Navigating tight deadlines, intricate design criteria, and unprecedented specifications, this project emerged as a harmonious blend of complexity and ingenuity.

Valued at $4 million, a team of 100 embarked on a journey through uncharted territories, grappling not only with technical challenges but also the weight of national prestige. What began as scepticism from some transformed into unwavering support from senior management, empowering the team to confront challenges with commitment and innovative solutions.

This project, categorized as a diamond in technological challenges, necessitated a groundbreaking system designed and constructed in India. As logistical hurdles, supplier intricacies, and multi-location coordination were surmounted, the team forged a path to success guided by transparent communication and meticulous planning.

Amidst high stakes, the project emerged triumphant, resonating through flawless soundscapes at the Presidential inauguration. The R&D team's innovation became a benchmark, with the system adopted as a standard offering by the parent organization. In this narrative of audacity, commitment, and technological prowess, the project not only surpassed expectations but also established a new benchmark for global technological achievements.

Keywords: Technology Innovation, Public Address System, International Sports Event, Project Management, Sound Reinforcement.

1. Introduction:

In the landscape of technological innovation and global leadership, a pioneering project unfolded under the auspices of an Indian division of a renowned multinational technology company. This venture was commissioned for a momentous occasion - the inauguration of an international sports event by the President of the country. The genesis of this project can be traced back to a Request for Proposal (RFP) initiated by the organizing committee responsible for the prestigious international event.

This undertaking bore immense significance as it not only showcased technological prowess but also carried the weight of national prestige. The project's inception was marked by a confluence of challenges: a compressed timeline of less than nine months, the intricate nature of the system design, and the demanding specifications that called for innovative features. Notably, the proposed system was poised to be a trailblazer, not just within the country but on a global scale, incorporating state-of-the-art concepts and critical microprocessor-based systems.

The unique challenge lay in the fact that the system had to be designed and built in India, as importing a complete system was not permissible. This added an extra layer of complexity to an already intricate project. Despite the scepticism of some within the organization who questioned the feasibility of undertaking such a sophisticated project in India, the senior management at both the Indian division and the European headquarters exhibited unwavering confidence in the appointed project manager. Consequently, the decision was made to undertake this ambitious project in India.

As the project unfolded, it assumed a classification denoting its exceptional challenges: a Technology Difficulty level of 4, a Complexity of Design at 5, a Novelty of Design rated at 5, and a Speed of Implementation level of 4. The specifications for the system were meticulously crafted by a technically skilled group of consultants in collaboration with the client's technical committee. The system, along with its variants, was slated for deployment across seven different stadiums, each with stringent technical specifications.

The project team faced unprecedented challenges, as the time constraints didn't allow for mature, field-tested systems. Despite these hurdles, the project moved forward with determination and a clear vision. This venture, positioned at the intersection of technology, innovation, and national pride, marked a defining moment in the realm of electronic development in India.

2. Project Initiation and Significance:

The genesis of this transformative venture lies in the proactive efforts of the Indian division of a global technology leader. Fuelled by a vision to showcase technological prowess on a grand scale, the project was initiated to craft an unparalleled experience for the inauguration of an international sports event, a ceremony graced by the esteemed presence of the President.

The significance of this project cannot be overstated. The international sports event represented a global platform, drawing attention to the prowess of the host nation not only in athletic competition but also in technological innovation. The inauguration by the President elevated the event's prestige, adding a layer of national importance to the project. The confluence of cutting-edge technology and a high-profile inauguration set the stage for a venture that went beyond routine projects, becoming a beacon of technological achievement on the global stage.

3. Challenges and Risk Assessment:

Embarking on the ambitious journey of orchestrating a ground-breaking project for the international sports event inauguration, the team encountered a myriad of challenges that demanded meticulous risk assessment and strategic planning.

Challenges and Risk Assessment:

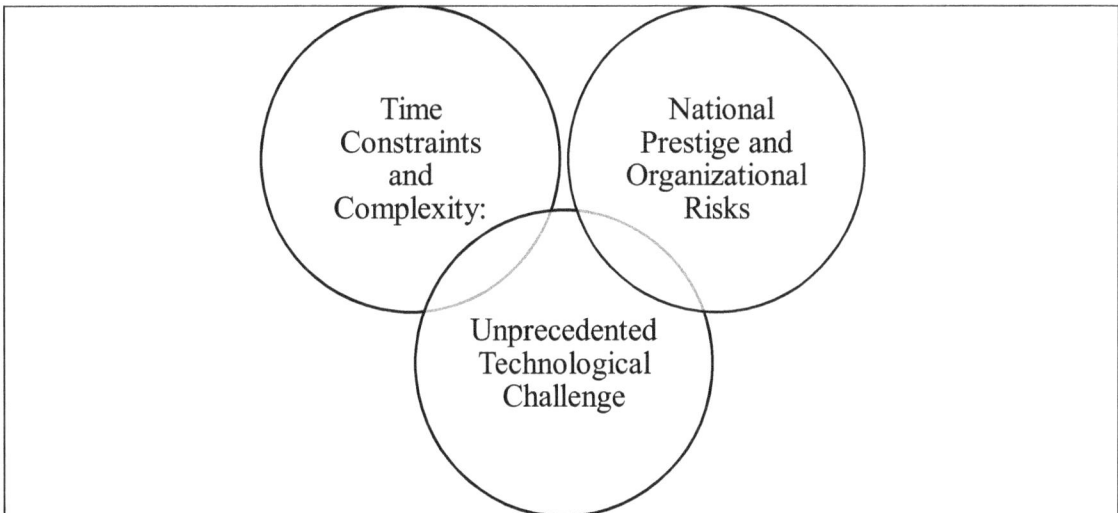

Figure 3. 1 - Challenges and Risk Assessment

Time Constraints and Complexity: The project operated within an exceptionally tight timeline, with less than nine months for design and implementation. This compressed schedule exacerbated the complexity of the task at hand, requiring the team to work seamlessly and with unparalleled efficiency.

Unprecedented Technological Challenges: Introducing a first-of-its-kind Public Address and Sound Reinforcement System not only in the country but globally, the project grappled with unparalleled technological challenges. The demand for innovative features and state-of-the-art concepts heightened the complexity of system design, pushing the boundaries of conventional technology.

National Prestige and Organizational Risks: The stakes were elevated by the involvement of national prestige. The success of the project wasn't just a matter of technological achievement; it had direct implications for the country's reputation. Failure was not an option, and the organizational risks were unprecedented, demanding a level of precision and commitment beyond the norm.

Navigating through these challenges required a strategic approach to risk assessment, ensuring that each obstacle was identified, analysed, and mitigated to safeguard the success of the project and the reputation of the nation. The project team had to balance innovation with risk management, addressing challenges head-on while maintaining a focus on the end goal.

4. Project Classification and Diamond Analysis:

The complexity and significance of the project were systematically assessed using a classification framework and a diamond analysis, providing a structured understanding of its nature.

Diamond Analysis of Project Complexity:

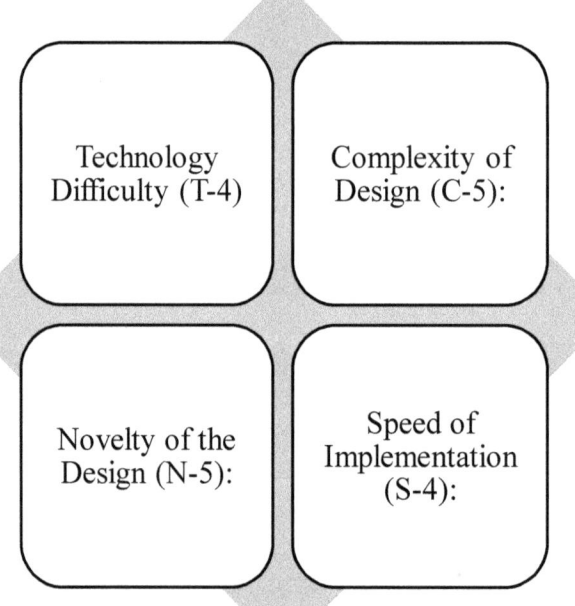

Figure 4.1- Diamond Analysis of Project Complexity

Technology Difficulty (T-4): The project's technological challenge was rated at Level 4, indicating a high degree of complexity. The innovative nature of the Public Address and Sound Reinforcement System, coupled with the demand for state-of-the-art concepts, pushed the boundaries of conventional technology. The team was tasked with navigating uncharted territory, contributing to the elevated T-4 classification.

Complexity of Design (C-5): With a Complexity of Design level set at 5, the intricacy of the system surpassed conventional norms. Crafting a first-of-its-kind system demanded a meticulous design approach, considering not only the innovative features but also the integration of critical microprocessor-based components. The project's complexity was thus classified at the highest level, denoted by C-5.

Novelty of the Design (N-5): The Novelty of the Design factor was classified at Level 5, emphasizing the ground-breaking nature of the project. The system's uniqueness, both nationally and internationally, sets it apart as a pioneer in the field. The demand for innovative features and a design that had never been implemented before underscored the project's novelty and its N-5 classification.

Speed of Implementation (S-4): Operating within a compressed timeline of less than nine months, the Speed of Implementation was rated at Level 4. The need for swift and efficient execution added another layer of complexity to the project. Balancing innovation with time constraints, the team worked diligently to meet the ambitious schedule, earning the project an S-4 classification.

This diamond analysis not only provides a quantitative assessment of the project's challenges but also offers a qualitative understanding of its ground-breaking and complex nature. The classification underscores the project's status as a technological marvel with unprecedented demands and a commitment to pushing the boundaries of innovation.

5. Specifications and System Design:

The crux of the project lay in the meticulous crafting of specifications and the intricacies of system design, both of which played pivotal roles in shaping the trajectory of the ground-breaking venture.

Specifications and System Design:

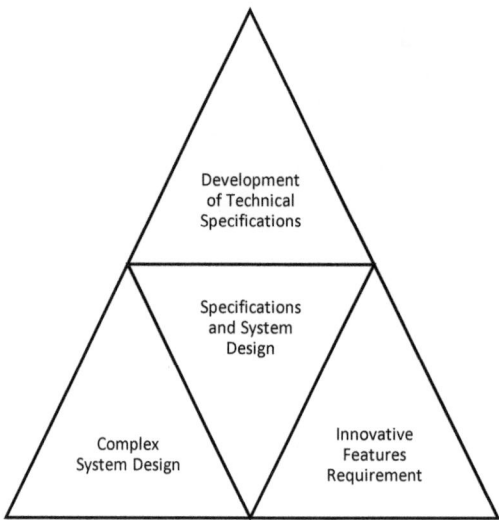

Figure 5 1 Specifications and System Design

Development of Technical Specifications: The specifications for the Public Address and Sound Reinforcement System were not just a set of requirements; they were a roadmap for innovation. A powerful and technically astute group of consultants collaborated with the client's technical committee in extensive discussions and negotiations to articulate specifications that would not only meet the demands of the international sports event but also set a new standard in audio technology.

Complex System Design: The complexity of the project manifested in the intricacies of system design. Crafting a first-of-its-kind system meant transcending conventional boundaries. The design had to incorporate innovative features, adhere to stringent technical specifications, and integrate critical microprocessor-based systems. It was not merely about functionality; it was about creating an immersive and flawless audio experience on a scale never attempted before.

Innovative Features Requirement: The system's design went beyond the ordinary, necessitating the incorporation of innovative features. Whether it was enhancing the clarity of sound in large stadiums or implementing cutting-edge concepts, the design phase was characterized by a commitment to pushing technological boundaries. The specifications, demanding in their nature, paved the way for a system that was not just functional but revolutionary.

The synergy between specifications and system design formed the backbone of the project. The specifications, forged through extensive consultations, provided the blueprint for the system's capabilities, while the design phase was an intricate dance between innovation and adherence to the unique demands of the project. Together, they set the stage for a technological marvel that would redefine standards in the realm of audio technology.

Logistics and Constraints: Navigating the intricate web of logistics and overcoming constraints presented a formidable challenge in the realization of the ground-breaking Public Address and Sound Reinforcement System.

Designing and Building in India: The stipulation that the system had to be designed and built in India imposed a distinctive set of challenges. This mandate not only underscored the commitment to domestic technological capabilities but also introduced logistical intricacies, including the need to develop a system that could rival international standards and withstand the scrutiny of a global stage.

Challenges of Import Restrictions: Import restrictions added a layer of complexity. The project demanded a unique approach as the system could not be imported as a complete unit. The team had to navigate regulatory frameworks and logistical intricacies to source critical components while ensuring compliance with import restrictions, thereby challenging conventional procurement practices.

Supplier Networks and Critical Components: The success of the project hinged on effective collaboration with a network of suppliers. Coordinating with over 25 critical component suppliers, the team faced the challenge of procuring and integrating essential elements into the system. The intricate nature of the project demanded a level of support and responsiveness from suppliers that went beyond the ordinary.

Meeting these logistical challenges and constraints required a strategic approach. The team had to forge strong partnerships with suppliers, devise innovative procurement strategies, and ensure that the constraints imposed by import regulations did not compromise the integrity of the system. The success of the project, despite these logistical complexities, underscored the resilience and strategic acumen of the project team in overcoming these challenges.

Team Structure and Leadership: The success of the ground-breaking venture was not only dependent on technological innovation but also on the strategic composition of the team and the adept leadership that steered it through uncharted waters.

6. Key Team Positions:

The team was meticulously crafted to bring together expertise from various domains crucial to the project's success as depicted in the following picture. Project Manager: Overseeing the entire project and ensuring its alignment with goals.

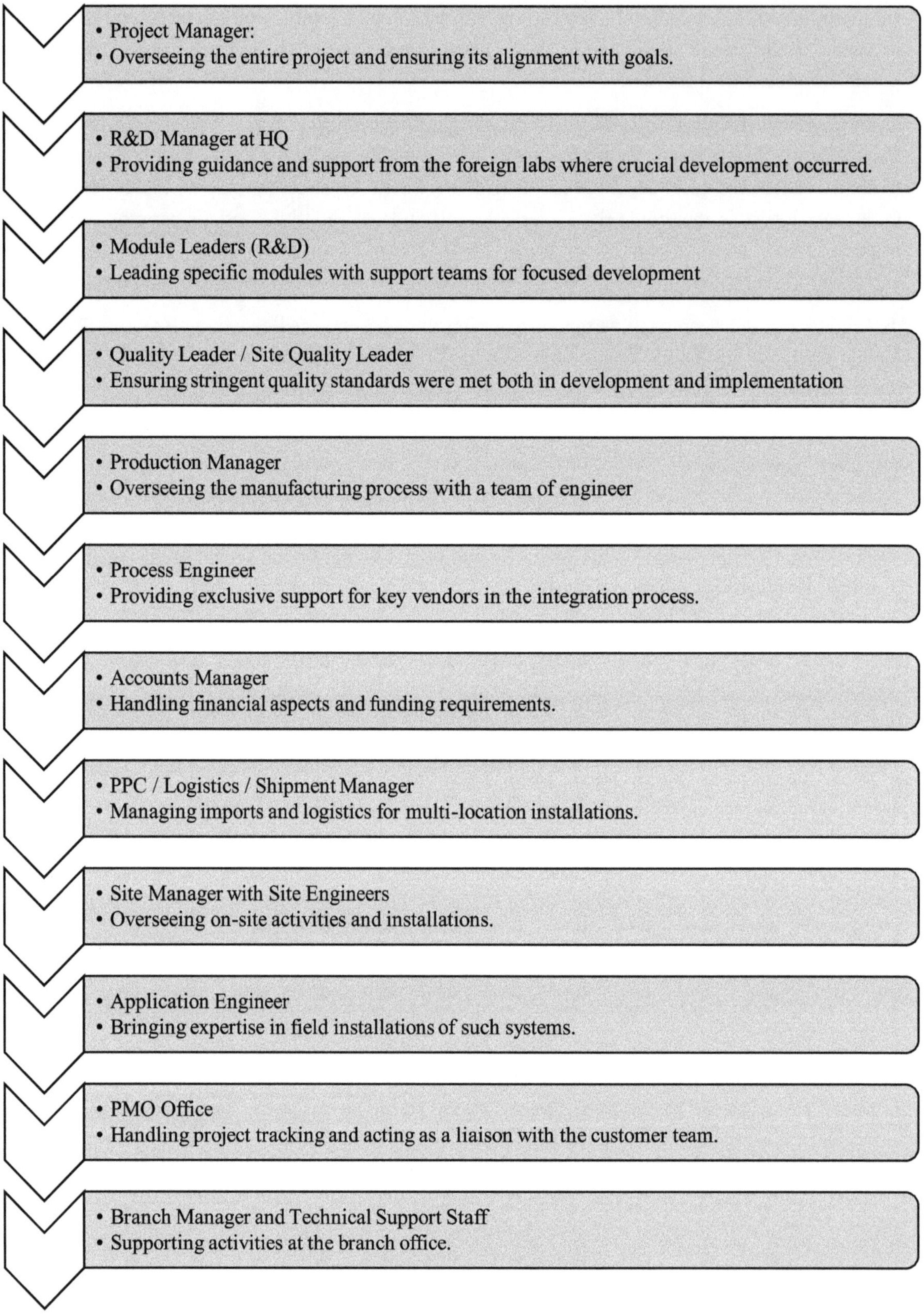

- **Project Manager:**
  - Overseeing the entire project and ensuring its alignment with goals.

- **R&D Manager at HQ**
  - Providing guidance and support from the foreign labs where crucial development occurred.

- **Module Leaders (R&D)**
  - Leading specific modules with support teams for focused development

- **Quality Leader / Site Quality Leader**
  - Ensuring stringent quality standards were met both in development and implementation

- **Production Manager**
  - Overseeing the manufacturing process with a team of engineer

- **Process Engineer**
  - Providing exclusive support for key vendors in the integration process.

- **Accounts Manager**
  - Handling financial aspects and funding requirements.

- **PPC / Logistics / Shipment Manager**
  - Managing imports and logistics for multi-location installations.

- **Site Manager with Site Engineers**
  - Overseeing on-site activities and installations.

- **Application Engineer**
  - Bringing expertise in field installations of such systems.

- **PMO Office**
  - Handling project tracking and acting as a liaison with the customer team.

- **Branch Manager and Technical Support Staff**
  - Supporting activities at the branch office.

Figure 6.1- Key Team Positions:

Leadership Competence:

The success of the project rested heavily on the competence of the leadership team, particularly the Project Manager. This individual, along with three seasoned seniors, possessed a track record of competence and experience, including exposure to international projects. The decision to entrust the project to this team was pivotal, and their confidence in navigating complex R&D projects proved to be a driving force.

1. Decision to Set Up Project in India:

The decision to set up such a high-stakes project in India was not without its sceptics. However, the unwavering faith of senior management in both the Indian and European headquarters played a decisive role. The Project Manager's competence, coupled with the trust bestowed upon the team, set the tone for a venture that defied conventional expectations.

The strategic alignment of key positions and the astute leadership provided a solid foundation for the project. The team's collective competence, guided by a seasoned Project Manager, instilled confidence and determination, crucial elements in steering a project with unprecedented challenges to success.

2. R&D Team Challenges:

The R&D team encountered a myriad of challenges throughout the design and development of the microprocessor-based Public Address System for seven stadiums. The primary hurdle was the novelty of the design, pushing the team to explore uncharted territories in electronic development. The compressed timeline of less than nine months posed a significant constraint, leaving little room for the luxury of matured, field-tested systems. The team of 15 members grappled with balancing innovation with the stringent specifications outlined for the system. Additionally, the lack of adequate testing infrastructure in India for the proposed system added complexity, requiring the team to devise innovative solutions to ensure the system's reliability and performance. Despite these challenges, the team's unwavering commitment and trust in their leader propelled them to overcome obstacles and deliver a ground-breaking solution. The leader and three seniors had field expertise with international projects

3. Testing and Field Implementation:

Testing and field implementation presented a unique set of challenges and innovative solutions for the R&D team. With insufficient testing infrastructure in India, the team opted for on-site testing, a decision driven by the project's time constraints. This risky approach required the team to anticipate potential issues and prepare extra components for on-the-spot modifications. Some imported components had to be modified in the field due to integration challenges. The coordination of multi-locational activities added another layer of complexity, demanding effective communication and collaboration. Despite these challenges, the active involvement of customer personnel and the cooperative support from suppliers and consultants played pivotal roles in ensuring the successful testing and field implementation of the system.

4. Success Criteria and Factors:

The success criteria for the project were carefully delineated to capture the multifaceted nature of the venture. Timely and simultaneous delivery of the system to seven different sites, 100% conformance to the specified Sound Reinforcement system requirements, the satisfaction of customers, consultants, and senior management, contentment of suppliers with reasonable margins, and the acknowledgement and appreciation of the project team were identified as key success factors. These criteria reflected not only the technical success of the system but also the satisfaction and collaboration of all stakeholders involved. The factors contributing to the success of the project included meticulous feasibility studies, clarity in scope and specifications, unwavering commitment from the senior management, a competent project manager, vigilant risk management, robust support from suppliers, effective communication, and exceptional teamwork from the entire task force.

Conclusion and Post-Project Reflection:

In retrospect, the project stands as a testament to the triumph of innovation and perseverance. The inaugural function, graced by the President, was an outstanding success, garnering praise from both national and international experts. The system developed by the R&D team not only met but exceeded expectations, becoming the standard offering by the parent organization. The success was not merely technological; it was a harmonious blend of meticulous planning, effective teamwork, and strategic decision-making. The challenges faced, from design intricacies to time constraints, were navigated with ingenuity and resilience. The project's positive impact reverberated beyond the technological realm, establishing a legacy of achievement for the entire team and contributing to the global recognition of India's capabilities in electronic development.

Questions:

1. As an R&D manager, how would you address the unique challenge of designing and developing a microprocessor-based Public Address System within a compressed timeline of fewer than nine months? What strategic approaches and resource allocations would you consider to ensure success?

2. Given the complex nature of the project, involving innovative features and stringent specifications, how would you foster a collaborative and innovative environment within the R&D team to overcome challenges and meet the project's objectives?

3. Considering the lack of matured, field-tested systems due to the project's time constraints, how would you approach the testing and field implementation phase? What measures would you put in place to mitigate risks and ensure the reliability of the system in diverse stadium environments?

Case No: 3 - A Triumph of Leadership and Expertise in Project Management: Navigating Complex Challenges in Airlines Solutions

Dr Jayasri Murali, Dr Sarita Samson

Associate Professor, IICMR, Pune, Assistant Professor, IICMR, Pune

Acknowledgements:

We extend our sincere gratitude to Dr Girish Kelkar, whose insightful thesis laid the foundation for the creation of this case study. Dr Kelkar's untiring efforts in the pursuit of knowledge and commitment to enriching the understanding of aspiring managers and industry experts practicing in the field have been truly commendable. Our dedication to advancing the discourse within the industry is reflected in the depth and quality of the material drawn from his thesis. We are privileged to have had the opportunity to build upon his work, and we acknowledge his invaluable contribution to the realm of management studies. His mentorship and scholarly endeavours have undoubtedly benefited those navigating the complex landscape of industry practice

Abstract:

This case study describes the development of a new revenue accounting system for a major airline. The project was complex and challenging, as the software had to be able to handle a wide range of regulations and rules. The company faced several challenges, including:

The software was for a relatively new segment of the market, so there were few domain experts available.

- The time pressure was enormous, as the airline needed the system in a short period.
- The team faced many technical challenges, such as database usage and network effectiveness.
- Preparing test data was a major challenge due to the complexity of the application and domain environment.

Despite these challenges, the project team was able to deliver the project on time and within budget. This was due to a number of factors, including:

- Close involvement of the customer.
- Commitment to documentation.
- Effective communication skills.
- Trust in each other and their leadership.
- Technical support from the customer IT team.

The project team did a good job of managing the risks associated with the project. They identified the risks early on and developed mitigation plans. They were also able to adapt to changes in the project scope and requirements. The project team's hard work and dedication paid off. They were able to deliver a complex and challenging project on time and within budget. This case study provides valuable lessons for other project teams.

Keywords: revenue accounting, airlines, success, project management, challenges, lessons learned.

1. Introduction:

In the heart of the thriving metropolis, where the technological heartbeat reverberated through the towering buildings, our protagonist, a seasoned software professional, found himself at a pivotal juncture in his career. The sun cast long shadows across the gleaming glass facades as he made his way to an evening meeting that would forever change the course of his professional journey.

The protagonist is an eminent expert who is far from an ordinary individual. With over two decades of industry experience under his belt, he has earned a reputation as a competent and quality-conscious software expert. His name resonated in the corridors of the organization he had called home for more than ten years. And now, his skills and leadership were about to be put to the ultimate test.

The organization he was a part of was a major player in the realm of software development. With a substantial turnover exceeding 400 crore and a workforce exceeding 2000 skilled professionals, it had the infrastructure and expertise to tackle complex challenges.

On that evening, he received an invitation from his boss, a meeting that held an atmosphere of eager anticipation. As he entered the office, he was greeted by an atmosphere charged with excitement and possibilities. His boss couldn't hide the smile of accomplishment.

With a gleam in his eye, the boss began to unveil an audacious plan. The organization, with its prior success in developing similar applications for a prominent Indian client, was setting its sights on an even grander endeavour - the creation of an "Airlines Revenue Accounting and Claims Settlement" system for one of the world's leading airlines. It was an opportunity of colossal proportions.

The knowledge and expertise accumulated during the successful execution of the previous project had fuelled the organization's confidence to compete on the international stage. In a fierce battle against four other vendors, the team had toiled tirelessly to craft a flawless Proof of Concept (POC). The international client's satisfaction with this endeavour was the final push needed to secure the monumental contract. And so, the deal was sealed, setting the stage for a project of immense significance.

The protagonist, with his wealth of experience and a deep understanding of the airline industry, emerged as the natural choice for the role of Project Manager. However, the enormity of this assignment was clear to everyone. The project was more than just a lucrative contract; it was a lifeline for the newly formed Airlines Application Division within the organization. Its success was not only imperative for the present but for the future, as the contract included the potential for Annual Maintenance Contracts (AMC) spanning the next five years.

With a contract size hovering around 5 million USD and a workforce of nearly 30 professionals, the task at hand was colossal. The clock was ticking, and there was immense pressure to deliver within a strict timeframe. The client's IT team had committed to an aggressive schedule, adding to the urgency.

This was no ordinary software project. It involved the intricate and high-stakes world of airline revenue accounting and claims settlement, a domain riddled with complex regulations, pricing structures, and agreements. Accuracy and precision were non-negotiable, and the team had to navigate a labyrinth of rules governing ticketing, cancellations, payments to other airlines, and intricate schemes.

Moreover, the technology landscape was evolving rapidly, and the chosen technology stack was relatively new in the Indian market. Domain experts were scarce, and time was of the essence, exacerbated by the impending closure of the existing plant.

However, despite these formidable challenges, there was an unwavering belief in the capabilities of the team, nurtured by robust support from the organization's senior management and the customers themselves. Clearances and logistics hurdles were met with determination, and the multi-location project coordination was tackled with precision.

As the protagonist stepped into this daunting yet exhilarating journey, he knew that his leadership would be tested, but he was resolute. The stakes were high, and the road was fraught with complexity, yet the vision was crystal clear - to craft a solution that would not only meet the client's expectations but also set new standards in the realm of airline revenue accounting.

This case, a narrative of ambition, challenge, and the pursuit of excellence unveil the importance of this project in the annals of software development and organizational growth. It embodies the spirit of innovation and unwavering commitment to deliver the extraordinary.

The airline industry, characterized by its dynamic nature and global reach, presents a myriad of intricate challenges that demand innovative solutions. As airlines strive to maintain operational efficiency, ensure passenger satisfaction, and optimize revenue streams, the complexities they encounter are multifaceted and ever-evolving.

2. Complexities in the Airlines Industry:

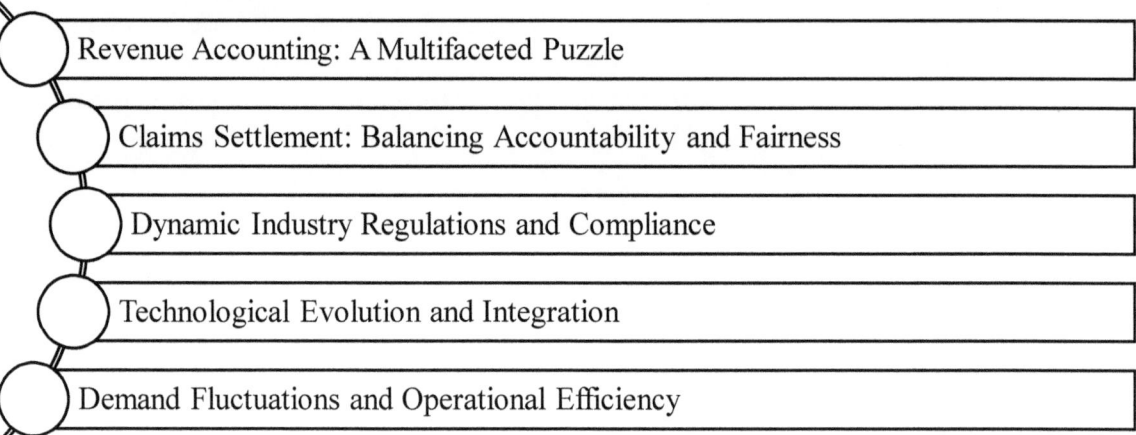

Figure 2. 1- Complexities in Airlines Industry

Revenue Accounting: A Multifaceted Puzzle:

The process of revenue accounting within the airline sector is a sophisticated process of intricate calculations, regulations, and agreements. Airlines must navigate a complex web of pricing structures, cancellations, rerouting, and ticketing regulations. This intricate dance requires precision to ensure accurate revenue recognition while adhering to industry standards and regulatory requirements.

Claims Settlement: Balancing Accountability and Fairness:

The landscape of claims settlement in the airline industry is equally intricate. Airlines must manage a plethora of claims from passengers, agents, and other stakeholders. The challenge lies in balancing accountability with fairness, ensuring that each claim is thoroughly assessed while maintaining operational efficiency and customer satisfaction.

Dynamic Industry Regulations and Compliance:

The airline industry operates within a framework of stringent regulations and compliance requirements. From safety protocols to financial reporting standards, airlines must adhere to a complex tapestry of rules. Keeping up with these regulations and ensuring their seamless integration into operations presents an ongoing challenge that requires meticulous attention.

Technological Evolution and Integration:

As the airline industry embraces technological advancements, the challenge of integrating new systems while maintaining operational continuity arises. Legacy systems, modern software solutions, and data management platforms must seamlessly coexist to ensure smooth operations and accurate data analysis for informed decision-making.

Demand Fluctuations and Operational Efficiency:

The airline industry is notorious for its demand fluctuations, influenced by factors such as seasons, economic shifts, and unforeseen events. Balancing operational efficiency with varying passenger volumes poses a continuous challenge, requiring proactive strategies to optimize resources and maintain service excellence.

In this intricate tapestry of challenges, the airline industry's pursuit of efficiency, accuracy, and customer satisfaction has given rise to ground-breaking initiatives. This case study probes into a remarkable journey undertaken by a leading software product and application development organization. With a turnover exceeding 400 crore and a workforce of over 2000 professionals, this organization embarked on a mission to create a cutting-edge "Airlines Revenue Accounting and Claims Settlement" system for a prominent airline.

At the heart of this endeavour lies the fusion of technical prowess, domain expertise, and relentless dedication. This case study unravels the complexities, triumphs, and strategic manoeuvres that propelled this audacious project from conception to completion. As we traverse through the following sections, the evolution of this visionary project, the challenges surmounted, and the transformational outcomes achieved will stand as a testament to the power of innovation and collaboration in the realm of modern airline solutions.

3. The Significance and Objectives:

The significance of this case study is that it provides valuable lessons for other project teams. The project team faced many challenges, but they were able to overcome them by working together effectively and using several project management best practices.

Technical Complexity and Innovation: The project involves the creation of a pioneering software application for airlines' revenue accounting and claims settlement. This application deals with intricate rules, regulations, and complex financial processes, such as pricing, cancellations, rerouting, payments, and various schemes. The fact that such a system was being developed for the first time in India adds to its technical significance.

Industry Impact: The successful development and implementation of this system would have a substantial impact on the airline industry. The accurate and efficient handling of revenue accounting and claims settlement is critical for airlines' financial stability and operational efficiency. This project, if executed successfully, could set a standard for similar systems in the Indian market.

International Collaboration and Prestige: The fact that an Indian software development organization secured a contract from a leading international airline adds to the prestige and recognition of the organization. It signifies the capability of Indian IT professionals to deliver sophisticated and high-quality solutions to global clients.

Risk Management and Timeliness: The project faces multiple challenges, such as evolving technology, tight timelines, a shortage of domain experts, and high expectations from the customer. Successfully managing these risks and delivering the project within the proposed time frame showcases the project management and execution skills of the team.

Business Expansion and Diversification: The creation of a new division within the organization dedicated to developing airline revenue accounting and claims settlement systems demonstrates the organization's intent to diversify its portfolio and enter a niche market. This expansion has the potential to open up new revenue streams and opportunities.

Coordination and Collaboration: The project's success relies on effective coordination among multiple teams located in different places. Managing communication, collaboration, and knowledge transfer among the teams is crucial for project success and highlights the importance of effective project management practices.

Management Support and Leadership: The strong support from senior management, including funding, administrative support, and motivation, underscores their confidence in the project team and their commitment to its success. The selection of a competent project manager with domain expertise and leadership skills further enhances the project's significance.

Business Continuity and Long-Term Relationship: The success of this project is pivotal for the newly formed Airlines Application Division and its future growth. The possibility of signing an Annual Maintenance Contract (AMC) for five years reflects the importance of maintaining a long-term relationship with the client and ensuring the system's ongoing support and enhancement.

In summary, this case is significant due to its technical complexity, industry impact, international recognition, risk management challenges, business expansion, coordination requirements, management support, and long-term implications. The successful execution of this project could establish the organization as a leader in developing advanced software solutions for the airline industry and contribute to its overall growth and reputation.

The case study shows that even complex and challenging projects can be successful if the team is committed to success. The case study provides valuable lessons on how to manage risks and how to adapt to changes in the project scope and requirements. The case study highlights the importance of close customer involvement and effective communication. The case study shows that trust and teamwork are essential for the success of any project. Overall, this case study is a valuable resource for project teams. It provides valuable lessons that can be applied to other projects.

In the challenging realm of modern airline solutions, where precision and efficiency are paramount, a project manager emerges as the linchpin in orchestrating success. This case study sheds light on a seasoned and capable software engineer who assumed the mantle of a project manager for a transformative endeavour.

4. The Protagonist:

At the centre of this narrative is the project manager – a veteran software engineer armed not only with technical prowess but also a profound understanding of project management principles. Beyond expertise, the project manager embodies effective communication, enabling the establishment of trust and rapport with the customer.

The Crucial Role:

The project manager's impact on the project's triumph cannot be overstated. A pivotal figure, the project manager's responsibilities encompassed various domains:

The Crucial Role of the Project Manager:

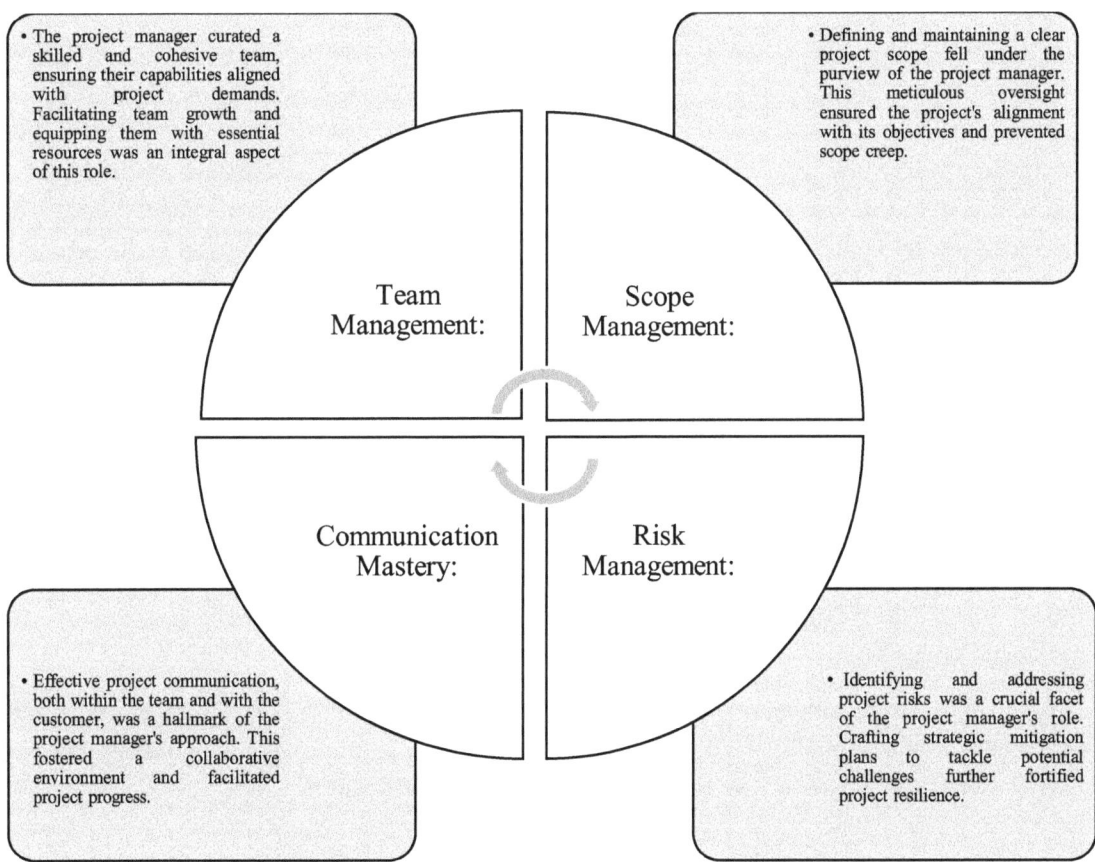

Figure 3 2- The Crucial Role of the Project Manager

Additional Insights on the Protagonist:

- The project manager's leadership was an inspiring force that galvanized the project team. Their ability to motivate and guide team members propelled collective efforts toward success.

- The project manager's adept communication extended beyond the team, forging a strong bond of trust with the customer. This rapport proved instrumental in aligning project goals with customer expectations.
- Skilfully wielding project management tools, the project manager navigated the project's complexities, ensuring adherence to timelines and budget constraints.

Ultimately, the project manager's expertise and leadership formed the bedrock of the project's accomplishments. Challenges were confronted head-on, and the project was delivered within the designated timeframe and budgetary parameters.

This case study illuminates the dynamic interplay of leadership, expertise, and project management acumen. It serves as a testament to the pivotal role a project manager plays in steering projects through uncharted territories and attaining triumphant outcomes.

5. Project Challenges:

The project's protagonists faced a multitude of challenges as they embarked on this prestigious endeavour. The contract, valued at around 5 million USD, required the collaboration of a workforce comprising approximately 25 developers and a QA/QC team of 5 individuals. Additionally, to ensure close coordination with the customer, 3 professionals were stationed on-site. With a tight timeline of 18 months, the pressure was palpable. The customer's IT team had committed to an aggressive schedule, and the proposed application's complexity demanded meticulous accuracy.

The realm of revenue accounting and settlement within the airline industry is fraught with intricacies. It involves navigating an intricate web of regulations, agreements, and rules. This encompasses pricing dynamics, passenger ticket management encompassing cancellations and rerouting, intricate payment structures to other airlines and agents, and the incorporation of specialized schemes. Adapting to changing conditions governed by time-reference tables adds another layer of complexity. Understanding and meticulously documenting this multifaceted business environment posed a significant challenge. Furthermore, sourcing domain experts was arduous due to the scarcity of individuals with the required experience and exposure to such specialized systems.

Compounding these challenges was the project's context within a period lacking matured systems operating in similar domains. This endeavour indeed stood as a formidable undertaking. Diamond analysis of project classifications further underscored its complexity:

6. Diamond Analysis of Project Classification:

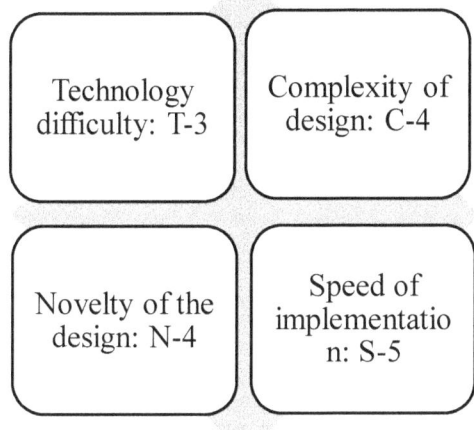

Figure 6.1- Diamond Analysis of Project Complexity

The project was characterized by its sheer size, involving an estimated 5 million USD budget (equivalent to INR 25-28 crore) encompassing manpower, overheads, travel, and incidental costs. The project team comprised 25 personnel within the Head Office and the QA/QC group, augmented by 3 on-site team members. The project's timeline spanned 18 months, with an estimated 20 months before the pilot test could commence at the customer's headquarters. Notably, this project marked the establishment of a new division within the organization, introducing a novel product line for "Airline Revenue Accounting & Claims Management System" - a pioneering venture in India at the time.

This project carried a heightened risk due to several factors: the adoption of a new concept and software application leveraging a new database version, the scarcity of domain experts in the relatively new Indian market, the time pressure stemming from the impending closure of an existing plant, and the customer's expectations driven by operational demands. Accurate and swift responses were non-negotiable for the proposed system.

Technology choice and maturity posed further intricacies. Although well-established in the USA and Europe's airline markets, the technology was being harnessed for the first time as a standardized product, amplifying the dearth of knowledgeable individuals equipped to handle both the technology and the domain applications.

Logistics and clearances emerged as logistical hurdles, compounded by governmental clearances, travel logistics, and visa processing - all intricate and time-consuming tasks. However, the customer organization provided robust support, streamlining the paperwork. Coordination across more than three locations - Mumbai, Pune, and the customer site - was facilitated with relative ease, while robust support from senior management translated into funding, administrative support, and motivation for the project team.

Customer involvement was a crucial pillar, with meticulous pre-project homework informing the Request for Proposal (RFP) release. However, scepticism about the capabilities of Indian software professionals posed an initial hurdle, demanding the project manager's and team's efforts to win their trust.

At the helm of this intricate endeavour stood a Project Manager chosen for competence, commitment, and expertise in software applications, bolstered by exposure to airline back-office processing.

7. A Pragmatic Strategy: Protagonist's Approach to Complex Challenges:

Amidst the labyrinth of challenges, Protagonist armed with his astute project management skills, navigated the project's complexities with a strategic approach. His leadership played a pivotal role in steering the project toward success.

Challenges in Complex Project Execution:

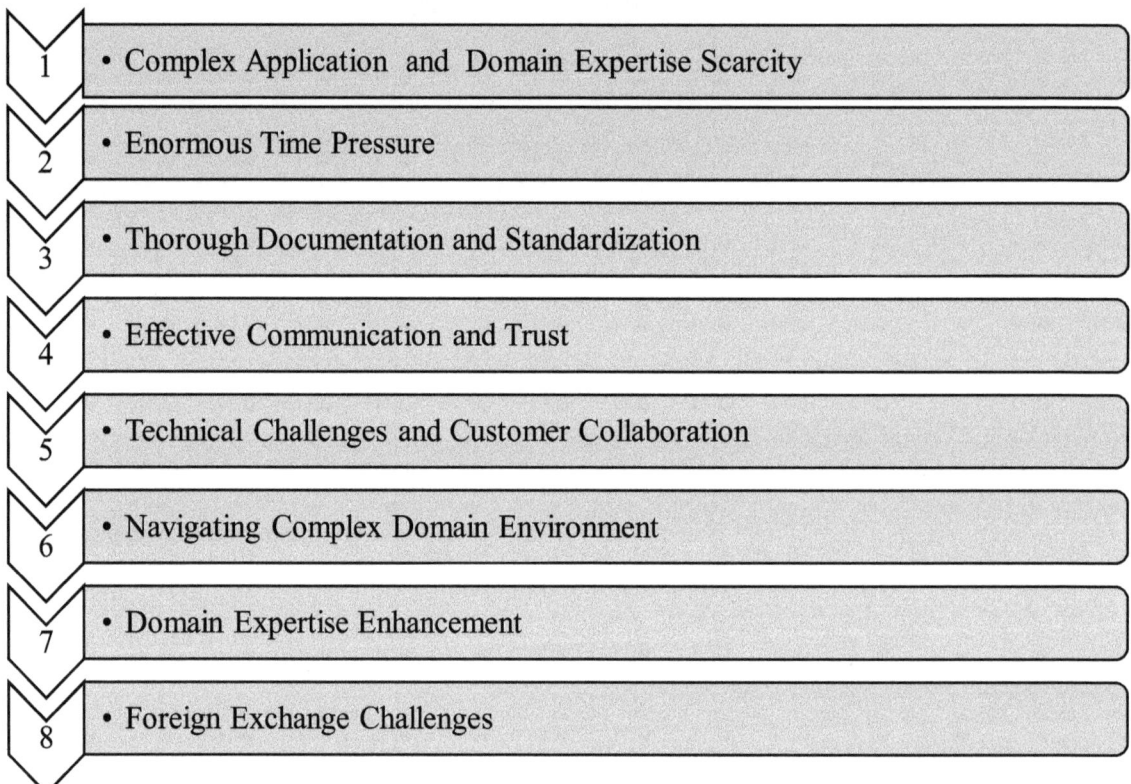

Figure 7.1 - Challenges in Complex Project Execution

Complex Application and Domain Expertise Scarcity: The software under development was a formidable application, navigating uncharted waters in a nascent market segment. The intricate web of business processes, industry regulations, and rules posed significant challenges. The scarcity of domain experts further intensified the complexity. However, the customer's active engagement and meticulous groundwork contributed to the effective management of this challenge.

Enormous Time Pressure: The project's stringent timeline created substantial pressure. Initial efforts were directed towards orienting the development team to grasp complex terminologies and processes. The dedicated training investments during the early stages proved instrumental in streamlining subsequent processes.

Thorough Documentation and Standardization: His team invested considerable time in establishing standardized documentation practices. The unwavering adherence to this practice ensured the team stayed on course. Every decision and meeting minute was documented, acting as a compass throughout the project's journey.

Effective Communication and Trust: Communication, both within the team and with customer representatives, was executed with precision. This efficient exchange of information was meticulously documented, providing a reference point for all stakeholders. Additionally, a culture of tacit trust within the team fostered harmony and facilitated a smooth workflow.

Technical Challenges and Customer Collaboration: The team grappled with technical roadblocks concerning database usage and network efficiency. Collaborative support from the customer's IT team proved invaluable, addressing these challenges in tandem.

Navigating Complex Domain Environment: The intricacies of the domain environment, especially in terms of preparing test data, presented hurdles. However, the high-quality groundwork conducted by the customer's team significantly aided in surmounting this challenge, supporting trials at both home and site offices.

Domain Expertise Enhancement: The scarcity of domain expertise within the team prompted him to emphasize training. His strategic approach, coupled with support from the customer's personnel, enabled the team to bolster their domain knowledge effectively.

Foreign Exchange Challenges: Currency exchange hurdles for travel presented a unique challenge. Protagonist resourcefulness was pivotal in addressing these issues.

Collaborative Efforts: Partnering with Stakeholders for Solutions: The project's positive environment was the culmination of collaborative efforts across multiple fronts:

8. Foundations of Success

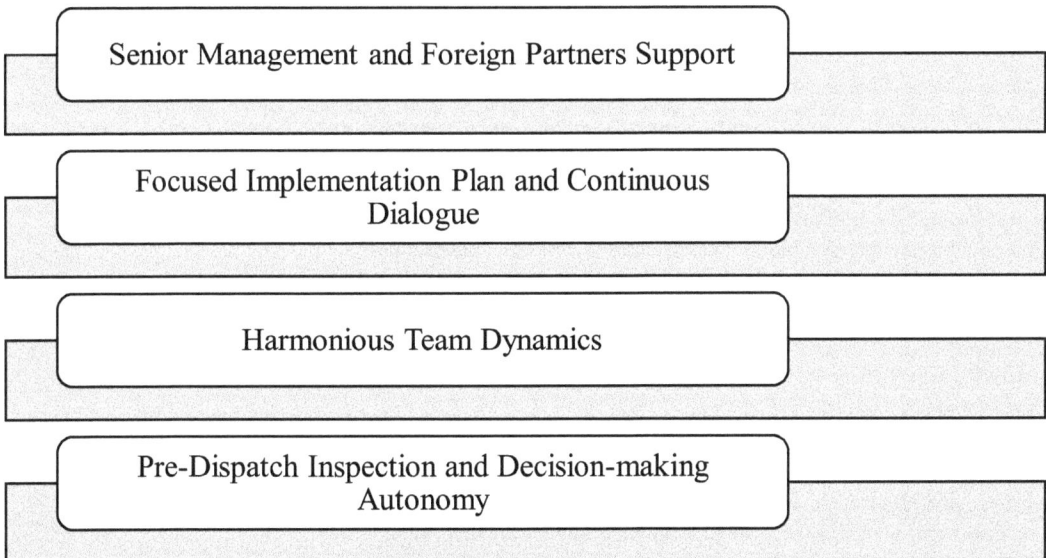

Figure 8.1 Foundations of Success

Senior Management and Foreign Partners Support: The unwavering backing of senior management and foreign partners created a conducive atmosphere for success.

Focused Implementation Plan and Continuous Dialogue: The project's team maintained a laser focus on a detailed implementation plan, in close cooperation with customer personnel. Regular dialogue between Customer PM and local PM expedited issue resolution, ensuring project completion within deadlines.

Harmonious Team Dynamics: A harmonious team dynamic fostered a work environment conducive to quality and productivity, ultimately contributing to the project's success.

Pre-Dispatch Inspection and Decision-making Autonomy: Rigorous pre-dispatch inspections, involving local and customer QA/QC teams, facilitated smooth on-site software implementation. The team's autonomy in decision-making streamlined operations.

Amidst these challenges, the Protagonist's strategic vision and collaborative approach emerged as the cornerstone of the project's triumph, underscoring the role of astute project management in overcoming complex hurdles.

9. "Project Success Criteria: Meeting Diverse Stakeholder Expectations for Triumph"

Organizational Expectations: A Comprehensive Outlook:

In the pursuit of executing the monumental project, the organization held a set of expectations that laid the foundation for its success and long-term impact. These organizational expectations were multi-faceted and encompassed a range of strategic goals and aspirations:

Critical Success Factors from the Organisation's Perspective:

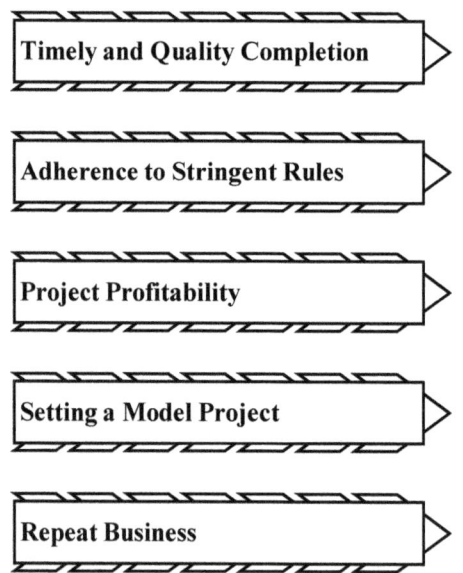

Figure 9.1 - Critical Success Factors from Organisation's Perspective

Timely and Quality Completion: The foremost aspiration was to ensure that the project was executed within the stipulated time frame while upholding the highest standards of quality. This commitment to meeting deadlines and delivering excellence underscored the organization's dedication to its clientele.

Adherence to Stringent Rules: The airline industry's intricacies demanded rigorous adherence to the intricate rules governing revenue accounting. The organization aimed to align the system with these regulations to ensure accuracy, compliance, and smooth operations for the airline partner.

Project Profitability: As a prudent investment, the project needed to yield profitable outcomes in line with the established financial projections. This aspiration underscored the organization's focus on generating tangible returns from the project's substantial investment.

Setting a Model Project: Beyond immediate gains, the organization envisioned this project as a pivotal model that could shape its future endeavour in the airline segment. The ambition was to create a reference point for excellence and innovation, positioning the organization as a leader in airline solutions.

Repeat Business: By exceeding expectations, the organization aimed to cultivate a strong relationship with the customer, leading to repeat business opportunities. This underscored the long-term vision of establishing enduring partnerships within the airline industry.

These organizational expectations collectively embodied the organization's commitment to excellence, innovation, and strategic growth. Through the successful execution of this project, the organization aspired to redefine its standing in the airline software development landscape.

Client / User Expectations: A Holistic Perspective:

The aspirations and anticipations of the client and end users played a pivotal role in shaping the project's objectives and outcomes. These expectations were multifaceted, reflecting the critical needs of the airline partner and its operational ecosystem:

Timely Delivery and Seamless Implementation: The airline customer set forth a paramount requirement for the project to be delivered within the agreed-upon timeline. The successful and efficient implementation of the system was of paramount importance to minimize disruptions to their operations.

Achievement of Committed ROI: The customer sought to realize a substantial return on investment (ROI) from the project. This expectation was grounded in the anticipation that the implemented system would contribute to cost savings, efficiency improvements, and revenue enhancements.

Critical Success Factor as per Client's Perspective:

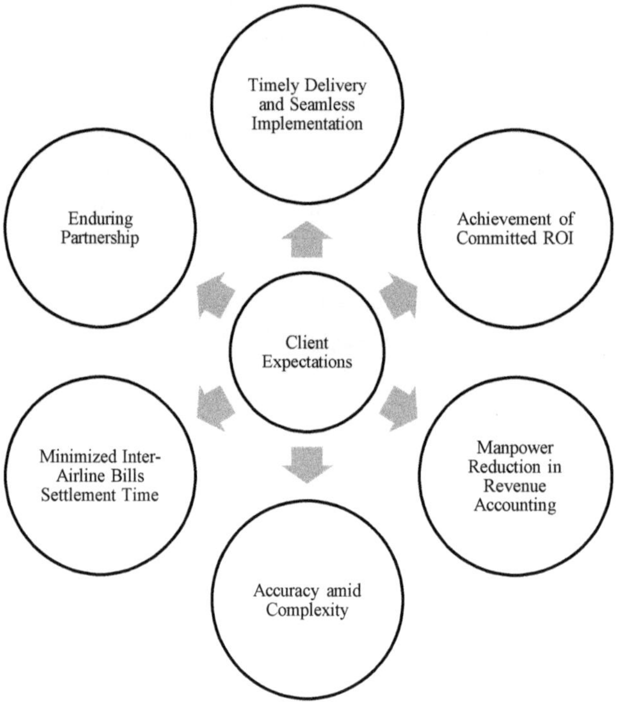

Figure 9.2 Critical Success Factor as per Client's Perspective

Timely Delivery and Seamless Implementation: The airline customer set forth a paramount requirement for the project to be delivered within the agreed-upon timeline. The successful and efficient implementation of the system was of paramount importance to minimize disruptions to their operations.

Achievement of Committed ROI: The customer sought to realize a substantial return on investment (ROI) from the project. This expectation was grounded in the anticipation that the implemented system would contribute to cost savings, efficiency improvements, and revenue enhancements.

Manpower Reduction in Revenue Accounting: Addressing operational efficiency, the customer aspired to streamline their revenue accounting division. The system was expected to automate and optimize processes, leading to a reduction in the need for extensive manual intervention.

Accuracy amid Complexity: Given the intricate rules, regulations, and complexities of revenue accounting in the airline industry, accuracy was non-negotiable. The customer expected the system to meticulously handle diverse scenarios, ensuring error-free accounting and settlement procedures.

Minimized Inter-Airline Bills Settlement Time: A significant challenge in the industry was the time-consuming inter-airline bills settlement process. The customer looked to the project to expedite these settlements, minimizing revenue leakage and enhancing financial control.

Enduring Partnership: Beyond the immediate project, the customer envisioned a collaborative partnership that would transcend this endeavour. They sought to establish a strong rapport with the software organization, fostering future collaborations for sustained growth and innovation.

These customer and user expectations were the cornerstones of the project's purpose, guiding the project team's efforts toward creating a solution that would not only meet but exceed the airline partner's operational needs. By comprehensively addressing these expectations, the project aimed to demonstrate its value and contribute to the customer's overarching goals in the airline sector.

Unveiling Retrospective Wisdom: Key Insights for Project Success:

The protagonist states that through candid conversations with the project team members and their esteemed Project Manager (PM), a compilation of critical success factors (CSFs) has emerged, providing invaluable retrospective insight. These factors, had they been contemplated before project initiation, could have significantly fortified the project's journey. It is worth noting that while these insights were not pre-emptively accounted for, they hold immense value for future endeavours.

Essential Factors for Project Success from Team Members' Perspective

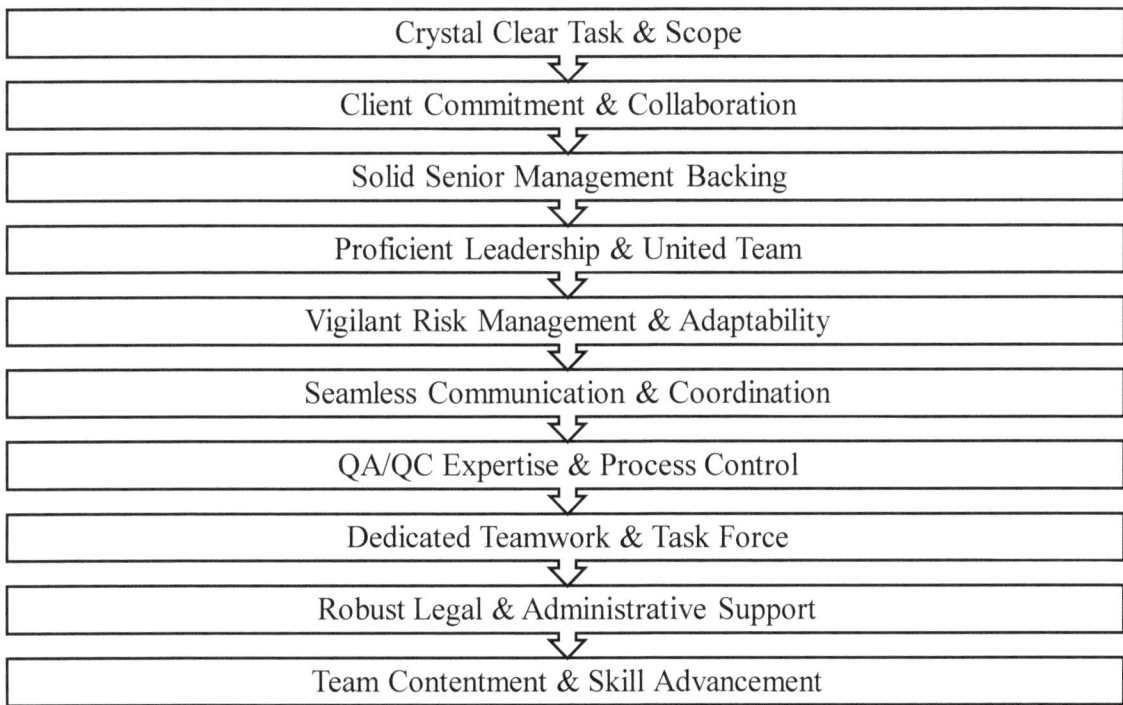

Figure 9.3 Essential Factors for Project Success from Team Members' Perspective

Clarity in Task and Scope Definition: A paramount realization was the need for absolute clarity in comprehending the task at hand, coupled with an unambiguous understanding of the project's scope and specifications. This, it's understood, would have propelled the team with greater focus and direction.

Customer Commitment and Participation: The value of unwavering commitment and active engagement from customer teams throughout the project lifecycle came to the forefront. Enhanced collaboration could have potentially alleviated challenges and streamlined the process.

Strong Senior Management Support: Acknowledging the significance of comprehensive backing from senior management and the freedom to exercise decisions, the team recognized that early alignment and assurance could have provided a more robust foundation.

Competent Project Management and Cohesive Team: The appreciation for a capable Project Manager and a cohesive, trustworthy team became apparent. Had the importance of these facets been recognized beforehand, assembling a well-versed team and appointing an adept Project Manager might have proven even more impactful.

Alert Risk Management and Timely Adaptations: Emphasizing alertness towards risk management, especially in the context of timelines and design changes during Proof of Concept (POC) and User Acceptance Testing (UAT), became evident. Integrating pre-emptive risk strategies might have led to smoother transitions.

Impeccable Communication and Coordination: The realization dawned on the indispensability of maintaining control over project progress through flawless communication and coordination. More proactive measures in this domain could have averted certain challenges.

Robust PMO Support and Issue Resolution: A standout realization was the importance of robust support from Project Management Office (PMO) personnel. Recognizing their role in stringent issue tracking and resolution might have expedited solutions.

The backbone of QA / QC Teams and Process Control Engineers: Acknowledging the pivotal role of Quality Assurance (QA) and Quality Control (QC) teams, alongside process control engineers due to well-established processes in the parent organization, it became evident that leveraging their support more strategically could have been advantageous.

Unwavering Teamwork and Dedicated Task Force: The power of unwavering teamwork and the tenacity of the task force members shone brightly. Nurturing these aspects from the outset could have bolstered the project's resilience.

Stalwart Support from Legal and Administrative Experts: The significance of sturdy support from Legal and Administrative experts became evident. Earlier integration of their guidance might have expedited certain procedures.

Team Satisfaction and Skill Development: The project's ultimate success depended on the satisfaction of team members and their skill development. Recognizing this early on could have steered efforts towards nurturing a more enriching environment.

In retrospect, these insights serve as a testament to the value of experience and the potential to transform challenges into stepping stones. While not all elements were anticipated, they now stand as pillars of wisdom for future undertakings, offering guidance and strategic foresight to approaching projects.

Key Lesson Learnt:

Some of the key lessons that can be learned from this case study include:

- The importance of close customer involvement. The project team worked closely with the customer to understand their needs and to ensure that the system met their requirements.

- The importance of documentation. The project team documented the project thoroughly, which helped them to stay on track and to communicate effectively with the customer.
- The importance of effective communication. The project team communicated effectively with the customer, the technical team, and each other. This helped to ensure that the project was completed smoothly.
- The importance of trust and teamwork. The project team was able to trust each other and work together effectively. This was essential for overcoming the challenges that they faced.

Conclusion:

In a resounding triumph, the project was deemed an unequivocal success, a testament to the team's unwavering dedication. Radiating with pride, the team celebrated their outstanding performance. The customer and senior management were elated with the outcome-timely completion and exceptional quality that exceeded all expectations. The gratified customer extended their commitment by signing a 5-year AMC contract.

Senior management's joy was palpable, prompting the establishment of a dedicated division for airline applications-an enduring venture that thrives to this day. The division's stellar reputation garnered the attention of four international airlines within two years, amplifying the organization's growth trajectory and ensuring sustained profitability.

Elevated to "Divisional Manager," the project manager assumed independent responsibility for this thriving business. The project's brainchild evolved into a flagship product, standing tall among the organization's accomplishments.

This victorious tale underscores the potential of visionary teamwork, strategic management, and unrelenting commitment, leaving an indelible mark on the organization's journey.

Questions:

1. How did the project manager's strong leadership and effective communication contribute to the successful completion of the complex airline revenue accounting system?
2. What were the key challenges faced by the project team, and how did they overcome these challenges through collaborative efforts and meticulous planning?
3. What were the critical success factors identified by the team members, and how did they play a pivotal role in ensuring the project's triumph, both from an organizational and customer perspective?
4. Imagine taking on the role of the protagonist in this case study. How might your innovative approach and strategic decisions have reshaped the project's trajectory, propelling it to unparalleled heights of success within the dynamic realm of airline solutions?

Case No 3: "A Triumph of Leadership and Expertise in Project Management: Navigating Complex Challenges in Airlines Solutions".

Introduction:

This case study probes into the development of a sophisticated revenue accounting system for a prominent airline, highlighting the complexities, challenges, and strategic manoeuvres that led to its successful completion. The case study showcases the interplay of effective project management, collaborative efforts, and stakeholder alignment in navigating the intricate landscape of airline solutions.

Learning Objectives:

- Understand the challenges and complexities associated with developing a revenue accounting system for the airline industry.
- Explore the significance of effective project management, leadership, and stakeholder collaboration in overcoming project challenges.
- Analyze the critical success factors identified by the project team and their impact on project outcomes.
- Evaluate the role of innovation and strategic decision-making in reshaping the trajectory of a complex project.

Discussion Questions:

How did the project manager's strong leadership and effective communication contribute to the successful completion of the complex airline revenue accounting system?

This question focuses on the pivotal role of the project manager in leading the team and ensuring effective communication with stakeholders. Students should highlight instances from the case study that demonstrate the project manager's leadership and communication skills, emphasizing their impact on project success.

What were the key challenges faced by the project team, and how did they overcome these challenges through collaborative efforts and meticulous planning?

Here, students should identify the various challenges outlined in the case study, including technical, domain-related, and timeline pressures. They should then discuss how collaborative efforts, customer engagement, and strategic planning played a role in overcoming these challenges.

What were the critical success factors identified by the team members, and how did they play a pivotal role in ensuring the project's triumph, both from an organizational and customer perspective?

Students should outline the critical success factors listed by the team members and elaborate on how each factor contributed to the project's success. They should highlight the alignment between organizational expectations and customer/user expectations, emphasizing how these factors collectively ensured a successful outcome.

Imagine taking on the role of the protagonist in this case study. How might your innovative approach and strategic decisions have reshaped the project's trajectory, propelling it to unparalleled heights of success within the dynamic realm of airline solutions?

This question encourages students to think creatively and apply their understanding of the case to propose innovative strategies that could further enhance project success. They should consider how they would address challenges, leverage strengths, and capitalize on opportunities to elevate the project's outcomes.

Teaching Plan:

- **Introduction and Background:** Provide an overview of the airline industry's challenges and the case study's focus on developing a revenue accounting system. Discuss the significance of effective project management in complex endeavours.

- **Discussion of Challenges:** Explore the challenges faced by the project team, including domain complexity, time pressure, and technical hurdles. Encourage students to analyse the multifaceted nature of these challenges.

- **The Role of the Protagonist:** Discuss the pivotal role of the project manager, highlighting their leadership, communication, and strategic decision-making. Explore how the project manager's actions influenced team dynamics and stakeholder engagement.

- **Organizational and Customer Expectations:** Analyse the expectations of the organization and the customer/user, emphasizing the importance of aligning project goals with stakeholder needs.

- **Critical Success Factors:** Examine the critical success factors identified by the team members and their impact on project outcomes. Encourage students to discuss how these factors could have been integrated earlier for enhanced project planning.

- **Innovative Approaches:** Facilitate a discussion on how students might approach the project differently if they were in the protagonist's role. Encourage them to propose innovative strategies, considering how these strategies would address challenges and leverage opportunities.

- **Lessons Learnt:** Summarize the lessons learned from the case study, highlighting the significance of effective communication, stakeholder collaboration, and strategic planning in project success.
- **Conclusion:** Reinforce the key takeaways from the case study and discuss the broader applicability of the lessons learned to other projects.

Assessment:

Assessment could include individual or group presentations where students are required to analyse and present their insights on various aspects of the case study, such as the role of the project manager, critical success factors, and innovative approaches. Additionally, essay-style questions could be included in examinations to evaluate students' comprehensive understanding of the case study's themes and lessons.

Case No 4: Strategic Transcendence: Pioneering an Independent Composite Material Company in India

Dr Jayasri Murali, Ms. Puja Gavande

Associate Professor, MBA@IICMR, Pune, Assistant Professor, MBA@IICMR, Pune

Acknowledgements:

We extend our sincere gratitude to Dr Girish Kelkar, whose insightful thesis laid the foundation for the creation of this case study. Dr Kelkar's untiring efforts in the pursuit of knowledge and commitment to enriching the understanding of aspiring managers and industry experts practicing in the field have been truly commendable. Our dedication to advancing the discourse within the industry is reflected in the depth and quality of the material drawn from his thesis. We are privileged to have had the opportunity to build upon his work, and we acknowledge his invaluable contribution to the realm of management studies. His mentorship and scholarly endeavours have undoubtedly benefited those navigating the complex landscape of industry practice.

Abstract:

This case study explores the challenges and successes faced by a large automobile manufacturing group in India as it ventured into establishing a new company for the manufacture and application of SMC (Single-sided moulded compounds) and DMC (double-sided moulding compounds) composite materials. The project aimed to replace outdated fibreglass technology with innovative composite materials in the auto and electrical industries.

The study delves into the complexities of technology adoption, project management, and strategic decision-making. Despite initial setbacks, the project team showcased technical success through successful Proof of Concept trials, though financial results initially indicated failure. The unwavering support from senior management and the strategic importance of the technology led to the project's continuation, ultimately resulting in substantial success over the subsequent decade.

Keywords:

SMC, DMC, Composite Materials, Project Management, Technology Adoption, Auto Industry, Strategic Decision-making, Proof of Concept, Financial Challenges, Senior Management Support, Innovation, Industrial Applications, Success Factors, Project Success Criteria, Risk Management, Coordination, Strategic Transcendence.

1. Introduction:

In the dynamic landscape of the Indian automobile manufacturing sector, this case study unfolds the strategic journey of a prominent group as it ventured into establishing a pioneering company dedicated to the manufacture and application of SMC (Single side moulded compounds) and DMC (Double-sided moulding compounds) composite materials. Against the backdrop of a successful fibreglass-based company within the group, known for its exclusive production of auto bodies for military and police applications, the group's headquarters recognized the need for a strategic shift to embrace innovative materials in response to evolving global auto markets.

The project's inception marks a significant strategic decision by the group to position itself at the forefront of technological advancements in the auto industry. This initiative aimed not only to replace outdated fibreglass technology but also to establish a unique position in the market through the adoption of SMC and DMC composites. The project's genesis, therefore, represents a strategic response to the changing dynamics of the industry, introducing complexities and challenges that would shape its trajectory.

2. Project Genesis:

The genesis of this transformative journey delves into the strategic considerations and decisions that marked the initiation of the project. It begins with the group's recognition of the evolving landscape in the global auto markets, prompting a decisive venture into the realm of SMC and DMC composite materials. The strategic importance of this project is underscored by the success of a specialized fibreglass-based company within the group, which had established a monopolistic market position in supplying auto bodies for military and police forces.

As the project took form, crucial decisions included the meticulous selection of a Project Manager with specific expertise in SMC and DMC composites. This Project Manager played a pivotal role in navigating the intricacies associated with technology adoption, project classification, and the inherent complexities of introducing novel materials in an industry accustomed to traditional practices.

The project's classification, as determined through a diamond analysis encompassing Technology difficulty, design complexity, Novelty, and Implementation speed, highlighted the multifaceted challenges it would encounter. The recognition of project complexity became integral to understanding the intricacies involved in its execution.

In summary, the genesis of this project represents a strategic response to the shifting tides of the auto industry. The complexities introduced by technology adoption, coupled with the group's ambition to lead in innovation, set the stage for a narrative that goes beyond conventional business ventures, providing insights into the strategic considerations and complexities that shaped its trajectory.

3. Leadership Selection:

The process of selecting the right leadership for the transformative project of establishing a company dedicated to SMC (Single-sided moulded compounds) and DMC (double-sided moulding compounds) composite materials was a critical aspect of the strategic initiative. Recognizing the unique challenges and complexities associated with introducing novel technologies in the auto industry, the group's leadership carefully considered key criteria in the appointment of a Project Manager to helm this ambitious venture.

Given the evolving nature of SMC and DMC composites in the global auto markets, the Project Manager's role was pivotal in steering the project toward success. The strategic decision-making involved the identification and recruitment of an individual with specific expertise and experience in the domain of SMC and DMC composites. The chosen Project Manager not only needed to possess a deep understanding of the technological intricacies but also the ability to navigate the complexities associated with such a pioneering initiative.

The appointed Project Manager brought a wealth of knowledge and experience in the field, having received specialized training in the UK and West Germany. His background included exposure to research and development processes in the international arena, particularly in the use of composites for industrial applications. Notably, the Project Manager had specific training in the UK and Germany, acknowledging the critical importance of tooling in the SMC and DMC market.

The significance of this leadership selection was underscored by the Project Manager's responsibility not only for establishing the new organization but also for overseeing the closure of the outdated fibreglass-based unit due to technological obsolescence. This dual responsibility required a leader with a comprehensive understanding of both the legacy processes and the innovative technologies at the core of the new project. Thus, the Project Manager's background and competencies played a crucial role in shaping the trajectory of the project and positioning it for success in a rapidly evolving market.

4. Diamond Analysis of Project Classifications:

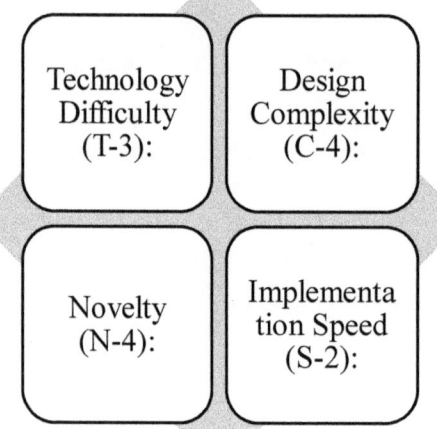

Figure 4.1 Diamond Analysis of Project Classifications

Technology Difficulty (T-3): The project involves the adoption and implementation of advanced technologies related to Single-sided moulded compounds (SMC) and Double-sided moulding compounds (DMC) composites.

The transition from traditional fibreglass technology to SMC and DMC composites introduces new manufacturing processes and materials, requiring a comprehensive understanding of the complexities involved.

Design Complexity (C-4): The design aspect of the project is marked by a high level of complexity (C-4). The shift from fibreglass to composite materials necessitates the revaluation of component designs, tooling, and production processes.

The intricate nature of designing components using SMC and DMC composites introduces challenges in terms of structural considerations, material behaviour, and the integration of these composites into existing auto industry standards.

Novelty (N-4): The project attains a high level of novelty (N-4) due to its pioneering nature. The introduction of SMC and DMC composites in the Indian auto industry, where traditional materials dominate, represents a ground-breaking shift.

The use of these innovative compounds for auto and electrical industry components positions the project as a trailblazer, facing the challenge of introducing a novel concept to an industry unfamiliar with such materials.

Implementation Speed (S-2): The speed of implementation for this project is rated at S-2. While the group recognizes the strategic importance of swift execution, certain factors, such as the shift in project location and the associated challenges, contribute to a moderate speed of implementation.

The intricacies involved in setting up a new organization, combined with the time required for comprehensive feasibility studies and the need to secure government clearances, impact the overall pace of implementation.

5. Scope Evaluation and Feasibility:

The project's initial scope was anchored in the establishment of a pioneering organization dedicated to the manufacturing and application of Single-sided moulded compounds (SMC) and Double-sided moulding compounds (DMC) composite materials. Originally conceptualized for the Pune-Mumbai vicinity, the project's scope encountered a transformative shift due to the intervention of a co-promoter, redirecting the project to an economically backward area. While this move aligned with conceptual ideals, the reality introduced significant challenges. The feasibility study, however, initially overlooked crucial shifts in the auto-component market trends, impacting the selection and deployment of capital equipment. Initially designed for medium-sized components, the project had to adapt to the auto industry's preference for larger components, incurring additional costs and delays. The scope, therefore, evolved dynamically, reflecting the intricate interplay of geographical considerations, market dynamics, and technological nuances, all of which played a pivotal role in shaping the project's feasibility and eventual trajectory.

6. Project Dynamics:

The dynamics of the project unfold as a complex interplay of technological innovation, market adaptation, and strategic decision-making. At its core, the project undergoes a transformative shift from traditional fibreglass technology to the cutting-edge realm of Single-sided moulded compounds (SMC) and Double-sided moulding compounds (DMC) composites. This technological evolution introduces intricacies in manufacturing processes, design considerations, and the application of novel materials in the auto and electrical industry components.

The geographical repositioning of the project from an urban setting to an economically backward area adds a layer of complexity. This shift, while aligned with broader conceptual goals, presents challenges related to land allocation, skilled manpower acquisition, and infrastructure development. The project dynamics further reflect the evolving trends in the auto-component market. Originally conceived for medium-sized components, the project adapts to the industry's prioritization of larger components, necessitating adjustments in capital equipment and incurring additional costs.

Time emerges as a critical factor, with the project facing pressures from proposed closure timelines of the existing plant and the imperative to swiftly establish the new organization. The project's dynamics also highlight the collaboration between the Indian team and foreign partners, navigating challenges in technology transfer, experimentation with new materials, and coordination across multiple locations.

The intricate web of project dynamics underscores the need for strategic decision-making, adaptability, and effective communication. Balancing technological innovation, market demands, and unforeseen challenges, the project's dynamics contribute to its narrative of transformation, resilience, and strategic transcendence in the dynamic landscape of composite materials in the Indian industrial sector.

7. Key Team Positions:

1. Project Manager:
2. Leader overseeing the entire project, making sure everything runs smoothly and aligns with the project's goals.

1. R&D Manager:
2. Focuses on research and development to ensure the new materials meet industry standards and contribute to the project's success.

1. Quality Leader:
2. Ensures the products meet quality standards, playing a crucial role in maintaining customer satisfaction.

1. Production Manager:
2. Manages the manufacturing processes, turning design ideas into actual products.

1. Process Engineer:
2. Supports vendors and ensures a smooth integration of materials into the production processes.

1. Procurement Engineer:
2. Handles sourcing materials and components, managing relationships with suppliers.

1. Accounts Manager:
2. Manages project finances, ensuring everything stays within budget.

1. Logistics Manager:
2. Plans and oversees logistics, making sure materials and products move efficiently.

1. Site Manager with Engineers:
2. Leads on-site activities, coordinating construction and installations.

1. Application Engineer:
2. Introduces new materials to customers, helping bridge the gap between technology and market needs.

1. PMO Office:
2. Tracks project progress, liaises with customer teams, and ensures smooth communication.

1. Legal Expert & Liaison Manager:
2. Manages legal aspects and relationships with stakeholders, ensuring compliance with regulations.

Figure 7.1: Key Team Positions

8. Challenges and Setbacks:

Facing an array of obstacles, the project encountered challenges that put the team's resilience to the test. One significant hurdle arose with the decision to move the plant from an urban to an economically disadvantaged area. This transition faced resistance, resulting in delays in acquiring land due to bureaucratic hurdles and local protests. The process, marked by a commissioner's refusal and subsequent government intervention, led to an avoidable two-year setback.

The shift in location also brought difficulties in securing trained manpower and support services. Qualified professionals were hesitant to relocate, prompting the recruitment of students from UDCT with special incentives. This not only highlighted the scarcity of skilled personnel but also added an unexpected layer of complexity to managing the human side of the project.

Time pressures intensified challenges, driven by the urgency to meet proposed closure timelines for the existing plant. The dynamic nature of the auto-component market, particularly the shift in priority from medium-sized to large components, introduced an unexpected setback. Initially designed for medium-sized components, the project had to recalibrate its approach, incurring additional capital expenses and causing delays.

Resistance to adopting SMC and DMC materials in the auto industry presented another layer of complexity. The slow response from auto manufacturers, even within the parent company, highlighted reluctance to embrace these innovative materials. Surprisingly, breakthroughs came from outside the group, particularly from electrical manufacturing units in Mumbai, revealing a deviation from initial investment expectations.

In essence, the journey was marked by bureaucratic hurdles in the geographical transition, unexpected shifts in market priorities, and resistance to innovative materials. Despite these formidable challenges, the team's determination and adaptability paved the way for eventual success after initial setbacks.

9. Positive Project Environment:

Within the project's positive environment, there existed a robust support system from senior management, foreign partners, and labs, underscoring the strategic significance of the initiative. The Group HQ provided unwavering support, offering timely funding, administrative backing, and motivational encouragement. The project team operated with considerable autonomy, fostering a sense of trust and confidence. Financial constraints were minimal, with the Project Manager empowered to allocate funds based on project needs. The team exhibited a high level of camaraderie, working cohesively and demonstrating a willingness to go above and beyond. Innovative ideas were welcomed, contributing to streamlined design and implementation processes. The matured processes within the parent organization facilitated effective process engineering, quality assurance, and quality control initiatives. Regular communication and coordination, coupled with meticulous risk management, further fortified the positive project environment. Despite external challenges, this collaborative and supportive atmosphere played a pivotal role in navigating complexities and achieving technical successes.

10. Success Criteria Determination:

The success criteria for the project were meticulously determined in consultation with senior management and sponsors. Central to these criteria was the successful completion of pilots for major auto companies and auto component manufacturers, ensuring the acceptance of Proof of Concept (POC) for critical components. Conformance to specified mechanical and electrical properties of trial components constituted a key success factor, emphasizing the importance of meeting industry standards. Additionally, satisfaction across all customer and technical consultant segments within the industry was identified as paramount, reflecting a holistic approach to success. Recognizing the integral role of suppliers, success criteria also encompassed their satisfaction, acknowledging their contributions to the introduction of new materials and methods. The overarching success criteria extended to the contentment and appreciation of the project team, principal HQ, and R&D personnel, forming a comprehensive framework for evaluating the project's achievements.

11. Factors Contributing to Success:

The project's eventual success, despite initial challenges and setbacks, can be attributed to several key factors. Foremost among these was the unwavering support from senior management, foreign partners, and labs, emphasizing the strategic importance of the project within the group. The Project Manager's autonomy in committing funds based on project needs played a pivotal role, ensuring financial considerations did not impede progress. The high level of team spirit and cohesion, coupled with a proactive approach to problem-solving, fostered an environment where individuals were willing to go the extra mile for project success. The cultivation of innovative ideas, particularly in simplifying design and implementation processes, contributed to overcoming obstacles. The project also benefited from matured processes within the parent organization, especially in areas of process engineering, quality assurance, and quality control. Effective communication, regular coordination, and robust risk management practices further fortified the project's success. Active participation from foreign partners and their consulting teams at the site provided crucial support, ensuring the smooth conduct of testing activities. In essence, a combination of leadership support, team synergy, innovation, and process maturity collectively underpinned the success of the project.

12. Financial Landscape:

The financial landscape of the project reflects a challenging trajectory over its initial years, marked by losses for the first four years and a breakeven achieved only in the fifth year. Cumulative losses amounted to approximately 1.5 crore in the initial phase. The divergence from projected turnover expectations, reaching 3.5 crores instead of the anticipated 5 crores in the fifth year, indicated financial hurdles. Despite these financial setbacks, the project continued with steadfast support from the Group HQ, aligning with the strategic importance of the technology. Noteworthy is the project's subsequent decade of success, achieving a turnover of around INR 85 Crores by the end of March 2015 and integration into the Auto Components division of the parent group. The financial landscape, initially marked by adversity, transformed into sustained success, demonstrating the long-term viability and strategic importance of the project.

13. Project Outcome and Reflection:

The project, despite facing significant challenges and setbacks, demonstrated resilience and ultimately yielded a mix of outcomes. Initial setbacks, including a two-year delay in land acquisition and shifts in market priorities, impacted the project's financial results, reporting losses for the first four years. However, the commitment from the Group HQ sustained the project, leading to a financial reversal in the fifth year with breakeven. The project's success was not solely measured by financial metrics; rather, it was underscored by noteworthy technical achievements. Successful Proof of Concept (POC) trials in the fourth and fifth years validated the project's technical success in introducing innovative SMC and DMC materials to the Auto and Electrical Industries. Subsequent orders from customers attested to the technology's acceptance. Although the project team perceived the first five years as a failure, the unwavering support from the Group HQ enabled the project to thrive in subsequent years, achieving a turnover of INR 85 Crores and integration into the parent group's Auto Components division. The project's trajectory, from initial challenges to sustained success, reflects a nuanced outcome where technical achievements eventually overshadowed initial financial setbacks.

Navigating the intricate landscape of a pioneering project brought forth valuable lessons that underscore the strategic role in decision-making. The foremost lesson involves the recognition of the dynamic nature of technology adoption. In the face of technological shifts, the project had to adapt swiftly to the obsolescence of fibreglass technology, emphasizing the importance of proactive decision-making in response to industry changes.

14. Conclusion: Strategic Transcendence:

The geographical relocation of the plant to an economically backward area revealed the significance of thorough feasibility studies. The insistence of a co-promoter to shift the project's location added unforeseen challenges, highlighting the importance of anticipating potential changes and conducting comprehensive analyses early in the project's lifecycle.

The prioritization shift in the auto industry from medium-sized to large components emphasized the need for flexibility in decision-making. Adapting to this change, while incurring additional capital expenses, showcased the strategic foresight required to align with evolving market trends.

Furthermore, the project highlighted the crucial role of collaborative decision-making. The active involvement of the senior management, financial institutes, and strategic partners played a pivotal role in overcoming hurdles. The unwavering support from these entities demonstrated that decisions made at the strategic level can significantly impact project outcomes.

In conclusion, the project's journey illuminated the strategic imperatives in decision-making amid complexities. Recognizing the dynamic nature of technology, conducting comprehensive feasibility studies, remaining flexible in the face of industry shifts, and fostering collaborative decision-making emerged as invaluable lessons that contributed to the project's ultimate success.

Questions:

1. If you were the project manager, how would you have formulated the project strategy to accommodate unexpected technological shifts?

2. In the event of a proposed relocation of the project site, how would you approach the decision-making process, considering potential challenges and benefits?

3. When faced with a shift in industry priorities affecting project scope and costs, how would you adjust your project plan and budget to align with the changing landscape?

Teaching Note:

Case No 4: Strategic Transcendence: Pioneering an Independent Composite Material Company in India.

Teaching Note

This teaching note guides discussing the case study "Strategic Transcendence: Pioneering an Independent Composite Material Company in India." The note includes suggested timings for each section to facilitate a comprehensive and structured discussion in a classroom setting.

Introduction (5 minutes):

- Briefly introduce the case study, highlighting the strategic initiative of establishing a company for SMC and DMC composite materials in the Indian automobile manufacturing sector.

- Emphasize the significance of the project in responding to industry changes and the complexities involved in technology adoption.

Project Genesis (10 minutes):

- Discuss the strategic considerations that led to the initiation of the project.

- Explore the importance of technology adoption, project classification, and the challenges associated with introducing novel materials in a traditional industry.

- Highlight the diamond analysis used to classify the project based on technology difficulty, design complexity, novelty, and implementation speed.

Leadership Selection (10 minutes):

- Examine the process of selecting the Project Manager, emphasizing the criteria for choosing an individual with specific expertise in SMC and DMC composites.

- Discuss the Project Manager's background, training, and the dual responsibility of establishing the new organization and closing the outdated fibreglass unit.

Diamond Analysis of Project Classifications (5 minutes):

- Review the diamond analysis of project classifications, focusing on technology difficulty, design complexity, novelty, and implementation speed.
- Discuss how these classifications shaped the understanding of project complexity.

Scope Evaluation and Feasibility (15 minutes):

- Analyze the initial scope of the project and its dynamic evolution due to geographical shifts and market trends.
- Explore the challenges faced during the feasibility study, including changes in auto-component market trends and their impact on capital equipment.

Project Dynamics (15 minutes):

- Examine the complex interplay of technological innovation, market adaptation, and strategic decision-making in the project.
- Discuss the challenges and adjustments related to the geographical relocation of the project and the shift in market priorities.

Key Team Positions (5 minutes):

- Review the key team positions and their roles in the success of the project.
- Discuss the importance of a well-structured and skilled team in navigating project complexities.

Challenges and Setbacks (15 minutes):

- Explore the significant hurdles faced by the project, including bureaucratic challenges, resistance to innovative materials, and unexpected shifts in market priorities.
- Discuss how the team overcame these challenges and the lessons learnt.

Positive Project Environment (10 minutes):

- Highlight the support system from senior management, foreign partners, and labs that contributed to a positive project environment.
- Discuss the importance of effective communication, coordination, and risk management.

Success Criteria Determination (10 minutes):

- Examine the success criteria determined in consultation with senior management and sponsors.
- Discuss the holistic approach to success, considering customer satisfaction, industry standards, supplier satisfaction, and team appreciation.

Factors Contributing to Success (10 minutes):

- Analyse the key factors that contributed to the project's success, including leadership support, team synergy, innovation, and mature processes.
- Discuss the importance of active participation from foreign partners and their consulting teams.

Financial Landscape (10 minutes):

- Review the financial trajectory of the project, emphasizing the initial challenges, breakeven in the fifth year, and subsequent sustained success.
- Discuss the role of Group HQ's support in overcoming financial setbacks.

Project Outcome and Reflection (10 minutes):

- Explore the project's mix of outcomes, including financial results and technical achievements.
- Discuss the lessons learned from the project's journey and the importance of strategic decision-making.

Conclusion: Strategic Transcendence (5 minutes):

- Summarize the key takeaways from the case study, emphasizing strategic imperatives in decision-making amid complexities.
- Discuss the lessons learned, including the dynamic nature of technology, the importance of feasibility studies, flexibility in decision-making, and collaborative decision-making.

Case No 5: Strategic Collaboration and Market Penetration: The Journey of a New Unit in Process Control Industries

Dr Jayasri Murali, Dr Vinod Bhelose

Associate Professor, MBA@IICMR, Pune, Assistant Professor, MBA@IICMR, Pune

Abstract:

This case study revolves around a technology project initiated with an estimated cost of $0.4 million over five years. The project aimed to establish a new unit for designing and developing process control devices and systems. However, it faced numerous challenges.

The team consisted of 32 members at its peak, dealing with uncertainties and risks associated with developing a new concept in process control technology. The project had both internal and external challenges, ranging from gaining customer confidence and managing finances to dealing with slow decision-making in the market.

Key issues included technology choices, management changes, communication breakdowns, and a lack of adequate domain expertise. Despite initial successes, the project faced setbacks in its later years due to strategic misjudgments, internal politics, and a refusal of technical collaboration.

This case study emphasizes the importance of customer involvement, competent team members, and strong project management for success. Ultimately, the project, while having some early successes, was deemed a failure after five years.

1. Introduction:

This case study delves into a comprehensive analysis of a technology project undertaken with an initial budget of $0.4 million over five years. The project's primary objective was to establish a pioneering unit dedicated to the design and development of cutting-edge process control devices and systems, particularly focusing on applications within the process industry.

The project's ambitious goals included completing licensing and registration processes, initiating dialogues with industry leaders, and achieving a substantial turnover within specific time frames. The endeavour, classified as a "New Greenfield Project," faced considerable risks and uncertainties due to its innovative nature and reliance on homegrown designs and local teams.

The team, comprising around 32 individuals at its peak, encountered multifaceted challenges spanning from internal issues like gaining customer confidence and managing finances to external factors such as slow decision-making in the market and intensifying competition. The project's trajectory unfolded against the backdrop of evolving technology, changes in market dynamics, and unforeseen management shifts.

This case study meticulously explores the internal and external challenges faced by the project team, shedding light on critical aspects like technology choices, management support, communication breakdowns, and the significance of domain expertise. Despite encountering initial successes, the project underwent a downward spiral in its later years, attributed to strategic misjudgments, internal political dynamics, and a reluctance to engage in technical collaborations.

Through a detailed examination of the project's journey, this study underscores the importance of factors such as customer involvement, a competent team, and robust project management for ensuring success in complex and dynamic environments. Ultimately, the project, marked by some early accomplishments, is evaluated as a failure after the completion of its five-year timeline.

2. Project Characteristics:

Visionary Scale:
1. Embarking on a groundbreaking journey with an initial investment of $0.4 million USD (INR 1.8-2.4 crore) over three years.
2. Constrained by the equity capital of 0.4 crore, challenging the team to innovate within financial boundaries.

Dynamic Team Dynamics:
1. A dynamic team of 12 in the inaugural year, expanding to 25 by the fifth year.
2. The ensemble included developers, QA/QC experts, sales maestros, domain aficionados, on-site engineers, and vital support services.

Orchestrating a meticulous 5-year Phase 1 plan.
1. Pioneering the first trial development within 24 months at the customer's doorstep.
2. Aiming for a dazzling turnover of over 6 crore and a robust 18% margin by the fifth year.

Greenfield Pioneering:
1. Classified as a "New Greenfield Project," pioneering a technology unit for innovative Process Industry Applications.
2. A bold challenge embraced by the project team.

Adventurous Risk-Taking:
1. Venturing into uncertainty, relying on promoters for the first two years.
2. A unique concept developed with homegrown designs and an Indian workforce.
3. Transitioning to self-generated cash-flow after the initial period.

Sponsorship Odyssey:
1. Early camaraderie among senior management evolved into tension.
2. Departure of the MD triggered a cascade of challenges, testing the resilience of the entire team.
3. A corporate drama influencing the nascent organization's destiny.

Tech Evolution and Adaptation:
1. Navigating the evolving tech landscape, drawing inspiration from global solutions in the USA, Europe, and Japan.
2. A strategic decision to locally develop low-end systems in-house, showcasing confidence in local engineering prowess.
3. A paradigm shift post-Chairman's exit, reshaping technological collaborations.

Strategic Supplier Synergy:
1. A judicious selection of suppliers, with emphasis on cultivating relationships with domain consultants.
2. Navigating complexities in obtaining industrial licenses and government registrations, demonstrating adept logistical management.

Coordination Complexity:
1. Juggling operations across three locations (Mumbai/Pune & customer site).
2. Streamlined communication investments facilitating seamless coordination.

Cohesive Team Tapestry:
1. Commencing as a tightly-knit team of 32 individuals, facing challenges head-on.
2. Early tensions gave way to unity after initial victories.
3. Resilient collaboration paving the way for innovation.

Customer Engagement Canvas:
1. Navigating initial skepticism from customers, transforming into active participation.
2. Customer involvement in developmental activities, fostering a symbiotic relationship.

Leadership Symphony:
1. A visionary Project Manager/CEO and a forward-thinking CTO, steering the ship with design and development prowess.
2. Augmented by a seasoned GM for sales, injecting strategic vigor into the team.

Fig 2.1 Project Characteristics

3. Project Challenges:

In a five-year journey marked by ambitious goals, the project team faced distinct challenges across defined phases. The initial focus aimed at establishing credibility and gaining trust from high-tech customers, presenting a formidable task for a newcomer in the intricate industry.

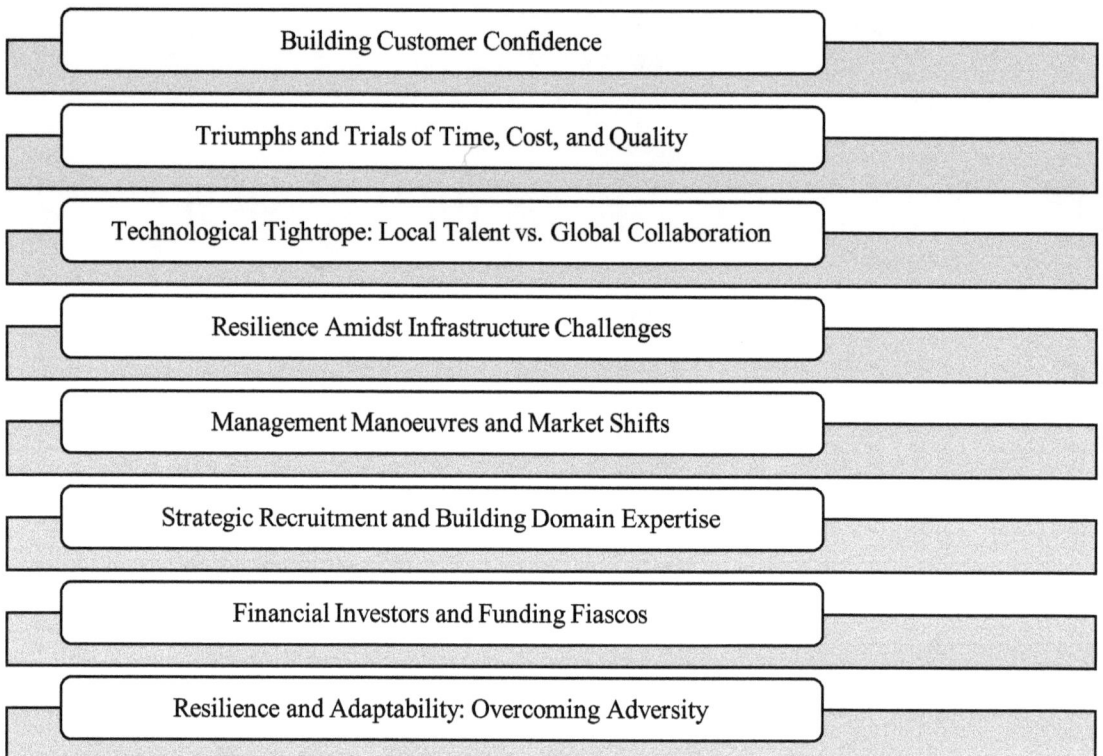

Figure 3.1: Project challenges

Building Customer Confidence: The project team successfully navigated the challenge of instilling confidence in customers through the combined expertise of the CEO and CTO. Leveraging the parent company's reputation played a crucial role in overcoming initial scepticism.

Triumphs and Trials of Time, Cost, and Quality: The trio of Time, Cost, and Quality emerged as perpetual challenges, with a funding commitment limited to the first 36 months. The team faced relentless pressure to deliver within tight timelines, and market dynamics added complexity with a shift towards integrated solutions.

Technological Tightrope: Local Talent vs. Global Collaboration: Navigating the absence of technical collaborations, the team relied on local talent for design and development, creating technological hurdles. Homegrown products faced delays and limitations, demanding swift adaptation to market shifts.

Resilience Amidst Infrastructure Challenges: Despite inadequate infrastructure and financial constraints, the team exhibited resilience. The project maintained a reputation for quality processes, showcasing the ability to thrive in challenging circumstances.

Management Manoeuvres and Market Shifts: Management decisions, including a refusal of foreign collaboration, introduced unforeseen challenges. Communication breakdowns with the new management exacerbated funding shortages, leading to a "step-child" treatment of the project.

Strategic Recruitment and Building Domain Expertise: Building domain expertise and recruiting competent manpower emerged as pivotal challenges. The team strategically handpicked initial members, understanding the critical importance of quality assurance in sensitive applications.

Financial Investors and Funding Fiascos: The project faced setbacks when financial investors turned indifferent, leading to confrontations over expansion plans. As the project unfolded, funds became a constant concern, aggravated by delays in the development of the General-Purpose Controller (GPC).

Resilience and Adaptability: Overcoming Adversity: Despite the myriad challenges, the project stands as a testament to the team's resilience and adaptability in the face of adversity. The ability to navigate through uncertainties and challenges underscored the team's commitment to turning ambitious goals into tangible successes.

4. Navigating External Challenges:

The success of the project was intricately tied to a multitude of external factors, each presenting unique challenges that demanded strategic manoeuvring.

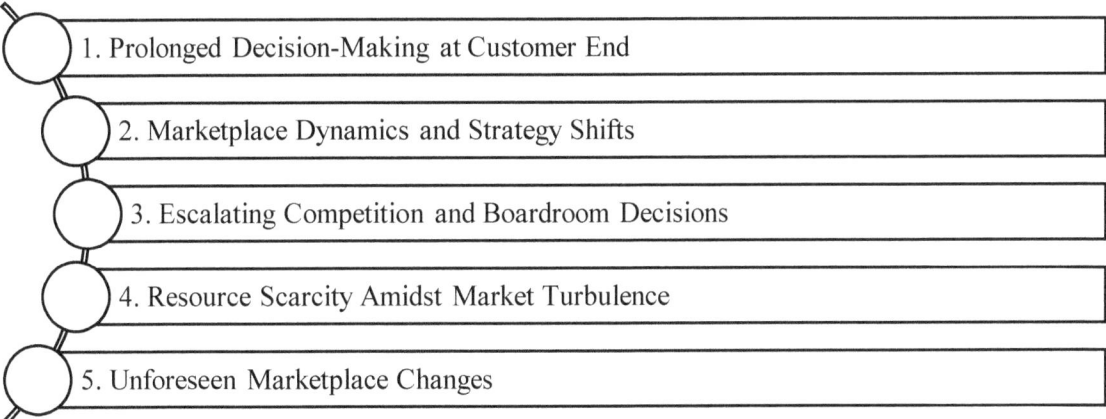

Figure: 4.1: Navigating External Challenges

1. **Prolonged Decision-Making at Customer End:** A persistent challenge lies in the slow decision-making processes at the customer's end. The timeline from the initial contact to finalizing contracts proved to be a considerable undertaking. Skilful management by the CEO and CTO duo was instrumental in streamlining these cycles during the initial two years.

2. **Marketplace Dynamics and Strategy Shifts:** The project encountered significant shifts in the marketplace, necessitating adjustments to the original strategy as early as the second year. While the project team implemented some changes, resource constraints limited the extent of their adaptability, highlighting the critical role of financial support.

3. **Escalating Competition and Boardroom Decisions:** Competition, initially subdued in the initial two years, intensified after the second year. The Board of Directors' reluctance to provide adequate support exacerbated the situation, creating a challenging environment for the project team.

4. **Resource Scarcity Amidst Market Turbulence:** The shortage of funds and resources posed a continual external challenge, hindering the team's ability to respond effectively to marketplace changes. The evolving landscape demanded swift adaptations, underscoring the crucial role of external support in ensuring project success.

5. **Unforeseen Marketplace Changes:** Market dynamics underwent unforeseen changes, impacting original market projections. The project team, constrained by financial limitations, grappled with mitigating these changes effectively, revealing the delicate balance between strategic flexibility and resource constraints.

In facing these external challenges head-on, the project team demonstrated resilience and adaptability, striving to steer the project towards success amidst a dynamic and often unpredictable external environment.

5. Diamond Analysis of Project Complexity:

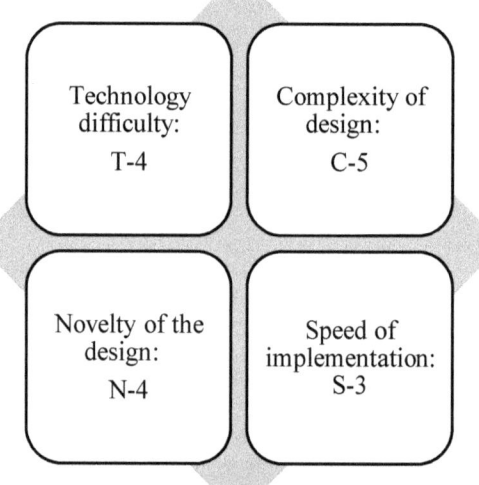

Figure: 5.1: Diamond Analysis of Project Complexity

Imagine the project as a dazzling diamond, each facet revealing a unique challenge. Picture the technology difficulty as a T-4, showcasing the project's journey through intricate, ever-evolving technologies. The complexity of design sparkles as a C-5, highlighting the intricate dance of creating complex products with local talent. In the novelty of design, marked N-4, envision the project as a pioneer, navigating uncharted territory in process control systems. Lastly, the speed of implementation, an S-3, captures the dynamic rhythm of racing against time and market changes. This project, like a radiant diamond, shines with technological challenges and innovative aspirations.

6. Key Positions in the Team:

1. Project Manager / Project Champion (CEO):
2. The visionary leader steering the ship, guiding the project with a blend of expertise and strategic insight.

1. CTO with R&D Orientation:
2. The maestro of product development, wielding a multi-disciplinary baton to harmonize innovative approaches.

1. Market Development & Sales Manager:
2. The virtuoso crafting melodies of market success, harmonizing the project's offerings with industry needs.

1. Business Analyst:
2. A melody weaver with a flair for R&D, sculpting the project's path through the intricate landscapes of Proteinomics & Genomics.

1. Business Domain / Process Experts / Consultants:
2. The skilled instrumentalists providing expertise in diverse domains and technologies, adding depth to the project's composition.

1. Delivery Manager:
2. The conductor of software applications for Engineering Applications, ensuring a seamless delivery performance.

1. Quality Leader / Site Quality Leader + 2 site engineers:
2. The guardians of quality, ensuring the project's outputs meet stringent standards in the delicate realm of diagnostic and analytical systems.

1. Accounts Manager:
2. The financial virtuoso managing the financial movements and funding, playing a critical tune in the project's financial composition.

1. PMO Office:
2. The silent yet powerful rhythm section, tracking and controlling project progress with precision and finesse.

1. Innovative Human Resource Personnel:
2. The catalyst for acquiring and nurturing talent, ensuring the team's composition resonates with the demands of the innovative project.

Figure: 6.1: Key Positions in the Team

7. Project Success Criteria:

The symphony of success for this visionary project was composed of distinctive notes, echoing the expectations and aspirations of both the organization and its discerning customers. The crescendo of triumph included completing the project in a harmonious blend of timely delivery and cost-effectiveness, with an unwavering commitment to unwavering quality standards. The composition reached its zenith when the project achieved profitability as planned, emerging as a model masterpiece in the business landscape-a reference point for future endeavours. The harmony extended to securing repeat orders, a sweet melody echoing customer satisfaction and trust. The satisfaction of the team members was the sublime undertone, fostering skill development and quality enhancement. The project's success criteria, much like a perfectly orchestrated symphony, reverberated across organizational, customer, and team dimensions, creating a harmonious legacy.

8. Project Success Factors:

The success of this intricate project can be attributed to a tapestry of factors that are intricately woven together to create a triumphant narrative. A clear understanding of the task at hand, coupled with a well-defined scope and specifications, laid the groundwork for success. The project's organizational structure, marked by smart decision systems, provided a stable framework for seamless operations. The commitment and active participation of customer teams throughout the project's lifecycle added a crucial layer, ensuring the alignment of deliverables with expectations.

Support from investors and joint venture partners emerged as a pillar of strength, fortifying the project's foundations. The project's heartbeat was the competent Project Manager and a trusted team, driving the endeavour with expertise and dedication. The development team's competence, coupled with the right attitude, brought a valuable dimension to the project's success. An alert risk management system, vigilantly addressing timelines and design changes, acted as a guiding compass through the project's complexities.

Behind the scenes, the Project Management Office (PMO) played a pivotal role, rigorously tracking issues and resolving them with precision. The robust support from Quality Assurance/Quality Control teams and process control engineers ensured that the project adhered to stringent standards. A tapestry of exceptional teamwork, coupled with unwavering support from the task force members, further enriched the success narrative. The project's success was a symphony of collaboration, innovation, and strategic prowess, showcasing a harmonious fusion of various success factors.

Conclusion:

In retrospect, the project, despite its early promise, encountered a tumultuous journey marked by misjudgments, internal politics, and strategic missteps. The Board of Directors (BOD) decisions, coupled with a lack of understanding of domain intricacies, cast a shadow on the project's trajectory. Heavy reliance on in-house development and the refusal to engage in technical collaboration emerged as critical errors.

While the R&D group's efforts were commendable, the system developed in India fell short of expectations. The CEO and CTO's decisions, though contributing to the organization's development, faced challenges due to situational and strategic factors. The project's failure, encompassing a few glimpses of success in its initial five years, serves as a valuable case study, underscoring the importance of strategic foresight, adaptability, and external collaboration in navigating complex project landscapes. Despite the setbacks, the dedicated efforts of the team and its leaders stand as a testament to resilience and commitment in the face of adversity.

The organization reported the following results for the first 5 years after the gestation period:

Year 12 months (Gestation period)

	1	2	3	4	5
Sales in crore	0.5	0.9	1.1	1.5	2
Margin As% (PBT / Sales)	(.80)%	(0.60)%	1.0%	2.00%	(4.0)%
*Bank OD					Around 1 Crore

Table 5.1

Questions:

1. **Comprehensive Strategy Overview:** As a manager leading this project, outline a comprehensive strategic approach to address both internal and external challenges. How would you balance the need for gaining customer confidence, managing finances, navigating technological hurdles, and responding to marketplace dynamics?

2. **Innovative Responses to Technology Challenges:** Considering the diamond analysis of project complexity and the identified technology challenges, propose innovative strategies and responses to ensure successful navigation through intricate technologies, design complexities, and the need for novel solutions. How would you foster adaptability and resilience in the face of technological uncertainties?

3. **Strategies for Long-Term Success:** Looking beyond the initial phases, discuss the strategies you would employ to ensure the long-term success of the project. Consider aspects such as customer involvement, team competence, collaboration with investors, and adapting to evolving market dynamics. How would you position the project for sustained success and overcome setbacks encountered in the later years?

Teaching Note

Case No 5: Strategic Collaboration and Market Penetration: The Journey of a New Unit in Process Control Industries.

Introduction:

The case study, "Strategic Collaboration and Market Penetration: The Journey of a New Unit in Process Control Industries," recounts a technology project with a $0.4 million budget over five years. Aimed at establishing a ground-breaking unit for process control devices, the project faced internal and external challenges. Despite ambitious goals, issues like customer confidence, financial management, and slow market decision-making emerged. Critical challenges included technology choices, management changes, communication breakdowns, and a lack of domain expertise, leading to setbacks. Despite initial success, strategic misjudgments and reluctance to engage in technical collaborations labelled the project a failure after five years. The study explores internal and external dynamics, emphasizing strategic foresight, adaptability, and collaboration in navigating complex environments.

Project Characteristics and Challenges:

- Emphasize the project's ambitious goals and the challenges faced in building customer confidence, managing time, cost, and quality, navigating technological hurdles, and overcoming infrastructure challenges.

- Highlight the importance of strategic recruitment, domain expertise, and the financial fiascos faced by the project team.

External Challenges:

- Discuss external challenges such as prolonged decision-making at the customer end, marketplace dynamics, escalating competition, resource scarcity, and unforeseen marketplace changes.

- Emphasize the team's resilience and adaptability in navigating these external challenges.

Diamond Analysis of Project Complexity:

- Illustrate the project as a diamond with facets representing technology difficulty, complexity of design, novelty of design, and speed of implementation.

- Discuss how each facet contributed to the overall project complexity.

Project Success Factors and Criteria:

- Identify success factors including a clear understanding of tasks, organizational structure, customer team participation, investor support, competent project management, and effective teamwork.

- Highlight success criteria involving timely delivery, cost-effectiveness, profitability, and customer satisfaction.

Conclusion:

- Summarize the project's journey, acknowledging early successes but ultimately deemed a failure.
- Stress the importance of strategic foresight, adaptability, and external collaboration in complex project landscapes.

Interactive Discussion Questions:

- **Comprehensive Strategy Overview**: Encourage participants to outline a strategic approach as if they were the project manager. Discuss how they would balance gaining customer confidence, managing finances, navigating technological hurdles, and responding to marketplace dynamics.

- **Innovative Responses to Technology Challenges:** Challenge participants to propose innovative strategies for navigating technological complexities and design challenges. Discuss fostering adaptability and resilience in the face of technological uncertainties.

- **Strategies for Long-Term Success:** Encourage participants to discuss strategies for ensuring the project's long-term success. Explore their perspectives on customer involvement, team competence, collaboration with investors, and adapting to evolving market dynamics.

Concluding Remarks: Sum up the teaching note by reinforcing the case's value in highlighting the intricacies of strategic management and the dynamic nature of technology projects. Encourage engaging discussions and critical thinking among students.

Case No 6: The Uncharted Path: Unravelling the Complex Tale of APC_Avanti's Project Journey

Dr Jayasri Murali, Dr Dipti Sharma

Associate Professor, MBA@IICMR, Pune, Assistant Professor, MBA@ IICMR, Pune

Abstract:

In the dynamic landscape of the controlled economy, APC_Avanti embarked on a challenging endeavour to establish a new manufacturing unit in the economically backward district of Satara-MIDC. Focused on producing innovative "Down the Hole Hammer" (DTH) bits for rock drilling applications, the project aimed to cater to the growing demands in water resource management and mining industries. Led by a dedicated core team, the project encountered various hurdles, from protracted regulatory processes to shifts in market demands.

This case study sheds light on the intricate journey of APC_Avanti over five years, outlining the team's objectives, challenges, and internal dynamics. The team, consisting of engineers with diverse expertise, faced hurdles such as delayed licensing processes, changes in market preferences, and technology adaptations. The project's technological complexity and the evolving nature of DTH technology in India added to the team's challenges.

Internal issues, including management pressures, communication breakdowns, and evolving team dynamics, further complicated the project's trajectory. Financial constraints, supplier issues, and inadequacies in infrastructure posed additional hurdles. The unforeseen switch in market preferences from cross bits to button bits significantly impacted the project's feasibility, leading to additional capital investments and delays.

Despite initially supportive sponsors, the project faced a downward spiral due to a lack of financial and strategic backing during challenging times. The team struggled with inadequate domain expertise, supplier support, and infrastructure, contributing to the project's ultimate evaluation as a failure.

This case study serves as a valuable exploration of the multifaceted challenges encountered by APC_Avanti, providing insights into the complexities of managing a high-risk, technology-driven project and the critical factors influencing its unexpected conclusion.

Keywords: Innovation, Resilience, Intricacies, Adaptability, Collaboration

1. Introduction:

In the realm of business innovation, APC_Avanti embarked on a ground-breaking venture by establishing a new manufacturing unit in the economically challenged district of Satara-MIDC. This endeavour took place during a time of strict economic control, making the process of setting up new industrial units arduous and time-consuming. Undaunted by these challenges, APC_Avanti, led by a group of skilled engineers, delved into the unexplored realm of manufacturing "Down the Hole Hammer" (DTH) bits - crucial components in rock drilling technology.

The project's origin coincided with an era dominated by a controlled economy, where intricate regulations made establishing new units a lengthy process. Despite these challenges, APC_Avanti emerged as a private limited company, founded by three engineers with over 12 years of experience each. Their backgrounds, shaped by dedication in a renowned multinational corporation, fueled their shared ambition to chart a new course in manufacturing.

The impetus for this ambitious venture arose from the growing demand in water resource management exploration, specifically for products used in drilling bore wells. Simultaneously, the mining industry provided an opportunity for the application of their envisioned mining products. The core team, consisting of engineers specializing in design, manufacturing, and quality assurance, collaborated seamlessly, setting the stage for a harmonious journey into this transformative project. The project's visionary leader, also the Chairman of the core team, took on the roles of Project Manager (PM) and project champion. The initial two years were marked by relative harmony and synergy, but the cumbersome process of obtaining business and industrial licenses posed a significant challenge, consuming over two crucial years and impacting the overall project timeline.

The inspiration for the new manufacturing unit arose from conversations with industry seniors engaged in mining activities in India. This dialogue informed the creation of a comprehensive project report covering market feasibility and technical aspects for the first five years. While robust in many aspects, the report lacked depth in risk analysis and sensitivity to market changes, setting the stage for challenges in the project's later stages.

Despite these hurdles, the project gained momentum as the report underwent fine-tuning and corrections, securing approval from the Small Industries Development Bank of India (SICOM). Simultaneously, the team acquired land in Satara-MIDC and sought overdraft limit approval from a reputed bank. With critical preparations in place, APC_Avanti stood on the brink of initiating project activities, ready to meet the increasing demand for DTH hammer bits.

As the organization geared up to capitalize on market opportunities, the project's objectives crystallized. APC_Avanti aimed not only to manufacture cutting-edge DTH products but also to make them cost-effective, using Indian raw materials and providing exceptional after-sales service. The design and development process prioritized user convenience, low maintenance, and easy integration with other equipment. A strategic goal was set to achieve breakeven within four years, with a projected turnover of 5 crores and a profit margin of around 18% by the end of the fifth year. The project's classification as a Technically Complex Project with considerable risks was underscored by its technological difficulty, design complexity, novelty, and speed of implementation. The estimated initial cost of the project stood at approximately 1 million USD, constrained by the equity capital of 1 crore from the promoters and their associates.

In the face of economic challenges and regulatory intricacies, APC_Avanti prepared to forge ahead into uncharted territory, driven by the collective expertise of its core team and a resolute commitment to technological innovation.

2. Objectives of the Project:

The goal of creating DTH hammer bits is to serve specific purposes in both water well drilling and mining activities. In simpler terms, these bits are designed to help drill holes effectively for accessing water in bore wells. Additionally, they find applications in the mining industry for drilling and exploration purposes. The objective is to make these bits technologically advanced and cost-effective, ensuring they meet the needs of users, especially in terms of the cost per foot of drilling. The aim is to manufacture these products using Indian raw materials, providing good after-sales service as needed. The focus is on making the application user-friendly, requiring low maintenance, and ensuring compatibility with other equipment and machinery. The ultimate target is for the organization to reach a break-even point within less than four years from the start, with a projected turnover of around 5 crores and a profit margin of approximately 18 % by the end of the fifth year.

3. Diamond Analysis of the Project Complexity:

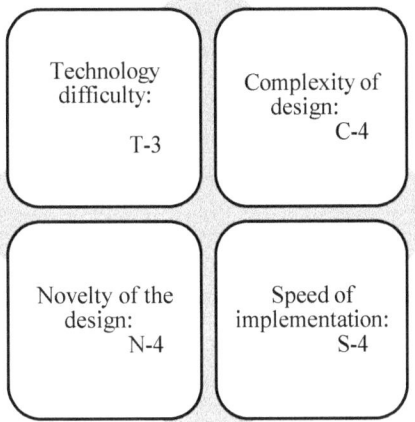

Figure 6. 1: Diamond Analysis of the Project Complexity

Technology Difficulty (T-3): The project involves a moderate level of technological complexity, marked by the challenges of introducing new manufacturing processes and designs for DTH hammer bits. The technology, though developed in advanced economies, faces initial stages of adoption in the Indian market.

Complexity of Design (C-4): Design complexity is relatively high, especially considering the shift from cross bits to button bits. This change necessitates adjustments in the planned designs, leading to challenges in the production process. The evolution in design adds a layer of intricacy to the project.

The novelty of the Design (N-4): The design novelty is notable, particularly in the context of the initial stages of introducing DTH hammer bits in the Indian market. The shift in market preferences and the need to adapt to button bits showcase the innovative aspects of the project.

Speed of Implementation (S-4): The project demands a moderately paced implementation due to regulatory hurdles, time-consuming licensing processes, and the need for approvals from various financial institutions. The intricate coordination required among multiple stakeholders contributes to the moderate speed of implementation.

By assessing these facets through the diamond analysis, it becomes evident that the project operates in a landscape marked by moderate to high levels of technological intricacy, design evolution, and innovative adaptations, all unfolding at a measured implementation pace.

4. Project Characteristics:

Size of the Project: The initial cost of the project was estimated at approximately 1 million USD (INR 46 crore in today's currency rates), including manpower costs, overheads, travel, and incidental costs.
The project cost was constrained based on the equity capital of 1 crore from promoters and their friends and relatives.

Number of People: The project involved around 45 individuals on average (and a maximum of 55) at any given point. This included 25 persons in the manufacturing unit, a QA/QC group of 5, and 15 team members at different sites for implementation.

Time Schedule: The project spanned five years in phases, with the pilot test expected to start at the customer location after 30 months from the initiation.
The target was to achieve a turnover of over 5 crores with a margin of 18% at that stage (PBT/Sales revenue).

Classification of Project: The project set up a new manufacturing unit for DTH bits for water well drilling and the mining industry, posing a challenge for the project team.
Considered a technically complex project, it involved considerable risks.

High-Risk Project: Uncertainties and risks arose due to the development of a "new concept" application using homegrown designs and Indian raw materials.
Changes in technology choice in the second year disrupted the initial capital outlay, necessitating additional funding and leading to ongoing problems.

Technology Choice/Maturity: The technology was evolving, with the new application being in its initial stages in India.
Attempts to collaborate with a US company faced resistance, impacting the project's progression.

Number of Suppliers: The project had many suppliers, with 15 critical suppliers for core activities.
Initially positive, the relationship soured later due to uneven cash flows.

Logistics/Clearances: Obtaining government clearances for orders, along with delays associated with order placement and payment cycles, posed significant challenges.

Location for Coordination: Coordination was required across more than four locations, including Mumbai, Pune, Kolhapur, and several customer locations.

Support from Sponsors: Initially strong, relations between senior management became strained due to different approaches and personalities.
Delays in fund release and pending accounts receivables further strained relations, creating a complex situation for the team.

Team Members & Effectiveness: The team initially worked cohesively but tensions emerged over time, driven by differences in convictions and competence.
This affected performance and led to confrontations and problems within the team.

Involvement of Customer: Customer support, particularly from government agencies, was mixed and sometimes hesitant during the initial phases.

Team Leader: The Project Manager, a competent and committed engineer with expertise in mining products and production, faced challenges due to the lack of higher authority, causing future problems for the project.

Fig 4.1 Project Characteristics

5. Navigating the Project Challenges:

Regulatory Hurdles and Delayed Approvals:	• The project encountered significant delays and challenges in obtaining business and industrial licenses. Regulatory approvals became a defining challenge, consuming more than two crucial years.
Financial Setbacks and Additional Funding:	• The initially estimated project cost faced drastic changes due to the switch to button bits in the second year. This disruption required additional funding, upsetting the feasibility of the entire project.
Technological Complexity and Collaboration Struggles:	• The project was classified as a Technically Complex Project with considerable risks. Attempts to collaborate with a US company faced resistance, impacting the project's progress in the evolving technological landscape.
Supplier Relationships and Cash Flow Issues:	• While there were many suppliers in the project, critical supplier relationships with 15 key entities turned problematic. Uneven cash flows led to strained relationships, affecting the smooth flow of project activities.
Logistical Challenges and Government Clearances:	• Logistics and obtaining necessary government clearances for orders proved to be a considerable challenge. Delays associated with order placement and payment cycles added complexity to the project's logistical aspects.
Multi-Location Coordination:	• Coordinating activities across more than four locations, including Mumbai, Pune, Kolhapur, and various customer sites, added an additional layer of complexity to the project's execution.
Strained Relations and Funding Delays:	• Despite an initial phase of strong support, relations among senior management became strained. Delays in the release of funds and pending accounts receivables created a complex and tricky situation for the project team.
Team Dynamics and Competence Issues:	• While the team initially worked cohesively, tensions surfaced over time. Differences in convictions and competence among team members created a challenging work environment, affecting overall project performance.
Customer Engagement and Government Agencies:	• The involvement of government agencies as major customers posed challenges. Managing customer relations, especially with government entities, became a significant aspect of the project's complexities.
Leadership Challenges and Lack of Authority:	• The competent Project Manager faced challenges due to a lack of higher position and authority, impacting decision-making and causing issues for the team throughout the project's lifecycle.

Figure 5.1; Navigating the Project Challenges

6. External Challenges Faced by APC_Avanti's Project:

Regulatory Complexity:	1. *Navigating Regulatory Red Tape* The project confronted intricate regulatory processes, facing delays in obtaining necessary business and industrial licenses. 2. Overcoming bureaucratic hurdles became a time-consuming and challenging aspect.
Financial Volatility:	1. *Unforeseen Financial Shifts* Drastic changes in the estimated project cost due to a switch to button bits in the second year led to financial setbacks. 2. The need for additional funding disrupted the financial stability, affecting the overall feasibility.
Technological Landscape:	1. *Adapting to Evolving Technology* The project operated in a technologically evolving period, introducing a new application that was well-developed in the USA and Europe but still in its initial stages in India. Attempts at collaboration faced resistance, impacting technology adoption.
Supplier Relationship Challenges:	1. *Managing Supplier Dynamics* The project involved numerous suppliers, but critical relationships with 15 key entities became problematic. Cash flow issues strained these relationships, affecting the timely supply of crucial components.
Logistical Complexities:	1. *Juggling Logistics and Government Clearances* Coordinating logistics for the project, especially obtaining government clearances for orders, posed considerable challenges. Delays associated with order placement and payment cycles added complexity to the logistical aspects.
Multi-Location Coordination:	1. *Coordinating Across Distances* The project spanned more than four locations, including Mumbai, Pune, Kolhapur, and various customer sites. Coordinating activities across these diverse locations presented additional challenges.
Market Dynamics and Customer Engagement:	1. *Navigating Customer Relationships* The involvement of government agencies as major customers introduced complexities. Managing relations with customers, particularly government entities, became a crucial aspect of the project's external challenges.
Global Economic Factors:	1. *Navigating Global Economic Trends* The project unfolded against the backdrop of a challenging economic landscape. Global economic factors influenced market conditions and added an external layer of uncertainty to the project.
Political and Policy Influences:	1. *Adapting to Political and Policy Shifts* Changes in political and policy landscapes introduced uncertainties. Adapting to these shifts and aligning the project with evolving political and policy frameworks became essential.
Competitive Industry Dynamics:	1. *Navigating Competitive Forces* The industry's competitive nature introduced external challenges. APC_Avanti had to strategize to position itself effectively amidst competition and changing market dynamics.

Figure: 6.3: External Challenges Faced by APC_Avanti's Project:

7. Key Positions in APC_Avanti's Project Team:

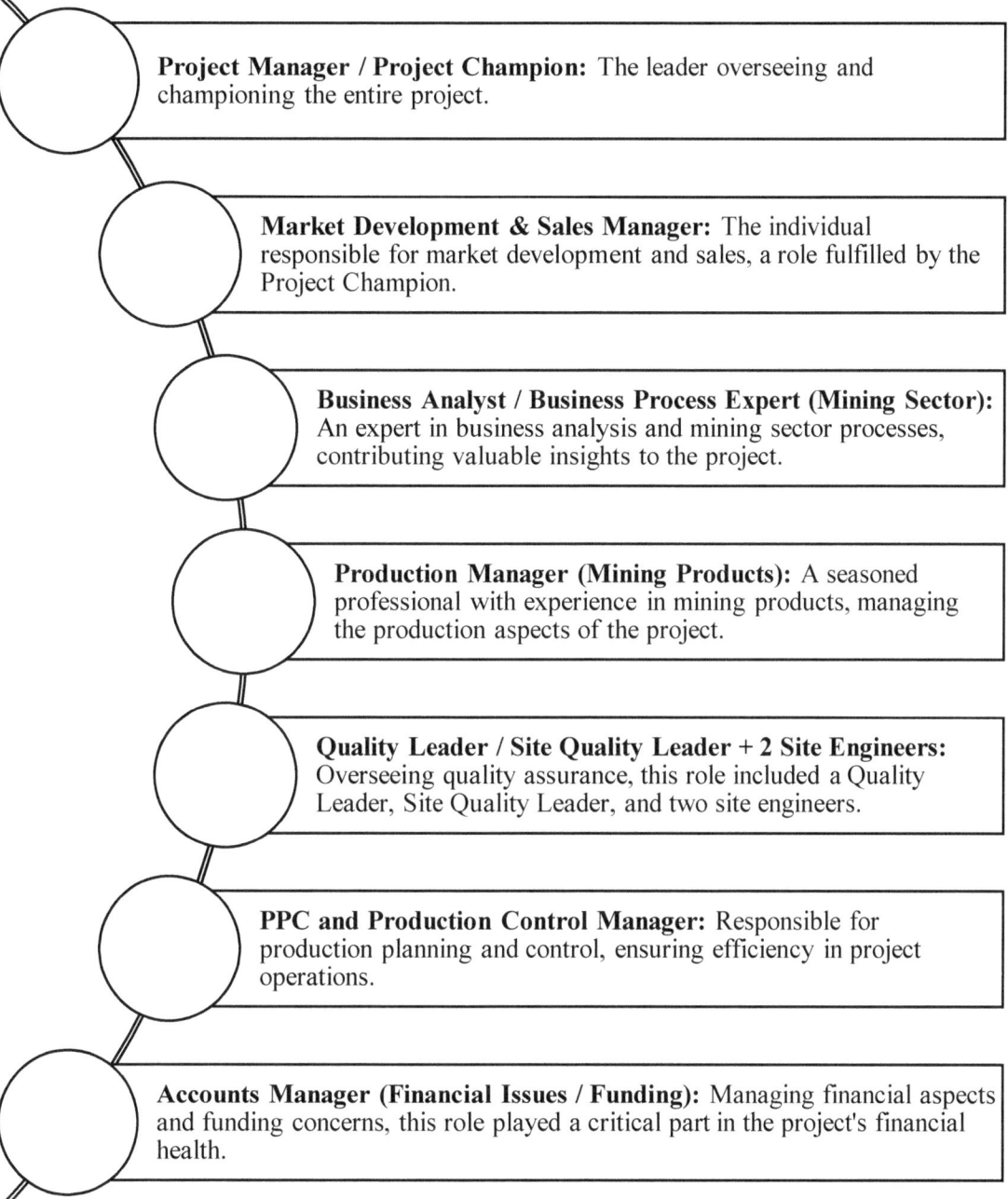

Figure 7.1: Key Positions in APC_Avanti's Project Team

These key positions collectively formed a diverse and specialized team, each contributing their expertise to different facets of the project, ultimately working together to overcome challenges and achieve the project's objectives.

8. Project Success Checklist:

Project Success Checklist for Our Team: Embarking on this journey, our team envisions success as a harmonious blend of timeliness, financial prudence, and unwavering commitment to quality. Our goal is not merely to complete the project but to do so within the allocated time and budget while upholding the highest standards of excellence. We thrive on the challenge of stringent field trials, aiming not just to meet but to exceed customer expectations through hands-on support and dedication to satisfaction. The bottom line: achieving the projected profitability, ensuring repeat business, and transforming our vision into a resounding success.

Project Success Criteria for Our Customers: From the customer's perspective, success translates into a seamless experience marked by punctuality and precision. We commit to delivering not only on time but also on the promise of reducing drilling costs per foot in the field, thereby ensuring a substantial Return on Investment. Beyond the transactional, our success is measured by the contentment of our dedicated team members, whose satisfaction and continuous skill development are paramount. We pledge to continually enhance our product design, elevating the quality of our offerings to consistently meet and exceed the evolving needs of our valued customers.

Conclusion:

In conclusion, the journey of APC_Avanti's venture into a new manufacturing unit for DTH bits, amidst the intricacies of a controlled economy and regulatory challenges, has been a saga marked by resilience and learning. The project, driven by a visionary core team, aimed to revolutionize the landscape of water well drilling and mining applications in India. However, as the narrative unfolded, unforeseen complexities arose, testing the mettle of the team and leading to an unexpected denouement.

The project's characteristics, spanning its size, manpower, and technological challenges, painted a vivid picture of ambition coupled with risks. Navigating through external challenges, the team faced hurdles in logistics, clearances, and strained relations with sponsors, contributing to the project's intricacies. Key positions within the team played pivotal roles, each bringing unique expertise to the table.

Despite the challenges, the success criteria, encompassing both organizational and customer expectations, were well-defined. Organizational goals centred on completing the project with unwavering quality, achieving profitability, and securing repeat orders. Simultaneously, customer expectations focused on timely delivery, cost reduction in drilling, team satisfaction, and product design improvements.

Reflecting on the project's success factors, the hindsight wisdom of the team revealed crucial elements like clarity of tasks, robust project organization, customer commitment, strong support from sponsors, meticulous risk management, and unwavering teamwork.

The story of APC_Avanti's venture is not just about the challenges faced but a testament to the tenacity and collaborative spirit of the team. The learnings from this journey serve as valuable insights for future endeavours, emphasizing the importance of foresight, adaptability, and cohesive teamwork in navigating uncharted territories of industrial innovation.

Questions:

1. How would you strategically address the challenges related to regulatory approvals and formalities that significantly impacted the project timeline? What proactive measures would you implement to streamline the process and ensure a smoother pathway for future projects?

2. Considering the complexities and delays in obtaining business and industrial licenses, what innovative strategies would you adopt to expedite the approval process without compromising compliance? How would you navigate through the regulatory intricacies to ensure timely project initiation?

3. Reflecting on the project's unforeseen complexities and financial constraints, what strategic financial planning and risk mitigation strategies would you implement to ensure the project's financial viability and sustainability? How would you approach the collaboration agreement with the U.S. company, considering the resistance faced by sponsors and banks, to enhance the project's technological maturity and market position?

Teaching Note

Case No 6: The Uncharted Path: Unraveling the Complex Tale of APC_Avanti's Project Journey.

Dr Jayasri Murali, Associate Professor, MBA@IICMR, Pune

Dr Dipti Sharma, Assistant Professor, MBA@ IICMR, Pune

Introduction (0:00 - 5:00):

- Briefly introduce the case study and its key components.
- Highlight the unique challenges faced by APC_Avanti in establishing a manufacturing unit for "Down the Hole Hammer" (DTH) bits in Satara-MIDC.

Objectives and Diamond Analysis (5:00 - 10:00):

- Discuss the objectives of the project and its classification using the Diamond Analysis.
- Emphasize the technological difficulty, design complexity, novelty, and speed of implementation.

Project Characteristics and Team Positions (10:00 - 15:00):

- Explore the project characteristics and key team positions in APC_Avanti's project team.
- Discuss how the diverse expertise of team members contributed to the project.

Navigating Project Challenges (15:00 - 20:00):

- Examine the internal and external challenges faced by APC_Avanti's project, as outlined in Figures 5.1 and 6.3.
- Discuss how the team navigated through these challenges and the impact on the project's trajectory.

Project Success Checklist and Criteria (20:00 - 25:00):

- Present the Project Success Checklist for the team and Project Success Criteria for customers.
- Discuss the importance of aligning organizational and customer expectations for project success.

Conclusion and Success Factors (25:00 - 30:00):

- Summarize the key points of the case study.
- Emphasize the success factors, including clarity of tasks, strong project organization, customer commitment, sponsor support, risk management, and teamwork.

Discussion Questions (30:00 - 40:00):

- Discuss strategic approaches to address challenges related to regulatory approvals and formalities. How can proactive measures streamline processes for future projects?
- Explore innovative strategies to expedite business and industrial license approvals without compromising compliance. How can regulatory intricacies be navigated for timely project initiation?
- Delve into strategic financial planning and risk mitigation strategies to ensure project viability. How would you approach the collaboration agreement with the U.S. company, considering resistance from sponsors and banks?

Assessment (40:00 - 45:00):

- Assess students based on their understanding of the case, and ability to apply strategic thinking to address challenges, and propose innovative solutions.
- Evaluate their critical thinking skills in reflecting on financial planning, risk mitigation, and collaboration strategies.

Conclusion and Key Takeaways (45:00 - 50:00):

- Summarize the key takeaways from the case study.
- Emphasize the importance of foresight, adaptability, and cohesive teamwork in navigating complex industrial innovation projects.
- Note: Timings are approximate and can be adjusted based on the pace of discussion and depth of analysis in each section.

Case No 7: Building a New Frontier: Analytical Software Development in Bio-Science

Dr Jayasri Murali, Dr Swapnisha Khambayat

Associate Professor, MBA@IICMR, Pune, Assistant Professor, MBA@IICMR, Pune

Abstract:

This case study probes into the intricacies of a transformative bio-science software development project that unfolded over five years. Focused on the challenges faced and overcome, the narrative unfolds with a discussion of the internal technical hurdles encountered by the multidisciplinary team. The need for a holistic view in the detection, analysis, and presentation of impurities set the stage for a paradigm shift in mindset, with leadership emphasizing one-on-one interactions and continuous training.

A pivotal factor for success was the establishment of a "first time right" approach, maintaining strict control over product and database design. The case study outlines the implementation of robust processes and feedback routines to ensure adherence to project scope. External challenges, including slow decision-making at the customer end and emerging competition, are explored, showcasing the strategic handling by the CEO and CTO.

Key team positions are outlined, highlighting the crucial roles of Project Manager, CTO, Market Development & Sales Manager, Business Analyst, Domain Expert, Delivery Manager, Quality Leader, and others. The success criteria, encompassing organizational and customer expectations, underscore the complexity of the project.

The retrospective insights of the team members reveal critical success factors, including clarity of task, smart decision systems, customer team participation, sponsor support, and a competent project manager. The project's positive outcome is emphasized, with the system developed in India becoming a standard offering globally. The case study concludes with reflections on the exceptional teamwork, support from diverse teams, and legal expertise that contributed to the project's resounding success.

Keywords: Bio-Science Software Development, Multidisciplinary Project, Technological Transformation,

Critical Success Factors, Project Leadership:

1. Introduction:

This case study unfolds against the backdrop of a ground-breaking bio-science software development initiative that spanned five years, providing a comprehensive examination of the challenges, strategies, and triumphs encountered by the involved stakeholders. The project, marked by its multidisciplinary nature, aimed to pioneer innovative solutions in the realm of protein-omics and genomics, requiring a seamless integration of technological expertise and business acumen.

The initial phase of the project grappled with formidable technical challenges, where the complexity of the technology surpassed the conventional understanding of many team members. While basic technological issues were acknowledged, the team lacked the requisite experience to navigate the intricate nuances specific to the application. This became a significant bottleneck in both the development and implementation cycles. The need for a "Holistic view for detection/analysis and presentation of impurities" emerged as a crucial aspect that demanded a paradigm shift in the mindset of the team members.

Leadership, embodied by the CEO and CTO, played a pivotal role in addressing these challenges. They undertook the task of instilling a holistic perspective through one-on-one interactions, constant training, and counselling sessions. The journey toward a unified approach to detection and analysis unfolded as a formidable challenge, demanding not only technological prowess but also a cultural shift within the organization.

Emphasizing a "first-time-right" approach became imperative in steering the project toward success. Strict control over product and database design emerged as a critical success factor. The establishment of robust processes and feedback mechanisms played a crucial role in keeping the project aligned with its scope. The case study explores the meticulous implementation of change control processes, specifically through the use of the "Engineering Change Control Notice," and evaluates how these measures contributed to the overall project success.

Beyond the internal technical challenges, the narrative extends to the external challenges faced by the project. Slow decision-making at the customer end posed a persistent hurdle, requiring deft handling by the leadership. Additionally, the emergence of competition, particularly in the sub-project domain, underscored the dynamic nature of the bio-science sector. The narrative sheds light on how the organization coped with these external challenges, with a focus on the strategic role played by the CEO and CTO during the initial five years of the project's lifecycle.

As the case study progresses, it delineates the key positions within the project team, emphasizing the critical roles of the Project Manager, CTO, Market Development & Sales Manager, Business Analyst, and various domain experts. These positions were vital in orchestrating a harmonious convergence of diverse skills and perspectives necessary for the success of the project. The interplay of roles and responsibilities within the team becomes a focal point in understanding how the project unfolded over time.

The success criteria for the project are outlined, encompassing both organizational and customer expectations. The intricate balance between completing the project within the defined time and budget constraints without compromising on quality emerges as a central tenet. Adherence to stringent field trials and FDA regulations, coupled with support for customer satisfaction, formed additional dimensions of success. Organizational aspirations, such as developing the application as a model project and securing repeat orders from the same customer, added layers of complexity to the success criteria.

The case study culminates in retrospective insights from the team members, shedding light on the success factors identified in hindsight. The clarity of the task, effective project organization structure, commitment and participation from customer teams, and strong support from sponsors are among the critical success factors discussed. The indispensable role played by competent and skilled development resources, coupled with vigilant risk management and project progress control, becomes apparent in the post-project reflections.

This sets the stage for a comprehensive exploration of a bio-science software development project that not only navigated intricate technical landscapes but also forged new paradigms in collaboration, innovation, and organizational adaptability.

2. Confronting Technological Transformation: Challenges and Solutions in a Bio-Sciences Endeavour:

The project embarked on a transformative journey involving significant technological changes, but the path was fraught with intricate technical challenges that demanded astute knowledge and experience. While the basic technology issues were understood by many team members, the project revealed a gap in their experience and exposure to the nuanced aspects of the application. This became a major bottleneck during the development and implementation cycles.

One of the pivotal challenges was the necessity for a "Holistic view for detection/analysis and presentation of impurities." The success of the application development efforts depended on multi-disciplinary technologies and addressing diverse issues. Many engineers and software professionals lacked this holistic viewpoint, which was crucial for the project. The leadership, primarily the CEO and CTO, faced the challenge of instilling this new approach. The process involved one-on-one interactions with team members and constant training and counselling. Developing individuals who could absorb and apply this new perspective proved to be a formidable task.

Moreover, the project emphasized a "first-time-right approach," necessitating strict control over product design and database design. This approach was crucial for the success of the sub-projects within the broader initiative. The team recognized the importance of keeping close track of specifications and change requests. Consequently, the organization implemented robust processes and feedback routines. This proactive stance allowed the team to maintain vigilance over project aspects, contributing significantly to its success.

The implementation of a strict process for change control through mechanisms like the "Engineering Change Control Notice" played a vital role. This approach ensured that changes were evaluated judiciously, preventing unnecessary disruptions. The organization's commitment to adhering to stringent processes positively impacted the overall project's success.

The technical challenges were manifold, encompassing the need for a holistic perspective, a "first-time-right" mindset, and robust change control processes. The leadership's role in driving these changes and ensuring their effective implementation was crucial for navigating the complex technological landscape.

3. Objectives of the Project: Forging a Path in Bio-Science Solutions:

In seizing the burgeoning market opportunity within the Bio-Science sector, the organization strategically leveraged its established relationships with key partners in the USA and North America. The positive response culminated in securing the first order for a feasibility study within the inaugural year, laying a robust foundation for the newly established unit.

The primary mission for the project team was to translate conceptual ideas into tangible solutions for the rapidly evolving Bio-Science markets globally. This endeavour was laden with challenges, and when probed further, the following insights emerged:

1. **Building Customer Confidence:** In the nascent stages, winning the confidence of the customer's technology team was paramount. Given the absence of a track record, the pivotal role played by the CEO and CTO in showcasing the organization's capabilities set the stage for subsequent inquiries and orders.

2. **Understanding Real Client Needs:** Efforts were directed towards comprehending the genuine needs of the client beyond apparent technological challenges. The challenge lay in deciphering vague ideas and articulating complex, multi-disciplinary expectations. The CEO and CTO adeptly navigated this challenge by identifying and representing "impurities" in clear engineering terms, a skill that became a critical success factor (CSF) for the project.

3. **Translating Ideas into Engineering Specifications:** Once the core issue and model were understood, the next step involved converting ideas into engineering specifications with the collaboration of domain experts. This effective collaboration, initiated from the very first project, instilled confidence within the project team despite the myriad challenges faced during the unit's inception.

Aligned with the vast potential of the market, the organization established the following objectives for the project:

4. Organizational Objectives for the Project:

1. **Analytical Software Development:** Develop analytical software products/solutions for the identification, analysis, and presentation of impurities in Bio-Science Equipment. Leverage domain knowledge, engineering design practices, and IT expertise in India for a global customer base.

2. **Cost-Effective Solutions:** Design and develop cost-effective solutions for Bio-Science Equipment in collaboration with customer R&D teams. Focus on identifying impurities and understanding cause-effect relationships using a modern multi-disciplinary approach.

3. **Indian Talent Utilization:** Utilize Indian talent to develop solutions and ensure continued services and support for international customers.

4. **User-Friendly Applications:** Design applications that are user-friendly and convenient for end-users in the field, ensuring low maintenance and modification needs.

5. **Break-Even and Profitability:** Reach the break-even point within three years of initiation, targeting a turnover of around 12 crores with profit margins exceeding 22% (PBT/Turnover) by the end of the fifth year.

These objectives collectively shaped the project's strategic direction, reflecting a commitment to innovation, collaboration, and sustained success in the dynamic field of Bio-Sciences.

5. Diamond Analysis of Project Complexity:

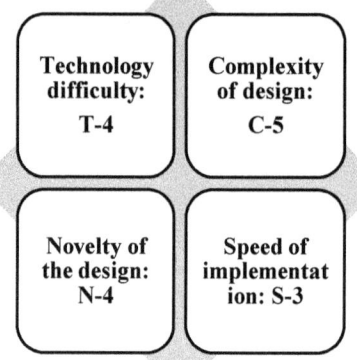

Figure 5. 1: Diamond Analysis of Project Complexity

The diamond analysis of the project underscores its intricate nature, with a technology difficulty rating of T-4, denoting a high level of technical challenges. The complexity of the design stands at C-5, indicative of a project requiring intricate design considerations. Furthermore, the novelty of the design is rated at N-4, emphasizing the innovative aspects inherent in the project. While the speed of implementation is marked at S-3, suggesting a moderate pace, the overall assessment positions the project within a challenging spectrum, necessitating adept handling of advanced technology, intricate design nuances, and innovative solutions for successful execution.

6. Project Characteristics: Navigating Challenges in a Bio-Science Software Venture:

- Size of the Project: Initial Cost: Approximately $0.5 million USD (INR 2-3 crore), encompassing manpower costs, overheads, travel, and incidental expenses.
- Capital Constraint: Limited by the equity capital of around 1 crore from promoters and associates.

- Number of People: Average manpower maintained at around 35.
- Year 1: Involved around 25 individuals in Mumbai/Pune.
- Year 5: Expanded to approximately 65, including Design & Development (45), QA/QC group (5), Sales (3), Domain Experts (2), Engineers at client sites (5), and Support Services (8).

- Time Schedule: Planned Phase: Initial phase set for 5 years.
- Trial Development: Estimated completion within 24 months at the customer's location.

- Financial Targets: Aimed for a turnover exceeding 12 crores with a margin of 18% in the fifth year (PBT / Sales revenue).

- Classification of Project: Designation: Classified as a New Project, establishing a software technology unit for developing Analytical Diagnostic Software Applications/Solutions for Bio-Science industry equipment.

- High-Risk Project: Uncertainties: Inherent risks due to the development of a new concept-based application using indigenous designs and Indian teams for Bio-Science industry clients.

- Financial Mandate: Funding covered expenses for the first two years, with subsequent operations relying on self-generated cash flows. No capital investment required for diagnostic equipment, provided by customers.

- Technology Choice/Maturity: Evolution: Technology evolving during the project period, with few solutions developed in the USA/Europe. The concept still in an evolutionary phase with various models being explored.

- Number of Suppliers/Consultants: Limited Need: Few suppliers but crucial reliance on domain consultants. Strong relationships established with leading consultants and testing agencies, contributing significantly to project delivery.

- Logistics/Clearances: Challenge: Managing logistics and obtaining government clearances for the import/return of customer equipment posed significant challenges.

- Location for Coordination: Multiple Locations: Coordinated activities across more than 3 locations (Mumbai/Pune & customer sites) facilitated by substantial investments in communication systems.

- Support from Sponsors: Initial Unity: Senior management acted as an integrated team with good relations. Later, differences in approaches and personalities led to tensions among promoters, creating a complex situation for the project team.

- Team Members & Effectiveness: Initial Cohesion: The team initially worked cohesively. Over time, tensions emerged due to differences in convictions and competence. Mixed and hesitant support among team members impacted overall performance.

- Involvement of Customer: Varied Support: Initially mixed/hesitant support from customers, engineers, and professionals. Confidence development led to effective coordination and communication.

- Team Leaders: Competent Leadership: The selected Project Manager/CEO, a committed Engineering Manager and born entrepreneur, possessed crucial expertise in product design and development. The CTO, a reputable R&D professional, together formed a potent duo, engaging effectively with customer personnel, a key strength for the project team.

Fig 6.1 Project Characteristics

7. Navigating Project Phases: Overcoming Challenges for Bio-Science Software Venture:

The project was intricately mapped across distinctive phases, each presenting its set of challenges and objectives:

Phase 1 (2 years): The initial focus was on navigating through licensing, registration, and other formalities. A critical milestone was to complete the Feasibility/Proof of Concept (POC) within 18 months from project commencement, aiming to commence invoicing before the conclusion of the first 2 years.

Phase 2 (1 year): The team aimed to initiate dialogues with prominent companies engaged in manufacturing analytic application equipment for impurity identification. The goal was to translate opportunities into customer orders, leveraging the newly developed concept/model. The ambitious target was to achieve a turnover exceeding 5 crores by the end of the third year.

Phase 3 (2 years): This phase's primary objective was to propel the organization towards a turnover of approximately 12 crores by the end of the fifth year, maintaining a robust margin of over 18% (PBT/Sales Revenue).

The outlined phases underscored the project's ambitious objectives, requiring the team to surmount numerous obstacles in their pursuit of success. The overarching goal for the project team was to bring to life a business endeavour that spanned from conceptualization to realization, specifically tailored for the rapidly advancing Bio-Science markets worldwide. Despite the inherent complexities, the team remained resolute in navigating these challenges throughout the project journey.

8. Exploring the Challenges in the Bio-Science Software Venture:

Internal Challenges: The project team encountered multifaceted challenges, and key aspects were highlighted by team members and the Project Manager:

Gaining Customer Confidence: Initiating a new unit without a track record posed the initial challenge of earning customer confidence. The CEO and CTO, leveraging their experience and domain knowledge, played a pivotal role in instilling faith through effective product design and development, winning the first order for feasibility analysis. Despite this success, the challenge persisted with each new customer until a solid organizational track record was established.

Time, Cost, and Quality: The pressure to complete the first project phase within 24 months, aligning with the initial funding window, presented a significant challenge. This demanded meticulous planning, cost control, and collective efforts from the team. The evolving market, shifting from product development to comprehensive R&D, added complexity, requiring a delicate balance between current projects and future developments.

Technology and Technical Infrastructure: Designing and developing innovative applications in diagnostic analysis without signed technical collaborations posed a formidable challenge. The team navigated this by relying on homegrown designs and technologies, supported by customers providing the necessary equipment for R&D purposes. Limited infrastructure funding, however, led to challenges in in-house testing, addressed partially by customer support.

Management Pressure and Priorities: The Board of Directors committed funding for the initial 24 months, creating perpetual pressure. While the management team had autonomy in decision-making, the constraint fueled tensions. This pressure was effectively managed without interference from the Board.

Communication & Coordination: Acknowledging the importance of communication, the CEO and CTO conducted regular briefing meetings and open town hall sessions to foster transparency and address concerns. This practice strengthened team cohesion and morale.

Domain Expertise: Recognizing the impossibility of having a team with complete experience, the organization cultivated relationships with external experts and consultants. Training sessions were implemented before new projects, ensuring a continuous learning curve for the team.

Customer Involvement: Departing from the traditional 'hands-off' approach, customers ensured close coordination with the project team, facilitating success in the initial period.

Manpower Availability: Limited funds constrained initial team selection. The leadership team personally handpicked members through referrals, emphasizing R&D inclination. Continuous technical training was adopted to bridge knowledge gaps.

Quality Assurance/Control: The criticality of deploying solutions in life-affecting applications demanded stringent quality standards. The organization established robust internal systems, improving and stabilizing over time.

PMO for Progress Tracking: A rigorous Project Management Office (PMO) plays a crucial role in reporting and controlling deviations, contributing to project success and adherence to standards.

HR and Training Role: The HR team faced the challenge of recruiting individuals with both technical expertise and R&D inclination. In-house training modules were implemented, proving valuable in long-term success.

Financial and Strategic Support: Initially supportive, the Board of Directors waning interest in operational activities led to confrontations during expansion plans, impacting the project in the eighth year.

Funds Management: Initial funding commitment for 24 months added uncertainty, but breakthroughs within 18 months allowed the team to sustain growth independently.

Additional Technical Challenges: The magnitude of technological changes posed intricate challenges, requiring astute technical knowledge and experience:

Holistic View for Detection/Analysis: Developing a holistic view for impurity detection, analysis, and presentation, crucial for multi-disciplinary technologies, demanded a shift in mindset. CEO and CTO led personalized interactions, training, and counselling to instil this approach.

Strict Control Over Design: Ensuring a 'first-time-right' approach necessitated strict control over product and database design. Strong processes and feedback routines were installed, ensuring project success.

Change Control Processes: Implementing a rigorous process for change control through Engineering Change Control Notices (ECCN) and judicious evaluation was achieved through the organization's strict process implementation.

The project team successfully addressed these challenges, showcasing resilience, adaptability, and strategic decision-making throughout the venture.

9. External Dynamics Impacting Project Success:

Several external factors were identified as influential elements that could shape the project's success probability:

Prolonged Decision-Making at Customer End: Slow decision-making processes at the customer end posed a persistent challenge in the market. The time and effort invested from the initial contact to contract finalization were substantial, often involving international visits. The adept handling of customers by the CEO and CTO played a crucial role in streamlining contract cycles, even with this inherent delay. The duo's effective management remained pivotal in the first five years of the project life cycle.

Emergence of Competition: While there was minimal competition initially, it started to develop over the first two years. However, the competition primarily centred around sub-projects rather than overarching R&D endeavours. The unit encountered strong competition, particularly in mathematical modelling aspects, learning valuable lessons in the process. Despite progressing into later phases, the organization struggled to make significant headway in achieving excellence in this domain.

10. Strategic Roles in the Team Setup

Establishing a robust team structure was imperative, comprising the following key positions:

Project Maestro / Visionary Leader (CEO):	Spearheading the project, the CEO assumed the pivotal role of Project Manager and Champion, steering the team with strategic acumen and foresight.
CTO with R&D Prowess:	The Chief Technology Officer (CTO) brought invaluable Research and Development orientation to product development, employing a multidisciplinary approach for innovation.
Market Dynamo & Sales Maven:	Initially managed by the Project Champion, the role of Market Development and Sales was crucial, ensuring proactive outreach to potential clients with active support from the CTO.
Versatile Business Analyst:	A Business Analyst with a penchant for multidisciplinary thinking and a flair for Research and Development in Proteinomics & Genomics played a pivotal role.
Domain Experts & Consultants:	Specialized experts in the Bio-Sciences sector, equipped with domain knowledge and technological expertise, contributed to the team's comprehensive understanding.
Delivery Maestro for Engineering Applications:	A Delivery Manager well-versed in software applications for Engineering Applications ensured seamless execution of project deliverables.
Quality Vanguard & Site Guardians:	The Quality Leader, accompanied by a Site Quality Leader and two site engineers, upheld rigorous quality standards, ensuring the integrity of life-affecting diagnostic and analytical systems.
Financial Steward - Accounts Manager:	Managing financial aspects and funding concerns, the Accounts Manager played a crucial role in the fiscal health of the unit.
Project Management Office (PMO):	The PMO office facilitated project tracking and liaised with customer teams for progress monitoring and issue resolution.
Innovative HR Navigator:	An innovative Human Resource professional, deeply attuned to the unique needs of the new unit, orchestrated talent acquisition and management strategies

Figure 10..1 Key Position

11. Project Success Criteria: A Holistic Perspective:

The project success criteria were meticulously crafted, harmonizing customer expectations with organizational aspirations:

Organizational Expectations and Achievements:

Timely and Cost-Effective Completion: Ensuring the project's timely completion within allocated funds, maintaining an unwavering commitment to quality.

Adherence to Stringent Regulations: Conforming to the rigorous standards of field trials, and FDA regulations, and providing on-field support for customer satisfaction through close collaboration with customer technology teams.

Financial Success: Achieving the targeted project profitability as envisioned by the organization, aligning with the expectations of investors and banks.

Model Project Development: Establishing the application as a model project, serving as a benchmark for future ventures in the Bi0-Sciences sector, leveraging Indian knowledge and skill sets.

Securing Repeat Orders: Gaining repeat orders from the same customer, signifying a crucial organizational requirement and the ability to foster enduring client relationships.

Customer/User Expectations:

Punctual Delivery with Precision: Ensuring on-time delivery and implementation, with a focus on accuracy and reliability, acknowledging the critical requirements of the Bio-Science industry.

Committed Return on Investment (ROI): Achieving the committed return on investment from the project, contributing to the cost reduction of diagnostic analysis in the field.

Team Members' Satisfaction:

Team Contentment and Skill Development: Prioritizing team satisfaction and fostering the development of new skills and domain expertise for future endeavours.

Enhanced Product Design Quality: Improving the quality of product design and standardizing approaches and routines for application development in the Bio-Science sector, promoting a culture of continuous enhancement.

Critical Success Factors Identified by Team Members:

In retrospect, the team members, along with their Project Manager, have highlighted key factors that could have significantly contributed to the project's success had they been considered at its outset. While these considerations weren't initially contemplated, they are deemed crucial by the team in hindsight:

Clarity in Task Definition: Ensuring a clear understanding of the task at hand, along with well-defined scope and specifications.

Effective Project Organization Structure: Establishing a robust project organization structure and implementing intelligent decision-making systems.

Customer Teams' Commitment and Participation: Securing unwavering commitment and active participation from customer teams throughout the entire project life cycle.

Sponsor Support and Decision Freedom: Enjoy complete support from sponsors and have the freedom to make decisions independently.

Competent Project Management and Trusted Team: Having a competent Project Manager and a team that is trusted and supportive.

Competent and Skilled Development Resources: Ensuring the availability of competent and skilled development resources with the right attitudes.

Alert Risk Management: Implementing vigilant risk management, especially concerning timelines and design changes for Proof of Concept (POC) and User Acceptance Testing (UAT).

Control Over Project Progress: Maintaining control over project progress through impeccable communication and coordination.

PMO Support for Issue Tracking: Receiving excellent support from Project Management Office (PMO) personnel for ruthless tracking of issues and their resolution.

Strong QA/QC Teams and Process Control: Benefiting from strong support from Quality Assurance (QA) and Quality Control (QC) teams, leveraging matured processes from the parent organization.

Exceptional Team Collaboration: Encouraging exceptional teamwork and receiving untiring support from task force members.

Legal and Administrative Support: Securing good support from legal experts and administrative teams.

Conclusion: Remarkable Success in the First Five Years:

The project, undertaken with ambitious goals and navigating through numerous challenges, emerged as an extraordinary success, receiving acclaim from all stakeholders involved. The R&D group in India, through dedicated and relentless efforts, developed a system that not only met but exceeded expectations. The parent organization acknowledged this achievement by adopting the developed system as a standard offering globally. The comprehensive success of the project was evident in the reported results for the initial five years of the gestation period.

The achievements and outcomes during this period can be summarized as follows:

Global Adoption of the System: The system developed by the Indian R&D group was not only recognized locally but also gained international acclaim. The parent organization embraced it as a standard system, extending its offering to a global audience.

Appreciation for Team Efforts: The untiring efforts of the project team did not go unnoticed. Stakeholders, including management, clients, and collaborators, expressed high appreciation for the team's dedication and hard work, which played a pivotal role in the project's overall success.

Positive Stakeholder Feedback: Feedback from various stakeholders, including customers, sponsors, and internal teams, was overwhelmingly positive. The project demonstrated an ability to overcome challenges, deliver on commitments, and establish itself as a reliable and innovative contributor to the Bio-Science sector.

Organizational Recognition: The success of the project contributed significantly to enhancing the reputation of the entire organization. The achievement was celebrated within the company, fostering a culture of innovation and excellence.

Financial Milestones: Financially, the project not only met but exceeded expectations. The reported results showcased a robust financial performance, indicating effective cost management, profitability, and adherence to the planned financial objectives.

Establishment as a Reference Project: The project's success positioned it as a reference project for future endeavours in the Bio-Science sector. It set a benchmark for leveraging Indian knowledge and skill sets in pioneering and complex technological applications.

In conclusion, the project's first five years stand as a testament to the resilience, expertise, and collaborative spirit of the team, leading to a ground-breaking success that reverberated throughout the organization and the industry at large.

12. The organization reported the following results for the first 5 years after the gestation period:

Year 1- 18 months		1	2	3	4	5
Sales in crores		0.5	2.4	6	8.6	10.7
Margin %		9	9.5	10.8	11.2	12.6

Table 12.1 Financial Performance

Teaching Note

Case No 7: Building a New Frontier: Analytical Software Development in Bio-Science.

Dr Jayasri Murali, Associate Professor, MBA@IICMR, Pune

Dr Swapnisha Khambayat, Assistant Professor, MBA@IICMR, Pune

Abstract:

This case study provides an in-depth exploration of a transformative bio-science software development project spanning five years. The narrative delves into the challenges faced and overcome by a multidisciplinary team, emphasizing internal technical hurdles, leadership strategies, and the establishment of a "first time right" approach. Key team positions, success criteria, and critical success factors are outlined, providing comprehensive insights into the project's complexities.

Learning Objectives:
- Understand the challenges and intricacies of a multidisciplinary bio-science software development project.
- Analyse the leadership strategies employed in addressing internal technical challenges.
- Explore the impact of external factors such as slow decision-making and emerging competition.
- Examine key team positions and their roles in orchestrating project success.
- Evaluate success criteria aligned with organizational and customer expectations.
- Identify critical success factors based on retrospective insights from the project team.
- Understand the financial milestones and organizational recognition achieved during the project.

Teaching Plan:

Introduction to the Bio-Science Software Development Project (15 minutes):
- Provide an overview of the case study.
- Introduce the authors and their roles.
- Highlight the transformative nature of the bio-science software development initiative.

Challenges in Technological Transformation (30 minutes):
- Explore the internal technical challenges faced by the project team.
- Discuss the necessity for a holistic view in the detection, analysis, and presentation of impurities.
- Analyse leadership strategies employed by the CEO and CTO to address these challenges.

Objectives of the Project (20 minutes):
- Examine the strategic objectives set for the project, including market opportunities and organizational goals.
- Discuss how the organization leveraged relationships and secured the first order for a feasibility study.

Diamond Analysis and Project Characteristics (15 minutes):

- Introduce the diamond analysis, highlighting the technology difficulty, design complexity, novelty, and speed of implementation.
- Discuss the project's characteristics and its positioning in terms of challenges.

Project Phases and Challenges (25 minutes):

- Explore the distinctive phases of the project, including licensing, feasibility/proof of concept, and dialogues with manufacturing companies.
- Discuss the challenges encountered in each phase, both internal and external.

External Dynamics Impacting Project Success (20 minutes):

- Analyse external factors such as prolonged decision-making and the emergence of competition.
- Highlight the strategic roles of the CEO and CTO in navigating these external challenges.

Key Team Positions and Success Criteria (25 minutes):

- Outline the key positions in the project team and their respective roles.
- Explore the success criteria aligned with organizational and customer expectations.

Critical Success Factors (20 minutes):

- Examine critical success factors identified by team members in hindsight.
- Discuss how these factors could have contributed to the project's success if considered earlier.

Conclusion and Achievements (15 minutes):

- Summarize the project's achievements in the first five years.
- Discuss the global adoption of the system, positive stakeholder feedback, and financial milestones.
- Emphasize the project's recognition as a reference project in the Bio-Science sector.

Q&A and Discussion (30 minutes):

- Encourage questions from students. Facilitate a discussion on lessons learned, strategic decisions, and the overall impact of the project.

Assessment:

- **Individual or Group Assignments (20 %):** Assign case-related questions or analyses to be submitted individually or in groups.

- **Class Participation (15%):** Evaluate students based on their participation in class discussions and engagement with case-related topics.

- **Case Presentation (25%):** Assign groups to present specific aspects of the case, such as challenges, success criteria, or critical success factors.

- **Final Examination (40%):** Include essay or discussion-based questions related to the case study and its key concepts.

Note: Adjust time allocations based on the specific needs of the course and class dynamics. Encourage students to relate the case study to real-world scenarios and discuss implications for future projects in the bio-science sector.

Case No 8: Revolutionizing Banking: A Tale of Total Branch Automation Project

Dr Jayasri Murali, Dr Rajendra Agawane

Associate Professor, MBA@IICMR, Pune, Assistant Professor, MBA@IICMR, Pune

Abstract:

This case study delves into the intricacies of a ground-breaking project titled "PDS- Development of Banking Application Software-Total Branch Automation Project," undertaken during a pivotal era in the banking industry's adoption of computerization. Faced with challenges such as strong unions, limitations in existing banking software, and resistance to computer usage, the Indian Banks Association (IBA) collaborated with nationalized banks to develop a new, comprehensive banking application.

The objectives of the project were ambitious, aiming to create a generic, flexible product that catered to nationalized, private, and cooperative sector banks while adhering to RBI norms. The project team, led by a dedicated Project Manager, encountered various internal and external challenges, including time pressure, management expectations, and a lack of domain expertise.

The scope of the project encompassed all branch-level banking operations, including savings accounts, term deposits, clearing operations, foreign exchange, and more. The challenges faced by the project team included internal issues such as time, cost, and quality management, as well as external challenges like slow decision-making processes, union interference, and changes in RBI policies.

The development approach involved a dedicated team of over 65 professionals, including a Project Manager, Business Analyst, Module Leaders, Database Expert, Quality Leader, and others. The technology difficulty, design complexity, novelty, and speed of implementation were classified as T-3, C-4, N-4, and S-5, respectively.

The project, estimated at around USD 3 million, successfully navigated challenges and uncertainties, showcasing a high-risk profile due to the novelty of the application and the evolving technology landscape. Despite the scarcity of domain experts and time pressure, the team achieved success through meticulous planning, documentation, communication, and collaboration with the customer.

Positives in the project environment included strong support from senior management, effective team coordination, and a harmonious working atmosphere. The project's success criteria aligned with both organizational and customer expectations, emphasizing timely delivery, adherence to banking sector rules, profitability, and reduced operational manpower.

Key success factors identified by the team included clarity about the task, commitment from customer teams, support from senior management, competent project leadership, risk management, effective communication, teamwork, and support from quality assurance teams.

In conclusion, the project achieved exceptional success, leading to the establishment of a dedicated banking division within the organization. The project manager was promoted, and the product became a flagship offering, contributing significantly to the organization's growth and profitability. The case highlights the transformative impact of strategic planning, collaboration, and perseverance in complex and pioneering projects.

Keywords: Banking Automation, Total Branch Automation, Project Management, Agile Bank.

1. Introduction:

In the era when computers were making their way into the banking industry, the atmosphere wasn't exactly enthusiastic. The challenge of introducing computer-based banking applications was compounded by the strong presence of unions in many banks.

The Indian Banks Association (IBA) took the lead in bringing modern technologies to the sector. However, the introduction of PC-based banking software, following IBA's specifications, faced significant hurdles. The older generation of banking personnel lacked confidence in computer usage, adding to the industry's challenges.

The existing banking products had limitations in software architecture, parameterization, and design flexibility. Some constraints included a lack of PC networking, each PC handling specific areas of the bank, and restrictions on the number of accounts per PC. These limitations hindered benefits and operational ease for customers.

In response, the Indian Banks Association consulted nationalized banks to develop new specifications that would address these constraints and provide additional benefits. The goal was to transform the way banks operated in India. Nationalized banks were encouraged to select branches where all functions could be computerized without limitations, integrating banking peripherals like passbook printers and swipe cards.

The objective was to harness the real potential of computerization, making banking operations more convenient for end customers. The IBA, in collaboration with banks, identified software houses and consultants capable of developing such products. The current organization, with a proven track record, was selected by IBA for this prestigious project.

Empanelled with IBA, the organization formed a dedicated project team. The experience of senior members in a study group set up by RBI played a crucial role in the organization's selection. Despite the challenges, the organization was motivated by its interest in the Banking & Financial sector, actively participating in this prestigious endeavour.

2. Objectives of the Project:

The organization saw an opportunity to kickstart the "Total Branch Automation project" and formed a dedicated team led by a Project Manager and experienced professionals. Focused on the vast potential of banking automation, the project aimed to achieve the following objectives:

Create a banking application that caters not only to the needs of nationalized banks but also addresses the requirements of private and cooperative sector banks, aligning closely with RBI norms and guidelines.

- To Develop a versatile product for the banking sector, featuring flexibility and parameterization to effectively handle bank-specific customization. This involved utilizing the core features and a robust design for comprehensive coverage.

- To Design the application to be user-friendly, ensuring that end-users find it highly useful and convenient in their banking operations.

- To ensure the product has low maintenance and modification needs, making it easy for interfaces and additions to enhance functionality.

- To Implement navigation and user-friendly features that can be effectively utilized even by novices, requiring minimal training or orientation.

- To Design the product to adapt seamlessly to the ever-changing banking guidelines issued by RBI.

- To Create a "database-independent" design, allowing end-user banks to select and choose a database of their preference.

- To Establish an architecture for the new application that supports inter-branch connectivity and embraces the concept of "anywhere banking."

3. Scope of the Project:

The project's scope encompasses a comprehensive software product designed to streamline all branch-level banking operations. The inclusive list of operations covers key banking functions, including but not limited to:

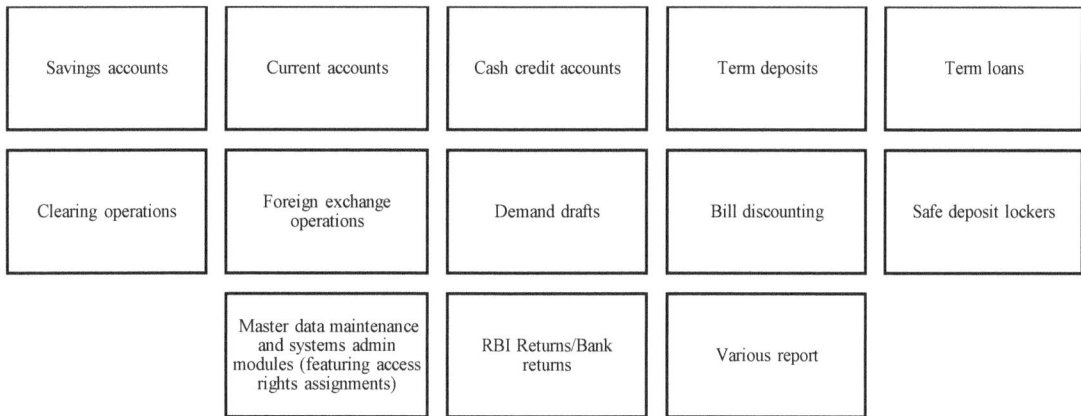

Figure 8. 1

While the listed items highlight essential banking functions, it's important to note that the scope is indicative. Additionally, the project includes the development of add-on modules and select features to facilitate seamless integration with other systems within the application suite.

4. Navigating the Project Challenges:

The project team faced an array of internal challenges, drawing attention to crucial aspects requiring the Project Manager's focus and collaboration with bank employees. Key challenges included:

Time, Cost, and Quality Conundrum: Meeting conventional project success factors and completing the project within 12 months posed a formidable challenge. With RBI guidelines setting time schedules for the switch to new banking applications, the team grappled with the onerous time pressure. Developing a generic software product demanded three times the effort of a bespoke application, adding to the complexity.

Management Pressure Cooker: The burgeoning excitement in software companies about the sector's potential led to management pressure. The urgency to launch products quickly replaced initial time estimates, exacerbating pressure on the development team to meet market demands.

Domain Expertise Dilemma: Insufficient domain expertise among team members and banking personnel created a significant hurdle. The team struggled to engage with individuals familiar with existing systems but lacked insight into how proposed changes would impact operations. Convincing senior banking personnel sceptical about computerized systems added to the challenge.

Team Dynamics in Flux: The prevalent issue of high employee attrition rates in the IT industry persisted. Despite the Project Manager's freedom to select the team, efforts were continually required to retain team members. The constant risk of key personnel leaving presented an ongoing challenge.

Banking Infrastructure Bottlenecks: Inadequate IT infrastructure in banks and incompatible hardware components necessitated considerable time and effort to procure necessary equipment. Bureaucratic hurdles in the procurement process frustrated the team in several locations.

Data Migration Dilemma: The success of a complex banking operations software relied heavily on clean and dependable data. Initial surveys unveiled a lack of accurate and comprehensive data in branches, posing serious impediments. Efforts to ensure data accuracy and fidelity became Herculean tasks, causing further delays.

In the face of these challenges, the project team navigated complexities, showcasing resilience and innovation to surmount obstacles and drive the Total Branch Automation project forward.

5. Surmounting Technical Challenges:

The ambitious technological transformation encountered a myriad of intricate technical challenges, demanding astute knowledge and experience from the project team. While basic technology issues were familiar to many, the lack of nuanced experience in this specific application proved to be a significant bottleneck in both the development and implementation phases.

- **Rigorous Control Over Design and Database:** The sheer size and complexity of the application necessitated a sophisticated architecture. The ongoing QA/QC cycles prompted fine-tuning of designs for optimal performance, sometimes requiring redesign efforts. The project team grappled with the enormity of the software, adapting and refining designs throughout the implementation journey.

- **Engineered Change Control Processes:** Effective change control through an "Engineering Change Control Notice" demanded a meticulous evaluation of requests. This critical aspect, pivotal for project success, required dedicated senior resources to ensure proper control throughout the project's duration.

- **Enforcement of Coding Standards:** With different teams dedicated to developing various modules, maintaining uniformity and standardization was paramount. Strict coding standards were implemented to facilitate consistent practices and methods. This control not only ensured process compatibility but also maintained data uniformity for integration.

- **Integration with Banking Peripherals and Existing Systems:** The absence of specific standards for hardware purchases across the banking community posed an ongoing challenge. Design teams had to consider local aspects and equipment availability, necessitating changes in the design, testing, and implementation stages to accommodate these variations.

- **Balancing Flexibility and Parameterization:** Achieving the right balance of flexibility and parameterization in design and database architecture was crucial. While these aspects are essential, an excess of flexibility and parameterization could make the system top-heavy, potentially impacting response times for various processes. The challenge was heightened by the expectation to develop a "Standard Product" rather than a bespoke application.

In overcoming these technical hurdles, the project team showcased resilience, adaptability, and a commitment to delivering a robust Total Branch Automation solution.

6. Overcoming External Challenges:

Several factors external to the project were identified as critical elements that could impact the project's likelihood of success.

The slow decision-making process at the bank's end, especially regarding design approvals and the acquisition of necessary hardware components, affected the overall development pace. The team's persistent efforts played a crucial role in resolving these issues.

The significance and interference of the bank employees' union served as an additional external influencing factor beyond the team's control. Collaboration with senior management and union representatives was essential to address these challenges. Without the cooperation of bank employees, resolving implementation and usage issues would have been nearly impossible.

Frequent changes in policies by RBI had a continual impact on the scope and specifications of various modules, posing an ongoing challenge for the project team. Business analysts had to stay vigilant about these changes, ensuring everyone involved was informed and incorporating adjustments into the final solution.

Cooperation from bank staff during the implementation phase initially raised concerns but gradually improved after discussions with union leaders and senior management. However, challenges persisted due to the lack of master data and delays in compilation from the working staff, leading to prolonged problem-solving processes.

Export/import obligations were time-consuming and represented non-value-adding activities, highlighting the potential for significant time savings.

- **Innovative Development Approach:** A dynamic team, spearheaded by a project manager, was entrusted with the monumental task of bringing this project to fruition. With over 65 professionals at its core (50 focused on development and QA/QC, plus 15 dedicated to implementation at five selected branches), the project faced various critical challenges, including:

- **Product Design Mastery:** Managing the enormity of the project required meticulous control over product design. Given the stringent accuracy expectations and adherence to RBI norms, uncertainties in rule interpretation could potentially introduce errors. Thus, the design control team played a pivotal role in ensuring the compatibility of field data at every stage.

- **Rationalizing and Standardizing:** Domain experts faced the challenging task of rationalizing and standardizing process routines. This complex endeavour demanded the expertise of professionals well-versed in banking operations. Dynamic changes in banking rules and regulations added an extra layer of complexity, requiring continuous attention to assess the impact on finalized designs and routines.

- **Module Leadership:** Module leaders shouldered the responsibility for individual modules, supported by programmers and quality control teams. Strict adherence to standards throughout the development and testing stages was crucial, although easier said than done.

- **Documentation Excellence:** A comprehensive system demanded high-quality documentation, a task further complicated by the multitude of applicable rules and regulations. The scarcity of IT professionals with a knack for thorough documentation posed a challenge. To address this bottleneck, the project team engaged bank professionals to form a task force dedicated to this challenging aspect.

During the developmental phase, the banking sector lacked matured systems based on these ground-breaking concepts. Introducing a completely new application concept to the Indian Banking sector naturally encountered resistance from existing employees, particularly bank staff. Undoubtedly, this project presented a myriad of challenges and opportunities for innovation.

7. Dimond Analysis of Project Classification:

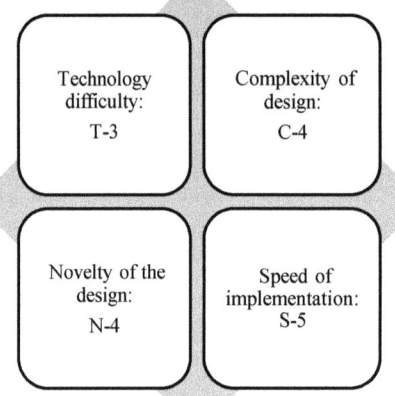

Figure 8. 2

The project, when subjected to a diamond analysis for classification, aligns with the following specifications:

- **Technology Difficulty (T-3):** The project exhibits a moderate level of technology difficulty, signifying that while there are challenges in the technological domain, they fall within a manageable range.

- **Complexity of Design (C-4):** The design complexity is classified at level 4, indicating a considerable level of intricacy in the design aspects. This suggests that addressing and managing design intricacies is a notable aspect of the project.

- **Novelty of the Design (N-4):** With a novelty classification of 4, the project introduces innovative and distinctive design elements. This suggests that the design incorporates novel features, pushing beyond conventional approaches.

- **Speed of Implementation (S-5):** The project's speed of implementation is marked at level 5, highlighting a rapid pace in executing the project. This implies a swift and efficient approach to bringing the project from conception to completion.

8. Project Characteristics:

1. Size of the Project:
2. Estimated at $3 million USD (INR 12-14 crore in today's currency rates), including manpower costs, overheads, travel, and incidental expenses.

1. Number of People:
2. Approximately 50 persons in Head Office for development and QA/QC.
3. An additional 15 team members deployed at 5 sites for implementation.

1. Time Schedule:
2. Planned project period: 12 months, with an expected pilot test initiation at customer branches/HQ within 14 months from the start.

1. Classification of Project:
2. A new project team was established for the existing organization, introducing a new product line for banking operations based on new requirements. This marked a pioneering effort in India, as no such product was available at that time.

1. High-Risk Project:
2. Uncertainties and risks due to the development of a new concept/software application using a new database version and connectivity.
3. Challenges in sourcing domain experts and managing time pressure with the proposed closure of the existing application.
4. High expectations from the customer, stringent accuracy and response time requirements, and concerns about union resistance in various banks.

1. Technology Choice/Maturity:
2. Evolving technology during the period, with the application being developed for the first time as a standard product in India.
3. Shortage of knowledgeable individuals in the market about this technology and domain applications.

1. Number of Suppliers:
2. Limited role for suppliers, with only a few professionals supplied during the project tenure.

1. Logistics/Clearances:
2. Significant challenges due to time pressure, requiring numerous government clearances, travel logistics, and visa processing. Support from the customer organization facilitated the completion of required paperwork.

1. Location for Coordination:
2. More than 8 locations (Mumbai/Pune and customer sites at 5-6 branch locations) manned with project team members. Effective coordination facilitated by excellent communication and infrastructure facilities.

1. Support from Senior Management:
2. Excellent support from senior management, providing timely funding, administrative support, and motivational encouragement throughout the project.

1. Involvement of Customer:
2. Mixed and hesitant support from banking personnel/professionals, with uncertainty about the impact of the new software on bank operations.
3. Willingness to participate in the exercise, provide support for specification development, and engage in pilot studies at select branch locations. However, some customer representatives had doubts about the abilities of Indian software professionals.

1. Team Leader:
2. Competent and committed Project Manager with expertise in software applications, coupled with exposure to airline back-office processing and ERP suite applications.

1. Key Positions in the Team

- **Project Manager / Project Champion:** Steering the project, ensuring overall success, and championing its goals.
- **Business Analyst / Business Process Expert:** Possessing expertise in the banking sector, especially in banking operations, to analyze and streamline business processes.
- **Module Leaders (4):** Overseeing critical aspects of the project and various modules, ensuring focused leadership for specialized areas.
- **Database Expert / Networking Expert:** Providing proficiency in database management and networking, contributing to the project's technological backbone.
- **Quality Leader / Site Quality Leader / Site Manager:** Managing quality control, site-specific quality assurance, and overseeing on-site implementation with the support of two site engineers.
- **Delivery Manager:** Assuming a crucial role, often taken on by a senior module leader, responsible for overseeing the timely and successful delivery of the project.
- **Accounts Manager:** Handling financial matters and funding to ensure the project's financial health.
- **PMO Office (Project Management Office):** Facilitating project tracking, maintaining liaison with the customer team, monitoring progress, and resolving issues efficiently.

Figure 8. 3

9. Navigating Challenges in Complex Banking Software Development:

Embarking on the development of a highly intricate banking software application presented a multitude of challenges, particularly revolving around the intricacies of banking processes and the regulatory landscape. Key challenges encountered and adeptly navigated by the project team included:

- **Scarcity of Domain Experts:** The scarcity of experts in the banking domain posed a significant challenge. However, active involvement and collaboration with customer professionals, coupled with diligent homework, empowered the project manager (PM) and the team to effectively address this challenge, resulting in the delivery of a high-quality product.

- **Enormous Time Pressure:** The project faced substantial time pressure for development. Initial investments in training and orientation proved crucial in helping the team swiftly grasp terminologies and process routines, ultimately expediting the overall development process.

- **Emphasis on Standardized Documentation:** The team dedicated considerable time to establishing standardized documentation practices. Rigorous adherence to this approach throughout the project ensured clarity in communication, and decision-making, and provided a robust foundation for success.

- **Efficient Communication:** Effective communication channels were established both with customer representatives and within the team. Thorough documentation of communications facilitated seamless reference, contributing to a smooth and well-coordinated workflow.

- **Trust and Harmony within the Team:** The team operated with implicit trust in each other and their leadership. This trust, coupled with effective communication, facilitated harmonious collaboration and established a rhythm within the team.

- **Technical Challenges with Database Usage:** Technical issues related to database usage and network effectiveness were encountered. The project's IT team collaborated closely with the bank's IT departments, providing necessary support to overcome these challenges.

- **Test Data Preparation:** Given the complexity of the application and the unique domain environment, preparing test data emerged as a major challenge. However, meticulous homework undertaken by the project team, coupled with support for trials both at the home office and on-site, proved invaluable in addressing this challenge.

- **Foreign Exchange Challenges for Travel:** Challenges related to foreign exchange for team members' travel were faced and successfully addressed, ensuring seamless collaboration and knowledge exchange.

- **Positive Dynamics in Project Environment:** Navigating the complexities of the project was complemented by several positive aspects within the project environment:

- **Endorsement from Senior Management and Foreign Partners:** The unwavering support from senior management and foreign partners provided a robust foundation for the project's success, instilling confidence and direction for the team.

- **Precision in Focus and Detailed Implementation Plan:** The team maintained a laser-sharp focus, aligning with a meticulously crafted implementation plan in collaboration with customer personnel. This precision contributed to streamlined execution.

- **Proactive Issue Resolution through Continuous Dialogue:** Continuous and open dialogue between Customer PM, local PM, and senior managers ensured immediate issue resolution. Monthly/quarterly project meetings involving leaders from both sides facilitated proactive decision-making and progress.

- **Harmonious Team Environment:** A harmonious team environment played a pivotal role in fostering quality work. The collaborative spirit within the team was instrumental in overcoming challenges and ensuring undisturbed progress.

- **Thorough Pre-Dispatch Inspections:** Rigorous pre-dispatch inspections, involving both local and customer QA/QC teams for every release, streamlined on-site software implementation. This meticulous approach minimized delays and waiting periods.

- **Empowerment for Decision Making:** The team enjoyed complete autonomy for decision-making and expenditure commitments, aligned with the decisions of the PM. This empowerment facilitated a smooth and efficient workflow for the entire team.

10. Success Criteria for Project Achievement:
The success criteria for this project were meticulously crafted to align with both organizational and customer expectations:

Organizational Expectations:

- **Timely and Quality Project Completion:** Completing the project within the designated timeline without compromising on quality.

- **Adherence to Stringent Banking Sector Rules:** Conforming to the rigorous operational and accounting regulations set forth by the banking sector.

- **Achieving Project Profitability:** Attaining the projected profitability outlined by the organization and ensuring financial success for the participating banks.

- **Model Project Development:** Establishing the application as a model project, serving as a reference for future endeavours in the banking segment.

- **Securing Repeat Orders:** Meeting the crucial organizational requirement of obtaining repeat orders from the same customer, showcasing sustained value delivery.

Customer/User Expectations:

- **On-Time Delivery and Implementation:** Ensuring punctual delivery and seamless implementation of the project within the agreed-upon timelines.

- **Committed Return on Investment (ROI):** Achieving the committed return on investment (ROI) as outlined in the project agreement.

- **Manpower Reduction in Banking Operations:** Effectively reducing the manpower required for various banking operations.

- **Accurate Bank Accounting:** Ensuring accuracy in bank accounting, navigating through complex rules and adapting to changes seamlessly.

- **Minimized Inter-Branch Accounting Time:** Streamlining inter-branch accounting processes to reduce cycle times and enhance overall efficiency.

Team Member Satisfaction:

1. **Ensuring Team Satisfaction:** Prioritizing the satisfaction of team members by fostering a positive and collaborative working environment.

2. **Development of New Skills/Domain Expertise:** Facilitating the development of new skills and domain expertise among team members, contributing to their professional growth for future endeavours.

3. **Critical Success Factors for Project Accomplishment** (As Perceived by Team Members)

4. Upon reflecting on the project journey, team members and their Project Manager identified key factors that significantly contributed to the project's success. While these factors weren't explicitly outlined at the project's commencement, their retrospective importance is evident:

5. **Clarity in Task and Scope:** Having a clear understanding of the tasks at hand, coupled with well-defined scope and specifications.

6. **Customer Team Commitment:** Active commitment and continuous participation from the customer teams throughout the project life cycle.

7. **Senior Management Support:** Wholehearted support from senior management, coupled with the autonomy to make necessary decisions and take action.

8. **Competent Project Leadership:** A skilled Project Manager leading a trusted and cohesive team, fostering a collaborative and reliable work environment.

9. **Vigilant Risk Management:** Proactive risk management, particularly concerning timelines and design changes for Proof of Concept (POC) and User Acceptance Testing (UAT).

10. **Effective Project Progress Control:** Maintaining control over project progress through seamless communication and coordination, ensuring alignment with objectives.

11. **Robust Support from Project Management Office (PMO):** Exceptional support from PMO personnel, diligently tracking issues and facilitating their swift resolution.

12. **Stalwart QA/QC Teams and Process Control Engineers:** Strong backing from Quality Assurance (QA) and Quality Control (QC) teams, supported by matured processes within the parent organization.

13. **Exemplary Team Collaboration:** Exceptional teamwork and unwavering support from task force members, contributing significantly to project milestones.

14. **Positive Contributions from Legal Experts and Admin Teams:** Positive contributions from legal experts and administrative teams, add value to the overall project dynamics.

15. **Triumphant Conclusion: A Stellar Project with Enduring Impact!**

The project stands tall as a resounding success, leaving the team brimming with pride for their exceptional performance. Both the customer and senior management expressed immense satisfaction with the project's outcome. Completed within the stipulated time frame, the project's quality surpassed all expectations, culminating in the signing of a 5-year Annual Maintenance Contract (AMC) by the customer.

Bolstered by this triumph, the senior management, recognizing the potential in the banking sector, made a strategic decision to establish a dedicated division for banking applications. This foresighted move has proven to be a game-changer, with the division thriving and contributing significantly to the organization's annual business. Over the next five years, an impressive 560 branches across various banks availed themselves of the division's expertise, marking a substantial milestone in the organization's growth and ensuring sustained profitability.

In recognition of his exemplary leadership, the Project Manager earned a well-deserved promotion to "Divisional Manager," entrusted with independently overseeing this burgeoning business segment. The project's product underwent further refinements and has evolved into a flagship offering for the organization, symbolizing the pinnacle of success achieved in the banking domain. Notably, the banking division's excellence attracted the attention of another software group, leading to its acquisition as part of its strategic expansion plans.

This project not only achieved its immediate objectives but also laid the foundation for enduring success, leaving an indelible mark on the organization's trajectory and industry standing.

Questions:

1. How would you address challenges related to the scarcity of domain experts in a critical project, ensuring that the team can effectively handle the complexities of the banking sector and deliver a high-quality product?

2. As a manager, how would you manage the significant time pressure for development, especially in the initial stages when team members need to understand complex terminologies and processes? What strategies would you employ to expedite the learning curve and ensure efficient project progress?

3. In the context of the project's success factors, how would you prioritize and ensure continuous support from senior management, effective communication within the team, and collaboration with key stakeholders, such as QA/QC teams and customer representatives, to maintain project momentum and quality throughout its lifecycle?

Case No: 8 Revolutionizing Banking: A Tale of Total Branch Automation Project.

Teaching Note

Objective:

This case study, "Revolutionizing Banking: A Tale of Total Branch Automation Project," serves as a comprehensive exploration of the challenges, strategies, and success factors involved in the development of a groundbreaking banking application. The objective is to provide insights into project management, technology implementation, and navigating complex environments, especially within the banking sector.

Teaching Plan:

- Session 1: Introduction and Project Overview.

Time: 30 minutes:

- Provide an overview of the case study and its relevance in the context of banking sector transformations.
- Discuss the key objectives of the Total Branch Automation Project.
- Session 2: Challenges Faced by the Project Team.

Time: 45 minutes:

- Explore the internal and external challenges encountered during the project.
- Discuss the team's approach to overcoming the scarcity of domain experts, time pressure, and issues related to team dynamics.
- Session 3: Technical Challenges and Development Approach.

Time: 40 minutes:

- Analyze the technical challenges faced in the development of the banking application.
- Discuss the project team's approach to design complexity, database usage, and integration with banking peripherals.
- Session 4: Success Criteria and Key Positions in the Team.

Time: 35 minutes:

- Examine the success criteria set by the organization and customers.
- Discuss the key positions within the project team and their roles.
- Session 5: Success Factors and Positive Project Environment.

Time: 50 minutes:

- Identify the success factors perceived by the team members.
- Explore the positive dynamics within the project environment, including support from senior management and effective team coordination.
- Session 6: Conclusion and Long-Term Impact.

Time: 30 minutes:

- Discuss the overall success of the project and its enduring impact on the organization.
- Explore the long-term consequences, such as the establishment of a dedicated banking division and the acquisition by another software group.

Discussion Questions:

As a manager, how would you address challenges related to the scarcity of domain experts in a critical project, ensuring that the team can effectively handle the complexities of the banking sector and deliver a high-quality product? (Session 2).

In the context of the project's success factors, how would you prioritize and ensure continuous support from senior management, effective communication within the team, and collaboration with key stakeholders, such as QA/QC teams and customer representatives, to maintain project momentum and quality throughout its lifecycle? (Session 5)

Reflecting on the challenges faced by the project team, how would you, as a manager, manage the significant time pressure for development, especially in the initial stages when team members need to understand complex terminologies and processes? What strategies would you employ to expedite the learning curve and ensure efficient project progress? (Session 2)

Case No 9: Transformation of Concept to Industry Standard: The Unveiling of Optessa and its Global Impact on Manufacturing

Dr Jayasri Murali, Ms. Pooja Nalawade

Associate Professor, MBA@IICMR, Pune, Assistant Professor, MBA@IICMR, Pune

Abstract:

This case study explores the successful transformation of a conceptual idea into an industry-standard software solution, Optessa, designed to optimize sequencing and scheduling in discrete component manufacturing, particularly focusing on the auto industry. Initiated by a team of entrepreneurs with extensive experience, the project addressed challenges in production planning and scheduling faced by the rapidly evolving auto industry. Overcoming initial hurdles and utilizing personal funding, the team strategically concentrated on developing a comprehensive solution tailored for auto manufacturing. The project's success was underscored by securing a pivotal order from the Honda Group, leading to widespread adoption across North America, Europe, and Asia. This case highlights the collaborative efforts, technological innovations, and strategic decisions that propelled Optessa to become a transformative force in the global manufacturing landscape.

Keywords: Optessa, sequencing, scheduling, discrete component manufacturing, auto industry, production planning, global impact, industry standard, entrepreneurial initiative, software solution, transformation, case study, success factors, technological innovation, strategic decisions.

Introduction:

In the current dynamic landscape of the business world, rapid changes are fundamentally reshaping how businesses operate. The pervasive influence of innovative technologies is accelerating these transformations, creating a complex environment that enterprises must navigate. Amidst these shifts, global changes are occurring at an unprecedented pace, requiring businesses to adapt swiftly. Core principles such as productivity, the quality of products and services, cost-effectiveness in operations, and sustained growth are paramount concerns for CEOs worldwide. In the contemporary era, customer expectations play a pivotal role, particularly evident in industries like automotive, where a "quick response" has become the defining ethos. This emphasis on responsiveness is crucial in meeting individual customer needs, necessitating effective sequencing, streamlined scheduling of manufacturing orders, and efficient operational processes. The pursuit of enhanced customer service underscores the imperative for robust optimization of sequencing and scheduling operations in the manufacturing sector.

Key Challenges Identified by the Automotive Industry:

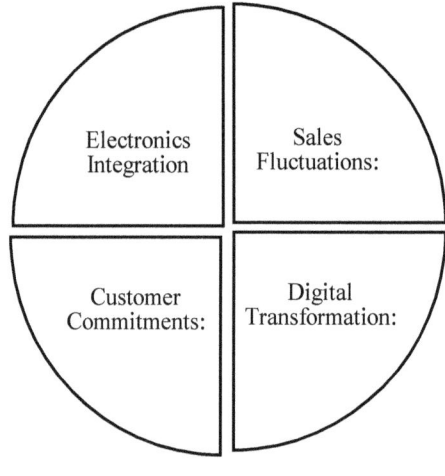

Figure 9. 1

The automotive sector faces significant challenges that demand strategic solutions. The industry contends with pronounced and rapid sales fluctuations, necessitating heightened flexibility in production planning and scheduling. Addressing this challenge requires an agile approach to activities and sequences. Furthermore, the industry is confronted with the imperative for holistic planning, implementation, control, and continual improvement of major manufacturing processes and resources. To achieve this, systematic adoption of a 'digital factory' is indispensable, integrating IT-based tools for informed management decision-making. Smart optimization of planning, sequencing, and scheduling applications is crucial to ensure timely deliveries aligned with customer commitments. Additionally, the escalating consumer demand for enhanced comfort and safety in vehicles is steering the automotive landscape towards increased incorporation of electronics, an essential component for driving innovations, including software advancements.

Pioneering a Paradigm Shift in Auto Industry Optimization:

In an era marked by relentless changes in the business landscape, the automotive industry faces a myriad of challenges, from fluctuating market demands to the integration of advanced technologies. Recognizing the need for a transformative solution, a dynamic team of entrepreneurs, comprising seasoned professionals from Canada and the USA, embarked on a journey to revolutionize sequencing and scheduling in manufacturing. Fuelled by the vision to address the specific needs of the auto industry, they delved into the intricate complexities of production planning, aiming to enhance efficiency, reduce costs, and ensure timely deliveries. This narrative unfolds the story of their venture, from identifying key challenges and conceptualizing an innovative algorithmic solution to successfully implementing it in collaboration with industry giants.

Charting the Course: Identifying Auto Industry Challenges: The automotive sector grapples with continual shifts in market and product requirements, necessitating a fine balance between process complexity and cost pressures. The integration of development, manufacturing, and logistics becomes paramount as product life cycles shorten. The team recognized the urgency for a global networking approach to counter diminishing added value from manufacturers. Out-to-delivery (OTD) timelines emerged as a crucial competitive advantage. This section details the specific challenges faced by the auto industry, setting the stage for the entrepreneurial journey.

Sequencing Success: The Genesis of a Game-Changing Solution: In response to the pressing need for better IT and optimization solutions, the entrepreneurial team, armed with diverse expertise, took centre stage. The decision to focus on the auto industry stemmed from its maturity and explicit awareness of the need for sophisticated sequencing and scheduling solutions. With one team member's extensive experience in the sector, a white paper outlining industry needs became the foundation for the project. The challenges were not only technical but also financial, as the team opted for a self-funded approach to safeguard intellectual property rights. This section unfolds the meticulous planning, from forming dedicated work groups to the critical decision-making processes that shaped the initial phase.

Navigating Complexity: Developing a Comprehensive Solution: As the team embarked on phase one, the intricacies of the proposed solution came into focus. The software had to address diverse ordering systems prevalent in different markets and incorporate terminology familiar to shop floor personnel. The emphasis was not just on classical operations research solutions but on enhancing the industry's competitive stance. Despite multiple offers from angel investors, the team maintained sole ownership of the intellectual property during the crucial initial stages. The narrative explores the challenges and triumphs of developing an algorithmic solution tailored to the auto industry's unique requirements.

From Vision to Reality: Triumph in the Face of Challenges: The project's success hinged on rigorous planning, innovative database design, and seamless coordination between teams in Canada, the USA, and India. A strategic timeline, spanning the first five years, outlined phases from prototype development to commercial orders. The pivotal moment arrived when the Honda Group endorsed the newly developed application, leading to standardized deployments across North America and Europe. The substantial savings and efficiency gains validated the project's significance. This section unravels the strategic decisions, triumphs, and lessons learned during the project's critical phases.

Beyond Boundaries: A Resounding Success and Industry Impact: In the competitive landscape of manufacturing optimization, this venture emerged as a resounding success. The narrative concludes by highlighting the significant milestones achieved, including the unit's remarkable growth to a turnover of 3.6 million USD within five years. The project not only succeeded in addressing the specific needs of the auto industry but also set a precedent for innovative solutions with far-reaching implications.

Strategic Goals for Project Success:

- Develop innovative business software products/solutions, namely "Optessa," introducing a ground-breaking approach to optimization for sequencing and scheduling applications, with a primary focus on the Auto Industry, particularly in Assembly Line and Paint Shop activities.

- Design and implement cost-effective solutions tailored for the Auto Industry, ensuring seamless integration with ERP and ERP Add-ons through collaborative efforts with customer teams.

- Leverage Indian talent to develop and deliver solutions, fostering a commitment to providing sustained services and support for international customers.

- Evolve the solution to cater to the unique needs of various industry verticals, to expand the application's versatility by the end of the fourth year.

- Craft an application that resonates with end-users, prioritizing usability and convenience in real-world scenarios.

- Engineer the product for minimal maintenance and modification requirements, ensuring easy interfaces with a diverse range of equipment and machinery.

- Achieve financial sustainability by reaching the break-even point within two years of inception. Initial projections indicate a turnover of approximately 3.5 million USD by the end of the fifth year, with profit margins exceeding 30% (PBT/Turnover) for the proposed joint venture.

Diamond Analysis of Project Classification:

The project exhibits the following characteristics based on the T-C-S-N Diamond analysis:

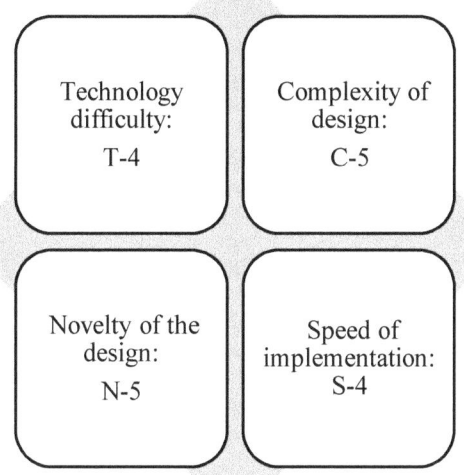

Figure 9. 2

Technology Difficulty (T): T-4 - The project involves a moderate level of technology difficulty, suggesting that while there are challenges, they are manageable with the right expertise and resources.

Complexity of Design (C): C-5 - The design complexity is high, indicating that intricate considerations and solutions are required for successful implementation.

The novelty of Design (N): N-5 - The design novelty is high, suggesting that the project introduces innovative and unique elements that may not have been extensively explored or implemented previously.

Speed of Implementation (S): S-4 - The speed of implementation is moderate, indicating that while there's a need for timely execution, there's room for careful planning and execution.

This analysis provides a snapshot of the project's key characteristics, highlighting areas that require special attention, such as the high design complexity and novelty. The moderate technology difficulty and speed of implementation suggest a balanced landscape that combines challenges with manageable aspects.

Project Characteristics:

- **Size of the Project:**
  - Budget of $0.5 million USD (INR 2.5 crore) for 5 years.
  - Initial phase of 18 months aimed at a turnover of over $3.5 million USD.

- **Number of People:**
  - Team of 20 in the Head Office, including QA/QC groups.
  - 3 team members at the site by the fifth year.
  - Initial 18 months involved approximately 8 persons, with a maximum strength of around 35.

- **Time Schedule:**
  - Initially planned for 12 months.
  - Pilot test expected within 18 months, challenging due to the absence of concrete orders.

- **Classification of Project:**
  - New unit by Indian Entrepreneurs in Canada/USA for global auto manufacturing plant market.

- **High-Risk Project:**
  - Inherent uncertainties and risks due to new concept/software application.
  - Time pressure added to challenges.

- **Technology Choice/Maturity:**
  - Evolving technology with inadequate existing solutions.
  - High risk due to a shortage of knowledgeable individuals and unknowns in the project environment.

- **Number of Suppliers:**
  - No specific role for suppliers.
  - Consultants and academicians played a critical role in optimizing algorithms.

- **Logistics/Clearances:**
  - Challenge due to time pressure and extensive travel requirements.
  - Effectively managed logistics and clearances for a multi-location team.

- **Location for Coordination:**
  - Coordination required across more than three locations (Canada, USA, and India).
  - Effectively managed without major challenges.

- **Support from Sr. Management:**
  - Excellent support from senior management.
  - Complete freedom for action and expenditures.

- **Involvement of Customer:**
  - Outstanding customer support, especially in the initial 18 months.
  - Initial doubts about Indian software professionals overcome over time.

- **Team Leader:**
  - Competent Project Manager with expertise in SW applications, international projects, and Auto Industry-based Sequencing/Scheduling.
  - Strong team-building skills and relationships with customers.
  - Expertise in Project Management Methodologies.

Key Roles in the Team:

The team was structured with essential roles, including:

- **Project Manager (Domain Expertise / Business Analyst / Business Process Expert):** Overseeing the project with a focus on domain expertise, business analysis, and process expertise.

- **Sales Manager / Sales Engineers (Role Played by CEO in the Initial Period):** Managing sales activities and customer engagement, initially handled by the CEO.

- **Module Leaders (3) for Various Critical Aspects of the Proposed Project & Development Team:** Leading modules crucial to the project's success and guiding the development team.

- **Database Expert / Network Expert:** Ensuring expertise in database management and network systems.

- **Quality Leader / Site Quality Leader / with 2 Site Engineers:** Spearheading quality assurance efforts, both centrally and at project sites, supported by two site engineers.

- **Delivery Manager for the Project (One of the Senior Team Members Played This Role):** Overseeing the timely and successful delivery of project milestones, managed by a senior team member.

- **Accounts Manager for Financial Issues / Funding:** Handling financial matters and funding requirements.

- **Site Manager PMO Office for Project Tracking and Liaison with Customer Team (In the Initial Part, This Role Was Played by CEO):** Managing the Project Management Office (PMO) and facilitating communication between the project team and the customer, initially managed by the CEO.

Figure 9. 3

Challenges Faced by the Project Team: Navigating Complexity and Innovation:

Understanding Business Implications: The primary challenge was grasping the economic and business implications of optimizing sequencing and scheduling in auto assembly plant operations. The concept needed to justify investment through on-time delivery, reduced cycle times, cost savings and enhanced competitive positioning.

Complex Software Development: The CTO faced challenges in developing a complex application with a novel approach. Overcoming issues related to Simulated Annealing, incorporating practical viewpoints, and addressing non-linear relationships were critical. Despite struggles, the team successfully demonstrated the application's effectiveness during the Proof of Concept (POC) stage.

Evolution of Interface Module: The interface module for data mobility underwent substantial changes during the initial years but was refined and stabilized. Adapting to complexities revolving around business process sequences, rules, and regulations across various industrial verticals was challenging, mitigated by close involvement with customer professionals.

Time Pressure for Development: Enormous time pressure necessitated initial investments in training and orientation for the development team. However, meticulous homework and training facilitated an expedited development process.

Standardized Documentation: Rigorous adherence to standard documentation proved crucial. Minutes of meetings and decisions were consistently documented, laying the foundation for project success by ensuring clarity and alignment.

Efficient Communication: Efficient communication within the team and with customer representatives, well-documented throughout the project, played a pivotal role. Tacit trust among team members and their leadership further facilitated harmonious collaboration.

Technical Issues and Collaborations: Technical challenges related to database usage and network effectiveness required dialogues with original equipment manufacturers (OEMs) of software platforms. Close collaboration with the customer IT team helped navigate and resolve these issues.

Test Data Preparation: The preparation of test data posed a significant challenge due to the complexity of the application and domain environment. However, the support and thorough homework by the first customer team proved instrumental in overcoming this bottleneck.

Scarce Domain Expertise: The scarcity of domain experts within the team necessitated an emphasis on training. The customer personnel's support during this phase played a crucial role in addressing the expertise gap.

Foreign Exchange Challenges: Challenges related to foreign exchange for travel were faced but had minimal impact on the overall project.

Positive Aspects of the Project Environment: Fostering Success Through Collaboration:

Strong Support from Stakeholders: The project benefitted from unwavering support from senior management, foreign partners, leading university professors, and retired professionals from AT&T in the USA. Their rich expertise proved invaluable in overcoming algorithmic challenges.

Focused Team and Detailed Implementation Plan: The team maintained a specific focus and adhered to a detailed implementation plan developed in collaboration with customer personnel. Challenges were tackled through mutual support and a willingness to put in extra hours when needed.

Effective Communication and Decision-Making: Continuous dialogue between the Customer Project Manager, local Project Manager, and senior managers from both sides ensured prompt issue resolution. Monthly/quarterly project meetings facilitated proactive decision-making, contributing significantly to project completion within the stipulated timeframe.

Harmonious Team Environment: A harmonious team environment played a pivotal role in creating a conducive work atmosphere. This positive dynamic was crucial for ensuring high-quality and undisturbed work, ultimately contributing to project success.

Efficient Pre-Dispatch Inspections: Rigorous pre-dispatch inspections involving local and customer Quality Assurance/Quality Control teams streamlined on-site software implementation. This approach minimized delays and waiting periods, ensuring a hassle-free deployment.

Freedom for Decision-Making: The team enjoyed full freedom for decision-making and committing expenses in alignment with the Project Manager's decisions. This autonomy facilitated smooth operations, complemented by continuous support from senior management throughout the project.

Project Success Criteria: Meeting Organizational, Customer, and Team Expectations:

Organizational Expectations:

Timely and High-Quality Project Completion: The primary organizational goal was to complete the project within the established timeframe without compromising on the quality of deliverables.

Adherence to Stringent Standards: Striving to meet the stringent standards set for the oil & gas and banking industries was a key organizational expectation, ensuring the developed solution met industry-specific requirements.

Achieving Planned Project Profitability: Organizational success criteria included achieving the anticipated project profitability as planned in the initial project assessments.

Model Project Development: Transforming the project into a model example within the industry aimed to set a benchmark for future business endeavours, emphasizing the significance of creating a reference project.

Securing Repeat Orders: A crucial organizational goal was to secure repeat orders from the same customer, highlighting the importance of fostering long-term client relationships.

Customer/User Expectations:

On-Time Delivery and Implementation: Meeting customer expectations involved ensuring on-time delivery and seamless implementation of the developed solution.

Committed Return on Investment (ROI): The project's success criteria included achieving the committed Return on Investment (ROI) as agreed upon with the customer.

Enhancing Competitive Business Stance: The project aimed to improve the competitive business stance of the customer organization, contributing to its overall market position.

Quality Support and Handholding: Providing exceptional support and handholding services during the implementation phase formed a crucial aspect of customer satisfaction.

Quality Documentation and Reduced Time Cycles: Meeting expectations involved delivering high-quality documentation and minimizing time cycles for the development of add-on modules, ensuring efficient and streamlined processes.

Satisfaction of Team Members:

Ensuring Team Satisfaction: A vital criterion for project success included ensuring the satisfaction of team members and fostering a positive and collaborative working environment.

Development of New Skills/Domain Expertise: Empowering team members to acquire new skills and domain expertise for future endeavours was integral to the success criteria, emphasizing continuous professional growth.

Key Success Factors Identified by the Project Team:

After thorough discussions with the project team and their Project Manager, several critical success factors (CSFs) have emerged, shedding light on aspects that significantly contributed to the project's success. While these factors weren't explicitly outlined at the project's outset, their retrospective identification proves valuable for future endeavours:

Clarity of Task and Scope: The importance of having a clear understanding of the task at hand, coupled with well-defined scope and specifications, emerged as a crucial success factor for the team.

Customer Teams' Commitment and Participation: The active commitment and continuous participation of customer teams throughout the project lifecycle played a pivotal role in its success.

Senior Management Support and Autonomy: Full support from senior management, coupled with the freedom to take necessary actions, was identified as instrumental in navigating project challenges.

Competent Project Manager and Trusted Team: The competency of the Project Manager and the trust within the team were recognized as foundational elements contributing to project success.

Alert Risk Management: Proactive risk management, particularly in terms of adhering to timelines and handling design changes during Proof of Concept (POC) and User Acceptance Testing (UAT), emerged as a critical success factor.

Effective Communication and Coordination: Impeccable communication and coordination played a key role in maintaining control over project progress issues, ensuring all team members were on the same page.

PMO Support for Rigorous Tracking: Strong support from Project Management Office (PMO) personnel for meticulous issue tracking and resolution added to the project's success.

Support from QA/QC and Process Control Engineers: Exceptional support from Quality Assurance/Quality Control (QA/QC) teams and process control engineers, backed by matured processes in the parent organization, contributed significantly.

Exceptional Teamwork and Task Force Support: The importance of exceptional teamwork and the untiring support of task force members were highlighted as crucial elements.

Support from Legal Experts and Admin Teams: Good support from legal experts and administrative teams was acknowledged for its positive impact on project success.

Consideration of Project Environments: The recognition of the impact of various project environments, including social, geopolitical, cultural, and local politics, on both the project and team members was deemed essential for effective project management.

Conclusion: A Resounding Success with Promising Prospects!

The project stands as a resounding success, with numerous achievements and positive outcomes that have surpassed expectations. The team takes great pride in their performance, delivering the project within the stipulated timeframe and meeting the highest quality standards. Both the customer and senior management express utmost satisfaction with the project's outcome, leading to the signing of a 5-year Annual Maintenance Contract (AMC). The developed products have found widespread adoption across North America, Asia, and Europe, with Honda standardizing the application for all its plants. Encouragingly, Ford Motors and General Motors have also embraced the application, inspired by the success witnessed with Honda. As the organization celebrates nine years of continued prosperity, it remains actively engaged and influential in the field, demonstrating the enduring impact of this highly successful project.

The organization reported the following results for the first 5 years after the gestation period

Year	18 months Gestation Period	1	2	3	4	5
Sales		-	0.5	0.8	1.1	3.6
Margin as % PBT			5.00%	-2.00%	7.20%	25.00%

Table 9. 1

Questions:

1. If you were in a managerial role, what actions would you have taken to address the challenges faced by the project team, especially in terms of understanding the business implications of optimizing sequencing and scheduling in auto assembly plant operations?

2. As a manager, what decisions or strategies would you have implemented to ensure the success of the project, considering the complexities of developing a new software application with a relatively new concept and approach?

3. In a managerial position, how would you have approached the situation of managing a multi-location team spanning Canada, the USA, and India? What steps would you have taken to overcome logistical challenges and ensure effective coordination among team members?

Teaching Note: Transformation of Concept to Industry Standard - Optessa and its Global Impact on Manufacturing.

Learning Objectives:

Understand the Challenges in Manufacturing Optimization: Explore the challenges faced by the automotive industry, emphasizing the need for optimized sequencing and scheduling in the manufacturing process.

Analyze Entrepreneurial Initiative: Examine how a dynamic team of entrepreneurs identified challenges, conceptualized a novel solution, and navigated complexities to bring Optessa to fruition.

Evaluate Success Factors: Analyze critical success factors identified by the project team retrospectively and understand their significance in project success.

Examine Project Characteristics: Explore the T-C-S-N Diamond analysis to understand the technology difficulty, design complexity, novelty, and speed of implementation in the project.

Assess Project Success Criteria: Evaluate the success criteria set by the organization, customers, and team members, and understand their role in project achievement.

Explore Global Impact: Understand how Optessa achieved widespread adoption globally, influencing manufacturing practices in North America, Europe, and Asia.

Teaching Pedagogy:

Case Analysis and Discussion: Begin with a thorough reading and analysis of the case, encouraging students to identify key challenges, project characteristics, and success criteria.

Group Discussion: Form small groups to discuss challenges faced by the project team and potential strategies to overcome them. Encourage diverse perspectives.

Role Play: Simulate a scenario where students take on the roles of project managers and discuss strategies to address challenges in understanding business implications, developing complex software, and managing a multi-location team.

Debate: Organize a debate on the significance of critical success factors and their impact on the overall success of a project. Encourage students to defend their perspectives.

Industry Expert Interaction: Invite industry experts or guest speakers to share insights on the challenges faced by the automotive industry and the impact of innovative solutions like Optessa.

Project Management Workshop: Conduct a workshop on effective project management, focusing on decision-making strategies, risk management, and communication in complex projects.

Case Presentation: Ask students to prepare and present a case study on another successful industry transformation project, drawing parallels and contrasts with the Optessa case.

Timing Action Plan:

Introduction (15 mins): Provide an overview of the case, its significance, and the learning objectives.

Case Analysis (30 mins): Allow students time to individually read and analyze the case, jotting down key points and challenges.

Group Discussion (45 mins): Form small groups to discuss challenges and potential strategies. Facilitate a lively exchange of ideas.

Role Play (30 mins): Simulate a role-playing scenario where students act as project managers addressing specific challenges faced by the Optessa team.

Debate (45 mins): Organize a debate on critical success factors, encouraging students to present arguments for and against their significance.

Industry Expert Session (60 mins): If possible, invite an industry expert to share insights related to manufacturing challenges and technological solutions.

Project Management Workshop (45 mins): Conduct a workshop on effective project management strategies, emphasizing decision-making and communication.

Case Presentation (30 mins): Assign student groups to prepare and present case studies on other successful industry transformation projects.

Conclusion and Q&A (15 mins): Summarize key learnings, address any remaining questions, and reinforce the broader implications of the case.

Assessment:

Individual Case Analysis: Evaluate individual understanding of the case through written analyses.

Group Discussion Participation: Assess active participation and contribution to group discussions.

Role Play Performance: Evaluate the effectiveness of role-playing scenarios in addressing challenges.

Debate Participation: Assess the quality of arguments presented in the debate.

Project Management Workshop: Evaluate engagement and participation in the project management workshop.

Case Presentation: Assess the quality of case presentations, focusing on parallels and contrasts with the Optessa case.

Overall Understanding: Evaluate students' overall comprehension of challenges, strategies, and success factors in industry transformation projects.

Case No 10: Mining the Challenges: A Comprehensive Analysis of a Mega EPC Project in the Indian Power Generation Sector

Dr Jayasri Murali, Mr Harshal Patil

Associate Professor, MBA@IICMR, Pune, Assistant Professor, MBA@IICMR, Pune

Abstract:

This case study delves into the complexities and triumphs of the SKG - EPC Project, a groundbreaking initiative by an Indian Power Generation organization to extract lignite from a large open mine. Valued at 6500 Million INR, this venture posed unprecedented challenges due to its sheer size, technological intricacies, and the involvement of various stakeholders. The project spanned 36 months, with an additional 24-month support period, making effective management and coordination critical.

The case study explores the classification of the project based on technology difficulty, design complexity, novelty, and speed of implementation. The specifications, prepared in consultation with reputed consultants, were vital for the project's success and its subsequent use in expanding the mines. The scope was extensive, involving numerous contractors, suppliers, and agencies, making coordination a Herculean task.

Challenges at various stages, from pre-sales preparation to execution and site work, are examined in detail. These challenges encompassed understanding intricate specifications, estimating costs, dealing with financial implications, and managing communication across a multitude of agencies. The proactive steps taken by the project team, including clarity in scope, strategic procurement, and meticulous logistics planning, are highlighted.

Key success criteria were established, focusing on timely delivery, conformance to specifications, and stakeholder satisfaction. The success factors identified include the importance of a feasibility study, commitment from customer teams, and robust risk management. The project's success is attributed to a competent project manager, strong teamwork, and meticulous planning, resulting in the adoption of the developed system as a standard offering worldwide.

While the project achieved remarkable success and recognition, the case study suggests areas for improvement, emphasizing the need for enhanced risk management and a more thorough analysis of logistics challenges in future large-scale EPC projects. Overall, the SKG - EPC Project stands as a testament to effective project management, collaboration, and overcoming challenges in a complex and dynamic environment.

Keywords: EPC Project, Large-Scale Mining, Logistics Challenges, Stakeholder Coordination, Project Success Factors.

Introduction:

The SKG - EPC Project emerged as a landmark initiative undertaken by an Indian Power Generation organization, signifying a significant foray into the extraction of lignite from a vast open mine. Priced at 6500 Million INR, this venture presented a distinctive set of challenges owing to its colossal scale, technological intricacies, and the involvement of diverse stakeholders. With a comprehensive duration of 36 months for the initial phase and an additional 24-month support period, the project demanded meticulous management and coordination to navigate through its complexities successfully.

This introduction aims to provide an overview of the project's magnitude and its implications within the realm of large-scale Engineering, Procurement, and Construction (EPC) endeavours. The classification of the project based on technological difficulty, design complexity, novelty, and speed of implementation sets the stage for a detailed exploration of the intricacies involved. The specifications, collaboratively devised with renowned consultants, take centre stage as the foundational blueprint for the project, underlining its pivotal role in future mine expansions.

The scope of the project extends far beyond the conventional, encompassing numerous contractors, suppliers, and agencies, each adding layers of complexity to the coordination and execution processes. As we delve into the challenges encountered at various stages - from pre-sales preparation to execution and on-site operations - a narrative unfolds, shedding light on the resilience and strategic acumen required to steer such a colossal project towards success.

This introduction establishes the context for a comprehensive exploration of the SKG - EPC Project, setting the scene for an in-depth analysis of its intricacies, challenges faced, proactive strategies employed, and the ultimate success achieved against a backdrop of innovation and complexity.

Diamond Analysis of Project Classifications:

In assessing the SKG - EPC Project, a diamond analysis provides a nuanced classification, highlighting key facets that contribute to the project's nature:

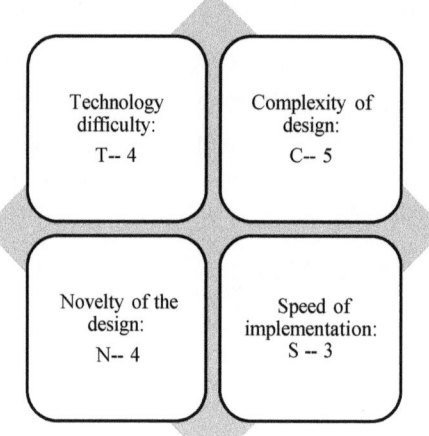

Figure 10. 1

Technology Difficulty (T): 4

The project grapples with a considerable level of technological complexity, earning it a T-4 classification. Innovations and advancements in technology are integral components, demanding expertise to navigate intricate engineering challenges.

Complexity of Design (C): 5

The project stands out with a C-5 classification, indicating an exceptionally high level of design complexity. The large-scale excavators, spreaders, and conveyors, each exceeding 42 meters, necessitate intricate design solutions, pushing the boundaries of conventional engineering.

Novelty of Design (N): 4

With an N-4 classification, the project embraces a novel approach to design. The uniqueness stems from the size and scale of the components involved, requiring innovative solutions to meet the project's specifications and objectives.

Speed of Implementation (S): 3

While not the fastest, the project maintains a moderately paced implementation with an S-3 classification. The size and intricacies of the components contribute to a measured speed of execution, balancing precision with the demand for timely completion.

This diamond analysis encapsulates the multifaceted nature of the SKG - EPC Project, acknowledging its technological challenges, design intricacies, innovative elements, and a balanced pace of implementation. The interplay of these factors forms the foundation for a comprehensive understanding of the project's dynamics.

Project Components and Challenges:

The specifications for the envisioned system were meticulously crafted by a highly influential and technically adept team of consultants, collaborating closely with the client's technical committee. The proposed system, along with its variations, held paramount importance as it was slated for utilization in the upcoming expansion of the mines. The project's scope was extensive, and intricate, and necessitated the involvement of multiple contractors, each handling distinct technical aspects. Notably, the directive stipulated that the system must be constructed within India, disallowing the importation of a complete system. Furthermore, a substantial portion of the system components had to be designed and manufactured within India, utilizing materials and components available in the country during that period. This mandate introduced a notable challenge to the project.

The SKG-EPC Project comprised four major components, each presenting unique engineering challenges. Excavators, spreaders, and two groups of conveyors, all exceeding 42 meters in size, demanded intricate assembly work on-site. The involvement of numerous subcontractors, suppliers, and agencies added layers of complexity, making coordination a formidable task.

Project Size and Classification: The project's sheer magnitude is reflected in various parameters, categorizing it as technically challenging, very complex, time-critical, and novel in approach. A comprehensive overview is presented through the following key parameters:

Value of the Project (INR 6500 Million): Signifying significant financial implications, any overruns in time or costs could impact both the customer organization and suppliers.

Periods (Basic Work 36 Months + Additional 48 Months for Support): The extensive duration poses challenges in retaining manpower and sharing knowledge, affecting motivation levels.

Volume of Work (Over 30,000 Tonnes of Materials/Steel): The substantial volume of materials, especially imported steel, heightens the risk, necessitating meticulous planning in the design stage.

Size of Land for Site Work (Over 100,000 Sq. Meters): Managing materials, ensuring safety, and addressing challenges like pilferage and property damage become critical on such expansive sites.

Design & Engineering (Over 500 Basic Drawings and 5000 Schematics): The challenge lies in providing an adequate workforce for design and engineering tasks and managing changes based on inspections and design reviews.

Size of Project Management Team (Over 400 People at Various Locations): Coordinating a team of this scale demands a strategic communication plan to avoid potential pitfalls and ensure smooth operations.

Various Agencies/Contractors/Consultants (Over 60 Agencies and 200 Personnel): Managing a diverse and large workforce from multi-cultural backgrounds poses communication and coordination challenges.

Logistics and Transportation (Over 15,000 Tonnes Imported and Local Steel): Coordinating transport from numerous locations and monitoring costs amid fuel price fluctuations adds complexity to the logistics.

Number of Commercial Contracts (Over 100 Contracts and 200 Purchase Orders): The extensive workload involves intricate negotiations, legal considerations, and alignment with customer guidelines.

Coordination with External/Internal Agencies (Over 10 National/International Agencies): Coordinating activities with multiple agencies and authorities requires meticulous attention to approvals and potential delays.

This comprehensive overview sets the stage for a deeper exploration of the challenges and proactive strategies employed throughout the SKG - EPC Project.

Major Challenges Encountered:

The challenges encountered throughout the various stages of this critical project were analyzed, and the following insights were gleaned:

Challenges during Pre-sales Stage Preparation / Estimation:

- Understanding and clarifying engineering specifications from the client's RFP posed a significant challenge, as some specifications were detailed while others were incomplete, impacting overall project progress.

- Estimating costs and time schedules was complex due to the project's size and complexity, requiring assumptions and cross-checking with customer approval, making the process time-consuming.

Challenges during Execution Stages (Engineering Design / Planning / Resources / Facilities / Infrastructure / Logistics):

- The project's sheer scale, volume, and strategic implications imposed a heavy burden on the team from the project's inception.

- Every decision carried substantial financial implications, especially in technical and procurement decisions, along with considerable costs in logistics and coordination.

- Coordinating with over 500 agencies and vendors, and adhering to procedural aspects and strict guidelines, presented significant challenges.

- Demanding customers emphasized documentation, leading to delays and potential loss of time and costs.

- Efficient execution required multi-functional expertise, challenging due to the numerous agencies involved, making coordination and communication formidable.

- The involvement of many individuals in planning, decision-making, and execution rendered control and reviews extremely cumbersome.

- Prolonged site work durations resulted in frustrations and lack of motivation, with continuous dialogue necessary to maintain team morale.

- Technically intricate issues with no precedent solutions, especially at the site, led to financial losses and delays.

- Facility planning complexities arose due to the enormity of sizes and logistics involved, requiring redesigns and customer vigilance approvals.

- Securing suitable sub-contractors at diverse locations, especially for site activities, presented a major challenge.

Challenges during Site Work:

- Coordinating across different locations and with numerous agencies posed an enormous communication challenge, risking potential disasters.

- Measuring completed work for stage-wise billing and reconciling with various agencies in a politically influenced setup was complex.

- Motivating the workforce at faraway sites with limited facilities and a large team size proved challenging.

- Untimely rains at the site caused havoc, submerging the entire plot, and leading to schedule setbacks and unplanned losses.

- Managing logistics and maintaining critical equipment at the site also presented several challenges.

Proactive Measures Leading to Success (Indicative List Only):

Clarity in Scope of Work: Meticulous care was taken in defining and gaining approval for the scope of work from customers and involved agencies, involving a dedicated team of senior professionals over six months.

Enlisting Support from Capable Vendors on Turnkey Basis: Proactive measures were taken to involve experienced and well-equipped vendors, especially for electrical and conveyor components, from the estimation stage onwards. This strategy streamlined coordination and logistics, controlled costs, and ensured international quality work.

Detailed Advance Financial Planning: The planning team forecasted, reviewed, and controlled funds flows and cash flows throughout the project period. Computer-based systems were employed to simulate project cash flows weekly, conducting "What If" analyses to anticipate the impact of changes and delays.

Proactive Planning and Cost Control in International Procurement: Strategic planning and cost control were employed in procuring major steel from the international market. Balancing imports with local purchases considered delays, emphasizing quality and reliability. Special attention was given to training local fabricators to meet expected standards.

Detailed Logistics Planning to Avoid Delays and Cost Overruns: The team paid special attention to logistics planning from the project's outset, conducting careful commercial negotiations with suppliers. Time-bound plans and instructions helped the project manager save costs by avoiding delays in logistics and transportation.

Crucial Facilities Planning - Manufacturing and Subcontractors: Meticulous planning for critical facilities and equipment at the site and other locations was essential. A dedicated team ensured proper action plans and tracking for the success of the project.

Utilization of Project Control Software: Software tools were employed for project management system (PMS) planning and control, resource optimization, tracking changes in work breakdown structure (WBS), risk assessments, regular reviews, and reporting. Collaboration with IT professionals and accountants was crucial.

Development of Ancillary Fabrication Contractors with Guidance: A special task force monitored and guided the development of ancillary fabrication contractors, a critical activity for overall project success. Senior management provided regular attention and support.

Systematic Manpower Planning: From the quotation stage, efforts were made to address the availability and retention of critical human resources. Challenges were faced due to the need for personnel to stay at sites for extended periods without adequate support facilities. While not completely satisfactory, planning for extra bonuses and incentives was explored to retain critical resources.

Project Characteristics:

- Size of the Project:
- Phase 1: Approximately 1000 Million USD (INR 650 crore in today's currency rates)
- Phase 2: Around 350 crore INR
- Total project value: INR 1000 crore (Approximately 155 Million USD)

- Number of People:
- Head Office (HO) / Design & Engineering Group: 25 persons
- Overall Project Team (including site personnel): 400 people (40 at site)

- Time Schedule:
- Project Duration: Less than 36 months
- Additional 24 months allocated for support at the site

- Classification of Project:
- Large Engineering, Procurement, and Construction (EPC) project with field implementation
- First of its kind in its category

- High-Risk Project:
- Uncertainties due to new design and time pressure
- High prestige and organizational reputation at stake
- Technical risks involved in modifying the German-designed basic structure using Indian materials
- Involvement of over 200 agencies contributing to the overall complexity

- Number of Suppliers:
- Several suppliers, with emphasis on 25 critical component suppliers
- Good support received from critical suppliers
- Various contractors engaged for specialized site work, including transport contractors

- Logistics/Clearances:
- Significant challenges due to time pressure
- Issues with logistics and transportation coordination, particularly over long distances
- Challenges in obtaining clearances for imported goods at the port, leading to delays in the project timeline

- Location for Coordination:
- Coordination required at more than 7 locations
- Multiple locations manned with project team members, posing communication bottlenecks

- Support from Senior Management:
- Excellent support provided by senior management
- Timely funding and administrative support
- Complete freedom granted to the team for technical and logistics actions

- Involvement of Customer:
- High involvement from customer personnel
- Keen interest expressed by the customer in project proceedings

- Team Leader:
- Team led by a highly competent and committed EPC professional
- Extensive track record, including experience working in German labs on complex EPC projects and international assignments

Key Roles within the Team:

The team was strategically structured with individuals assuming crucial positions to ensure the project's success. The key positions included:

Project Manager: Responsible for overall project coordination and management.

Design Engineers and Application Engineers at HQ in Germany: Engaged in the design process and application-specific aspects at the headquarters in Germany.

Design/Module Leaders (Design & Engineering) with Application Expertise: Led the design and engineering teams, providing expertise in specific applications.

Quality Leader/Site Quality Leader: Oversaw quality control measures both at the site and within the overall project.

Production Manager with Requisite Engineers in Workshop for Complex Jobs: Managed the production processes, including overseeing complex tasks in the workshop.

Process Engineer/Process Engineer for Exclusive Support of Key Vendors: Provided specialized support to key vendors and managed the processes associated with them.

Procurement Engineer/Logistics Manager: Handled procurement activities and efficiently managed the complex logistics involved.

Accounts Manager for Financial Issues/Funding: Managed financial aspects and funding requirements for the project.

PPC/Logistics/Shipment Manager: Coordinated Production Planning and Control (PPC), logistics, and shipment activities, particularly in the context of the intricate and multi-location nature of the project.

Site Manager with 7 Site Engineers with Good PR Abilities: Oversaw on-site operations, supported by a team of seven site engineers with strong interpersonal skills.

Application Engineer with Expertise and Some Experience in Installation of Systems: Brought expertise in applications and hands-on experience in installing similar systems in the field.

Project Management Office (PMO) for Project Tracking and Liaison with the Customer Team: Ensured efficient project tracking and maintained communication with the customer team.

Branch Manager and Technical Support Staff at Branch Office: Managed operations at the branch office, supported by technical staff to address specific project-related needs.

Project Success Criteria:

After thorough discussions with the project team and the Project Manager, the following criteria were established as essential benchmarks for the project's success, considering inputs from customers and their consultants:

Timely and Simultaneous Delivery of the Four Basic Equipment Groups Required at the Sites: Ensuring the prompt and synchronized delivery of the four fundamental equipment groups to the designated sites.

100% Conformance to the Specifications of the Proposed Systems for the Mine: Achieving complete adherence to the specifications outlined for the mine's proposed systems.

Satisfaction of All Customers, Consultants, and Senior Management of the Project: Garnering contentment and approval from all stakeholders, including customers, consultants, and senior management involved in the project.

Satisfaction of Suppliers for the Project with Reasonable Margins and Appreciation for Their Contributions: Ensuring suppliers' satisfaction by providing them with reasonable margins and acknowledging their valuable contributions to a project of national prestige.

Satisfaction and Appreciation of the Project Team: Fostering a sense of satisfaction and appreciation among the project team members for their dedicated efforts and contributions.

Satisfaction of the Principal HQ and EPC/Design & Engineering Personnel at Headquarters: Gaining approval and appreciation from the principal headquarters and the key personnel involved in Engineering, Procurement, and Construction (EPC) at the headquarters.

Project Success Factors (As Perceived by Team Members):

Upon discussions with the team members and their Project Manager, it is evident that the following list of factors would have served as Critical Success Factors (CSFs) for this project. It is important to note that while a formal list was not prepared during project execution, this compilation is based on the team's experience and feedback from customer teams. The identified CSFs that were tracked throughout the project duration include:

Need for a Reliable "Feasibility Study": Emphasizing the importance of a dependable feasibility study to lay a solid foundation for project planning.

Clarity About the Task at Hand & Scope and Specifications at Every Stage: Ensuring clear understanding and transparency regarding tasks, scope, and specifications at each project stage.

Commitment and Participation by the Customer Teams: Securing commitment and active involvement from the customer teams throughout the project lifecycle.

Complete Support from Senior Management: Garnering unwavering support from senior management to facilitate smooth project operations.

Competent Project Manager & Trusted Team: Appointing a skilled Project Manager and assembling a team that instils trust and confidence.

Risk Management, Especially in Terms of Timelines and Design/Changes: Prioritizing effective risk management, particularly concerning timelines and design changes, which could have been addressed more comprehensively from the project's outset.

Full Support from the Supplier Network: Securing comprehensive support from the supplier network to streamline the supply chain.

Smart and Timely Support from Respective Managers Working Closely with the PM: Ensuring timely and strategic support from managers closely collaborating with the Project Manager.

Strong Logistics Planning & Execution: Implementing robust logistics planning and execution to overcome challenges associated with project scale and multi-location operations.

Control Over Project Progress Issues Through Impeccable Communication and Coordination: Exercising control over project progress challenges through effective communication and coordination.

Excellent Support from Project Management Office (PMO) Personnel for Ruthless Tracking of Issues: Receiving outstanding support from PMO personnel for rigorous issue tracking and resolution.

Strong Support from QA/QC Teams and Process Control Engineers: Leveraging robust support from Quality Assurance/Quality Control (QA/QC) teams and process control engineers, benefiting from mature processes within the parent organization.

Exceptional Teamwork and Untiring Support from Task Force Members: Fostering exceptional teamwork and securing unwavering support from task force members dedicated to project success.

Conclusion: Remarkable Success with Valuable Insights:

The project stands as a remarkable success, earning high praise from all stakeholders deeply involved in its execution. The system crafted by the EPC group in India has been embraced as a standard offering worldwide by the parent organization, a testament to the exceptional accomplishments of the project team. The relentless and dedicated efforts of the team were duly acknowledged and highly appreciated.

However, in reflection, the team recognizes areas where improvements could enhance future project endeavours. Specifically, there is a consensus on the importance of bolstering 'Risk Management' practices. A more thorough and proactive approach to anticipating and mitigating potential risks could have further fortified the project's overall resilience.

Furthermore, the team underscores the need for heightened attention to the prior analysis of logistical challenges. While the project achieved immense success, a more in-depth exploration of potential logistical hurdles during the planning phase could have positioned the team to manage the project even more effectively.

The Project's triumphant outcome underscores the team's competency and commitment, serving as a valuable foundation for future endeavours. The insights gained through this experience provide a roadmap for refining strategies, ensuring that future projects benefit from an even more robust framework.

Teaching Note:

"Mining the Challenges - A Comprehensive Analysis of a Mega EPC Project".

Total Duration: 4 Sessions (Assuming each session is 1.5 to 2 hours).

Session 1: Introduction and Project Overview (1 hour):

- Introduction to the case study and its significance (15 mins).
- Overview of the SKG - EPC Project, its scope, and key parameters (30 mins).
- Diamond analysis: Technology Difficulty, Complexity of Design, Novelty, Speed of Implementation (15 mins).

Session 2: Project Components, Challenges, and Classification (1.5 hours):

- Detailed analysis of the four major project components (20 mins).
- Exploration of challenges at various stages: Pre-sales, Execution, Site Work (40 mins).
- Understanding project characteristics: Value, Periods, Volume of Work, etc. (30 mins).
- Group discussion on classification and characteristics (20 mins).

Session 3: Strategies, Team Roles, and Success Criteria (1.5 hours):

- Proactive measures leading to success: Clarity in scope, vendor selection, financial planning, etc. (30 mins).
- Key roles within the team and their significance (20 mins).
- Project success criteria and factors (30 mins).
- Role-playing scenarios and group discussions (30 mins).

Session 4: Critical Analysis, Debates, and Conclusion (1.5 hours):

- SWOT analysis of the SKG - EPC Project (30 mins).
- Group projects: Developing hypothetical plans for mitigating challenges (30 mins).
- Debates on critical success factors and alternative approaches (30 mins).
- Individual reflections and conclusion (15 mins).

Teaching Pedagogy:

- Encourage active participation, group discussions, and interactions.
- Consider inviting guest speakers with relevant industry experience.
- Allocate time for Q&A and addressing students' queries.
- Provide resources for further reading and exploration.

Assessment:

- Case study report (individual or group) - 40%
- Class participation - 20%
- Group project presentation - 20%
- Individual reflections - 20%

Case No 11: Riding the Wave of Technological Evolution: A Case Study on the Development of a Novel Banking Application

Dr Jayasri Murali, Mr Harshal Patil

Associate Professor, MBA@IICMR, Pune, Assistant Professor, MBA@IICMR, Pune

Abstract:

This case study delves into the intricacies and challenges faced during the development of an Enterprise-wide Application Software for Investment Management System, focusing on the financial sector's transition to computerization. Initiated in the late eighties and partially completed by the mid-nineties, the project aimed to revolutionize the loan processing cycle in India by introducing efficient transaction processing and overcoming limitations in existing banking products.

The project, funded by the World Bank, posed numerous challenges, including resistance to computer-based applications from senior management and strong unions, evolving regulations, and the need for a generic product adaptable to various banking institutions. The objectives included developing a user-friendly, low-maintenance application compliant with banking guidelines, offering database independence, inter-branch connectivity, and adhering to evolving RBI norms.

The project team faced internal challenges such as scope changes, time pressures, and inadequate domain expertise, coupled with external factors like slow decision-making, union interference, and policy changes by RBI. The technological difficulties were categorized as high, with challenges in product and database design, change control, source code management, and interface with peripherals.

The project was classified based on technology difficulty (T-3), design complexity (C-4), novelty of design (N-4), and speed of implementation (S-5). The estimated project cost was around $3 million, involving over 65 professionals.

Key project positions included a Project Manager, Domain Expert, Module Leader, Database Expert, Quality Leader, Delivery Manager, and Accounts Manager. Success criteria focused on timely completion, adherence to banking regulations, profitability, becoming a reference project, and obtaining repeat orders.

Despite facing numerous challenges, the project was considered a failure, with incomplete outcomes and financial setbacks. However, the Project Manager's efforts were acknowledged, and the developed framework became valuable for subsequent projects, contributing to partial recovery of costs. The study concludes by highlighting the lessons learned and the silver lining in utilizing project elements for future endeavours.

Keywords: Banking Software, Enterprise-wide Application, Investment Management System, World Bank-Funded Project, Project Challenges

1. Introduction:

The financial landscape witnessed a transformative era in the late eighties as the introduction of computerization gradually penetrated banking and financial institutions. This case study unfolds the narrative of a ground-breaking project initiated during this period - the development of an Enterprise-wide Application Software for an Investment Management System. The project, partially completed by the mid-nineties, was a response to the challenges faced by a Government-owned Financial Institute in the computerization of its Loan Processing System.

In an environment characterized by the nascent stage of computer-based banking applications and resistance from strong unions, this project aimed to redefine the loan processing cycle in India. Spearheaded as a World Bank-funded initiative, it held prestige and garnered constant monitoring from the Project Management Office (PMO). The financial institute, recognizing the limitations of conventional banking products, envisioned a new banking software application that would introduce efficiency, design flexibility, and parameterization to meet the evolving needs of the sector.

The objectives set for the project encompassed not only the development of a product aligned with Reserve Bank of India (RBI) norms but also the creation of a generic banking application capable of handling institution-specific customizations effectively. Emphasizing user-friendliness and adaptability, the goal was to develop a low-maintenance application capable of accommodating ever-changing banking guidelines. The proposed architecture aimed to be database-independent, promoting inter-branch connectivity and the concept of anywhere banking.

As we delve into the complexities and challenges faced by the project team, including internal management issues, domain expertise gaps, and external factors such as changing policies and union interference, this case study aims to dissect the intricacies of a pioneering project that, despite encountering setbacks, left a lasting impact on the trajectory of banking software development.

2. Project Objectives:

Seizing the opportunity presented, the organization initiated the "Total Branch Automation Project" by assembling a dedicated team led by a Project Manager and seasoned professionals. Recognizing the vast potential of banking automation, the organization outlined the following objectives for the project:

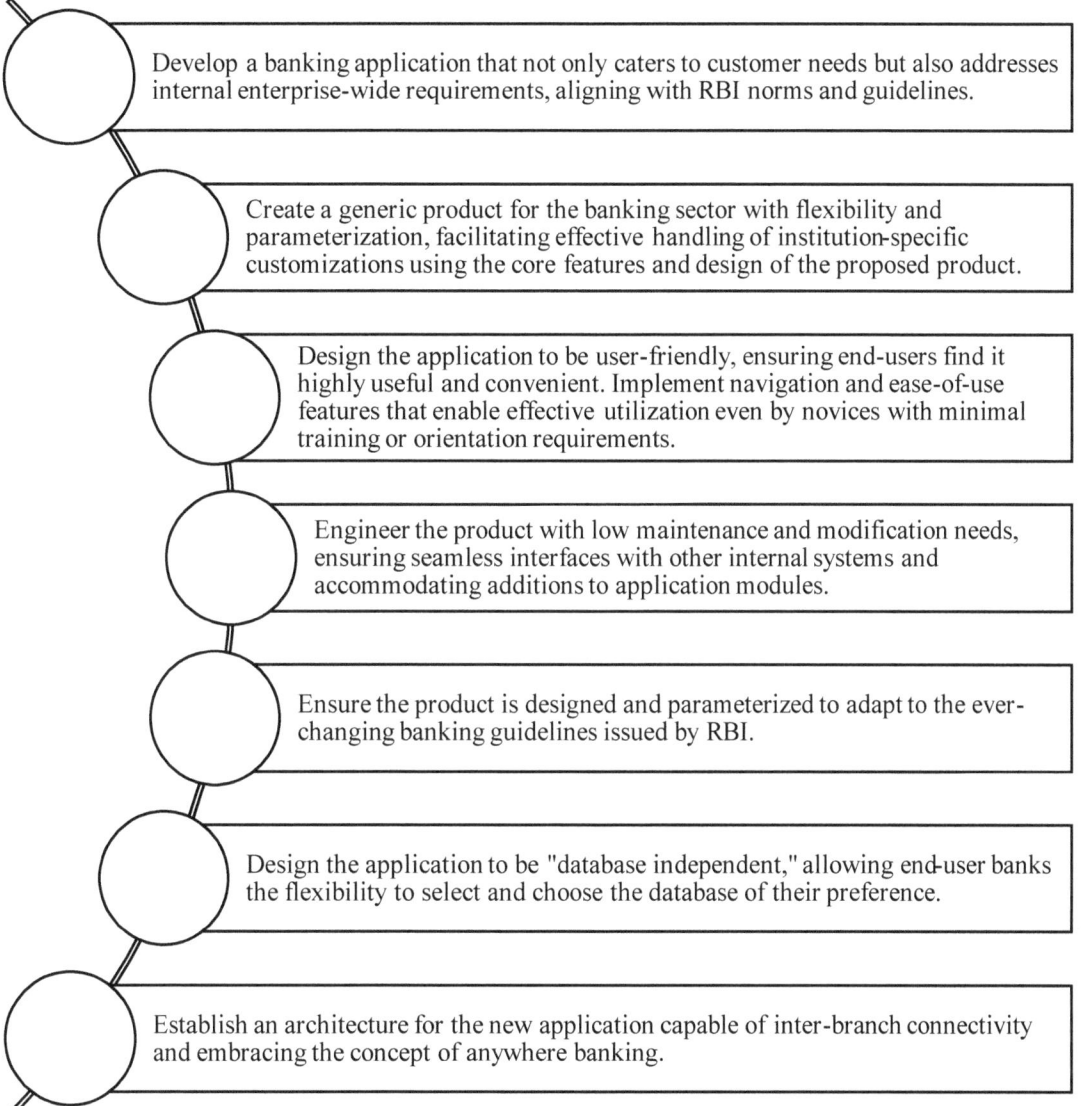

Figure 11. 1

3. Internal Project Management Challenges:

The project team, including the Project Manager (PM) and bank employees, faced several internal challenges that demanded attention. Some of these issues are outlined below:

Scope/Time/Cost/Quality Dynamics Changes: The primary challenge was aligning with conventional project success factors and completing the project within 24 months, as per RBI guidelines for transitioning to new banking rules.

Developing a generic software product demanded significantly more time and effort compared to a bespoke application, posing an unexpected challenge for the team.

Management Pressure and Regulatory Changes: The software industry perceived a significant opportunity in the banking sector, leading to excitement and urgency among management to launch products quickly.

Intense pressure resulted in shortcuts and mistakes. Time estimates were disrupted by new regulations, creating challenges for the project team.

Domain Expertise Gap: The team lacked adequate domain expertise in banking processes, with many personnel unfamiliar with how to adopt proposed changes by government authorities.

Convincing banking personnel of the benefits of new systems proved to be a significant pain point, especially among senior personnel uncertain about the effectiveness of proposed applications.

Internal Politics and Groupism: Internal divisions within the customer organization, involving MD and office staff, user departments, and the powerful IT group, led to conflicts during the acceptance of scope and specifications.

The initial development of the Request for Proposal (RFP) by the IT group without involvement from the user department caused conflicts, requiring intervention from the MD to reach compromises.

Scope assessment discrepancies between IT and user groups resulted in delays and cost escalations, leading to demotivation among the project team.

Staffing Challenges: High employee attrition rates, prevalent in both the project and customer organizations, persisted throughout the project. Despite the PM's freedom to choose the team, efforts were continually needed to prevent team members from leaving.

Infrastructure Challenges: Inadequate IT infrastructure in banks, with past hardware components incompatible with the proposed solution, required significant time and effort for procurement.

Data Integrity and Migration Challenges: Success in developing complex banking operations software relied heavily on clean and dependable data, which posed challenges due to the unavailability and inaccuracy of current branch data.

Loan accounts reconciliation was neglected initially, leading to inaccurate status, and demanding substantial efforts for correction.

Addressing these internal challenges was crucial for the success of the Total Branch Automation Project.

4. Technical Challenges Faced by the Team:

Implementing technological changes of this magnitude presented numerous intricate technical issues that demanded astute technical knowledge and experience. The project team's lack of requisite experience and exposure to the nuances of the application emerged as a primary bottleneck during the development and implementation phases.

Product and Database Design Control: Designing an application of this scale required effective and intelligent architecture to address the various modules and routines involved.

The sheer enormity of the application posed challenges, leading to the need for fine-tuning designs during QA/QC cycles. The team, lacking specific experience in such a vital activity, resulted in shortcuts, wrong compromises, and numerous rejection and rework episodes.

Change Control Processes: Enforcing strict control through "Engineering Change Control Notice" and judiciously evaluating change requests was crucial.

Despite best intentions, this activity fell short, with inadequate recording of all changes, demanding attention from the Project Manager (PM) and senior resources to ensure proper control throughout the project.

Source Code Control: Developing modules with different teams necessitated adherence to standard practices and methods to ensure uniformity and standardization.

Strict coding standards were implemented to maintain control over processes, compatibility, and integrated approaches in the final implementation stage. Meticulous and smart updates to the Work Breakdown Structure (WBS) database were essential for data compatibility and integration.

Interface Challenges: Considering the absence of specific standards for hardware purchases in the customer organization, the design teams faced ongoing challenges throughout the project's design, testing, and implementation stages.

Changes were sometimes required at the site based on local considerations and equipment availability when interfacing with banking peripherals and other existing systems/auxiliary modules.

Flexibility and Parameterization Impact on Design Complexity: Balancing flexibility and parameterization during the finalization of design architecture and database designs was crucial. Excessive flexibility and parameterization could make the system top-heavy, potentially affecting response times for various process routines in such a large system. The expectation to develop a "Standard Product" rather than a bespoke application for a bank introduced additional challenges and issues during the design and implementation stages.

Addressing these technical challenges was imperative for the successful development and implementation of the Total Branch Automation Project.

5. External Challenges:

Several external factors were identified that could impact the project's likelihood of success. These external influences included:

Slow Decision-Making at the Customer End: Delays in design approvals from the customer end had a direct impact on the development speed of the entire project. Persistent and diligent efforts from the team members were crucial in resolving these issues and maintaining project momentum.

Influence of Bank Employee's Union: The importance and interference of the bank employee's union stood out as an additional and critical external factor beyond the team's control. Collaboration with senior management of the bank and union representatives played a significant role in handling these issues. Cooperation from bank employees was essential for resolving implementation and usage challenges.

Frequent Changes in RBI Policies: The project team faced ongoing challenges due to frequent changes in policies by the Reserve Bank of India (RBI). The business analyst had the responsibility of meticulously tracking these changes, keeping all stakeholders informed, and ensuring their incorporation into the final solution.

Cooperation from Bank Staff during Implementation: Cooperation from bank staff during the initial stage of implementation was questionable. Gradual improvement occurred after a series of discussions with union leaders and senior management from the banks. Overcoming challenges related to the lack of master data and delays in compiling data from the working staff was a complex task, consuming considerable time and resources.

Addressing and navigating these external challenges was vital for the project team to successfully execute the Total Branch Automation Project.

6. Project Approach:

To tackle the challenges of the Total Branch Automation Project, a dedicated team, led by a project manager, was assigned to the initiative. This team consisted of over 65 professionals, with 50 individuals dedicated to development and quality assurance/control, and an additional 15 people involved in the implementation at five selected branches. Key aspects of the approach included:

Product Design Team Oversight: Managing the extensive size of the project was a daunting task. Accurate results, aligned with Reserve Bank of India (RBI) norms, were imperative for the bank application. The product design team played a crucial role in controlling and ensuring the compatibility of field data at every stage, addressing uncertainties in the interpretation of rules to minimize errors across application modules.

Rationalizing and Standardizing Process Routines: Domain experts faced the challenging task of rationalizing and standardizing process routines. This required an experienced professional with in-depth knowledge of banking operations. Changes in banking rules and regulations added complexity, demanding continuous attention to estimate their impact on finalized designs and routines. This dynamic aspect of the project brought moments of frustration for the entire team.

Responsibility of Module Leaders: Module leaders took on the responsibility for individual modules, supported by programmers and quality control teams. Meticulously adhering to set standards throughout development and testing was critical but challenging.

Introduction of a New Concept in Banking: During the project's development period, the banking sector did not have matured systems based on the introduced concepts. The application concept was entirely new for the Indian banking sector, leading to resistance, particularly from existing bank employees. Overcoming this resistance added another layer of complexity to the already challenging project.

This multifaceted approach aimed to address the intricacies and novel aspects of the Total Branch Automation Project, ensuring a comprehensive and coordinated effort from the dedicated team.

Diamond Analysis of Project Classification:

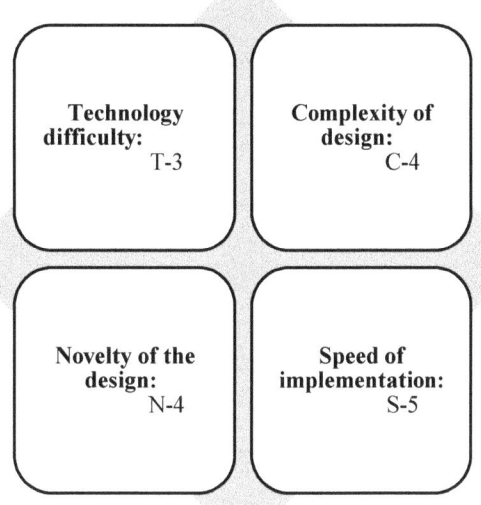

Figure 11. 2 - Diamond Analysis of Project Classification

Technology Difficulty (T-3): The project is rated at T-3, indicating a moderate level of technology difficulty. This suggests that while there are technological challenges, they are not extremely complex or insurmountable. The team should be equipped to handle moderate technological intricacies.

Complexity of Design (C-4): The project design complexity is rated at C-4, signifying a high level of intricacy. This indicates that the design aspects of the project are quite challenging and may require sophisticated solutions. The team needs to invest significant effort in managing the intricacies of the design.

Novelty of the Design (N-4): The novelty of the design is rated at N-4, suggesting a high degree of innovation and uniqueness. This implies that the project involves introducing new and groundbreaking concepts, making it crucial for the team to navigate uncharted territory and possibly face resistance from traditional practices.

Speed of Implementation (S-5): The speed of implementation is rated at S-5, indicating a high urgency and pressure for rapid deployment. This suggests that there are tight timelines and a need for swift execution, possibly driven by external factors such as regulatory requirements or market demands.

The project faces moderate technological difficulty, high design complexity, a high degree of design novelty, and an urgent need for speedy implementation. This diamond analysis provides a quick overview of the key characteristics and challenges associated with the project classification.

7. Project Characteristics:

- **Size of the Project:**
  - The project is valued at approximately $3 million USD (INR 10-11 Crore in today's currency rates), encompassing manpower costs, overheads, travel, and incidental costs.

- **Number of People:**
  - Around 50 personnel were involved in development and QA/QC at the Head Office, and 15 team members were dedicated to implementation at five different sites.

- **Time Schedule:**
  - The planned project duration was 24-28 months according to the feasibility study, with an expected start of the pilot test at the customer branch or HQ within 24 months from the initiation.

- **Classification of Project:**
  - A new project team was established for the existing organization, introducing a new product line for banking operations based on novel requirements. This marked a pioneering effort in India, as there was no comparable product available at that time.

- **High-Risk Project:**
  - The project carried significant uncertainties and risks due to the development of a new concept and software application using a new database version and connectivity. Sourcing domain experts was challenging, and time pressure was heightened by the proposed closure of the existing application. Customer expectations, especially regarding accuracy and response time, added to the complexity, along with potential issues related to union presence in banks.

- **Technology Choice/Maturity:**
  - The technology was in an evolving phase, being applied for the first time as a standard product. Knowledgeable individuals in the market were limited regarding this technology and domain applications based on the new rules and norms.

- **Number of Suppliers:**
  - There was minimal involvement of suppliers, except for one contractor responsible for software resources.

- **Logistics/Clearances:**
  - Logistics and clearances were not significant challenges as all team members were based in Mumbai. However, coordination with site staff posed a challenge, requiring the Project Manager to dedicate considerable time.

- **Location for Coordination:**
  - Coordination was managed across three locations (Mumbai + 2 additional locations) with project team members. Offices were well-equipped with excellent communication and infrastructure facilities.

- **Support from Sr. Management:**
  - Senior management provided consistent support, including timely funding, administrative support, and motivational encouragement throughout the project. The team was granted complete freedom for action and expenditures

- **Involvement of Customer:**
  - There was mixed and somewhat hesitant support from banking personnel and professionals. Customer teams were uncertain about the impact of new rules and software on bank operations but were willing to participate in the process, offering active support for specification development and pilot studies at select branch locations.

- **Team Leader:**
  - The Project Manager chosen was a competent and committed software professional with expertise in software applications and some exposure to airline back-office processing.

Figure 11. 3- Project Characteristics

8. Key Positions in the Team:

The team structure included the following essential roles:

Project Manager / Project Champion:
- Responsible for overseeing the entire project, ensuring its successful delivery and aligning with project goals.

Domain Experts / Business Analyst / Business Process Expert:
- Individuals with expertise in the banking sector, especially regarding banking operations, serving as key resources for domain knowledge and business analysis.

Module Leaders (4):
- Leaders assigned to various critical aspects of the project and its modules, ensuring focused and effective management of key project components.

Database Expert / Networking Expert:
- An expert responsible for database management and networking aspects, ensuring the robustness and efficiency of the technical infrastructure.

Quality Leader / Site Quality Leader / Site Manager:
- Leading quality assurance efforts, including site-specific quality management during implementation at branches. Supported by two site engineers for on-site implementation.

Delivery Manager:
- A senior module leader assuming the role of Delivery Manager, overseeing the timely and successful delivery of project outcomes.

Accounts Manager:
- Handling financial issues and funding matters, ensuring effective financial management within the project.

PMO Office (Project Management Office):
- Responsible for project tracking and maintaining liaison with the customer team. Ensured progress tracking and played a crucial role in issue resolution.

Figure 11. 4-Team structure

9. Project Success Criteria:

The criteria for project success were established by considering both customer expectations and organizational goals:

Organizational Expectations:

- Complete the project within the specified timeframe without compromising on quality.
- Adhere to the stringent rules governing banking sector operations and accounting standards.
- Attain the planned project profitability for both the organization and the partner banks.
- Develop the application as a model project, serving as a reference for future business endeavours in the banking segment.
- Secure repeat orders from the same customer, emphasizing the importance of building lasting relationships.

Customer / User Expectations:

- Ensure timely delivery and successful implementation of the project.
- Achieve the committed Return on Investment (ROI) from the project.

- Reduce manpower requirements in banking operations.
- Attain requisite accuracy in bank accounting, considering the complex set of rules and changes.
- Minimize the cycle times for inter-branch accounting, contributing to efficiency improvements.

Team Member Satisfaction:

- Ensure team satisfaction by providing opportunities for skill development and domain expertise.
- Facilitate the acquisition of new skills, preparing team members for future challenges and opportunities in the industry.

Critical Success Factors for the Project (as perceived by the team members now):

After discussions with the team members and their Project Manager, it becomes evident that the following points would have been valuable Critical Success Factors (CSFs) for this project. However, it should be noted that this aspect was not considered before the project commenced.

- A clear understanding of the task at hand, including clarity about scope and specifications.
- Commitment and active participation by the customer teams in the system development throughout the project life cycle.
- Full support from senior management, providing freedom for necessary actions.
- Competent Project Manager and a trusted team.
- Vigilant risk management, particularly in terms of timelines and design/changes for Proof of Concept (POC) and User Acceptance Testing (UAT).
- Control over project progress issues through seamless communication and coordination.
- Outstanding support from Project Management Office (PMO) personnel for rigorous issue tracking and resolution.
- Robust support from Quality Assurance (QA) / Quality Control (QC) teams and process control engineers, leveraging strong and matured processes in the parent organization.
- Exceptional teamwork and unwavering support from task force members.
- Good support from Legal Experts and Administrative teams.

10. Conclusion:

Navigating Challenges with a Silver Lining:

The project, in retrospect, is labelled as a failure due to the incomplete implementation of various components in the envisaged software application. A significant contributing factor to this setback was the prolonged delay of three years, primarily stemming from critical issues on the customer's end. Compounding the challenge was the inability of the project organization to fully recover the designated financial resources and professional charges from the customer, resulting in a financial setback.

Despite the obstacles and the project falling short of its intended outcomes, the project team takes pride in their earnest efforts under challenging circumstances. The unwavering dedication and contributions of the Project Manager (PM) were particularly noteworthy, earning recognition from both the customer and the senior management. Interestingly, the PM strategically repurposed the foundational framework developed during this project for subsequent clients. This strategic move played a crucial role in partially recuperating the financial deficit experienced in this venture.

While the project faced adversity and is retrospectively classified as unsuccessful, the positive recognition garnered by the team and the pragmatic utilization of the groundwork laid during the project contribute a silver lining to an otherwise intricate and demanding endeavour.

11. Questions:

1. **Strategic Decision-Making:** How would you advise the project team to navigate slow decision-making at the customer end, especially in obtaining design approvals? Propose strategies that balance the need for comprehensive decision-making with the project's urgency.

2. **Change Control Processes:** Given the challenges in enforcing strict change control processes, what specific measures or tools would you recommend to ensure effective recording and evaluation of engineering change requests? How can the team enhance the overall change management strategy?

3. **User Acceptance and Team Satisfaction:** Drawing from the case study, outline a plan to enhance user acceptance during the implementation phase. Additionally, how would you ensure team satisfaction, considering the challenges faced in internal politics, groupism, and high employee attrition rates?

Teaching Note: "Riding the Wave of Technological Evolution: A Case Study on the Development of a Novel Banking Application".

Objective:

The case study is designed to provide insights into the complexities and challenges faced during the development of Enterprise-wide Application Software for Investment Management Systems in the late eighties and mid-nineties. The focus is on technological evolution in the financial sector, project management challenges, and lessons learned.

Teaching Plan:

Introduction and Project Overview (30 mins):

- Briefly introduce the case study, its authors, and the context.
- Highlight the significance of the project in the evolution of banking applications.

Project Objectives and Approach (45 mins):

- Discuss the objectives set for the Total Branch Automation Project.
- Explore the team's approach to tackle the challenges, emphasizing the roles of key team members.

Internal Project Management Challenges (1 hour):

- Analyse internal challenges, including scope changes, management pressure, and domain expertise gaps.
- Discuss strategies to manage internal dynamics, considering scope, time, cost, and quality.

Technical Challenges Faced by the Team (1 hour):

- Delve into technical challenges such as product and database design, change control, source code management, and interface issues.
- Discuss how the team could have addressed these challenges effectively.

External Challenges (45 mins):

- Examine external factors like slow decision-making, union interference, and policy changes by RBI.
- Discuss strategies to navigate external challenges beyond the team's control.

Diamond Analysis and Project Characteristics (30 mins):

- Introduce the diamond analysis framework (Technology Difficulty, Complexity of Design, Novelty of Design, Speed of Implementation).
- Analyse the project's characteristics based on the diamond model.

Key Positions, Success Criteria, and Critical Success Factors (45 mins):

- Discuss the key positions in the team and success criteria from both organizational and customer perspectives.
- Explore critical success factors identified by the team members.

Conclusion and Lessons Learned (30 mins):

- Summarize the case study, highlighting the project's outcome, recognition, and setbacks.
- Discuss lessons learned and the silver lining in repurposing the project's foundational framework.

Interactive Session (30 mins):

- Facilitate an interactive discussion, encouraging students to share their perspectives on strategic decision-making, change control, and team and user satisfaction.
- Address questions and foster critical thinking.

Assignments and Assessment (15 mins):

- Assign case-related tasks, such as analyzing a specific challenge or proposing alternative strategies.
- Discuss the assessment criteria for case study reports, ensuring a balance between individual and group contributions.

Case No 12: Project Phoenix: The Rise, Fall, and Lessons from AmanK's Chemical Chronicle

Dr Jayasri Murali, Ms Dipti Bajpai

Associate Professor, MBA@IICMR, Pune, Assistant Professor, MBA@IICMR, Pune

Abstract:

This case study delves into the ambitious venture of AmanK, a multinational corporation, in establishing a plant to produce polyester resins, gel coats, and bonding paste on the outskirts of Pune, Maharashtra, India. The project, initiated due to the demand from a major customer in the wind energy sector, faced numerous challenges from its inception.

The USA-based project team, overlooking local conditions and underestimating the expertise of Indian engineers, encountered setbacks related to unrealistic time and cost estimates. The decision to involve a local team came too late, leading to a cascading series of misjudgments, including a misguided choice of EPC contractor and the adoption of incompatible Chinese designs.

The narrative unfolds with obstacles ranging from environmental clearances and political interventions to complications with EPC contractors. Poor planning, lack of local engagement, and oversight of crucial project elements resulted in substantial delays and cost overruns. The case outlines the lessons learned from neglecting due diligence, the importance of dynamic feasibility studies, and the significance of adapting global practices to local conditions.

The project's success criteria, including customer satisfaction, adherence to specifications, and team appreciation, were far from achieved. The aftermath led to a complete overhaul of leadership, but the financial toll and dissatisfaction lingered. The study concludes with a critical analysis of the factors contributing to the failure and offers insights for organizations venturing into complex, cross-cultural projects in dynamic environments.

1. Introduction:

The narrative of AmanK's endeavour to establish a new company to produce polyester resins, gel coats, and bonding paste on the outskirts of Pune, Maharashtra, India, unfolds a tale of challenges, miscalculations, and a quest for redemption. Originating from a large multinational corporation in the USA, known for its expertise in toxic and hazardous substances, the project aimed to respond to the demand from windmill blade manufacturers in India.

Initiated by the USA-based project team, the project encountered initial resistance due to a lack of trust in local Indian engineering talent. The team, driven by their experience in setting up similar plants across Asia, underestimated the unique challenges of the Indian environment. Their approach included finalizing land, signing contracts with a local EPC contractor, and formulating ambitious plans without involving local expertise.

The project faced setbacks, including a halt due to environmental clearances, local political interventions, and resistance from the workforce. The lack of respect for local conditions, coupled with an ill-informed choice of EPC contractor, led to rejection, rework, and substantial financial losses. The attempt to adopt Chinese plant design further complicated matters, highlighting the significant differences in standards between China and India.

Multiple changes in EPC approaches resulted in a standstill, prompting the involvement of UHDE Engineers & Consultants. Despite their professional handling, the cost skyrocketed to INR 50 crore, pushing the project to the brink of financial infeasibility. The blame game ensued, affecting team morale and creating a reluctance to take responsibility.

The investigation into the project's challenges revealed negligence by the law firm regarding local clearances, leading to heavy losses and a change in project management. The construction was eventually completed, but the full-fledged production was yet to commence, marking a journey fraught with hardships, lessons, and the pursuit of redemption for AmanK.

2. Challenges Faced by the Project Team:

The project team grappled with several challenges, primarily stemming from the choice of the project site and the selection of inappropriate EPC contractors. However, a major failure lay in neglecting fundamental principles and checklists crucial for effective project management. After careful discussions and a thorough review of available data, the main challenges identified for the project are as follows:

Inadequate Due Diligence on EPC Contractor: The failure to conduct comprehensive due diligence on the EPC contractor before awarding a contract of such magnitude was a critical oversight. Insufficient scrutiny of the contractor's facilities, resources, and background experience during the vendor shortlisting process proved to be detrimental.

Overly Ambitious Planning & Control Processes: The planning and control processes employed were not only inadequate but also overly ambitious, failing to align with the project objectives. Overconfidence on the part of the USA team emerged as a significant cause of failure.

Flawed Scope/Time/Cost Estimates: Hastily prepared estimates for scope, time, and costs, based on experiences in other countries, deviated from practical realities in India. Despite warnings from local team members about the disparities, the suggestions were ignored, leading to significant problems. The lack of adjustment to Indian conditions occurred twice during the project's tenure.

Insufficient Engineering Readiness: The overall engineering readiness for the project was lacking, resulting in subsequent issues. A failure to review the concept and design considering Indian conditions from the project's inception proved to be fatal and incurred substantial costs.

Last-Minute Decision-Making for Piping Routes: Critical decisions, particularly regarding piping routes and layouts, were made hastily at the eleventh hour on-site without adequate detailing. This led to extensive redesigning and re-engineering, causing delays and financial setbacks.

Lack of Trust in Local Talent: The USA team's lack of trust in the abilities of local engineers and project managers became evident. While the local team was eventually brought in to salvage the project, it was a delayed decision and exceeded cost estimates from the feasibility report stage.

Imposition of Chinese Designs: Imposing Chinese designs and system concepts on the Indian project, despite previous negative experiences, proved to be a fatal mistake.

Failure to Consult Local Team: The USA team neglected to consult the local team before assigning contracts and selecting consultants, leading to disastrous outcomes, especially in the case of the law firm in New Delhi.

Lack of Detailed Risk Analysis: Failure to conduct a detailed risk analysis, particularly concerning local conditions, environment, and applicable regulations, resulted in numerous challenges and bottlenecks throughout the project.

Neglecting Local Community Relations: The need to establish relationships with local community members and influencers was not anticipated, causing bottlenecks during various project phases. This aspect improved only when the local team took charge.

Inadequate Review Mechanism: There was a lack of a stable and comprehensive review mechanism to control project activities despite facing initial impediments.

Logistics Planning Challenges: Logistics planning became a significant problem due to the backward location of the plant, with a lack of support from an industrial service network nearby. Delays ensued as every requirement necessitated trips back to Pune or Mumbai, persisting as an issue for the plant.

Mishandling of Clearances: The New Delhi team of consultants mishandled both factory inspector office clearance and environmental clearance. The Maharashtra Pollution Control Board (MPCB) threatened plant closure, requiring extensive persuasion to obtain permissions.

Overloaded Senior Project Manager: The heavy workload of the senior project manager in the USA team resulted in inadequate attention to the Indian project.

Localities Influence: The plant's peculiar location, controlled by the local mafia, led to significant interference in the industrial belt. Insufficient attention in the initial phase resulted in severe penalties for negligence, emphasizing the need for proactive consideration of such possibilities.

3. Project Characteristics:

- Size of the project:
- Approximately $10 million USD (INR 63-65 crore in today's currency rates, including Building, Capital Expenses Capitalized, Other Equipment + Accessories).

- Number of people:
- 25 persons in Head Office (R&D group, Engineering, Project Management Personnel) + 150 people overall, including Site personnel and support staff.

- Time schedule:
- Originally planned for 3 years as per the feasibility study.
- Estimated/expected production start after 30 months from the project's initiation.

- Classification of project:
- New organizational setup as a green field project.
- First of its kind activity in India at that stage, with no existing plants in India having specific experience in running such facilities (except for a small plant in South India).

- High-risk project:
- Numerous uncertainties and risks due to the introduction of new materials in India for the first time.
- Risk associated with acceptance and suitability of these materials in the Indian Market.
- Time pressure due to proposed supply of locally manufactured materials to the Wind Energy segment.

- Technology Choice/Maturity:
- Evolving technology gaining acceptance in the US, Europe, and Asian Markets.
- However, new and not established in India, with a shortage of knowledgeable people in the market about this technology and its applications.

- No of suppliers:
- Several suppliers of raw materials, support services, Designers & Project Engineers/EPC contractors, and suppliers of various equipment and consumables.
- Major challenge with EPC contractors.

- Logistics/Clearances:
- Significant challenge due to time pressure and lack of requisite facilities and service structures in the site location.
- Government clearances/licenses essential for overall project activities, making logistics/legal matters crucial for project success.

- Location for co-ordination:
- More than 3 locations manned with project team persons: USA, Pune office, and Site office.
- Coordination challenging due to financial institutes and various Govt/Semi-Govt agencies in the initial phase of the project.

- Support from Senior Management:
- Mixed support (Excellent & timely support for funding/Good admin support & motivational support but inadequate engineering & EPC support).
- Local team given complete freedom for actions and expenditures later in the project.
- Some equity taken up by a famous financial institute, generating constraints for the project team.

- Involvement of Customer:
- No initial support from customers.
- Some customers had apprehensions about the use of these materials in the industry sector, creating constraints for the marketing team.

- Team Leader:
- Senior Project Manager selected was a competent/committed production engineer with good expertise in the technology.
- However, overloaded with assignments, resulting in less time for the Indian Project.
- The local PM also had competent design/engineering and project management experience.

Figure 12. 1-Project characteristics

4. Key Team Roles:

To ensure the project's success, the team was structured with essential positions, each playing a pivotal role in the overall execution:

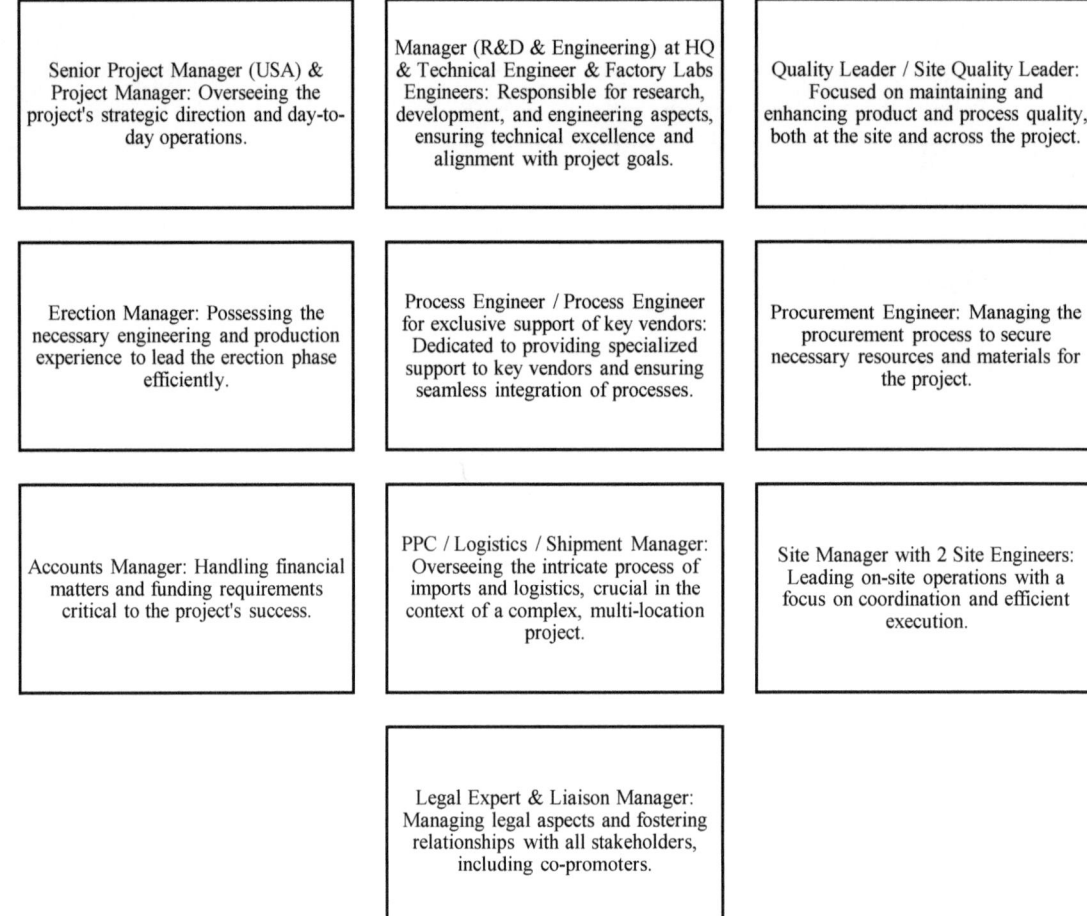

Figure 12. 2-Key Team roles

5. Project Success Criteria :

- The predetermined success criteria for the project, established in consultation with senior management, sponsors, and project team members, are as follows:

- The primary objective of the project is to successfully deliver locally manufactured chemicals and chemical products through the proposed Indian Plant, with strong support from senior management during this critical phase.

- Adherence to specified chemical, mechanical, and electrical properties of the proposed trial components is identified as a key success criterion for the project.

- Achieving overall satisfaction from customers and technical consultants in the relevant industry verticals is a pivotal measure of success, aligning with discussions held with senior management.

- Ensuring the contentment of suppliers for the project, including providing reasonable margins and recognizing their contributions to the introduction of new materials and methods, is considered essential.

- Securing satisfaction and appreciation from the project team is a critical success factor.

- Meeting the expectations of the principal headquarters and garnering approval from R&D personnel at the project office are integral components of the project's success criteria.

6. **Project Success Factors (as perceived by the current team members):**
   - **Clarity about the Task at Hand:** Clear understanding of the project scope and specifications.
   - **Customer Team Commitment:** Active participation and commitment from customer teams in developing basic products using locally available Indian raw materials.
   - **Senior Management Support:** Full support from senior management throughout the project.
   - **Competent Project Management:** Competent Project Manager leading a trusted and capable team.
   - **Alert Risk Management:** Proactive risk management, particularly concerning timelines and design changes for Proof of Concept (POC).
   - **Supplier Network Support:** Comprehensive support from the supplier network.
   - **Effective Communication and Coordination:** Control over project progress issues through impeccable communication and coordination.
   - **PMO Personnel Support:** Excellent support from Project Management Office (PMO) personnel for rigorous tracking of issues and prompt resolution.
   - **QA/QC and Process Control Support:** Strong support from QA/QC teams and process control engineers, leveraging robust processes in the parent organization.
   - **Exceptional Teamwork:** Exceptional teamwork and unwavering support from task force members.
   - **Legal and Administrative Support:** Good support from legal experts and administrative teams.

7. **Conclusion: Project Debacle:**
In evaluating the project against the backdrop of established success factors, it becomes evident that this endeavour was nothing short of a catastrophe. Satisfaction eluded every stakeholder involved. Through meticulous study and extensive discussions with the project team, it is unequivocal that this project stands as a glaring instance of failure, even though it staggered across the finish line, leaving the project promoters and owners far from content.

The project, initially slated for completion within 18 months, spiralled into a prolonged ordeal, extending over 24 months beyond the original feasibility study estimates. Financially, the cost projections skyrocketed from the modest INR 24 crore to a staggering INR 64 crore. Despite the relentless efforts of the local team, their hard work did not translate into contentment with the project's outcomes.

Upon closer examination, it's apparent that the critical success factors (CSFs) crucial to the project's triumph remained elusive. The financial ramifications were severe, inflicting continued distress upon the organization. The narrative of this project serves as a stark reminder of the importance of meticulous planning, thorough risk assessment, and unwavering commitment to achieving success in complex ventures.

8. Questions:

- Strategic Planning and Due Diligence: If you were the project manager, how would you ensure a comprehensive due diligence process for selecting an EPC contractor? What specific criteria would you consider avoiding the pitfalls faced by the AmanK project?

- Dynamic Feasibility Studies and Local Adaptation: In the context of dynamic feasibility studies, how would you approach adapting global practices to local conditions, especially in a cross-cultural project? What measures would you take to ensure the project's plans align with the unique challenges of the Indian environment?

- Team Collaboration and Risk Management: As a manager, how would you foster trust and collaboration between the USA-based project team and the local Indian team? Additionally, what proactive risk management strategies would you implement to prevent delays, cost overruns, and complications with vendors in a project of this nature?

9. Teaching Note:

Pedagogy: This case study is designed to engage students in a comprehensive analysis of a real-world project, emphasizing the complexities and challenges associated with cross-cultural ventures. The following pedagogical approaches are recommended:

- **Interactive Discussion (0:00 - 10:00):** Start with an interactive discussion, encouraging students to share their initial thoughts on AmanK's project. Facilitate a brief brainstorming session on potential challenges in multinational projects.

- **Critical Analysis (10:00 - 20:00):** Guide students through a critical analysis of the challenges faced by the project team. Encourage them to identify key issues related to due diligence, planning, and the impact of cultural differences on project outcomes.

- **Group Activities (20:00 - 30:00):** Divide students into groups and assign each group a specific challenge faced by the project team. Have them discuss and present potential solutions or preventive measures. This promotes collaboration and diverse problem-solving approaches.

- **Application Questions (30:00 - 40:00):** Engage students with the application questions for managers. Encourage them to think strategically, considering the specific context of the AmanK case. Facilitate group discussions to share insights and strategies.

- **Case Simulation (40:00 - 50:00):** Conclude the session with a case simulation exercise. Present a hypothetical scenario where students must apply lessons learned from the AmanK case to manage a similar project. This allows them to practically apply their understanding.

10. Assessment:

Assessment strategies should encompass both individual and group components, evaluating students on their understanding of project management principles, critical thinking skills, and ability to apply theoretical knowledge to real-world scenarios.

- **Individual Reflection (Written Assignment):** Assign an individual reflection where students analyze the AmanK case, highlighting key takeaways, lessons learned, and personal insights regarding effective project management in cross-cultural settings.

- **Group Presentation:** Evaluate group presentations on the assigned challenges and proposed solutions. Assess the depth of analysis, clarity of communication, and the feasibility of suggested strategies.

- **Application Questions Responses (Individual):** Assess individual responses to the application questions for managers. Evaluate the depth of understanding, strategic thinking, and the ability to apply project management principles to complex situations.

- **Case Simulation (Group):** Evaluate group performance in the case simulation exercise. Consider their ability to integrate lessons from the AmanK case into a simulated project management scenario, focusing on decision-making and risk mitigation.

- **Class Participation:** Encourage active participation in class discussions, giving credit to students who contribute thoughtfully to the analysis of challenges, lessons, and potential strategies throughout the session.

Case No 13: Master Plan for Sustainable Development: Holistic Approach to Water Management, Agriculture, Health and Education

Dr Jayasri Murali, Ms Puja Gavande

Associate Professor, MBA@IICMR, Pune, Assistant Professor, MBA@IICMR, Pune

Project Name: Project Dudhna 'Tushar Samriddhi': Restoring Water Conservation Structures & Implementing Watershed Plus Initiatives.

Project Overview:

The project, named 'Tushar Samriddhi,' embarked on the restoration of inactive water conservation structures along the Dudhna River in Shelud-Chartha Villages, Taluka & Dist. Aurangabad. Employing a participatory approach, the initiative sought to enhance agro-based livelihoods through 'watershed plus' activities.

Abstract:

This document presents a detailed account of Project Dudhna, an ambitious initiative led by a non-governmental organization (NGO) focused on sustainable water management. The project aimed to address water scarcity challenges in a specific region, employing a multidisciplinary team and innovative technologies. The founders of the NGO took on key roles as Project Champions, steering the endeavour through various challenges.

The team composition encompassed social workers, technical experts, tech leaders, trainers, supervisors, treasurers, auditors, and trustees, forming a cohesive unit dedicated to the successful execution of the project. Positive aspects of the project environment included strong support from senior management, effective collaboration with corporate organizations, and continuous dialogue with government officials and local stakeholders.

The success criteria, considering both organizational and customer expectations, emphasized timely delivery, adherence to regulatory requirements, and the development of a sustainable model for future initiatives. Factors contributing to project success, as identified by the team, included clarity of scope, committed customer participation, strong leadership, risk management, effective communication, and support from various stakeholders.

The document concludes with an evaluation of the project's success over its initial five years, highlighting achievements such as significant water harvesting, positive impacts on good recharge, critical irrigation support, and successful mobilization of additional contributions. Despite initial challenges and partial success, the project laid the foundation for continued social initiatives by the NGO.

Major lessons learned during the project implementation involved mid-term changes in excavation plans, innovative approaches to structure strengthening, and the importance of community adherence to guidelines. The document stresses the need for water structure rejuvenation as a replicable model, attracting volunteers, donors, and developmental agencies.

In summary, Project Dudhna stands as a highly successful initiative with measurable positive impacts on water resources, agriculture, and the community. The project's legacy extends beyond its initial scope, serving as a model for future endeavours in sustainable water management.

Keywords: Project Dudhna, Sustainable water management, NGO, Project Champions, Team composition, Corporate collaboration, Government partnership, Project success criteria, Customer expectations, Organizational expectation

1. Introduction:

In response to the critical water scarcity challenges prevalent in drought-prone regions, particularly in Maharashtra, India, a ground-breaking initiative named 'Tushar Samriddhi' was launched by a dedicated NGO in Aurangabad. The project aimed to address the pressing issue of water availability and offer essential support for survival in affected communities.

Led by a highly esteemed social worker with a proven track record in community service, 'Tushar Samriddhi' set out to confront the water scarcity challenge through innovative and constructive means. The project focused on rejuvenating river beds and restoring defunct water conservation structures along the Dudhna River, specifically in Shelud-Chartha Villages, Taluka & Dist. Aurangabad.

The core objective of the initiative was not only to ensure a sustainable and efficient water management system but also to enhance Agro-based livelihoods in the region. Through a participatory approach, the project sought active involvement from the local community, emphasizing collaboration and shared responsibility.

Acknowledging the gravity of water-related issues across the country, the NGO recognized the need for a positive and proactive solution. 'Tushar Samriddhi' was conceived as a holistic response, addressing both the immediate challenges of water scarcity and the long-term goal of fostering a resilient and thriving community.

As the project unfolded, it became a beacon of hope for the affected villages, showcasing the potential impact of community-driven initiatives in tackling complex societal problems. The following sections delve into the key aspects, successes, challenges, and outcomes of the 'Tushar Samriddhi' project, providing a comprehensive overview of its evolution and contribution to sustainable water management and community development.

2. Project Objectives:

In addressing the critical water scarcity faced by the Shelud-Chartha villagers, particularly during the arduous summer months, the primary objective of the project was to alleviate their acute water shortage. The dire situation is marked by a high prevalence of waterborne diseases due to

thorough investigation and discussions with the local community identified the core issue as the "non-availability" of good potable water.

To combat this challenge, the NGO initiated the ambitious 'Tushar Samriddhi' project, focusing on reviving water sources within the riverbed by cleaning it. Although similar approaches had been successful elsewhere, this specific method had not been attempted in the region. The project aimed not only to re-establish water tables in the immediate village but also to extend its impact along the riverbed in the district.

3. Current Situation Overview:

The project unfolded against the backdrop of a challenging environment, marked by half the annual rainfall, severely affected crops, and a critical shortage of drinking water in the villages. The 2012 drought forced the NGO to establish a cattle camp, highlighting the severity of the situation. The need for the project was evident not only in rescuing agriculture but also in ensuring the health and well-being of the local population.

4. Challenges and Unique Contributions:

The enormity of the challenge was met with genuine efforts from the NGO, which strategically formed a task force to investigate further. Convincing the sceptical villagers and gaining their wholehearted support was a major hurdle. Fortunately, enthusiastic engineers volunteered their expertise, contributing significantly to the technical aspects of the project.

5. Main Objectives of the Project:

Integrated Rural Development: Establish an initiative focusing on water management and healthcare in Shelud-Chartha village.

- **Corporate Support:** Secure funding from corporate organizations through CSR programs for effective water management.

- **Community Participation:** Encourage villagers to contribute financially to the project, overcoming initial scepticism.

- **Technical Data Dissemination:** Provide detailed technical information in the local language through discussion groups to garner support.

- **Comprehensive Solution:** Develop a sustainable master plan covering water management, agriculture, health, and education for long-term success.
- **Discussion Forums:** Establish forums through local leaders to facilitate open communication and ensure a shared understanding of the project.
- **Stakeholder Engagement:** Initiate contacts with corporate organizations, foreign agencies, and high-net-worth individuals for funds and support.
- **Volunteer Management:** Identify, select, counsel, and induct volunteers for the diverse activities of the organization.

6. Innovative Approach and Holistic Solutions:

The project embraced an innovative approach by not only addressing immediate water scarcity but also formulating a comprehensive master plan. This included a ridge-to-watershed development plan, short-term drainage lines, percolation dams, artificial ponds, and strategies for soil conservation. The holistic design aimed at ensuring a sustained impact on the community, requiring continuous dialogue, and a mindset shift for long-term success.

7. Challenges Faced by the Project Team:

The project team encountered various internal challenges that demanded attention, particularly from the Project Manager. Key issues include:

- **Enlisting Senior-Level Volunteer Support:** Enlisting commitment from volunteers at a senior level posed a significant challenge initially. The decision not to compensate founders, trustees, or volunteers added complexity. This hurdle was partially overcome by leveraging the network of founder trustees and their influence in renowned social organizations. The commitment of highly qualified volunteers played a crucial role, contributing significantly to the project's success despite early uncertainties.

- **Lack of Activity Plans and Organizational Processes:** The absence of well-defined activity plans, processes, and standards for planning presented another challenge. NGOs often face difficulties in organizing efforts into disciplined working methods. Decision-making, especially in a democratic setup, proved challenging, causing delays and missed opportunities.

- **Scope, Time, and Cost Challenges:** NGOs, reliant on funding from corporate CSR or other sources, face challenges in planning activities due to unpredictable fund availability. Flexibility in plans and schedules becomes imperative, influencing the overall project direction, scope, and timelines.

- **Enlisting Local Support:** Enlisting support from the local population was critical, considering the project's long-term benefits for them. Overcoming pressure groups and gaining trust required a patient approach. The formation of a steering committee from the local personnel, along with sustained dialogue and involvement, proved effective.

- **Attracting Technical Volunteers:** Attracting qualified technical volunteers for challenging on-site engineering work was another hurdle. Leveraging a network of volunteers from Mumbai and Pune helped secure the expertise needed for project planning and execution.

- **Coordinating with Multiple Agencies:** Effective coordination with various agencies involved in different project steps, such as socio-economic surveys, project advocacy, and water structure surveys, presented its own set of challenges. Skilful leadership helped resolve coordination issues.

- **Infrastructure Challenges:** The lack of funds posed challenges in establishing a well-equipped office and basic infrastructure for the new organization. While the parent organization provided some support, securing funds for essential amenities remained a hurdle.

- **Volunteer Recruitment and Management:** Recruiting new volunteers and managing a strong volunteer base were ongoing challenges. The dependence on personal contacts and the need for continuous efforts to engage volunteers for critical projects remained a persistent concern.

- **Operational Management by Volunteers:** While a volunteer-driven approach has its merits, ensuring that core team members are consistently available for key project activities, especially in the initial years, posed challenges. Enforcing corporate discipline in voluntary organizations is inherently complex.

- **Affordability of Professional Services:** Affordability of professional services for finance and legal matters remained a challenge. NGOs face constraints in allocating funds for essential services, leading to compromises and reliance on external support.

- **Communication Challenges:** Communication among volunteers became challenging due to a lack of computer knowledge and internet/email usage. Despite attempts at training and canvassing, this issue persisted, impacting operational efficiency.

- **Tedious Approval Processes:** Time-consuming and tedious formalities for permissions from corporations and approvals from the Charity Commissioner's office added delays to the project. Procedural hurdles and lackadaisical attitudes from local authorities complicated matters.

- **Field Work Knowledge Gap:** Volunteers lacking knowledge of actual fieldwork posed difficulties in gaining a proper perspective. Motivated volunteers without a social work background needed significant training and orientation to manage sensitive social projects effectively.

- **Public Relations and Fundraising Challenges:** The absence of strong PR machinery to approach donors, maintain follow-ups, and secure additional funds remained a challenge. Fundraising efforts relied on records and personal contacts, often resulting in unsatisfactory outcomes.

- **Data Management and Analysis:** Inadequate attention to data management and analysis emerged as a challenge. The absence of a professional approach to handling data, despite attempts to improve, reflected a weak area. Budget constraints hindered seeking professional help.

Addressing these challenges required strategic leadership, effective communication, and continuous efforts to adapt and overcome obstacles. The commitment and persistence of the project team played a crucial role in the project's success.

8. Social Issues Impacting Project Performance:

Undertaking any social initiative involves the challenging task of altering the mindset of key stakeholders, requiring dedicated efforts from pioneering teams right from the project's inception. Addressing such significant changes involves navigating complex social, economic, and emotional issues, demanding astute expertise, practical knowledge, and experience. This project was no exception, and despite a basic understanding of social issues among team members, the lack of experience and exposure to the intricate nuances posed a major obstacle in the project's development and implementation cycles.

- **On-Site Behaviour and Conduct:** Controlling on-site behaviour and conduct from employees and committed volunteers proved to be a crucial area requiring attention. Resource persons often lacked the necessary experience and skill sets to handle the current environment and site-specific issues. While continuous training was a solution, it fell short on various project modules. Founder members invested considerable time in gearing up the team, emphasizing the need for strict control to avoid potential issues resulting from misjudgments by field-level personnel.

- **Project Progress Reviews:** Implementing a strict process for reviewing project progress and accommodating changes in plans was essential. Founder members took meticulous steps to make this a standard practice within the organization. However, the challenge of maintaining flexibility in planning due to funding sources and timing persisted throughout the organization's activities.

- **Collaboration with Other Organizations:** Establishing interfaces with various organizations for lateral cooperation in social initiatives is vital for ensuring the success of similar projects. This collaborative approach is crucial in consistently and effectively communicating the importance of such projects among all concerned NGOs.

- **Flexibility in Plans and Operations:** Projects of this nature demand flexibility in plans and operations. However, corporate organizations, as funding agencies, may not always appreciate this approach due to potential financial impacts. This discrepancy can lead to issues and misunderstandings, affecting the timely delivery of the project. Balancing the need for flexibility with funding constraints remains an ongoing challenge for the organization.

9. Diamond Analysis of the Project Classifications:

The application of the diamond analysis framework to classify the project reveals specific characteristics in key dimensions. Let's delve into each aspect.

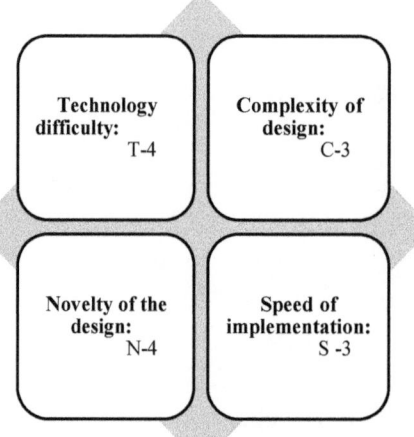

figure 13. 1-Diamond Analysis of the Project Classifications

- **Technology Difficulty (T-4):** The project is marked by a high level of technology difficulty, denoted by the 'T-4' classification. This indicates that the technological aspects involved in the project implementation are intricate and require advanced expertise. The challenges in technology may encompass various aspects, such as the use of sophisticated tools, innovative solutions, or intricate systems that demand a high level of technical proficiency.

- **Complexity of Design (C-3):** The complexity of design is identified as 'C-3,' suggesting a moderate level of intricacy in the project's design. While the project's overall design presents challenges, it does not reach the highest levels of complexity. This implies that certain elements of the project require careful planning and design, but the overall structure is manageable.

- **The novelty of the Design (N-4):** The novelty of the design is classified as 'N-4,' indicating a high degree of innovation in the project. This suggests that the project incorporates novel and ground-breaking design elements that may be pioneering in its field. The emphasis on novelty implies a departure from conventional approaches, possibly introducing innovative solutions or methodologies.

- **Speed of Implementation (S-3):** The speed of implementation is categorized as 'S-3,' reflecting a moderate pace in executing the project. While there is a commitment to timely implementation, the project does not operate at an exceptionally rapid pace. Factors such as funding timelines, external approvals, or resource availability may contribute to a moderate speed of implementation.

- The diamond analysis of the project classifications highlights a technologically challenging initiative with a moderately complex design, marked innovation, and a balanced pace of implementation. This classification provides insights into the project's key characteristics, aiding stakeholders in understanding and addressing specific challenges and opportunities associated with each dimension.

10. Project Characteristics:

Size of the Project:
Estimated at 0.2 million USD (INR 1.0-1.25 crore today), covering revenue expenses sourced from donations, encompassing manpower costs, overheads, travel, and incidental costs.

Number of People:
Initially, a core team of 5-6 volunteers expanded to around 12-14 members and eventually to 150, including part-time workers and village residents.

Time Schedule:
Original plan spanned 48 months, adapting to the flexible nature of the initiative, relying on pilot tests and responsive expansion.

Classification of Project:
Represents a new startup NGO, pioneering water management and rural development in Aurangabad.

High-Risk Project:
Undertaken in uncertain circumstances, facing challenges in recruiting senior volunteers without compensation, and recruiting experienced social workers.

Number of Suppliers/Affiliates:
Relies on proven approaches and mindsets, leveraging the experience and confidence of renowned social workers in the founding team.

Suppliers/Affiliates Role:
Critical role for low-margin suppliers, funding partners, and associations with similar initiatives. Personal goodwill and networks played a crucial role.

Logistics/Clearances:
Obtaining certifications, licenses, and permissions posed challenges, with initial support from the parent NGO for office space and expenses.

Location for Coordination:
Operates across more than 6 locations, facing coordination challenges, but receiving support from corporate organizations and the parent NGO.

Support from Sr. Management:
Senior management provided timely guidance, though funding and admin support were initial challenges.

Involvement of Customer:
Mixed support initially, but gained full backing as the village witnessed dedicated work. Government department cooperation improved over time.

Leader:
Competent and committed Project Manager, supported by a dedicated team of trustees, navigated challenges with patience and professionalism.

figure 13. 2- Project Characteristics

11. Key Roles within the Team:

- **Project Champions:** Occupied by the Project Director and Project Manager, who are the founders and driving forces behind the NGO.
- **Social Workers and Technical Experts:** A team of professionals well-versed in social work and technical expertise, particularly experienced in projects with a social orientation.
- **Tech and Module Leaders:** Initially two, now expanded to over six leaders overseeing critical aspects and modules of the project.
- **Training Experts:** Responsible for conducting soft skills training and ethical behavior exercises to foster the right attitude within the workgroups.
- **Module and Field Supervisors:** Overseeing the execution of modules in the field, managing volunteers, and ensuring smooth operations.
- **Treasurers and Auditors:** Handling financial matters, funding, and auditing processes, with auditors serving as advisors.
- **Trustees' Office:** Engaged in project tracking, facilitating communication with customer teams, and ensuring alignment with the beneficiaries' needs.

figure 13. 3-Key roles within the team

Positive Aspects in the Project Environment:

- **Strong Support from Senior Management and Corporate Organizations:** The project received unwavering backing from senior management and corporate entities, providing a solid foundation for success.

- **Focused Team with Detailed Implementation Plan:** The team maintained a specific focus and diligently followed a detailed implementation plan in collaboration with customer personnel.

- **Effective Communication with Government Officials and Customer PM:** Ongoing dialogue with government officials, customer project managers, and local project managers demonstrated a commitment to promptly address issues. Regular monthly or quarterly meetings involving senior managers facilitated proactive decision-making.

- **Harmonious Team Collaboration:** The cohesive and harmonious teamwork created a conducive environment for high-quality and uninterrupted project work.

- **Overcoming Local Resistance through Steering Committee:** Initial resistance from residents diminished after the formation of a Steering Committee, allowing them the freedom to decide project priorities.

- **Empowered Decision-Making and Expense Commitment:** The team enjoyed complete autonomy in decision-making and the commitment of expenses based on the decisions made by the Project Manager, ensuring a smooth workflow.

12. Project Success Criteria:

Organizational Expectations:

- **Timely Project Completion with Uncompromised Quality:** Complete the project within the designated timeframe without compromising service quality.

- **Adherence to Charity Commissioner's Office Regulations:** Conform to the stringent regulations set by the Charity Commissioner's Office governing NGO operations.

- **Achievement of Project Delivery Targets:** Meet the planned project delivery objectives for the targeted population as defined by the organization.

- **Development of Model Project Modules:** Develop project modules as exemplary models, serving as a reference for future activities.

- **Repeat Requests from Communities:** Garner repeats requests from various communities where services were provided, indicating the project's success and impact.

- **Enlistment of Local Support and Participation:** Successfully enlist the support and active participation of local communities in the project.

Customer/User Expectations:

- **Timely Delivery to Solve Water Availability Challenges:** Ensure timely delivery and implementation to address both short-term and long-term water availability challenges.

- **Achievement of Targeted Population and Frequency:** Achieve committed target population and frequency as outlined in the community service plan.

- **Accuracy and Efficiency in Operations:** Attain the requisite accuracy and efficiency in project operations, incorporating a complex set of rules and changes.

- **Effective Handling of Emotional and Social Issues:** Effectively manage emotional and social issues that may arise during the project's execution.

- **Satisfaction of Team Members, Trustees, Volunteers, and Beneficiaries:** Ensure satisfaction among team members, trustees, volunteers, and program beneficiaries.

- **Team Satisfaction and Skill Development:** Guarantee team satisfaction and facilitate the development of new skills and domain expertise for future endeavours.

- **Sustainability of the Project for the Future:** Establish a foundation for the project's sustainability and continued success in the future.

Project Success Factors (as perceived by the team):

- **Clarity of Task, Scope, and Specifications:** Clear understanding of the project task, scope, and specifications from the outset.

- **Customer Team Commitment and Participation:** Active commitment and participation from customer teams in developing the right ecosystem throughout the project lifecycle.

- **Support from Senior Management and Freedom for Actions:** Complete support from senior management with the freedom to take necessary actions for project modules.

- **Competent Project Manager and Trusted Team Members:** The presence of a competent Project Manager and a team of trusted members.

- **Alert Risk Management:** Vigilant risk management, especially concerning timelines and scope changes, although improvements were needed.

- **Control Over Project Progress through Communication and Coordination:** Effective control over project progress through impeccable communication, coordination, and regular reviews.

- **Support from PMO Personnel:** Strong support from Project Management Office (PMO) personnel for rigorous issue tracking and resolution.

- **Strong Support from Audit Teams and Process Control:** Strong support from Audit teams and robust process control, facilitated by matured processes in the organization.

- **Exceptional Teamwork and Support from Founding Members:** Exceptional teamwork and unwavering support from the founding members, are particularly crucial in the initial stages.

- Support from Legal Experts and Admin Teams: Timely support from legal experts and administrative teams whenever required.

13. In-depth Conclusion: A Project of Remarkable Success with a Few Challenges:

The project, while achieving significant success in its first five years, encountered internal process and efficiency concerns from the original team of founder members. Despite this, corporate CSR funding agencies, although only partially satisfied due to licensing delays, recognized the project's high quality. Notably, Corporate CSR program officers continued their support, and the senior management's contentment led to the establishment of additional teams for new social initiatives. The NGO perseveres, consistently contributing to various social issues.

14. Significant Achievements:

- Successful harvesting of 40 million litres of water, is a commendable feat considering recent low rainfall.

- Positive impact on well recharge, leading to increased water extraction for irrigation.

- Crucial irrigation support for horticulture crops, safeguarding 71 acres of orchards and benefiting 37 farmer families.
- Strategic water storage in farm ponds, ensuring a substantial income of Rs 70 lakhs for farmers.
- Sustained functionality of hand pumps, providing reliable drinking water even in low rainfall conditions.
- Strengthening of 300 meters of Kachcha Road using excavated material, showcasing resourcefulness.
- Mobilization of additional contributions from key suppliers and local farmers by SPMESM, reflecting collaborative success.

15. Valuable Lessons Learned:
- Flexibility with a mid-term change in excavation plans for optimal groundwater recharge.
- Cost-effective strengthening of side wings of structures using excavated material.
- Modification of the cut-off trench with the creation of a support buffer zone near the base.
- Recognition and encouragement of farmers lifting water from adjacent wells for farm pond irrigation.
- Adherence by Shelud Chartha farmers to guidelines against direct water lifting during scarcity.
- Emphasis on the importance of water structures rejuvenation, attracting support from volunteers, donors, and developmental agencies.
- "Tushar Samriddhi" as a replicable model, gaining recognition as a focal point in the region.
- Growing interest from various stakeholders in Project Dudhna, signalling an extension of work across the entire basin.

Teaching Note: Master Plan for Sustainable Development": Holistic Approach to Water Management, Agriculture, Health, and Education.

Overview:

This teaching note provides an overview of the case study on Project Dudhna 'Tushar Samriddhi,' focusing on sustainable water management and community development. The case study covers project objectives, challenges, successes, and lessons learned. It is designed for discussions in classrooms or training sessions related to project management, social initiatives, and sustainable development.

Timing:

The case study discussion is estimated to take approximately 90 minutes. The suggested breakdown is as follows:

Introduction and Background (15 minutes):

- Briefly introduce the case study.
- Discuss the background of Project Dudhna, its objectives, and the key challenges faced by the project team.

Diamond Analysis and Project Characteristics (10 minutes):

- Introduce the diamond analysis framework and its application to classify the project.
- Discuss the technological difficulty, complexity of design, novelty, speed of implementation, and implications for stakeholders

Team Composition and Positive Aspects (15 minutes):

- Explore the team composition, roles, and positive aspects of the project environment.
- Discuss the significance of strong support from senior management, effective collaboration with corporate organizations, and continuous dialogue with government officials.

Project Success Criteria (20 minutes):

- Examine the organizational and customer expectations outlined in the project success criteria.
- Discuss the importance of meeting timelines, conforming to regulations, and achieving targeted objectives for the organization and customers.

Project Success Factors (20 minutes):

- Analyse the factors contributing to the project's success as perceived by the team.
- Emphasize the role of clarity, commitment, support from senior management, and effective communication in achieving success.

Conclusion, Achievements, and Lessons Learned (20 minutes):

- Discuss the overall conclusion of the project, major achievements, and lessons learned during the implementation.
- Explore the legacy of the project and its impact on future social initiatives by the NGO.

Q&A and Group Discussion (10 minutes):

- Encourage questions, reflections, and group discussions.
- Facilitate a conversation about the challenges faced in social initiatives, the importance of community participation, and the replicability of the project model.

Facilitation Tips:

- Encourage active participation and diverse perspectives.
- Relate project management concepts to real-world challenges.
- Discuss the implications of the case study on sustainable development practices.

Assessment:

- Evaluate participants based on their understanding of project management principles.
- Assess critical thinking skills through discussions on challenges and solutions.
- Encourage participants to propose alternative approaches to overcome project obstacles.

Case No 14: Rebuilding Lives and Villages - A Tale of Rehabilitation and Transformation After the 1994 Marathwada Earthquake

Dr Jayasri Murali, Ms Puja Gavande

Associate Professor, MBA@IICMR, Pune, Assistant Professor, MBA@IICMR, Pune

Abstract:

This project, titled "Project Phoenix," recounts the remarkable journey of rehabilitation and transformation initiated by the Renowned NGO in response to the devastating earthquake that struck Marathwada in 1993. Focused on the rehabilitation of villages, particularly "Harali" and its surrounding areas, the project aimed to restore normalcy and rebuild the lives of over 50,000 affected residents.

Led by a seasoned social reformer and dedicated project manager, the initiative faced numerous challenges, from immediate medical assistance and housing to enlisting local support and generating financial aid. The Project Director's hands-on approach, quick decision-making, and transparent communication played a pivotal role in overcoming these challenges and gaining the trust of the affected communities.

The objectives of the project included providing urgent mental and physical support, educating the masses about overcoming natural calamities, offering free medical services, and establishing a task team for temporary housing. The project also emphasized social awareness programs, engaging local volunteers, initiating discussions through local leaders, and seeking support from corporate organizations, foreign agencies, and high-net-worth individuals.

Despite internal challenges and bottlenecks, the project successfully evolved into a transformative force, giving rise to a range of sustainable activities at the "Harali Center". These activities encompassed education, agriculture, technology, women empowerment, environmental initiatives, and more. The project's success prompted its expansion to other locations, positioning it as a role model for community-driven self-sufficiency projects.

The abstract highlights the project's challenges, successes, and the indispensable role of local collaboration, financial support, and dedicated volunteers. "Project Phoenix" stands as a testament to the resilience of communities in the face of natural disasters and the potential for transformative change through concerted, compassionate efforts.

Keywords: Rehabilitation, Earthquake, Community Transformation, NGO Initiatives, Self-sufficiency

1. Introduction:

Natural disasters can create unprecedented challenges for humanity, destroying both infrastructure and human lives. In such moments, society must embark on immense efforts to rehabilitate affected areas and restore normalcy and dignity to the affected population. The undertaking requires significant human dedication and motivation from individuals and the common person on the street to rectify the situation promptly.

This project exemplifies such a scenario, dating back to September 1993. A group of villages near Harali village in Umaraga Taluk, Sholapur district, Maharashtra, faced complete devastation, with over 5,000 houses and structures destroyed during a powerful earthquake. The region, home to more than 50,000 residents, lost all their homes due to the seismic event.

The initiative to reconstruct this area was spearheaded by the Pune-based NGO, 'Renowned NGO,' with an active branch in Sholapur. Established in 1962 with the motto "Motivating Intelligence for Social Change," the organization's scope has expanded across various realms of social work. Its primary objective is to cultivate leaders capable of addressing and solving India's myriad challenges, fostering leadership qualities, motivation, and attitudes geared towards problem-solving.

Renowned NGO engages in diverse fields such as education, research, rural development, health, and youth development. Its presence extends to multiple locations in Maharashtra, including Pune, Nigdi, Salumbre, Sholapur, Harali, and Ambajogai. The organization has initiated three schools in Nigdi, Sholapur, and Sadashiv Peth, Pune.

Following the massive earthquake in South Marathwada in 1993, the renowned NGO - Sholapur, swiftly responded. Well-wishers and past students contributed a substantial sum of 40 lakhs for relief efforts in the affected area. Initially selecting two villages for vocational rehabilitation and medical services, the NGO later responded to the villagers' request in Harali by establishing a primary and secondary residential school in 1995. In 2006, an agricultural polytechnic offering a three-year diploma after 10th standard, affiliated with Marathwada Agricultural University, was inaugurated. Facing an 8-hour power cut in the area, Renowned NGO embraced alternative energy sources like solar, bio-gas, and wind.

Crucially, the NGO does not rely on government grants for its schools, and it does not charge fees to rural students. The marketing of fruits and fruit products serves as an income source, providing employment opportunities for rural women. Presently, the activities in Harali have catalysed transformations in the surrounding villages, instigating a vibrant resurgence in the population that suffered from the calamitous earthquake.

2. Project Objectives:

The primary aim of the project was the rehabilitation of the devastated village near Harali, encompassing neighbouring villages and housing over 50,000 residents. Beyond housing and reconstruction support, a crucial focus was on organizing immediate, high-quality medical assistance for the affected individuals post-earthquake. The exemplary motivation of project volunteers demonstrated through tireless efforts over several months, successfully re-established Harali as a thriving community once again-an admirable objective indeed!

3. Outlined below are the main project objectives for quick reference:

- To offer both mental assurance and urgent physical assistance to the population, emphasizing a commitment to a better future. Immediate actions, such as fundraising by the parent NGO, involving thousands of volunteers and school children, generated over 40,00,000 INR within weeks, enabling the project team to operate efficiently on-site.

- To educate the masses about the prevailing situation and effective strategies to overcome the aftermath of a natural calamity. This objective aimed at garnering support and active participation from the community in the collective march towards the rehabilitation of the village and its surroundings.

- To prioritize providing necessary medicines and medical services free of charge to the affected population, addressing the urgent health needs resulting from the earthquake.

- To establish a task team with active involvement from residents for the swift provision of temporary housing facilities, often necessitating makeshift arrangements in many cases.

- To form a 'Social Awareness Programs Group' consisting of local volunteers dedicated to assisting underprivileged individuals within the community. This was achieved with active participation from both seniors and youth from the local population.

- To create discussion forums for villagers facilitated by their local leaders, ensuring accurate and genuine information about the project was shared and fostering the right mindset for sustaining efforts post-project completion.

- To initiate contacts with Corporate Organizations, Foreign agencies, and High Net Worth Individuals (HNIs) to secure funds and support for conducting various medical and social initiatives as specified in the activities outlined above.

- To identify, select, counsel, and induct volunteers for the proposed activities of the new organization. Emphasis was placed on launching multiple initiatives aimed at assisting those affected by natural calamity, promoting a quality life through education, technical training, enterprising agriculture, character formation, and motivation-building education for students.

- To enlist and nurture the development of young volunteers who would continue providing services on an ongoing basis, acknowledging the persistent challenge even in the present day.

4. "Empowering Change: The Transformational Leadership of the Project Director:

The individual spearheading the project, known as the Project Director, was a seasoned social reformer and dedicated project manager. Possessing ample experience and skills to handle such a sizable disaster, his hands-on approach and rapid decision-making capabilities were significant assets for initiating the project. His noteworthy speed in organizing activities and charismatic, down-to-earth behaviour played a crucial role in soothing the villagers right from the project's inception.

Upon reaching the location after the earthquake, the Project Director efficiently mobilized a group of over 40 volunteers. The financial aid provided by the headquarters, along with additional volunteers, proved instrumental in kickstarting relief work. Notably, most volunteers were current and former students from Pune and Sholapur, groomed in a highly disciplined work culture and dedicated to selfless service. This facilitated the Project Director in promptly forming the necessary modules and work groups, each assigned specific tasks for the project.

Enlisting the confidence, support, and participation of seniors from nearby villages in the project for rehabilitating the devastated areas posed a critical challenge. The Project Director's social orientation, transparent communication, and behaviour earned him the confidence of seniors during the initial phases. A Sarpanch from a neighbouring village even contributed a piece of his land for the project, significantly boosting the morale of the villagers. The project witnessed substantial progress in its early months, prompting the Renowned NGO to establish a new school in the region. This development enabled the Project Director to introduce various new initiatives at Harali.

The subsequent paragraphs probe into specific details of initiatives undertaken at Harali, highlighting the considerable success of the original project and the expanded vision from the Project Director. This transformative effort has not only turned the project into a legendary endeavour in the state of Maharashtra but has also achieved remarkable self-sufficiency in the area. The Project Director's visionary and tireless efforts have yielded substantial dividends, turning the team's dream of transformation into a reality. Indeed, the dream has come true!

5. Harali Center: A Vibrant Hub of Diverse Initiatives and Sustainable Development:

The Harali Center is currently abuzz with a myriad of activities, including:

- A rural residential school catering from 1st to 10th standard.

- An Agricultural polytechnic offering a 2-year diploma course.

- Computer training centers.

- Fruit plantations featuring 7000 fruit trees such as Amla, Guava, Lime, Mango, Tamarind, cashew nut, etc.

- A fruit processing unit providing employment opportunities for rural women.
- Water and soil testing lab.
- Drip and sprinkler irrigation systems.
- Vermiculture activities.
- Sheep rearing.
- Implementation of solar, wind, and bio-energy.
- Rainwater harvesting and bore recharge initiatives.
- Government-approved plant nursery.
- Fabrication shop.
- Production of fly-ash blocks.
- Centre for spiritual studies and meditation.
- Residences for Working Women.
- Govt.-recognized Agri-tourism centres.
- Venue for training programs available to government and non-government agencies, industries, and educational institutes.

6. The Challenge and Its Complexities:

Undoubtedly, the challenges faced by the project were formidable, yet the underlying need was undeniably genuine. To ensure the success of the project in one location, there was an imperative to extend its transformative concept to other areas where villages needed to attain self-sufficiency. Thus, the project was inherently strategic, serving as a role model for similar endeavours across the country.

Challenges Encountered by the Project Team:

Upon interaction with project team members and the Project Manager, several key challenges emerged, providing valuable insights from a project management perspective. The following points outline the internal issues and bottlenecks observed during the project:

- **Urgent Activity Plans and Hope Generation:** The immediate challenge was to generate activity plans that offered a ray of hope for the affected villagers. The Director of the NGO, an accomplished social reformer, took charge, setting up a camp within hours after the earthquake to provide urgent medical help, food, clothes, and daily essentials to the needy.

- **Enlisting Local Support:** Pacifying the disturbed minds of the local population, who had lost everything, required careful handling. The Project Director actively involved locals in planning and decision-making through a Steering Committee, establishing confidence and cooperation over time.

- **Generating Adequate Finances:** Securing financial support from Corporate Organizations, High Net Worth Individuals (HNIs), and other NGOs was crucial. The parent NGO mobilized funds initially, and later, contacts with NRIs and foreign social organizations sustained funding for the project's various initiatives.

- **Senior-Level Volunteer Support:** Enlisting support and commitment from senior-level volunteers, especially the initial teams, posed a significant challenge. The decision not to offer market-rate compensation for founders, trustees, and volunteers required strategic recruitment of highly qualified individuals committed to working with the core team.

- **Lack of Activity Plans and Processes:** The absence of detailed plans and standard processes for planning presented a significant challenge. While basic plans were prepared, the dynamic nature of the project demanded flexibility, requiring decisions based on careful planning and communication with locals.

- **Scope, Time, Cost, and Project Plans:** Unprecedented challenges related to project scope, time, costs, and overall plans were inherent in natural disaster-based projects. The fluid nature of such projects required flexibility, with decisions based on current situations and available resources.

- **Local People's Support:** Enlisting the support of the local population was critical for the project's success. The Project Director and team actively engaged with locals set up a steering committee, and allowed locals to prioritize their needs, fostering confidence and cooperation.

- **Technical Personnel Recruitment:** Recruiting qualified technical volunteers for onerous engineering work in adverse conditions was challenging. The strong network of volunteers through the parent NGO facilitated the recruitment of technical experts.

- **Coordination with Multiple Agencies:** Coordinating with various agencies involved in the project required close monitoring and coordination. Active support from government and semi-government agencies was crucial for the project's completion.

- **Infrastructure Development:** Establishing well-equipped hospital facilities and basic infrastructure was hindered by a lack of funds in the initial phase. Dedicated efforts were made to secure support from various sources, ensuring the development of essential facilities.

- **Volunteer Recruitment and Retention:** While the volunteer base was strong, recruiting new volunteers posed difficulties. Dependence on personal contacts and tireless efforts were necessary, as part-time volunteers might not be suitable for critical project activities.

- **Operational Management by Volunteers:** Most operational management was handled by volunteers, posing challenges in the long run. Enforcing corporate discipline in voluntary organizations was not feasible, requiring flexible methods and effective man-management skills.

- **Professional Services Affordability:** Affordability of professional services for finance and legal matters was a challenge. The parent NGO provided support where possible, alleviating some of the financial constraints.

- **Communication Challenges:** Communication within volunteers became challenging due to a lack of knowledge of computers, the internet, and email. Despite training courses, the lack of basic infrastructure and trained staff continued to affect operating efficiency.

- **Lengthy Approvals Process:** Obtaining permissions, dealing with formalities, and paperwork for the Charity Commissioner's office were time-consuming and tedious. Naive volunteers faced challenges in managing procedural and statutory conformances, often leading to mental agonies.

- **Lack of Fieldwork Knowledge:** Volunteers lacking knowledge of actual fieldwork posed difficulties in gaining a proper perspective. Motivated workers without social work backgrounds required training and orientation to handle sensitive project issues.

- **Public Relations Challenges:** Limited PR manpower and machinery for approaching donors, maintaining follow-ups, and securing more funds posed challenges. The parent NGO's experienced team supported the project in this regard.

- **Data Management and Analysis:** Data management and analysis were neglected areas due to budget constraints and a lack of expertise. Recent initiatives to address this issue lacked professional direction and experienced oversight.

- **Social Issues Impacting Performance**: Addressing complex social, economic, and emotional issues affecting project performance was a major challenge. The lack of experience and exposure among team members in managing such nuanced aspects posed bottlenecks, which were gradually addressed with the inclusion of professionals in the organization.

The multifaceted challenges encountered by the project underscore the intricate nature of social initiatives, demanding adaptive strategies, strong leadership, and a sustained commitment to overcome hurdles and drive meaningful change.

7. Project Classification Based on Diamond Analysis:

- **Technology Difficulty (T-3):** The project falls under Technology Difficulty Level 3, signifying a moderate level of technological complexity. While not the most advanced, the project involves technologies that require a certain degree of expertise and understanding.

- **Complexity of Design (C-2):** Complexity of Design is classified as Level 2, indicating a moderately intricate design. The project involves design elements that go beyond simplicity but do not reach the highest level of complexity.

- **Novelty of the Design (N-4):** The Novelty of the Design is rated at Level 4, suggesting a high degree of innovation and uniqueness. The project introduces novel concepts or solutions, setting it apart from conventional approaches.

- **Speed of Implementation (S-4):** The Speed of Implementation is categorized as Level 4, indicating a rapid and efficient implementation process. The project demonstrates a high ability to translate plans into actions swiftly.

This Diamond Analysis provides a comprehensive classification, emphasizing the project's technological demands, design intricacies, innovative nature, and efficiency in implementation.

8. Project Characteristics:

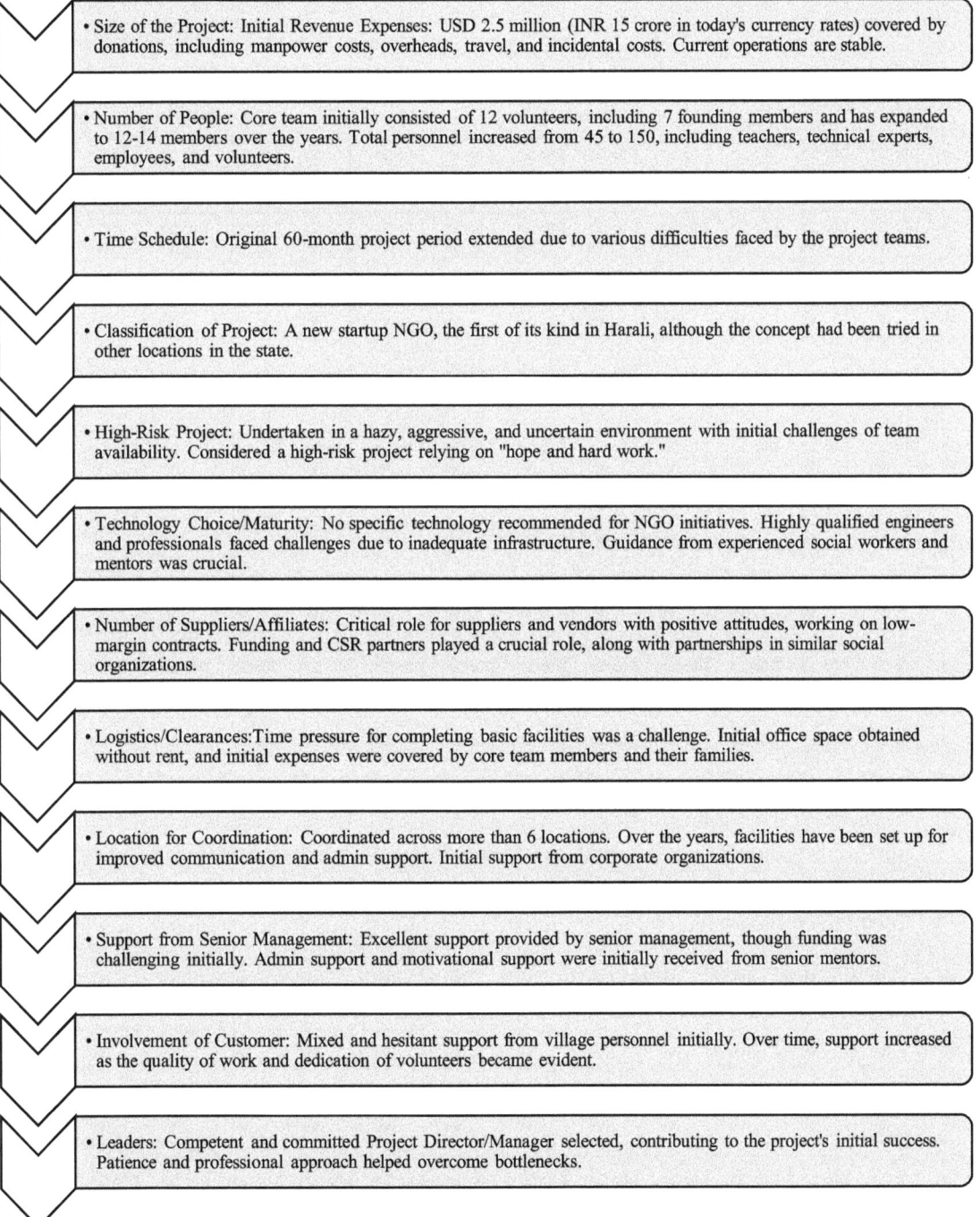

Figure 14. 1- Project Characteristics

Key Roles within the Team:

- **Project Champions:** Project Director/Project Manager (Founders of the NGO) leading the initiatives.

- **Social Workers and Technical Experts:** Team comprising social workers and technical experts with experience in similar socially oriented projects.

- **Tech Leaders/Discipline Leaders:** Initially 5 and now over 16 leaders overseeing critical aspects and modules of the proposed project.

- **Training Experts:** Specialists responsible for conducting soft skills and ethical behavior training exercises for workgroups.

- **Technical Consultants:** Diverse group of experts including Civil Engineers, Agriculturists, Architects, Technicians, Food Industry Specialists, Workshop Managers, and Non-conventional Power experts, especially in solar energy.

- **Financial Management:** Treasurers handling financial issues, funding matters, and advisors (auditors).

- **Trustees' Office:** Responsible for project tracking and maintaining liaison with volunteers, teams, and beneficiaries

Figure 14. 2- Key Roles within within the team

9. Positive Aspects in the Project Environment:

- **Strong Support from Senior Management and Corporate Organizations:** The project received unwavering backing from senior management and corporate entities.

- **Focused Team with Detailed Implementation Plan:** The team maintained a specific focus and adhered to a detailed implementation plan, working collaboratively with mentors.

- **Effective Communication with Government Officials and Customer Project Managers:** Continuous dialogues with government officials, customer project managers, and local project managers facilitated immediate issue resolution. Regular strategic and critical decision-making meetings were conducted monthly or quarterly, proving beneficial for the team.

- **Harmonious Team Collaboration:** A harmonious team environment contributed to high-quality and undisturbed work, playing a crucial role in the project's success.

- **Overcoming Local Resistance:** Initial resistance from local communities diminished after the formation of the 'Steering Committee,' empowering them to decide their priorities.

- **Freedom for Decision-Making and Expense Commitments:** The team enjoyed autonomy in decision-making and committing expenses based on the decisions of the Project Team (Founder Members), ensuring smooth operations.

10. Project Success Criteria:

Consideration of both customer expectations and organizational goals played a pivotal role in defining the success criteria for the project:

Organizational Expectations:

- **Maintain Harmony and Peace in Harali & Surrounding Areas:** Uphold a peaceful and harmonious environment in Harali and its surrounding regions.

- **Timely Project Completion with Uncompromised Quality:** Complete the project within the scheduled timeline, ensuring no compromise on the quality of service.

- **Adherence to Charity Commissioner's Office Rules:** Strictly conform to the stringent regulations set by the Charity Commissioner's office governing NGO operations.

- **Achieve Project Delivery Targets as Planned:** Accomplish the project's delivery for the targeted population as initially planned by the organization.

- **Develop Model Project Modules for Future Reference:** Create project modules that serve as a model for reference in future activities and initiatives.

- **Generate Repeat Requests from Communities Served:** Obtain repeat requests for services from various communities where assistance was provided, demonstrating the impact and effectiveness of the organization's efforts.

- **Enlist Support and Active Participation of Local Communities:** Successfully secure support and active participation of local communities in the project, a goal that was effectively realized.

Customer/User Expectations:

- **Ensure Timely Delivery of Medical Services with Proper Diagnosis:** Guarantee the timely delivery of medical services, including accurate diagnosis and comprehensive medical care in all operational aspects.

- **Achieve Committed Target Population and Service Frequency:** Meet committed targets for the population served and the frequency of services, maintaining a high level of quality and unwavering ethics.

- **Attain Accuracy and Efficiency in Operations:** Ensure operational accuracy and efficiency in the face of complex rules, challenges, and medical regulations.

- **Effectively Handle Emotional and Social Issues:** Address emotional and social issues adeptly within the core team and among other participants involved in the project.

- **Ensure Satisfaction of Team Members, Trustees, Staff, and Beneficiaries:** Secure the satisfaction of team members, trustees, staff, and beneficiaries, particularly those considered "the needy."

- **Ensure Team Satisfaction and Foster Skill Development:** Prioritize team satisfaction and facilitate the development of new skills and domain expertise for future endeavours.
- **Ensure Sustainability of the Project for the Future:** Establish a foundation for the project's sustainability, laying the groundwork for ongoing success and positive impact.

Project Success Factors (Team Perspective):

Through discussions with team members, project managers, and project directors, it is evident that the following factors were instrumental in the success of the project. It's important to note that these considerations were not necessarily comprehensively thought out before the project commenced.

- **Clarity of Task and Scope with Flexible Approach:** Having a clear understanding of the task at hand, scope, and specifications, coupled with a flexible approach to adapt to the challenging environment.
- **Commitment and Participation of Core Team Members:** The commitment and active participation of core team members in developing the right ecosystem throughout the entire project life cycle.
- **Complete Support from Senior Management:** Obtaining complete support from senior management, coupled with the freedom for actions for project and module leaders.
- **Competent Project Manager and Trusted Consultants:** The presence of a competent project manager, trusted consultants, and a professional team with diverse expertise.
- **Alert Risk Management:** A vigilant approach to risk management, particularly in terms of timelines and scope changes, although there were areas that needed improvement at various stages.
- **Control over Project Progress through Communication and Coordination:** Exercising control over project progress through impeccable communication, coordination, and regular reviews.
- **Excellent Support from Mentors:** Benefiting from excellent support from mentors and the rigorous tracking of issues with a commitment to their resolution.
- **Exceptional Teamwork and Support from Founding Members:** The exceptional teamwork and unwavering support from the founding members during the initial stages of the project.
- **Support from Legal Experts and Administration Teams:** Good support from legal experts and administrative teams whenever required.

Conclusion: Highly Successful Project with Notable Achievements:

The project achieved significant success in its first five years, delivering substantial benefits to the beneficiaries. While the internal processes and efficiency were commendable, the founding members continued to strive for perfection. A key success indicator was the acceptance of the initiative by local villagers, who now take pride in being integral members of the team—a realization of their dream.

Corporate CSR funding agencies expressed satisfaction, and the increasing number of students enrolling in the school and diploma programs further affirmed the project's success. The continuous positive outcomes make it a source of pride as the dream project delivers exceptional results. Truly, a great success!

Questions:

1. **Strategic Decision-Making**: Assume you are part of the project team during the immediate aftermath of the earthquake. The Project Director is faced with the decision of prioritizing either immediate medical assistance or temporary housing for the affected residents. Discuss the factors that should influence this strategic decision. What considerations would you propose, and how might this decision impact the project's overall success?

2. **Stakeholder Engagement and Communication**: You have been assigned the role of a communication manager for the project. The local community is sceptical and resistant to external assistance. Outline a comprehensive stakeholder engagement and communication strategy to build trust and encourage active participation. How would you tailor your communication to address the emotional and social concerns of the local population? Provide specific communication tactics and channels you would employ.

3. **Sustainability and Long-Term Impact**: The project has completed its immediate relief efforts and initiated various sustainable activities at the "Harali Center". As a sustainability consultant, propose a detailed plan for ensuring the long-term impact and self-sufficiency of the project. Identify specific initiatives or practices that contribute to the ongoing success of the project, considering economic, social, and environmental sustainability. How would you measure and evaluate the effectiveness of these sustainability measures over time?

Teaching Note

Case No 14: Project Phoenix: Rebuilding Lives and Villages - A Tale of Rehabilitation and Transformation After the 1994 Marathwada Earthquake.

Introduction:

The case study "Project Phoenix" details the remarkable journey of a rehabilitation and transformation initiative in response to the 1994 Marathwada Earthquake. The project, led by a seasoned social reformer and a dedicated project manager, aimed to rebuild villages and restore normalcy to over 50,000 affected residents. The case covers project initiation, challenges faced, strategies employed, and the subsequent transformative impact on the communities.

Learning Objectives:

- Understanding Project Management in Social Impact Initiatives:
- Explore the unique challenges and considerations in managing projects with a social impact.
- Analyse the role of leadership, communication, and stakeholder engagement in such projects.

Project Initiation and Planning:

- Examine the critical steps in initiating a project, especially in the aftermath of a natural disaster.
- Understand the importance of stakeholder analysis, risk management, and project planning.

Project Execution and Monitoring:

- Explore strategies for effective project execution in challenging environments.
- Discuss methods for monitoring and controlling project progress in dynamic situations.

Social Impact and Sustainability:

- Analyse the social impact of the project on the affected communities.
- Evaluate the sustainability of initiatives beyond immediate relief efforts.

Teaching Methodology:

Case Study Analysis:

- Break down the case into segments for in-depth analysis.
- Encourage students to identify key challenges, decision points, and lessons learned.

Group Discussions:

- Facilitate discussions on ethical considerations in project management.
- Explore the social, economic, and emotional aspects impacting project performance.

Role Plays:

- Conduct role-playing scenarios based on decision-making challenges faced by the project team.
- Encourage students to think critically about leadership and team dynamics.

Guest Speaker Sessions:

- Invite guest speakers with expertise in project management, social impact, and community development.
- Connect theoretical concepts with real-world experiences.

Classroom Activities:

- Assign small group projects focusing on developing a social impact proposal.
- Organize debates on the role of NGOs, corporate entities, and government agencies in disaster recovery.

Assessment:

- Case Study Analysis Report (30%):
- Individual or group analysis of specific aspects of "Project Phoenix."
- Group Project - Social Impact Proposal (40%):
- Develop a comprehensive proposal for a hypothetical social impact initiative.
- Class Participation and Discussions (20%):
- Active engagement in class discussions, role plays, and debates. (10%)

Conclusion:

The case study "Project Phoenix" provides a rich context for exploring the complexities of managing projects with a social impact. Through analysis, discussions, and practical exercises, students will gain valuable insights into effective project management, ethical considerations, and the transformative potential of community-driven initiatives. The case encourages critical thinking, decision-making, and application of project management principles in real-world scenarios.

Case No. 15: Innovation Amidst Challenges: A Deep Dive into the Implementation of a Cutting-Edge Telecom Project in India

Dr Jayasri Murali, Dr Sarita Samson

Associate Professor, MBA@IICMR, Pune, Assistant Professor, MBA@IICMR, Pune

Abstract:

This case study delves into a pivotal project undertaken during the telecom boom in India, marking the era of liberalization and privatization. The project, initiated by a renowned Indian group, aimed to establish a cutting-edge backbone for national internet services and regional data centres, contributing to the evolution of communication infrastructure. Commencing as a Phase 2 expansion in 1996-97, the project faced multifaceted challenges, encompassing internal management issues and external hurdles such as regulatory clearances and changing government policies. The objectives included developing a high-speed network conforming to international standards, catering to retail and corporate customers, and setting up regional data centres.

As the project unfolded, the team encountered internal challenges like delays in regulatory approvals, management pressures for swift execution, a shortage of domain expertise, high employee attrition rates, and the need for a robust testing infrastructure. External challenges involved grappling with government authorities resistant to change, competition from existing agencies, and navigating through policy changes by the Department of Telecommunications (DOT). Despite these obstacles, the team managed to establish the main backbone network, regional hubs, private VPNs, an R&D lab, and a robust support system.

This case study sheds light on the complexities of managing a large-scale telecom project in a dynamic environment, addressing the intricate balance between time, cost, and quality, adapting to evolving technologies, and ensuring regulatory compliance. It offers insights into overcoming internal and external challenges, showcasing the significance of strategic decision-making, team resilience, and adaptability in the successful implementation of a transformative telecom initiative.

1. Introduction:

During this period, India witnessed the emergence of a telecom boom, marking a new era of liberalization and privatization driven by government policy changes. Previously, communication services were predominantly under government control, and the shift towards liberalization and privatization was well-received by the public and business community. It was within this transformative landscape that a significant project was undertaken by a prominent Indian group known for its contributions to basic communication infrastructure.

Having already established a presence in setting up telecom infrastructure and providing value-added services during Phase 1, which included an X.400-based telecom framework offering email facilities and special services, the organization decided to embark on Phase 2. This expansion, initiated in 1996-97 and completed by 2000-01, aimed to leverage state-of-the-art technology to enhance services and solidify its position as a key player in the evolving Indian telecom market. The project's total outlay amounted to around 250 Crore INR (> 600 Crore INR in current terms).

Notably, this period coincided with unprecedented technological advancements in the telecom domain. The project team faced the crucial task of evaluating the impact of these developments on their undertaking. Keeping abreast of technological progress and incorporating the latest advancements into the proposed network architecture was imperative to align with market needs and international standards. Meeting these requirements posed a significant and challenging responsibility for the project team during this dynamic period.

2. Project Objectives:

In seizing the opportunity, the organization initiated the establishment of a "Comprehensive Internet/VPN Services Backbone Network" for both local and international services. The appointment of a Project Director and Senior Program Manager (Head of Technology) marked the formation of a team comprising over 40 personnel for this prestigious endeavour.

Considering the vast potential of the telecom market, the organization outlined the following objectives for the project:

1. Implement a cutting-edge, high-speed network adhering to international standards, ensuring technical superiority over potential competitors through collaboration with global leaders in the segment.

2. Develop a Telecom Backbone Network with high speeds catering not only to the needs of retail customers but also offering specialized services for Corporate and Institutionalized customers following DOT norms and guidelines.

3. Establish Regional Data Centres to provide connectivity with a high-speed network backbone using state-of-the-art technology.

4. Build infrastructure and capabilities to provide Private Networks for Corporate and Institutional Customers, incorporating special value-added features with high speeds.

5. Develop an excellent support services network, ensuring 24x7 support with low maintenance and modification needs, and ease of interfaces and additions.

6. Create special service packages and applications for customers, ensuring efficient utilization of the proposed network's unique features in the country.

7. Design and parameterize the product to adapt to ever-changing Telecom application needs, aligning with guidelines specified by the Department of Telecommunications (DOT) and banking guidelines issued by RBI.

8. Ensure the scalability of the design/architecture of the proposed network, enabling seamless connections to various international networks.

9. Ensure that the proposed architecture of the new application allows for inter-location connectivity and the establishment of private secure networks.

3. Project Scope:

The project encompassed the establishment of cutting-edge infrastructure for telecom services, addressing the burgeoning demand in the country while offering value-added services compatible with international networks.

The scope involved the setup of various centres at different locations, including:

- Implementation of the main Backbone network at the Head Office.
- Establishment of regional hubs in more than 8 cities with connectivity to BSNL/VSNL.
- Configuration of Private VPNs tailored to customer requirements, adhering to necessary information security standards and guidelines.
- Establishment of an R&D Lab in Pune for continuous development initiatives.
- Creation of a 24x7 service support group aligned with proposed Service Level Agreements (SLAs).
- Implementation of an efficient system for handling and addressing customer complaints, ensuring a prompt and effective resolution of any issues.
- While the mentioned functions provide a broad overview, it's important to note that additional modules and select interfaces were developed as part of the application suits to enhance the overall project functionality.

4. Challenges Faced by the Project Team:

Internal Challenges:

- **Time, Cost, and Quality:** The team encountered a significant challenge in adhering to conventional project success factors (Scope/Time/Cost & Quality) to complete the project within 36 months. Delays in obtaining permissions and licenses from the Department of Telecommunications (DOT) for the proposed architecture and network lines posed a substantial hurdle, resulting in a budget escalation of over 15% and a schedule delay exceeding 25%.

- **Management Pressure:** Intense competition in the telecom sector led to heightened management pressure for early project completion. The urgency to launch services quickly led to undue pressure on engineering, development, and site teams, fostering shortcuts and subsequent rework, causing unnecessary costs and delays.

- **Inadequate Domain Expertise:** The project team faced a challenge in adapting to new technologies, particularly in terms of banking processes. Many telecom personnel lacked judgment on how to adopt proposed changes and their implications on systems. Senior personnel expressed reservations about the effectiveness of new technologies, highlighting a shortage of expertise in the new domain.

- **Staff Turnover:** High employee attrition rates, a common issue in the telecom and IT industry, persisted throughout the project. Despite the project manager's efforts to select and retain a dedicated team, turnover continued to be a challenge, necessitating ongoing training initiatives.

- **Telecom Infrastructure Availability:** The lack of infrastructure posed a hurdle, but proactive support from senior management ensured funding for development labs. However, procurement challenges, driven by approval processes controlled by accountants, consumed substantial time, money, and effort.

- **Requisite Interfaces and Integration:** Developing interfaces for diverse equipment, protocols, and modules in the proposed solution presented a formidable challenge. With basic modules from different sources and non-compatible protocols, the development team invested significant time and effort in R&D before achieving seamless integration.

- **Data Migration and Accuracy:** Ensuring accurate and reliable data files for the complex telecom operations software proved challenging. Initial surveys revealed inaccurate or unavailable data in branches, necessitating Herculean efforts and time loss for the project team.

- **Application Software Development:** Creating sophisticated system applications for efficient customer management, usage tracking, and billing modules posed a complex challenge. The evolving configuration and complexity of the task demanded extensive efforts from the entire team to meet tight deadlines.

5. Project Execution Approach:

A dedicated team, led by a project manager, was assigned to undertake this extensive project. The team consisted of over 45 professionals, with 35 individuals focused on development and quality assurance/control (QA/QC), and an additional 10 personnel involved in implementation at select locations/branches. Key aspects of the approach included:

- **Product Design Team Oversight:** Given the enormity of the project, precise results were imperative for the Telecom application, aligning with norms specified by the Department of Telecommunications (DOT). Uncertain interpretation of rules could introduce errors in the application suite. Thus, effective control over design and ensuring data compatibility at each stage became a critical aspect for the design control team.

- **Rationalizing and Standardizing Process Routines:** This challenging task required domain experts with substantial knowledge of Telecom Network operations. Frequent changes in DOT rules added complexity, necessitating constant attention to assess their impact on finalized designs and routines. The dynamic nature of this aspect kept the entire team on their toes, leading to occasional moments of frustration.

- **Module Leader Responsibilities:** Module leaders, supported by programmers and quality control teams, shouldered the responsibility for individual modules. Strict adherence to standards throughout the development and testing stages was crucial, making this seemingly simple task challenging.

- **Technical Writers for Documentation:** The complex system demanded high-quality documentation, considering the myriad of rules and regulations. However, finding professionals with expertise in documentation within the IT industry was a bottleneck. A task force, comprising bank professionals, was formed to address this challenge.

- **Educating Customer IT Departments**: Introducing new concepts and technologies posed a challenge in gaining cooperation from customer IT departments. In an era where matured systems for these concepts were lacking in the country, resistance from existing employees, particularly from old government departments, presented a significant challenge throughout the project.

6. Diamond Analysis of Project Classification:

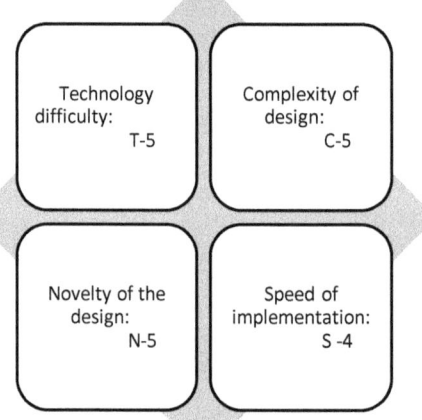

Figure 15. 1- Project Classification

Technology Difficulty (T-5): This dimension indicates a high level of complexity and difficulty associated with the technological aspects of the project. The project likely involved advanced and intricate technological solutions, demanding a comprehensive understanding of cutting-edge systems.

Complexity of Design (C-5): The complexity of design is assessed to be at a significant level (C-5). The project's design requirements were intricate, requiring careful consideration and detailed planning to ensure the successful integration of various components.

Novelty of the Design (N-5): The novelty of the design is rated at a maximum level (N-5). This suggests that the project involved innovative and pioneering design elements, possibly introducing new concepts and solutions that were not prevalent in the industry before.

Speed of Implementation (S-4): The speed of implementation is evaluated at a slightly lower level (S-4).

While the project aimed for a reasonably fast implementation, it faced challenges or constraints that prevented it from achieving the highest rating in this dimension.

This project was characterized by a high level of technological difficulty, design complexity, and design novelty. Although it aspired to achieve rapid implementation, certain factors may have hindered its speed of execution, leading to a rating of S-4 in that dimension.

7. Project Characteristics:

- Size of the Project: Estimated at USD 40 million (INR 240-260 crore in today's currency rates), inclusive of manpower costs, overheads, travel, and incidental expenses.

- Number of People: Approximately 50 individuals in Mumbai/Pune, comprising developers, QA/QC personnel (5), and 15 team members at 5 implementation sites.

- Time Schedule: Initially planned for a 36-month project period. Delays occurred, extending the completion timeline by an additional 14 months due to licensing issues.

- Classification of Project: Treated as a new project for the organization, introducing phase 2 with the first-time market offering in India for Telecom operations based on new requirements.

- High-Risk Project: Inherent uncertainties and risks due to the use of a new paradigm, technology, and software applications. Sourcing domain experts was challenging.

- Technology Choice/Maturity: The technology was in the evolving stage. Although well-developed in the USA/Europe, it was being implemented for the first time as a standard service/product in India.

- Number of Suppliers: Limited critical role for suppliers, but active participation from technology partners and associates was crucial for project success.

- Logistics/Clearances: Significant challenge due to time pressure in obtaining licenses and permissions. Government clearances were required at multiple locations, but there was strong support from the Head Office and senior management.

- Location for Coordination: More than 6 locations (Mumbai/Pune & Customer sites at 6 branch locations) with excellent communication and infrastructure facilities, making coordination manageable.

- Support from Senior Management: Senior management provided excellent support, timely funding, administrative assistance, and motivational support throughout the project, granting the team autonomy.
- Involvement of Customer: Mixed and hesitant support from department personnel. Some customer representatives doubted the abilities of Indian Telecom/Software professionals for this critical application, making the situation complex for the project team.
- Team Leader: Project Manager, a competent and committed telecom engineer with domain expertise, excellent exposure to software applications, and some experience with international projects and telecom standards.

8. **Key Positions in the Team:**
The team was structured with the following crucial positions:

- **Project Director / Project Manager as 'Project Champion':** The Project Director is a senior leader responsible for strategically guiding and overseeing project execution.
- **Business Analyst / Business Process Expert:** Expertise in the Telecom sector, especially concerning new concepts, technologies, and operations.
- **Module Leaders (4):** Responsible for overseeing various critical aspects of the proposed project and its modules.
- **Database Expert / Networking Expert:** Proficient in database management and networking, this expert ensures seamless integration and optimal performance of the project's technical infrastructure
- **Quality Leader / Site Quality Leader / Site Manager:** Assisted by 2 site engineers for implementation at branches.
- **Delivery Manager:** One of the senior module leaders assumed this role.
- **Accounts Manager:** Handling financial issues and funding matters.
- **PMO Office (Project Management Office):** Responsible for project tracking and liaison with the customer team for progress monitoring and issue resolution.

9. **Issues and Challenges:**
- **Scarcity of Domain Experts:** The banking software development faced a significant challenge due to a lack of domain experts in the initial stages. The intimate involvement of customer professionals and thorough homework helped the project manager (PM) and the team handle this challenge effectively. The result was the production of a high-quality product.
- **Time Pressure for Development:** Enormous time pressure exists for software development. The initial investment in training and orienting the development team members regarding terminologies and process routines helped expedite the processes effectively.

- **Documentation Standardization:** The team invested considerable time in deciding ways to document processes in a standardized manner. Ruthless adherence to documentation standards proved crucial and significantly contributed to the project's success. Meeting minutes and decisions were noted and documented meticulously throughout the project's duration.

- **Efficient Communication:** Communication within the team and with customer representatives was carried out efficiently and well-documented. Transparent communication fostered a positive work environment and contributed to the project's success.

- **Trust Among Team Members:** The team exhibited tacit trust in each other and their leadership.

- This trust helped the PM maintain harmony and establish a rhythm of working within the team.

- **Technical Challenges:** The team faced numerous technical challenges related to new technologies and the integration of various modules. Close cooperation with concerned personnel, and government officials, and garnering required support proved instrumental during the project tenure.

- **Test Data Preparation:** Due to the complexity of the application and domain environment, the preparation of test data posed a major challenge. Thorough homework and support for trials at both the home office and on-site were crucial in overcoming this challenge.

- **Integration of Modules:** Challenges were encountered in integrating various modules supplied by partners and aligning them with the Indian infrastructure of the day for the telecom industry.

10. Positives in the Project Environment:

- **Senior Management Support:** Full support from senior management and foreign partners provided a solid foundation for the project.

- **Focused Team and Detailed Implementation Plan:** The team's focus on a detailed implementation plan in cooperation with customer personnel contributed to project success.

- **Continuous Dialogue:** Continuous dialogue with government officials, customer PM, and local PM helped address issues immediately and facilitated proactive decision-making.

- Regular project meetings involving senior managers from both sides ensured smooth progress.

- **Harmonious Team Environment:** A harmonious team environment paved the path for good quality and undisturbed work.

- **Pre-dispatch Inspection:** Pre-dispatch inspections involving local and customer QA/QC teams facilitated hassle-free on-site implementation of modules without delays.
- **Freedom for Decision-Making:** The team had the freedom for decision-making and commit expenses based on the PM's decisions, ensuring a smooth workflow.

11. Project Success Criteria:

The project's success criteria were designed to meet both organizational and customer expectations:

Organizational Expectations:

- Complete the project on time without compromising quality.
- Adhere to stringent rules set by the Department of Telecommunications (DOT) for telecom sector operations.
- Achieve planned project profitability for the organization.
- Develop the application as a model project for future reference in the telecom segment.
- Obtaining repeat orders from the same customer, a crucial organizational requirement.

Customer/User Expectations:

- Ensure on-time delivery and implementation.
- Achieve the committed Return on Investment (ROI) from the project.
- Attain requisite accuracy and efficiency in operations with a complex set of rules and changes.

Satisfaction of Team Members:

- Ensure team satisfaction and the development of new skills/domain expertise for the future.

Project Success Factors :

After discussions with team members and their PM, it is evident that the following actors were crucial for the success of the project. While these might not have been comprehensively considered before the project started, they emerged as key success factors:

- Clarity about the task at hand, including scope and specifications.
- Commitment and active participation by customer teams throughout the project lifecycle.
- Complete support from senior management and freedom of action.
- Competent Project Manager and a trusted team.

- Alert risk management, especially regarding timelines and design/changes for Proof of Concept (POC) and User Acceptance Testing (UAT).
- Control over project progress issues through impeccable communication and coordination.
- Excellent support from Project Management Office (PMO) personnel for tracking and resolving issues.
- Strong support from Quality Assurance (QA) and Quality Control (QC) teams, along with process control engineers.
- Exceptional teamwork and untiring support from task force members.
- Good support from legal experts and administrative teams.

12. Conclusion: Highly Successful Project with Few Silver Linings!

The project was deemed a resounding success, with the team rightfully proud of their outstanding performance. Despite facing delays in licensing and permissions, the project was evaluated as a complete success, meeting and even exceeding expectations in terms of quality. The customer, as well as senior management personnel, expressed great satisfaction with the project outcome, leading to the signing of an Annual Maintenance Contract (AMC) for the next 5 years.

Recognizing the success achieved, the senior management decided to establish additional teams dedicated to handling Telecom sector applications. This division not only thrived but also expanded its business significantly each year. The high-quality work showcased in this project attracted additional customer accounts from various corporate organizations, enhancing the organization's overall growth and ensuring sustained profitability.

In recognition of his leadership and contributions to the project's success, the project manager was promoted to the position of "SBU Head," overseeing this business independently. The product developed during the project has undergone further refinement and has evolved into one of the flagship products of the organization, contributing significantly to its continued success in the market.

Questions:

1. How did the external environment, including government policies, impact the project's timeline and budget?
2. What role did leadership play in overcoming internal challenges, such as high employee turnover and inadequate domain expertise?
3. Discuss the implications of the high level of technological difficulty and design novelty on the project's success.

Teaching Note

"Innovation Amidst Challenges: A Deep Dive into the Implementation of a Cutting-Edge Telecom Project in India".

Abstract:

This case study explores the challenges and successes of a significant telecom project in India, initiated during the telecom boom era. It covers the period from 1996-2001 and delves into the complexities faced by the project team, both internally and externally. The study emphasizes the importance of strategic decision-making, team resilience, and adaptability in successfully implementing transformative telecom initiatives.

Teaching Objectives:

- Understand the challenges and opportunities in managing large-scale projects in dynamic environments.
- Analyze the impact of external factors, such as government policies, on project execution.
- Explore the balance between time, cost, and quality in project management.
- Examine the role of leadership, team dynamics, and adaptability in project success.
- Evaluate the importance of communication, documentation, and risk management in project execution.

Teaching Methodology:

- **Case Discussion (60 mins):** Encourage students to analyze the challenges faced by the project team and identify critical success factors. Discuss possible alternative strategies that could have been employed.
- **Role Play (30 mins):** Divide students into groups to role-play scenarios reflecting challenges faced by the project team. Emphasize decision-making under time constraints and the importance of effective communication.
- **Guest Lecture (20 mins):** Invite a guest speaker with experience in managing large-scale telecom projects. Allow students to ask questions and gain insights from real-world experiences.
- **Debrief and Analysis (40 mins):** Facilitate a class discussion on the guest lecture, connecting it with the case study. Discuss how real-world experiences align with theoretical concepts learned in class.

Assessment:

- **Individual Reflection (20 mins):** Assign a short reflection essay where students discuss key takeaways from the case study and guest lecture, linking them to project management theories.

- **Group Presentation (30 mins):** Each group presents their analysis of the challenges and successes of the project, emphasizing critical success factors and proposing alternative strategies.

Discussion Questions:

- How did the external environment, including government policies, impact the project's timeline and budget?

- What role did leadership play in overcoming internal challenges, such as high employee turnover and inadequate domain expertise?

- Discuss the implications of the high level of technological difficulty and design novelty on the project's success.

Conclusion:

This case study provides a comprehensive understanding of managing telecom projects in dynamic environments. It encourages students to think critically about project management strategies and offers real-world insights through a guest lecture. The emphasis on teamwork, communication, and adaptability aligns with essential skills for future project managers.

Part 2
Case Studies

Case No. 16: Setting up a new greenfield project to design and manufacture Auto Components for OEMs

Dr Jayasri Murali, Dr Sarita Samson

Associate Professor, MBA@IICMR, Pune, Assistant Professor, MBA@IICMR, Pune

Extract: The Auto and Component markets in India have witnessed substantial growth in the past four decades, attracting young entrepreneurs, particularly in the western region. Amid the surge of new units from 1991 to 2000, government initiatives fueled the aspirations of emerging professionals. In 1995, two first-generation friends, one an engineer in metallurgy and the other in electrical engineering, initiated a venture in Baroda to manufacture special ferrous and non-ferrous auto components. Despite their diverse backgrounds, their complementary skills and experience paved the way for the project. However, internal discord, lack of formal documentation, and unforeseen challenges led to the project's failure, emphasizing the importance of strategic partnerships, legal agreements, meticulous feasibility studies, and proactive decision-making in entrepreneurship.

Introduction:

The Auto and Component markets in India have grown over the last 4 decades and have attracted the attention of many young entrepreneurs in the last few years. Many young professionals nurture an ambition to set up new green fields/start-up units for auto components in the western part of India. The growth of the Auto / Auto Components industry saw the entry of many new units in India, especially in the Western belt, from 1991 to 2000. Several new initiatives set up by the Government also provided a new impetus and boost to young entrepreneurs to set up new units for this vital sector, which was seen as an engine for economic upliftment and growth of the Indian Economy.

This unit was set up by a team of two first-generation entrepreneurs who were personal friends from the school time, and classmates from the same college. One of them is an engineer with a Metallurgical Engineering specialization and the other has a background in Electrical Engineering. The person who took the initiative had worked for over 25 years in the industry, mainly in the Auto and Auto Components Industries. He had travelled abroad and had undergone specialized training for the manufacturing and processing of auto components/parts and sub-assemblies during his tenure with the industries. He had gained good experience in these sectors and was able to establish good contacts across the segments, based on his personal skills and networking abilities. The other person had managed to immigrate to the UK based on the contacts and family relationships where his wife was working. This person was involved in trading various types of commodities and was desirous of returning to India and setting up his activities.

These two persons had good family backgrounds and wanted to set up a new unit for the design, manufacture and supply of special ferrous and non-ferrous auto components for a variety of applications on an OEM basis. The idea was finalized in 1994 and the project was initiated in 1995. Two middle-aged persons, the senior person with an engineering background, and the other with a commercial background, decided to set up such a new unit in Baroda in 1995. These two persons were They decided to contribute initial equity of around ₹1.05 crore, in the proportion of 60:40. Later the promoters decided to approach the bank for a loan of around ₹2.5 crore in GIDC estate. The feasibility report along with market analysis was prepared, and over a period, the bank gave a green signal for the project, considering the background experience of the promoters. The land was acquired, and the building was constructed in the first 12 months. The unit was now ready for the launch.

Objectives:

The main aim of the newly initiated project was to design/develop and manufacture auto components for the OEMs in the Auto sector in India & over the years become one of the suppliers of auto components for the Auto majors in Western countries.

The main objectives for the proposed unit were formulated as follows:

- To set up a state-of-the-art manufacturing unit for the design/development of "Gears & Shafts" for two and four-wheeler vehicles, based on the requirements of the select OEMs in the country.

- To set up an India network of dealers for the sale of these components to auto sector customers (OEMs + after-sales markets) based on the market analysis carried out.

- To become one of the suppliers of auto components for the Auto majors in the western countries.

- To develop such a product/system that will be the state of art in terms of technology, and cost-effective in terms of the sales price for the end users (cost per foot of drilling).

- To ensure requisite automation where possible, in the manufacturing unit, to ensure a high level of productivity and efficiency.

- To provide good after-sales service where required.

- To ensure that the product will require low maintenance/modification, and will have easy interfaces required for other ranges of equipment and machinery.

- To ensure that the organization will reach the break-even point in less than 3 years from the beginning. (The initial report indicated that the turnover by the end of the 5th Year will be around ₹25 crores with profit margins of around 18% (PBT / Turnover)).

- To explore the opportunities for IPO around the 4th year of the operation and prepare for the IPO around the 5th year subject to achievement of the objectives / set goals by the end of 4th year.

Based on the 'Diamond Analysis' of the project classifications one can classify the project as specified below:

- Technology difficulty: T-3
- Complexity of design: C-4
- The novelty of the design: N-3
- Speed of implementation: S-4

About the project case:

Sr No	Project Characteristics	Comments
1	Size of the project:	1 million (INR 6.5 crore in current currency Rates (including manpower costs + overheads + travel + incidental costs) was estimated as the initial cost of the project. The total amount of the project cost was constrained based on the equity capital of the equivalent of ₹1.05 crore from the promoters and their friends and relatives. The actual cost was more than INR 7.5 Cr.
2	The number of people:	The number of developers and other staff/workers involved in the Baroda office & factory was around 25, including QA / QC group 5 In addition, 15 team members were involved in different operational departments at the start of the project. Thus, total manpower was around 45 on average (and 55 maximum) at any point of time in the project, as per the initial projections. Around 18 people were qualified engineers & others were 12th-standard pass-outs.
3	Schedule:	5 years in phases as specified below. It was estimated/expected that the Pilot tests were to start at the customer location after 30 months from the start. It was expected that the project should achieve a turnover of over 25 crore and a margin of 18% at that stage (PBT / Sales revenue) by the 4th year of the project after the plant was commissioned.

4	Classification of project:	A New Project was set up as a new manufacturing unit, for Auto Components, especially, for the auto industry along with Industrial machinery manufacturers. This was indeed a challenge for the project team for this start-up unit.
5	High-risk project:	There were many uncertainties/risks because "new concept-based technology proposed for manufacturing" based development & application was expected to be developed using homegrown designs and Indian raw materials. The financial outlay assumed in the feasibility stage underwent drastic changes due to the switch over to button bits in the 2nd year. This disturbed the initial capital outlay and created a need for additional funding. This upset the feasibility of the total project as such and the company continued to face problems till it was closed at a later stage.
6	Technology Choice / Methods Maturity:	The technology was evolving in this period. These application methods, although well-developed in Western countries, were still in the initial stages in India. There was a shortage of knowledgeable persons in the market about this technology and domain applications. The organization had an opportunity to sign a collaboration agreement with a company from the USA, but the partner from the UK /Sponsors and banks refused to support this move because of the large sums involved at the beginning of the project. The PM tried his level best to see this collaboration through but in vain.
7	No of suppliers:	In this project there were many suppliers, but the number of critical suppliers number 15 for the core activities, at the beginning of the project. Initially relationship with this group was good but was turned into a major problem due to a lack of uniform cash flow for the project. Such relationships turned sour when the market became aware of the rift in the partners at an early stage.
8	Logistics / Clearances:	This was quite a challenge, due to time pressure, the requirement of a lot of Government clearances for their orders, and delays associated with order placement and payment cycles. The promoters had no idea about the risks and possibilities of the delay involved. The initial timelines were upset right from the beginning.
9	Location for co-ordination:	More than 3 locations (Mumbai / Baroda & site at GIDC). However, the location-based control was not a major challenge, since the senior promoter was handling all the issues from his office in Baroda.

10	Support from Sponsors:	Senior management acted as an integrated team, and relations were good in the initial phase. However, they started being indifferent to each other due to major differences in the financial commitments from the promoters. The junior partner never sent the funds in time and hence created major bottlenecks for the unit. Naturally, there was an air of tension among promoters. The delays in the release of funds, and pending accounts receivables, stretched the relations further, and tensions continued for a long time. This led to a complex/tricky situation for the team and their life became miserable. Finally, the approach adopted by the junior partner staying in the UK became unbearable, and led to the rift between the promoters, finally ending in a legal battle resulting in the closure of the unit. The situation became worse when the junior partner gave his power of attorney to one of the political musclemen in Baroda. This created grave problems and finally, the project was called off. The current loans had to be paid off only by the senior partner, who had signed all the documents with bankers. This amounted to almost cheating by the partner in the UK. A good project idea was ruined in the end.
11	Team members & effectiveness:	Initially, the team worked as a cohesive team and was working well together. However, over a period, tensions began surfacing. This was mainly because there was a considerable difference in the convictions and competence of the team members. This issue surfaced when the project faced severe problems and the relations were always tense from this stage onwards, till the operations were closed. There was mixed/hesitant support from the team members to each other and this certainly affected the performance.
12	Involvement of Customer:	There was mixed/hesitant support from the customer/customers' engineers/professionals during the initial phases. The government agencies were major customers and managing them was quite a challenge.
13	Team Leader:	The Project Manager selected was a competent/committed engineer (good expertise in mining products and production). He should have been given a higher position and authority due to his contributions and abilities. However, this was not done due to equal equity holding and this caused major problems for everyone in the future.

The challenges of the project team:

The project was defined in terms of the following phases:

Phase 1 (2 years):

- To complete the licensing/registration & other formalities and to complete the building activities before the end of the first 2 years:

Phase 2 (1 year):

- To initiate the manufacturing of the initial product range before the end of 3rd year:

Phase 3 (2 years):

- To ensure that the organization reaches a turnover of around 5 crores by the end of 5th year with a margin of over 18%

- As can be seen from the phases explained above, the objectives set for the organization were quite ambitious and the team had to get over many impediments before they could achieve the goals set for them. Team members pointed out various aspects of the challenges faced during the tenure of the project and indicated some of the actions that were initiated to get over the challenges.

- The following points were noted based on the interaction with the project team members and Project Manager. The key issues are specified below for quick reference:

Internal challenges:

Many internal issues/aspects needed attention from the project team, especially for the PM. Some issues warranted attention from the bank employees as well. Some of these issues are specified below:

- **Changes in market priorities and product mix:**

During the initial 2 years, when the groundwork was being carried out, there were few changes in the product mix because of changes in the market. The initial study indicated the use of relatively simple components to be designed and produced. However, the delay in the initial approvals led to a delay in the startup of the new units. This delay hit the plans of the new units considering that such low-end components were already established by various units and hence the line of the products had to move to a higher platform and more complex/intricate components. This meant changes in the plans and changes in feasibility reports/payback periods. This meant a change of all the designs and investments in additional capital equipment that were already ordered and procured. This led to a waste of time and effort and an additional burden for capital investments. This was a setback in the initial period itself apart from all other problems.

- **Time, Cost and Quality:**

The main challenge for the team was to conform to the conventional project success factors and complete the first project phase in less than 24 months. This was a challenge since GIDC approval/agreements took a lot of time. Additionally, the GIDC team suggested that the organization should approach Banks for additional funds given the projected market growth. This process took a lot of time. Bankers approved overdraft limits only after getting confirmation from experts and professional bodies, such as ACMA. With this complex coordination, the fund's flow was never timely further compounding the problems.

This also threw out of gear all the assumptions about the product concept and affected the schedule and costs for the project. The capital investments had to be enhanced, and this was quite a heavy burden on the project, which had not even begun.

- **Technology and technical infrastructure :**

This was an important issue for the newly formed unit for manufacturing products. The team had decided to design and develop all the products and had not signed any technical collaboration. The homegrown designs and technology used had their share of problems and challenges. Difficulties arose when they had to change a few specifications of the products based on feedback from some of the key customers. There were many trial and error cycles before the designs and processes could be standardized.

The heat treatment also posed challenges to the team. The specific Industrial Estate did not have an adequate engineering support structure of dependable suppliers for various issues and every now & then one had to go to Ahmedabad or Mumbai for support. This became a major headache for the project members. Such issues also added to operating costs and delays.

Additionally, the infrastructure for testing was far from adequate, mainly due to the inadequacy of funds. This created problems in the field since they were not diagnosed in-house. This meant additional costs and delays for the team.

- **Management pressure:**

The BOD members & officials from the Bank saw an unprecedented opportunity in this sector at this stage for the new project, without understanding the field-level issues. This made the life of the promoters miserable. Bankers always forced the project team to commit to unrealistic time schedules that were not easy to achieve.

- **Communication & Co-ordination issues:**

In the initial period, the communication was very good, but this was deteriorating over a period (after the first 2 years). This certainly affected the smooth working within the team, and it also converted the friendly and positive atmosphere into a vitiated atmosphere and tensions in the project environment. This was mainly on account of funds shortage and working capital shortages. This tension continued almost throughout all the remaining periods.

- **Domain expertise for new processes was not adequate:**

The core team had some working knowledge about the product range but once the production cycle started, they realized that their knowledge was not adequate to respond to the market demands and technical issues raised by the end users. This compounded the problems multiple-fold. Then this took a toll on the core team's time since they had to attend to such issues on priority. The solutions were found mainly by the trial-and-error method, which is not very cost-effective.

- **Support from the suppliers' network:**

Traditional manufacturing products have a lot of materials costs (>65%) and depend upon many types of suppliers. In the initial period, the suppliers were very cooperative. However, over a period, they had problems because of late payments due to the financial crunch for the project. Additionally, the batch quantities from the new unit were very small and hence the margins were also under pressure for the suppliers. This compounded the problems & in reality, this problem continued throughout the tenure of the project.

- **Availability of adequate infrastructure for the project unit:**

Due to high pressure on available funds, the initial choice of the proposed infrastructure was quite inadequate. Additionally, the changes in the market conditions compounded this problem further. Some of the already installed capital equipment became redundant and new items had to be procured. Lack of funds was a perpetual problem for this project and despite the right thinking and decision-making, none of the new initiatives could fructify in time.

- **Lack of support from the bank for working capital for the project:**

The cycles of manufacture were long, and the customer outstanding was very high (>90-120 days) in general. This itself was a problem and was further compounded due to enormous delays due to a prominent portion of the market controlled by Government agencies. This became a deadlock for the project throughout the tenure of the project.

- **Lack of financial support and strategic support from investors (Financial Investors) :**

Although the initial support from the sponsors and investors was good, when the unit started facing problems and financial crunch, these agencies were indifferent to the requirements despite a lot of pleading and justification from the core team members. This escalated the problem and the company went into tight fiscal clutches. This continued for the period of the last 4 years of the project. The bankers changed their stance and even cut out part of the overdraft limits. This sent the organization into total spin and the unit suffered heavy losses from year 2 to 5.

Additional Technical Challenges:

Technology changes of this magnitude involve a lot of complex technical issues that cannot be addressed effectively without astute technical knowledge and experience. This was evident in this project. Although basic technology issues were known to many team members, they did not have the requisite experience and exposure to the nuances involved in this application. This was one of the main bottlenecks in the development and implementation cycles for the project.

- Strict control over product design and changes requested by OEM customers.

- Strict process for change control through "Engineering Change Control Notice" and judicious evaluation of such requests in line with quality norms of the customers.

- Flexibility/parameterization and its impact on design complexity that was not within the control of the new unit. Customer approval was responsible for the resultant delays.

External Challenges:

Several external factors were identified as eternal factors that could affect the probability of success of the project.

- Slow decision-making at the customer end was a perpetual problem in this market. Some of the OEM customer orders were cancelled due to changes in the Management policies on the OEM side.

- Additionally, some of the small manufacturers and dealers started carrying out business on a cash basis which created problems for organized sector companies.

- The importance and interference of the employee's union was an additional and critical external influencing factor that was not really under the control of the team. However, with the help of the senior management of the bank and representatives of the union, such problems were handled.

- Frequent changes in policies by the Government affected market growth and margins.

- Additionally, there was an obvious emergence of the Chinese on roads, which compounded the problem.

Key positions in the team:

The team had to be manned with the following key positions:

- Project Manager / Project Champion.

- Market development and sales manager (This role was played by the Project Champion).

- Business Analyst / Business Process Expert with expertise in the Auto sector.

- Production Manager with experience in the Auto Industry with experience in non-ferrous metals.

- Quality Leader / Site Quality Leader + 2 site engineers .

- PPC and production control Manager for the project.

- PMO office for project tracking and liaison with customer team for progress tracking & resolving issues. Many of these activities had to be carried out by the promoter himself and this was a burden.

Project Success Criteria:

The project success criteria took into consideration customer expectations and organizational expectations:

Organizational expectations/achievements:

- To complete the project in time / available funds without any compromise on quality.
- To conform to stringent rules of field trials and support on the field for customer satisfaction.
- To achieve the project profitability as planned for the organization and the investors/banks.
- To develop this application as a model project so that it can become a reference project for future business in the mining segment.
- To get repeat orders from the same customer was an important organizational requirement.

Customer / User Expectations:

- To ensure on-time delivery and implementation.
- To achieve committed ROI from the project (To reduce cost in the field).

Satisfaction of the team members:

- To ensure team satisfaction and development of new skills/domain expertise.
- To improve the quality of product design.

Project Success Factors:

Based on the discussions with the team members and their PM it becomes clear that the list of the following points would have been useful for them as CFSs for this project. However, it must be noted that this aspect was not thought of before the project started.

- Clarity about the task at hand & clarity about scope and specifications.
- Project organization structure.
- Commitment and participation by the customer teams in the development of the product throughout the tenure of the project life cycle.
- Complete support from the sponsors/banks & freedom of action.
- Competent Project Manager & trusted team/team support.
- Alert Risk Management especially in the form of timelines and design/changes for POC / UAT.

- Control over project progress issues through impeccable communication and coordination.
- Excellent support from PMO personnel for ruthless tracking of issues and resolving them.
- Strong support from QA / QC teams and process control engineers (support received due to strong and matured processes in the parent organization).
- Exceptional teamwork and untiring support from the task force members.
- Good support from Legal Experts and Admin teams.

Conclusion:

Failed the project despite Herculean efforts from the core team!

The project was evaluated as a failure and the team was very disappointed that despite their hard work, they had not achieved the goals. The customer was happy but had their share of issues about quality and late deliveries. Senior sponsors and banks were not at all happy about the carry-forward losses. The organization had been led into spiralling problems mainly on account of cash crunch and problems of shortage of capital funds. Some parts of the project were finished in time, however, the turnover reached only 1.5 crore in the fifth year with heavy losses.

This company continued to run as a sick unit for a very long time. However, the project was not treated as a success at all. There were certain additional complex problems because one of the promoters left the project midway. The situation went from bad to worse and the operations had to be closed in due course of time.

Learnings from the Case Study:

The critical learnings from the case study can be specified as follows:

- It is critical for every new start-up unit that the right partners (and right first team members are selected right from the beginning with due attention and care), since mistakes in judging this will certainly lead to disasters and more than 'certain failures' for the project. This case is riddled with such nasty situations between 2 very good childhood friends, and the discord led to complete failure on the part of the prompter partner.
- The friendship and partnership mustn't be the same. One lesson is to ensure that appropriate documentation and legal aspects are specifically pinned down, and should not lose any attention, to help avoid future problems and land mines, as one can see in the bespoke study. Trust, once lost, cannot be rebuilt through societal means. In modern times, all statutory and legal aspects must be well formatted as applicable along with all necessary registrations, certifications, and agreements.
- It is important to ensure that the basic understanding between the proposed partners is documented in the form of a detailed contract covering all the basic terms and conditions agreed upon by both parties. This needs to be done very carefully, identifying areas of unique contributions by both parties. This will avoid future problems ensure/enforce the terms and help the parties to contribute their parts as per the agreed terms. Such a contract

also helps 'exit' conditions (based on original understanding) and specific responsibilities to be discharged by the respective parties to the contract. Such a formal process is essential before one can embark on the project activities.

- The feasibility study must be carried out with requisite details and with due diligence. Without such homework, it may not be prudent to start the project in modern times.

- It is also clear that such projects need very good planning functions and ensure that all right areas of the operations are covered. However, certain flexibility must be provided in planning functions. For such SMS units, it is funds that drive the project progress, control parameters being 'scope/time/costs & quality'.

- One should note that interference from political leaders can cause great damage to the project's health and welfare and hence political interference has to be completely avoided.

- It is also important to learn that if one observes that whatever happens to the project, and you do not have confidence that things are going well, you must take the final decision even to abandon the project. This may look contrary to common sense, but it has its' own sense. Such a precipitative policy may help save embarrassment and additional decisions.

Discussion Points:

Selecting the Right Partners:

- Discuss the importance of choosing suitable partners for a startup, considering their skills, experience, and compatibility.

- Explore how personal relationships, as seen in the case study, may not necessarily translate into effective business partnerships.

Distinguishing Friendship and Partnership:

- Examine the distinction between personal friendships and professional partnerships, emphasizing the need for clear documentation and legal frameworks.

- Analyze the consequences of overlooking legal aspects and the impact of strained relationships on business outcomes.

Detailed Contractual Agreements:

- Delve into the necessity of a detailed contract outlining terms, contributions, exit conditions, and responsibilities to avoid conflicts.

- Discuss how a well-structured contract can serve as a roadmap for the partners and help in resolving potential disputes.

Thorough Feasibility Study:

- Explore the significance of conducting a comprehensive feasibility study with due diligence before initiating a project.
- Discuss how a thorough feasibility study can identify potential challenges and contribute to informed decision-making.

Balancing Planning and Flexibility:

- Examine the role of effective planning in project success and the need for flexibility within the planning process.
- Discuss how balancing structured planning with adaptability can contribute to the smooth progression of projects, especially in terms of funds and control parameters.

Avoiding Political Interference:

- Discuss the detrimental impact of political interference on project health and the importance of establishing mechanisms to avoid such interference.
- Explore strategies for startups to navigate potential political challenges and create a conducive business environment.

Decisive Project Abandonment:

- Analyze the counterintuitive concept of abandoning a project when confidence is lost, emphasizing the importance of proactive decision-making.
- Discuss the potential benefits of a decisive approach in saving resources and mitigating further challenges, even if it may seem contrary to common sense.

Case No 17: Setting up a new NGO to provide requisite support to handle difficulties of Destitute Women / Girl Children and Orphans

Dr Jayasri Murali, Harshal Patil

Associate Professor, MBA@IICMR, Pune, Assistant Professor, MBA@IICMR, Pune

Extract: Amidst the challenging social landscape in the country, a notable social worker embarked on a noble initiative to aid destitute women and children through a newly formed NGO. With 45 years of selfless social work experience, she leveraged her reputation to create a platform for positive change. Despite facing delays in licensing and permissions, the project achieved substantial success in its first five years. Although internal processes drew criticism, corporate CSR funding agencies were partially satisfied. The organization's quality outcomes garnered ongoing support, leading to the establishment of additional teams for new social initiatives. This enduring NGO continues to thrive, securing funding from various corporate CSR units due to its impactful work.

Introduction:

The current social situation in the country is very challenging and many in the society need help and support even for basic survival, especially destitute women, and children. Such situations are seen all over the country and pose a major challenge to the society as such. There is a need to confront this challenge in a constructive and positive mode that can help address such issues in the country, especially through NGOs.

This new initiative was started as an effort towards facing and resolving the challenges faced by society at large. The leader, and initiator, was one of the most renowned social workers of repute in the country, who decided to form this new NGO. This new project was her brainchild. She had an accomplished career. Her reputation and her 'Noble Values' were known to many on account of selfless social activities carried out by her over the previous 45 years of experience, in terms of social work and social initiatives. She had set up social organizations in her past career and hence she had adequate experience and know-how about issues involved in setting up social initiatives and such challenging projects.

Objectives:

The main objective of the project was to provide help for the needy destitute women and girl children in the city of Pune and surrounding areas as explained earlier. The main challenge of the newly initiated project was to develop a going organization of 'selfless volunteers' that will study, understand and resolve problems faced by destitute women/girls and children in the economically challenged strata of society and, provide them ongoing support, care and career opportunities that will lead them to better quality of life, and provide opportunities for growth and stability. This is quite a challenge indeed. It is important to note that such an initiative needs lots of funds for setting up facilities, and infrastructure, enlisting support of the committed volunteers, and achieving results during the first 5 years. The objectives for the new organization set-up were as follows:

- To set up a new social initiative in Pune to take care of the needs of destitute women, underprivileged girls and children to rehabilitate them and provide various educational & career opportunities for them for further advancement in life.

    - To ensure that within the first year, the following types of activities are set up in Pune, as part of the ongoing exercise for the newly formed organization:

    - To set up a 'Counseling Centre for distressed and needy women' in Pune.

    - To set up a 'Vocational Guidance Centre' for young women and adolescent girls.

    - To provide educational aid to needy female students, especially for school and higher education, through ongoing funds/donations based on corporate organizations and individual donors, as an ongoing exercise.

    - To set up 'Study Centres' with adequate facilities for the students from slum areas (1 near Pune and 1 in Pimpri) to promote good education and reading habits for students from challenged strata of society with the help of few CSR initiatives.

    - To set up a daycare centre for street children in red light areas, provide them food/clothes / basic education and training, and enrol them in good schools for further studies, with active help from other NGOs.

    - To identify, select & appoint newly identified 'volunteers. Additionally, to cultivate and conduct comprehensive training for volunteers in the organization to develop adequate skills and competencies for social initiatives indicated above.

    - To conduct training and motivation for the current senior volunteers and trustees to develop social acumen for them to provide quality services to the society at large, and enlist support from them for various activities.

- To initiate contacts with Corporate Organizations, Foreign agencies and HNIs (High Net Worth Individuals) to avail funds and support for conducting various social initiatives indicated for activities specified above.
- To identify, select, counsel, and induct volunteers for the proposed activities of the new organization. This activity is not as simple as it may appear to be.

The challenges of the project team:

The following challenges/points, and issues were noted based on the interaction with the project team members and Project Manager.

The key issues are specified below for quick reference:

Internal issues and bottlenecks observed:

Many internal issues/aspects needed the attention of the project team, especially for the PM. Some of these issues are specified below:

- **Enlisting support and Commitment of the volunteers at the senior level:**

This was one of the main challenges for the founding team at the beginning of the project. This problem was partially solved using a network of the founder trustees, and their influence over some of the renowned social organizations. The challenge was mainly because the NGO had decided that none of the founders/trustees or volunteers would be paid any compensation. This was a great bottleneck right from the beginning. The problem was partially solved when a group of highly qualified women decided to participate in the activities of the NGO. They committed, that they would work with the senior members, and get field experience in social projects, and then gradually handle the projects/modules independently. However, all said and done the availability of competent volunteers continues to be a major challenge for this project even now.

- **Lack of activity plans, and required processes, routines and standards, for planning:**

This was the next challenge. One must realize that sheer enthusiasm and dedication do not result in the achievement of the organizational goals and the success of the projects at hand. Many NGOs face this type of challenge, and it is not easy to organize such efforts into disciplined methods of working. At times, the non-availability of various personnel for the decision-level meetings would result in delays and missed opportunities for NGOs. Additionally, the decisions are expected to be made democratically and conscientiously, resulting in unprecedented challenges. One must realize that in NGOs, leaders cannot enforce the decisions down the line so easily, and this continues a challenge for this NGO even now.

- **Challenges related to Scope / Time and Costs:**

The projects undertaken by the NGOs are a challenge for many types of NGOs. Such problems crop up because activities can be planned only after assurance of funding from the corporate CSR or HNIs. There are many supportive organizations (local and foreign) but their timing for approval is not fixed hence making definitive plans and time schedules is quite a challenge for the

NGOs. The plans and schedules need to be flexible and modified as per the availability of funds. This is an inherent problem for all the NGOs even now. This is possible to be solved when the predictability of the cash flows can be established in advance. This NGO also faced these challenges and had to depend on many flexible/fluid plans in the beginning.

- **Getting a proper well-equipped office and basic infrastructure for running the new organization was not possible due to a lack of funds:**

One can easily appreciate the difficulty faced by the NGO about the basic infrastructure due to acute shortages of funds. The funds are primarily generated through donations, and it is improbable that corporate organizations are willing to release funds for administrative expenses. They are not keen to allocate funds for basic amenities and office set-up, especially in the initial phase. This NGO started in a very small two-room office on a rental basis before it could ramp up the facilities. However, it is easy to appreciate that without original plans being sound and worthy of implementation, a project to implement will remain only a dream without realization

- **The volunteer base is at present strong but getting new volunteers is difficult:**

This is a perpetual challenge for any NGO. They need to depend on personal contacts and carry out tireless efforts to enlist the interest of prospective volunteers, willing to work for the NGOs without getting paid for their time and contributions. These days many younger persons are willing to spend part of their free time on such efforts. This will continue to be a challenge for NGOs in general. Part-time volunteers, although they are useful, cannot depend on part-timers for serious and critical projects.

- **Most of the operational management is done by volunteers, which may not be desirable in the long run:**

One can appreciate that for any successful project, the core team members must be available for most of the key activities of the project continuously, at least in the initial few years. This is not so easy for NGO organizations. These organizations need very flexible methods of work, and one cannot enforce corporate discipline in such voluntary organizations. Everything depends on personal priorities and the motivation of the individual members of the team of volunteers. This creates problems and impediments in the smooth working of many projects.

- **Professional finance services and legal matters are not affordable:**

In the modern era, it is very important that any organization, public or private, needs to conform to statutory norms and compliances. This task is not as easy as it seems. Such tasks need requisite professional expertise and experience to ensure that these tasks are handled judiciously and with due care. Such professionals need not necessarily be willing to work without compensation, and NGOs are not in a position to pay market rates for their services. However, the quality of accuracy and conformance to regulations cannot be compromised. This poses quite a challenge for the NGOs and this project was no exception for the same. NGOs must cut corners in many other aspects, and conserve money to pay for the professional services as explained above. This is certainly not easy.

- **Due to CSR regulation, funds become available but the reporting and other procedures are difficult to understand and follow for persons who do not know modern techniques and computerized systems:**

This results in many delays, reworking and hence loss of efficiency and effectiveness, for the NGO-controlled projects. This was a problem faced by the current project under consideration. Although the senior volunteers were qualified and were aware of the use of the systems, they did not have adequate exposure and training in the concepts, methods and use of such sophisticated data compilation and reporting systems expected to be used by the corporate CSR program directors and senior management of the funding companies. This would result in delays and unwarranted explanations to the authorities resulting in a reduction of the funds available. On many occasions, such activities had to be stage-managed and led to compromises in terms of values and principles accepted by the NGO. This was quite difficult for the leaders of the NGO.

- **Communication among volunteers becomes sometimes difficult due to lack of knowledge of computers, internet/email:**

This point is already explained above and was difficult to solve, despite certain training courses conducted, and canvassing carried out by the leaders. This issue continues to affect the operating efficiency of this organization even now. Corporate CSR organizations in a few cases are supportive of help, but lack of basic infrastructure and lack of trained staff continues to plague this aspect.

- **Permissions from corporations, formalities and paperwork for the Charity Commissioner's office are time-consuming and tedious and take a long time for approvals:**

Procedural and statutory conformance is one of the most burdensome matters for NGO organizations that do not have any source except for donations-based funding. Many of the volunteers are naïve and do not have adequate knowledge or personality, to manage such affairs smoothly. This can cause many mental agonies and impediments in the smooth running of such projects. In addition to this, many local authorities, instead of helping such NGOs, add to the miseries of the NGOs. Their lackadaisical attitudes cause a loss of effectiveness and a wastage of resources at times. This aspect is very painful for many NGOs.

- **Lack of knowledge of actual field work causes difficulty in having a proper perspective of the work since volunteers do not necessarily have a social work background:**

Getting motivated workers and volunteers has been a challenge as explained above. Additionally, even if one found willing volunteers to work free of charge, there was another difficulty faced by the NGO. These volunteers, however smart, did not have adequate training and exposure to manage social projects that have very sensitive issues to be handled and managed with kid gloves. This is mainly because many stakeholder groups have different expectations and perceptions about the outcome. There are strong emotional stances and very vocal (many times unnecessary) explanations. The atmosphere in any project can be vitiated quickly by the slightest provocations. One must have requisite dexterity and judicious methods to handle such tricky situations. NGOs of any type can face many new challenges due to this type of project environment. Training and orientation of the volunteers can help address such issues, but only in partial ways. The field supervisors have to spend a lot of effort and time in counselling sessions dedicated to solving such problems in the field, and this is not easy.

- **The organization does not have strong PR manpower and machinery to approach donors, keep follow up with past donors, and avail more funds:**

For CSR funding also, such machinery is necessary, but is non-existent. Presently fundraising happens due to the record of running the projects well, and through personal contacts of volunteers. On many occasions, such efforts are far from satisfactory and result in unprecedented problems at the beginning, or during the execution of the projects at hand. The senior professionals in PR areas are not willing to be part of such outfits due to a lack of compensation. There are no easy solutions for this type of problem of NGOs.

- **Data management and analysis is another area which is expensive and not well looked after till now:**

This has been an area that has not received due attention right from the beginning of the project and even now continues to be rather a weak area, despite few attempts to improve the same. Since the organization has a data bank of 20 years of various social projects, it is advisable to create a proper data bank, data analysis, and also research on the topics. Such initiative is not yet observed, though there is some similar activity recently taken up, it is not carried out professionally since no one in the team has the expertise and experience to direct and manage such efforts. Professional help sought from outside has not helped since the budgets are quite inadequate and not financed by CSR funding.

Social issues that affect the performance of various projects and initiatives:

Any social work involves a 'change in the mindset' of the main stakeholders in the society at large. It also entails dedicated work by the 'pioneering volunteer teams' right from the beginning. Changes of such magnitude involve a lot of complex social /economic and cultural/emotional issues that cannot be addressed effectively without astute expertise, working knowledge and experience. This was evident in this project. Although basic social issues were known to many team members, they did not have the requisite experience and exposure to the nuances involved in this effort. This was one of the main bottlenecks in the development and implementation cycles for the project.

- **Strict control over on-site behaviour and conduct of the employees and committed volunteers is an area that needs attention:**

The resource persons do not have adequate experience and appropriate skill sets to handle the current environment and issues at the site. Training continuously was, therefore, the main solution, but was far from adequate on many project modules. The founder members had to spend a considerable amount of time gearing up the team of volunteers and trustees (to nurture & control the teams and individual members) to reach an acceptable level of performance. Misjudgments on the part of field-level personnel can create a lot of issues, and if the issues are not controlled in time, they can cause severe setbacks for the project as well as for the NGO organizations. It is necessary to create proper training/orientation analysis, training mechanisms and review systems to avoid such problems.

- A strict process of reviews for project progress and change in plans was essential and was carried out meticulously by the founder members right from the beginning and now this has become a norm in the organization. But this was not an easy task. The flexibility required in planning due to the source of funding and timing of funding continues to be a challenge for the organization, even at this stage of activities. It may be necessary to build flexibility in the basic approach towards planning and scheduling of activities.

- Interface with various other organizations for lateral cooperation for such social initiatives is essential to ensure the success of similar projects in the field as such. This is vital to ensure that the importance of such projects is communicated consistently and effectively from all the concerned NGOs in unison. The founders of the organization were clear about this, and their network helped establish such cooperation. This type of initiative has given the NGO informal leadership in the related circuit of NGO activities.

- Flexibility in plans and operations is essential to manage projects of such nature as described earlier. However, the funding agencies do not appreciate such an approach since it generates financial impact and this does not suit the corporate organizations. This can generate many issues and misunderstandings from time to time and can affect the delivery of the project at hand.

Problems faced at project levels:

- **Women are not keen to attend the programs and get themselves trained/equipped to handle their problems:**

This is a special problem seen in India. Many times, the relatives, and friends of such an affected woman stop these women from seeking help, either based on lack of knowledge or certain ulterior motives of these relatives. One can appreciate that due to such issues, women or girls are unwilling to seek help. Social NGOs in India face such problems across the country and this is a challenge indeed for all.

- The general public is still not sensitive enough to women's problems, therefore difficult to get financial help/support to run such counselling centres and conduct awareness generation programs. This continues to haunt the NGOs in a variety of services. However, there is no choice but to pursue such mass efforts to educate society at large.

- Girls are still neglected in families and do not get preference for education, nutrition, or even medical treatments. The situation has improved in the last decade but still, such cases are found in plenty. Many girls (more than 50% from the lower economic class) are anaemic due to malnourishment. Even after getting financial support and counselling, some of the girls cannot complete their education due to health problems right from childhood. The senior family members, especially in rural areas are against girls getting educated and this is still a problem in our country. This is a challenge indeed for such

NGOs. The organization, over the years, has done pioneering work for the last few decades to carry out mass awareness about such issues plaguing society.

- For educational programs conducted in communities, the response is very low. Attendance decreases considerably towards the end of the program. It is noticed that anything available free for the participants is seen as 'not so useful and important'. This not only is a challenge for 'the organization but for the entire nation at large. It is going to take considerable effort and time for NGOs all over the world, to overcome this challenge.

- Community girls are many times not allowed to go out of the community for various reasons. This means one needs to conduct programs for them in the community itself. However, it is difficult to get a proper place, which is clean, safe and with proper light and surroundings. Many such locations are also full of anti-social elements and the volunteers and staff working in these areas are harassed on many occasions. For support classes and other activities conducted in communities also, the same problem arises. The organization has been able to take care of some of these issues with the help of local municipal corporations and they have received good cooperation from these authorities.

- For projects for certain groups of children like Aids affected / infected children, getting financial help is very difficult as these children have short lives and no prospects of living for a long time. Many agencies and individuals are reluctant to help such children. This of course restricts the availability of funds for such programs. However, one must realize that things are changing for the better due to dialogues and public forum discussions on such subjects. However, as a nation, we have a long way to go, to publically accept such issues in society.

- For another group of children of sex workers, there are safety problems. The children in such programmes are taken away by antisocial elements or they run away. Getting staff to work for them is difficult, and also, there is a lot of political interference and a range of problems. The police personnel often help on such occasions, but their help is available for a few aspects only, and that too not on a full-time basis. Sadly, it is noticed that anti-social elements try and exploit such situations and it is quite a task for NGOs to ensure the proper safety and care of such women & children.

- Awareness among parents about quality education is non-existent in many families. Even in this era, due to a lack of basic education and awareness, many retrograde thinking patterns are seen in society at large. Sometimes weird opinions and viewpoints are prevalent. Opinions in many families are not proactive and are in favour of generic education. Creating such awareness is also a difficult task for the NGOs.

Based on the diamond analysis of the project classifications one can classify the project as specified below:

- Technology difficulty: T-4
- Complexity of design: C-3
- The novelty of the design: N-3
- Speed of implementation: S-2

Project:

Sr No	Project Characteristics	Comments
1	Size of the project:	0.3 million USD (INR 2.1-2.25 crore in today's currency rates, as Revenue Expenses based on donations from various sources in the society (HNIs + CSR + Common man on the street) including manpower costs+ overheads + travel + incidental costs).
2	People:	The core team of volunteers included 5-6 members in the founding team, consisting of reputed social workers, which has now expanded to around 12-14 members over the years. The total numbers were around 25 in the beginning and have now grown to 210 including part-time workers and part-time counsellors. The NGO now has 4 offices and has acquired its office place during the last 3 years due to the expansion of the activities involved.
3	Schedule:	The original plan of 60 months was planned project period as per the 'Feasibility - Study'. It was estimated/expected that the pilot test would start right from the beginning and the speed of expansion would depend upon the response from the 'needy' and various funding agencies approached. However, as can be seen from the records, the concept was very well supported by society at large and many corporate organizations and hence the NGO has been able to expand its activities over the last decade and is on a growth path. This was possible only due to the flexible approach and untiring efforts of the initial team.
4	Classification of project:	This is a case of a new startup NGO. Although the basic concept was already tried out in Mumbai, this was the first of its kind NGO in the city of Pune. The City of Pune has many NGOs and charitable organizations, but there was no NGO that had the plans/vision to undertake multifaceted activities under the auspices of a single NGO. It was felt that Pune should support such efforts for the upliftment of destitute women and children based on the support of the society at large and support from CSR allocations from the corporate sector as such.
5	High-risk project:	There were many uncertainties/risks in the project. The project was undertaken in a very hazy and uncertain environment without the availability of team members at the beginning. This was indeed a challenge. Additionally, it was difficult to enlist senior volunteers since it was decided that there would be no compensation for such

		volunteers who would commit to work without remuneration or honorarium. Again, it was difficult to recruit social workers with adequate exposure/experience and training for such activities. The project was indeed risky in many ways, and 'hope' was the only resource based on which the project was undertaken by the group of 'experienced social work seniors.
6	Technology Choice / Maturity:	There is no specific technology as such recommended for such NGO Initiatives. However, for any such social initiatives, there are specific methods, proven approaches and certain mindsets that pave the foundation of future success for such 'amorphous' activities, where the motivation of the founding team and their previous experience are the main assets, based on which such startup initiatives are undertaken. Luckily for this project, there was a group of highly experienced group of renowned social workers in the form of founder members who had the requisite confidence for successful project completion.
7	Suppliers/affiliates	For this project, there was not much of a critical role for suppliers, but there was a role for the funding /CSR funding partners. Additionally, partnerships and close associations in similar initiatives / social organizations were critical for initiating such an organization. Personal goodwill and the network of the founding members were very useful in the initial stage of the project. Support from similar organizations and active support from 'The Charity Commissioner's Office' was essential to lay strong foundations for the project.
8	Logistics / Clearances:	This was quite a challenge due to the time pressure to obtain appropriate 'Certifications / Registration / Licenses and permissions' were a challenge, as explained earlier. In many cases, NGO is a facade for other anti-social activities and hence getting proper clearance and certification from all the authorities was an important consideration before the activities could be launched. Initially getting the office space without rent was a challenge indeed. However, with kind help from one of the NGOs working for the 'old' people in Pune city, this problem was solved. Initial expenses for the newly set up organization were taken up based on individual abilities and managed by senior members through their networks.

9	Location for co-ordination:	More than 6 locations (Pune City has 4 locations & Work locations in Undre / Pimpri-Chinchawad-total locations 6 hence more than 10 over a period) that were manned with project team members. Coordination was a challenge since the project organization did not have enough budget to provide computer network-based coordination systems. Over the years this organization has set up the requisite facilities and as such the overall admin support is better. Additionally, a few of the initial 'Corporate' customers also provided active support during the implementation period in the first 5 years including providing office space and admin assistance at a few locations. However, coordination continues to be a problem for this organization.
10	Support from Sr. Mgt:	Senior management provided excellent support and timely inputs. However, Funding was a challenge in the initial period due to a shortage of funds. Similarly, there was no specific admin support in the beginning. The trustees themselves were carrying out all the activities as and when possible. Initially, Admin Support and motivational Support were received from the senior management and trustees. The team was given complete freedom for action and expenditures.
11	Involvement of Customer:	There was mixed support / hesitant support from the 'Corporate Organizations' but people were willing to listen and help. Over a period, they saw the quality of work and observed dedicated work done by the volunteers and they gave full support for the initiatives taken up. Government Department personnel were difficult to convince and started putting a lot of conditions and creating bottlenecks, but this was solved over a period. The customer teams were cooperative from the beginning. They were willing to provide active support for the development of specifications and pilot studies at the select branch locations. PM and the team had a difficult task of winning over their minds. This made the situation quite complex for the project team.

12	Project Leader Project Champion:	The project Manager selected was a competent/committed social worker of repute. This helped in the initial period. Her patience and professional approach to social work help solve many bottlenecks and impasse situations. The team of trustees was very supportive and took an active part in handling issues of teams and beneficiaries.

Key positions in the team:

The team had to be manned with the following key positions:

- Project Director / Project Manager as 'Project Champions' (The founders of this NGO).
- Team of social workers and experts with expertise in similar projects with social orientation.
- Module Leaders (4 initially and now over 12) for various critical aspects of the proposed project & modules.
- Training experts for soft skills and ethical behaviour and attitude-building exercises for the workgroups.
- Module / Field supervisors and volunteer in charge.
- Treasurers managing financial issues/funding and auditors (advisors).
- Trustees' office for project tracking and liaison with customer teams and beneficiaries.

Positives in the project environment:

- There was full support from senior management and foreign partners / corporate entities
- The focus of the team was very specific and worked toward a detailed implementation plan in cooperation with the customer personnel. This was one of the most important factors for success along with the dedication of the pioneering team of volunteers.
- Continuous dialogue with Govt officials / Customer PM and local PM with resolve to address the issues immediately helped the team to complete the project in the required time. The senior managers from both sides attend project meetings monthly / quarterly to make decisions and move forward proactively. This was useful for the team.
- Harmonious teamwork paved the path for a good quality / undisturbed work environment. This was crucial for the success of the project.
- Pre-dispatch inspection for every release involving local and customer QA / QC teams helped hassle-free on-site implementation of the modules without delays and waiting periods.
- The team had full freedom for decision-making and commitment to expenses as per the decisions of the PM. This paved the path for smooth working for the team.

Project Success Criteria:

The project success criteria took into consideration customer expectations and organizational expectations:

- Organizational expectations.
    - To complete the project in time without any compromise on quality of service.
    - To conform to stringent rules of the Charity Commissioner's office for the NGO operations.
    - To achieve the project delivery for the targeted population as planned by the organization.
    - To develop project modules as a model project so that they can become reference projects for future activities.
    - Getting repeat requests from various communities where services were provided was an important organizational requirement.
- Customer / User Expectations
    - To ensure on-time delivery and implementation.
    - To achieve a committed target population and frequency of the project in the community service.
- To achieve requisite accuracy & efficiency in operations that have a complex set of rules & changes. Similarly handling emotional and social issues effectively.
- Satisfaction of the team members Trustees / Volunteers / Staff and beneficiaries of the programs.
    - To ensure team satisfaction and development of new skills/domain expertise for the future.

Project Success Factors:

Based on the discussions with the team members and their PM it becomes clear that the list of the following points would have been useful for them as CFSs for this project. However, it has to be noted that this aspect was not necessarily thought about comprehensively before the project started.

- Clarity about the task at hand & clarity about scope and specifications.
- Commitment and participation by the customer teams in the development of the right ecosystem throughout the tenure of the project life cycle.
- Complete support from the senior management & freedom for actions for project modules.
- Competent Project Manager & trusted team members.

- Alert Risk Management especially in the form of timelines and scope/changes. This was done well but was not up to the mark at all times/stages.

- Control over project progress issues through impeccable communication and coordination/reviews.

- Excellent support from PMO personnel for ruthless tracking of issues and resolving them.

- Strong support from Audit teams and process control (support received due to strong and matured processes in the organization that have been developed over a period) through frequent reviews and communications in the small teams working on the modules.

- Exceptional teamwork and untiring support from the founding members in the initial period.

- Good support from Legal Experts and Admin teams as and when required.

Conclusion:

Highly successful project with few silver linings!

The project was evaluated as a great success in the first five years. Although good work was done for the beneficiaries, the original team of founder members were not very happy about the internal processes and internal efficiency. The corporate CSR funding agencies were partially happy. The project was not finished in the requisite time due to several licensing and permissions delays, but the quality of the project outcome was completely satisfactory as per the expectation. The corporate CSR program officers continued to support the organization for many such initiatives. The senior management was very pleased and decided to constitute additional teams to handle new Social initiatives. This NGO is still in existence and is doing good work every year. Due to the quality of the work carried out in this project, additional CSR units from various Corporate Organizations continue to fund such programs.

Learnings from this case study:

There are many learning opportunities for the NGO projects.

- The most important learning is that if the team is committed and dedicated to the cause, the NGO, then they can deliver a successful project for the stakeholders, despite the hurdles and challenges faced by the team. This is important learning for all types of project details.

- It is critical, that despite the project size and nature of activities, preparation of a project plan with adequate flexibility is essential. One may tend to make simplistic assumptions while preparing a plan then we may be wrong at times but not planning at all will send everything topsy-turvy. NGOs need to develop their framework for planning and adopt a few ideas from the conventional corporate approach for industrial organization. NGO plans need to be flexible, and adaptable, and resource commitments need to be bare minimum, to ensure that one can quickly adopt another set of priorities when there is a need.

- It is noticed that such NGO types of projects need a lot of PR / Liaison and coordination to ensure that the project is smoothly running. This team also faced unprecedented attacks from local goons and village-based activists taking advantage, for that are based on their perception of their professional powers. In the last set of elections, this has been seen on many occasions across the country, so this project was not an exception, but the challenges are real and omnipresent.

- The development of volunteers is another project feat that the project has been able to achieve. This is important leadership learning from this case study. It very significant feat for typical NGO initiatives.

- It is important that even for NGO projects, it is critical to carry out a feasibility study before one can embark on the project activities only based on a 'gut feel'. Once again it is important to emphasize that flexible and adaptable planning approach has to be used for planning such projects, especially NGO projects. This is because, for NGO projects, one is heavily dependent on outside donations & funding under CSR. The quantum & timing of such cash flows are not easily predictable. This makes planning extremely difficult for the project team.

- Clarity of purpose and effective communication are also equally important for the success of any project. This aspect needs constant attention & involvement of senior / core team members, who need to take care of these aspects to keep the project on an even keel and also to keep the motivation of the team at a high level.

- For every NGO project, there is always a paucity of infrastructure & facilities. This is mainly on account of a shortage of funds, and a feeling that generating such facilities is additional overhead for the project. However, it it needs to be understood, that basic facilities are essential for even NGO projects. Such facilities increase the effectiveness of the team and help the project to progress faster. This is important learning for the future generation of project professionals.

- For the success of the project, it is essential to make a basic 'budget for operations and financial resources'. Many people in NGOs feel that for NGOs such efforts are not required. This notion is faulty and real-life experience indicates that on the contrary 'budgeting activity is a must' for every type of activity including NGO projects.

- In most of the NGOs, many senior members work as volunteers, and they are not paid any compensation. However, they expect respectful treatment from the organization. In many NGOs, it is observed that such aspects are not considered well, and the availability of volunteers is taken for granted. This is not correct and the seniors for the NGO should pay a lot of attention to this soft aspect for the overall success of the organization in general and the NGO project in particular. If this aspect is not handled well, the organization may lose such useful senior resource persons. That is certainly not desirable for any organization.

- Every NGO project is largely dependent on outside funding (Donors & CSR aid). This is not an easy task at all, and every NGO needs to develop a dedicated team for such efforts. Future leaders need to pay attention to this soft aspect.

- Additionally, every NGO needs to develop good working relationships with the concerned authorities and agencies. This relationship goes a long way in terms of getting clearances and approvals quickly. The investment of time in this aspect is very useful and helps make the project successful. Young future project management professionals need to learn this well and practice the same in the field.

Discussion Points:

Commitment and Dedication to NGO Projects:

- Explore how the commitment and dedication of a team can lead to successful NGO projects despite facing challenges.
- Discuss examples of teams overcoming hurdles through perseverance and commitment to the cause.

Importance of Flexible Project Planning:

- Examine the critical role of flexible project planning in NGO initiatives, considering the unpredictable nature of funding and external donations.
- Discuss how NGOs can blend conventional corporate planning approaches with their unique requirements.

PR, Liaison, and Coordination Challenges:

- Analyze the significance of effective public relations, liaison, and coordination in ensuring the smooth running of NGO projects.
- Discuss real challenges faced by the team, including attacks from local elements, and explore strategies for managing such situations.

Development of Volunteers as a Leadership Learning:

- Discuss the importance of developing volunteers as a leadership accomplishment in NGO projects.
- Explore how empowering volunteers contributes to the success of typical NGO initiatives.

Feasibility Studies in NGO Projects:

- Examine the necessity of conducting feasibility studies for NGO projects instead of relying solely on intuition.
- Discuss the unique challenges of planning in NGO projects, especially given the dependence on unpredictable external funding.

Clarity of Purpose and Effective Communication:

- Discuss the role of clarity of purpose and effective communication in the success of NGO projects.
- Explore how constant attention from senior/core team members can maintain project focus and team motivation.

Importance of Basic Infrastructure for NGO Projects:

- Examine the common paucity of infrastructure in NGOs due to funding constraints and the need for a shift in perspective.
- Discuss how basic facilities can enhance team effectiveness and project progress.

Budgeting for Operations and Financial Resources:

- Explore the misconception that budgeting is unnecessary for NGO projects and highlight its importance.
- Discuss the impact of budgeting on the success of different types of activities, including NGO projects.

Respectful Treatment of Senior Volunteers:

- Analyze the need for respectful treatment of senior volunteers within NGOs.
- Discuss how neglecting this aspect can lead to the loss of valuable senior resources, affecting overall organizational success.

Dependency on External Funding and CSR Aid:

- Explore the challenges of dependency on external funding, donors, and CSR aid in NGO projects.
- Discuss the importance of developing dedicated teams for fundraising efforts.

Building Relationships with Authorities and Agencies:

- Discuss the significance of building good working relationships with authorities and agencies for NGO project success.
- Highlight the investment of time in nurturing such relationships and its positive impact on obtaining clearances and approvals.

Case No.18: Building Rajiv Gandhi Setu - Bandra Worli Bridge - one of the unique and prestigious bridges in Mumbai - a long - awaited solution to traffic congestion in the Mega City innovative concept that has now become a role model in the country

Dr Jayasri Murali, Mrs Dipti Bajpai

Associate Professor, IICMR, Pune, Assistant Professor, IICMR, Pune

Extract: The Rajiv Gandhi Sea Link, a remarkable 8-lane cable-stayed bridge in Mumbai, connects Bandra to Worli, reducing travel times from 45–60 minutes to just 15 minutes. Part of the proposed West Island freeway system, the Rs.1600 crore project by MSRDC and executed by Hindustan Construction Company was inaugurated on July 1, 2009, by Sonia Gandhi. The Sea Link alleviates congestion on Mahim Causeway, providing a faster route between the western suburbs and central Mumbai. Its construction, though 5 years behind schedule, showcases India's capability in handling intricate engineering projects. The innovative use of mobile explosive scanners ensures safety, while the project's success emphasizes the importance of strategic planning and collaborative efforts.

Introduction:

The Rajiv Gandhi (Bandra-Worli) Sea Link is an 8-lane, cable-stayed bridge with pre-stressed concrete viaduct approaches, l linkings Bandra and the western suburbs of Mumbai, with Worli and central Mumbai, and is the first phase of the proposed West Island freeway system. The Rs.1600 crore ($400M approx) project of Maharashtra State Road Development Corporation (MSRDC) is being executed by Hindustan Construction Company. Designs and Project management are by M / S DAR Consultants. The bridge was inaugurated on 30 June 2009 (Postponed and inaugurated on 1 July 2009) by UPA Chairperson Sonia Gandhi. The Sea Link would enable speedy travel between Bandra and Worli, cutting travel times from 45–60 minutes to 15 minutes. One can appreciate that such savings in time for every 'Mumbaikar' every day.

The Bandra-Worli Sea Link, officially called Rajiv Gandhi Sea Link, is a cable-stayed bridge, with pre-stressed concrete-steel viaducts on either side, that links Bandra in the Western Suburbs of Mumbai with Worli in South Mumbai. Rajiv Gandhi Sea Link Project has been one of the most highly recommended projects of all the transport studies done for the metropolitan region. Previously, Mahim Causeway was the only link connecting the western suburbs with the island city of Mumbai. Therefore, this existing 'North-South' traffic corridor was very congested and during the peak hours resulted in a bottleneck at Mahim Causeway.

Construction of this link provides an additional fast-moving outlet from the island city to the western suburbs & vice versa, thereby providing much-needed relief to the congested Mahim Causeway. This link also forms a part of the western freeway. The sea link reduces travel time between Bandra and Worli during peak hours from 60–90 minutes to 20–30 minutes. The first four of the eight lanes of the bridge were opened to the public on 30th June 2009. All eight lanes were opened on 24th March 2010. The project was 5 years behind schedule.

The bridge uses mobile explosive scanners for vehicles travelling on the sea link. Scans take less than 20 seconds for each vehicle with sensors above and below the vehicles. Over 180 cars can be scanned per hour by each scanner. The pillars and the towers supporting the bridge are protected by buoys designed to withstand explosions and collisions. These inflated buoys surround each pillar of the sea link to avoid any damage.

Facts about Bandra-Worli Sea Link (BWSL): 13 Interesting, Mind Blowing and Amazing Facts:

1. The construction of the bridge started in 2000 and completed in 2010. It took 10 years to be completed and fully functional.

2. The bridge was constructed by the Hindustan Construction Company, India.

3. A few people know the real name of this bridge, "Rajiv Gandhi Sea Link". The bridge is popularly known as the Bandra-Worli Sea Link.

4. The bridge cost US$250 million or Rs. 16 billion Indian rupees.

5. Bandra-Worli Sea Link had an average daily traffic of 37,500 vehicles (approx.).

6. The bridge was designed by Seshadri Srinivasan.

7. The bridge's height is 126 m or 413 ft. BWSL's width is 66 ft.

8. Bandra-Worli Sea Link's largest pylon towers are 128 m or 420 ft in height.

9. The BWSL helps to reduce the travel time between two points from 60-90 minutes to 6-8 minutes.

10. The cost of illuminating the bridge was Rs. 9 crores!

11. The initial planned cost of the bridge was Rs. 1,306 crores and it increased to Rs. 1,650 crores due to delay in the project.

12. The bridge consumes 1,000 KW of power a day, enough to fulfil the need for electricity of 100 households.

13. The Bandra-Worli Sea Link was inaugurated by UPA Chairperson Sonia Gandhi in Mumbai on 30th June 2009.

Extract of article written by a journalist: (Mr Mrityunjay Bose works with Sakaal Times. 2009):

A Marvel in Engineering:

It is gigantic. It is majestic. It is an engineering marvel and an architectural wonder too. The first of its kind in India (the first bridge to be constructed in open-sea conditions), the 5.6-km-long, eight-lane, approximately Rs 1,600-crore Bandra-Worli Sea Link (BWSL), which has now been renamed as the Rajiv Gandhi Sea Link, is an engineering marvel that aims to ease traffic in Mumbai, India's commercial capital.

The construction is a miracle on the Arabian Sea that has an imposing presence on the Western horizon of Mumbai. One can imagine the strength and might of the bridge given the fact that it weighs nearly 50,000 African elephants and the length of steel wires used in the project is equivalent to the circumference of the Earth. And it has made a difference: the distance which earlier took nearly 45 minutes - from Bandra till Worli if one uses the old road – now takes just eight minutes.

It is the first time that cable-stay bridges have been attempted on open seas in India. Coupled with the fact that the aesthetically designed pylons have an extremely complex geometry and one of the longest spans for concrete decks, the challenges encountered were indeed formidable. With its cable-stayed towers soaring gracefully skywards, the bridge was constructed by Hindustan Construction Co Ltd (HCC), an engineering, construction, infrastructure and integrated urban development and management giant and designed by UK-based Dar Consultants for Maharashtra State Road Development Corporation (MSRDC). It has today emerged as one of the prominent landmarks of Mumbai and a popular tourism destination.

HCC Chairman and Managing Director Ajit Gulabchand said:

"Construction of the Bandra-Worli Sea Link has been one of the most challenging infrastructure projects undertaken in recent times in India. We took on this project with the quest to set new benchmarks in precision engineering and prove India's infrastructure development capabilities. Reflecting on the hard work of our engineers and over 3000 workers who have raised this Sea Link in rough open sea conditions, I am proud to say we have truly built a monument to human skills, enterprise and determination."

Bulky Equipment:

Construction of the mammoth bridge structure required some huge cranes and several other heavy construction equipment. Some of these included Jack-up platforms, floating barrages, boats, crawler cranes, tower cranes, gantry cranes, derrick cranes, launching trusses, placer booms, diesel generators, diesel & air compressors, concrete pumps, transit mixers, reverse circulation drilling machines and 'A' frame barrage. The equipment was brought together from various countries. A total of 130 pieces of equipment were used and the cost was Rs 190 crore. Twenty-five pieces of equipment were imported for Rs 78 crore. It is significant to note that some of the equipment had to be imported or brought into the country on rental. Availability of such complex equipment also meant delays over 6-8 months and the project had to reconcile with major delays only due to such complex time schedules and logistics involved in the same.

Building Challenge:

Building the Bandra-Worli Sea Link was a challenge indeed. The Link Bridge consists of twin continuous concrete box girder bridge sections for traffic in each direction. Each bridge section except at the cable-stayed portion is supported on piers typically spaced at 50 metres. Each section is meant for four lanes of traffic complete with concrete barriers and service sidewalks on one side. The bridge alignment is defined with vertical and horizontal curves. The highlights of the Bandra-Worli Sea Link are the two aesthetically designed cable-stayed bridges, viz., the Bandra and Worli Cable-Stayed Bridges of 500 and 150-metre spans, respectively, with the highest towers soaring to a height of 126 metres, equivalent to the height of a 43-storied building.

The cable-stayed design allows the free movement of fishing boats. The cable-stayed portion of the Bandra channel is 600 metres in overall length between expansion joints and consists of two 250-metre cable-supported main spans flanked by 50-metre conventional approach spans. A centre tower with an overall height of 128 metres above the pile cap level supports the superstructure utilizing four planes of stay cables in a semi-fan arrangement. The cable-stayed portion of the Worli channel is 350 metres in overall length between expansion joints and consists of two 150-metre cable-supported main spans flanked by 50-metre conventional approach spans. A centre tower with an overall height of 55 metres above the pile cap level supports the superstructure using four planes of stay cables in a semi-fan arrangement.

According to Mr Araby EL Shenawy (Engineer and head of the Project management Consulting team from Egypt), "The method of balanced cantilever was adopted for the construction of the deck for Bandra Cable-stayed Bridge. This is considered to be one of the biggest cable-stayed bridges in the world with a concrete deck built with this method of construction. It was, therefore, a real challenge to monitor the behaviour of the structure during all erection stages and to compare the same with the behaviour of the corresponding theoretical computer model of the bridge, to ensure the achievement of the desired geometry at the end of the construction. It was also essential to control the stresses in the critical bridge elements during every single construction stage to ensure the adequacy of the bridge elements all the time."

Safety & Security - a major challenge for the project!! Big Brother Watching!

Safety & Security of the Bandra-Worli Sea Link is a major issue. The Mumbai Police has factored in the security concerns and has taken a series of measures by putting up a high-tech security system. A special team of officers led by the Joint Commissioner of Police (Traffic) monitors the traffic flow and is responsible for safety and security. However, the task at hand is not at all simple. Safety & security is very critical for the project manager and his team and hence it must receive its due share of attention seen from the complex nature of work in this newly initiated project. Apart from this, this specific project is of national pride and importance, hence safety and security assume additional prestige associated with the same.

Continuous Power Supply:

For the entire project, a reliable power supply has been arranged. It will also house diesel generator sets and auto mains failure panels to cater to critical loads, e.g. monitoring, surveillance, and communication equipment, and emergency services like aviation obstruction lights. Adequate lighting levels have been maintained, and energy-saving luminaires installed. Special emphasis has been given to incorporating lightning protection at bridge towers and control room buildings to protect those buildings/structures and the sophisticated monitoring and communication equipment installed therein. A built-in feature of providing reliability and availability of equipment is achieved through duplicate cables for such equipment. Facade lighting for the bridge tower and special lighting in the landscaped area are also included.

Main Objectives of the project:

The objectives for the new organization set-up were as follows:

- To build a bridge with new technology and help provide faster traffic between Bandra and Worli for four-wheelers to avoid congestion in Mumbai city (45 minutes to be reduced to less than 10 minutes).

- To ensure that international quality standards right from the stages of concept design to final delivery (EPC standards).

- To ensure that this project is completed within the stipulated time of 60 months (in reality, it took over 110 months due to various constraints).

- To ensure that the design and architecture are modern, styling should be such that it becomes a landmark bridge without any compromising in Engineering Standards and Specifications.

- To ensure that the design is such that it will allow easy passage for the marine vessels to pass under the bridge.

- To ensure that the design and engineering construction incorporates safety and security measures, and provide uninterrupted power supplies for the ultra-modern equipment and facilities provided for in the design.

- To incorporate "Energy and Environmental" friendly construction and make use of natural (non-fossil based energy sources) as far as possible.

- To ensure the safety and security of the personnel and society at large during and after the construction of the bridge.

The challenges of the project team:

The following points were noted based on the interaction with the project team members and Project Manager. The author had a chance to meet Brig. Satish Diwanji (working at HCC at that time), Project Manager who is the main Champion & experienced PM. The author had a chance to ask him about the challenges faced during the project execution. The key issues discussed are mentioned below for quick reference:

Internal issues and bottlenecks observed:

Some internal issues/aspects needed the attention of the project team, especially for the PM. Some of these issues are:

Too many agencies were involved in the decision-making and approval process (at times no one knew who was responsible and accountable for the decisions and the impact of the decisions)

Too many agencies were involved in the decision-making process, and this created many unnecessary complications for the project team, leading to delays and losses due to higher costs (some of these avoidable). The following main agencies were involved in the project:

- Maharashtra State Road Development Corporation (MSRDC).
- Bombay Municipal Corporation.
- Govt. of Maharashtra (PWD) and Police Department.
- Govt. of India Coordinators.
- Bankers and Financial Institutes.
- A variety of consulting firms and individual consultants (Local and International).
- A variety of Inspection agencies (Local and International).
- Senior management from the project organization had the basic responsibility to manage the project as per the specifications and within scope/time/cost constraints.
- Range of political party leaders and their Offices.

Although the project organization had defined lines of reporting and, well-defined authority structures, these at times were rendered ineffective on account of interventions by the agencies specified above. This was one of the unique challenges for such a complex project. The coordination among the agencies was a nightmare for the project team. All these agencies in concept were focused on the project objectives, they had their points of view, approach to work, internal processes and priorities for the work. This made life very miserable for the project teams. Additionally, every agency had an **'Own Ego'** that compounded the problem dimensions. The team had a tough time due to this aspect. Better cooperation amongst the agencies would have helped avoid delays, cost overruns and stress for the project coordinators. Due to internal politics and own priorities, the nodal agencies were not able to organize.

The project is an 'Engineering Marvel' and very complex in terms of Engineering Design and Construction, Structural Engineering Designs and Confirmations and Concept Testing Site Work Challenges.

While talking to the Project Manager, the following major issues/challenges/issues were identified from an engineering angle:

- Engineering Design/Construction/Technology Choice and associated Technical Challenges. (Complexities increased due to the enormous size of the project compounded by aggressive project conditions, working in the sea with high wind speeds).
- Meeting challenges of open sea conditions without adequate and right type of equipment, and personnel with previous relevant experience. Many engineering professionals had no direct experience nor adequate exposure to tough working environments.
- Ground Stabilization (this was a tough challenge and was compounded on account of unpredictable weather conditions and wind speeds).
- Piling installation in hard rock without overburden.
- Pile cap construction below tide levels.
- Working in Inter-tidal areas.
- Initial erection of Trusses.
- Relocation of Trusses.
- Construction of cable-stayed bridge with one of the world's longest and heaviest concrete decks.
- Stringent standards & precision levels are to be achieved during the construction of the bridge.
- Construction of Pylon tower legs/Geometry control.
- Working during the monsoons (was a unique challenge given the Mumbai rains).
- Erection of Pier table segments.
- Logistics in marine locations.
- Link bridge.
- Stringent requirements towards aesthetics: High Geometric Control, Immaculate Grooves in the concrete surface, Excellent finish of the concrete surface.
- Innovations at every stage of work and one had to observe strict engineering guidelines for the innovations as well. Every workday came up with a new challenge. This went on for long periods.
- Psychological Conditioning of the people to work without a 'chalata hai' attitude was also a big challenge. They were not at all used to working to such standards and engineering accuracies and methods of work.

One can easily understand that with such conditions, where everything that can change the basic design/concept and the impact of these issues can drive the project personnel crazy at times, especially when the changes are significant. Since the project was the first of its kind in India, there were not many people to consult within India. For everything, one had to depend on foreign experts and their approval was crucial before anything could change site.

Permissions from Govt Authorities/Municipal Corporations/and other statutory authorities and completion of other formalities:

The senior management of the newly formed division of the company (for this project) had decided from the beginning that they would complete all the formalities and certifications from the competent authorities cleanly and judiciously and would refrain from cutting corners and making adjustments.

One can easily appreciate that getting approval for such a huge and ambitious project is a herculean task and one needs to face many impediments to obtain permission. This is a tough task indeed. One of the major challenges was to obtain permission to set up such a modern bridge through a private enterprise. The Government authorities were also perplexed about such a new venture that was unprecedented in history. There were too many unknowns and anxiety to approve itself was a challenge at times for the officials. They were not at all convinced that such a project is feasible in terms of its practicality and acceptance (since there was no parallel in the recent history of the construction and infrastructure industry).

Despite several visits and presentations made by the core team, the Government authorities were reluctant to grant permissions and clearances from several ministries involved. However, through untiring efforts and focus, the core team could obtain all the requisite permissions and certifications from the competent authorities. However, this resulted in considerable delays and avoidable costs for the project organization.

Funding and bank finances was also a major challenge:

Funding and project financing for such a large infrastructure project is not at all a simple task for any agency. Additionally, due to being the first of its kind in the country with lots of uncertainties and risks, this project provided full scope for anxiety, confusion, confrontations and egos of everyone involved leading to further complications.

Like getting all the requisite permissions from the authorities, getting a nod from the banks and financial institutions was also a great challenge faced by the project team. The core team had to go through an agonizing period since the bankers were very reluctant to even look at the proposals submitted since they were more than convinced that such a project would not at all take off the ground. Additionally, the size of the funding requirement was considerable and hence carried heavy risk in the transactions involved.

Nobody was willing to discuss even the basic feasibility report prepared, and they thought that the idea itself was 'crazy' and had no chance of success in terms of practical reality. This created a lot of frustration and anxiety for the promoters who had staked all their fortunes for the project. Approval was soon becoming a mirage for the team. However, through the intervention by the CMD (he was a great supporter of the project idea) and some of the Senior Officials of the Government, the issues were resolved. However, getting the right type of funding continued to be a challenge for the promoter team. Over a period, through the BMC and ministries of the Govt. of

Maharashtra, help from the CM's Office, and finally the PM's office the final arrangements for the financial requirements were tied in and then the green signal was given to the project.

The challenge faced was the sheer 'size of the project':

This was the next challenge. One has to realize that the sheer volume/size and complexity of the project were enormous, and the issues involved had to be dealt with with due care and attention. Enthusiasm and dedication were not good enough to set up strong foundations for the success of the project. Very dedicated efforts, patience and due diligence had to be used to ensure proper designs, structural analysis, site planning, infrastructure availability and detailed project planning and scheduling for the workmen and resources.

Proactive planning was the key to the project's success. The planning engineers involved in the project had to undergo proper training and orientation along with the change of conventional mindsets to handle such a challenging and voluminous project. One had to develop a holistic view and an ability to deal with the details at the same time. This is not as easy as it may seem to be in the beginning. This was quite a challenge right from the beginning for the entire team. One can easily understand that the planning team's challenge was to keep the plans quite flexible on one side but at the same time had to be reasonably accurate and realistic with the plans/schedules and estimates. Any wrong assumptions or mistakes would have significant implications on the costs and time schedules. This was quite a challenge for the planning team. However previous experience and dedicated efforts by a few of the core team members helped handle the situation well without any major hiccups or delays. The sheer size of the project had an impact on the design & engineering and planning teams throughout the tenure of the project.

The complexity of the design and estimation efforts is due to size/complexity and the use of a non-conventional approach to the entire project:

As one can imagine, the design & engineering and estimation were all intertwined in the complexity of the project. Additionally, due to new concepts and a lot of unknowns, all the matters related to design and engineering had to be checked and checked again and again through the design & engineering process. Similarly, 'Engineering Change Request' was one more source of confusion and tension. Many things had to be checked again and again if they had any additional impact on other designs.

The complications increased further because the methods proposed for the project envisaged the use of state-of-the-art technologies for the project. Some of the concepts, designs and methods of construction proposed, were never used in this type of infrastructure and construction industry in India. Additionally, the type of project equipment envisaged for the project was not normally used in India. Some of this equipment was not even considered while preparing the basic feasibility study and had an impact on the project plans and budgets.

The team of promoters had to ensure that all types of Engineering experts (Design Experts/Architects, Construction Site Engineers with relevant experience) were inducted into the project. Every new member in such teams was interviewed and short-listed personally by the

Core team of the organization to ensure appropriate fit in terms of competencies/skills and the right attitude towards the challenges right from the beginning of the project.

Challenges related to Scope/Time and Costs (needs flexibility in approach):

Projects of such gigantic proportions undertaken by the PM render all the conventional methods and practices inadequate and insufficient. This is quite a challenge, as one can imagine since there is no precedence and standards for such innovative projects. The task at hand is quite challenging and highly onerous for the planning team.

While discussing this point, the Program Manager explained that:

"Under such an environment one had to adopt a completely flexible approach for planning and sometimes recast the scope/schedules and costs again and again without compromising the promise made to the promoters of the project. This may sound contrary to the basic approach and tenets of project management in the conventional sense, but keeping the primary direction the same, one had to make changes, and sometimes significant changes, to the scope of the proposed activity, leading to a lot of changes for the projects. However, when adoption of the best technologies and modern facilities are the critical success factors for the project, one needs to use flexibility in the approach for finalization of the scope (and hence impact on schedules and costs). This was part of life throughout the tenure of the project. One needs to understand that innovations and adoption of new approaches is a dynamic process in case of such projects, and flexibility in approach helps determine long-term success". One can easily appreciate that without 'Flexibility' in approach and methods of work (hence in scope/time and costs) it would have been impossible to achieve the desired success.

However, 'flexibility' certainly does not mean a 'carte blanche' approach to the project team. Every new suggestion and proposal for new methods/type of equipment was analyzed and scrutinized before clearances for the same. This was an important aspect otherwise one may lose sight of the main objectives, and the scope may drift in its essence without getting due attention.

Getting a proper well-equipped office and basic infrastructure for running the new organization was not possible due to a lack of funds:

One can easily appreciate the difficulty faced by the PM in the initiating phases of such a project, but very soon such facilities were created, and the PM insisted that the best modern facilities and tools were available to the team over a while. The additional funds were infused by the corporate office right from the beginning (this was possible only on account of continued support from the CMD of the project organization. CMD and senior managers in the organization were convinced about the success and (hence prestige of the project) right from the beginning and were willing to take risks.

Setting up a flexible but effective organizational set-up was one more challenge faced by the newly set-up organization:

This is a perpetual challenge for any large project organization. Judicious choice of personnel and effective but flexible organization the needed for every large-sized project.

Such a need demands able leadership and balance between 'people Vs tasks' issues for large project organizations. Additionally, despite the requisite skills, it was essential to assess the fit of the person in the team and his mindset for unstructured situations was also a challenge for the selection of the core team. This had to be undertaken with due care and attention by the HR team.

Considerable efforts and discussions with experts led to the development of an organisational structure suitable for such a large project. However, getting the right fit of professionals with the right competencies/skills and experience was an additional challenge. However, this problem was handled by the HR team supervised by the CMD. He ensured that apart from technical skills, due importance was given to candidates with the appropriate mindset.

Most of the operational management is done by site engineers. Without proper and well-oiled internal systems and control methods of work, it is difficult to carry out such a large project without problems:

One can appreciate that for any successful project, the core team members must be available for most of the key activities of the project continuously, at least in the initial few years. This is not so easy for dynamic project organization. These organizations need very flexible methods of work, and one cannot enforce corporate discipline in such organizations. This creates problems and impediments in the smooth working of many projects.

Considerable time and efforts were spent by the senior management personnel to ensure that the right type of systems and controls were developed in the newly formed organization to ensure proper work instructions, reviews of progress as per the plans, and internal controls to ensure smooth working for the people at the site. The development of simple but effective systems paved the path for the success of the project. This activity was judiciously carried out throughout the tenure of the project.

Development of support infrastructure and support network of the vendors and sub-contractors was also a challenge for this project:

In the modern era, it is very important that any organization, public or private, has developed a good and reliable network of support organizations (in the form of resource providers, sub-contractors and vendors for specialized artefacts and engineering services). In terms of modern project management practices, this aspect is seen as one of the CSFs for the success of any project.

However, this aspect was not well handled in the initial phases of this project. One of the challenges for this PM was that the 'Feasibility Study' was not carried out with due attention and some of the support services were simply not included in the basic assumptions made for the estimates (hence not provided for in the Budget).

For example, the provision of a crane to lift the trusses was not provided for in the original assumptions since no one had anticipated such a need. This was discovered at a later stage after the initial designs were replaced by the modified approach for the trusses. This meant two things, one original estimate had to be redone and the costs for the cranes had to be provided which were simply missing from the original budget. This created a lot of issues since the project did not have the financial prowess to purchase them as capital equipment only for this project. The alternative solution was to hire them from Singapore, which was very costly and meant delays for the cranes to arrive at the site from Singapore. However, there was no choice but to hire them and wait for their arrival. This was very embarrassing for everyone concerned.

Additionally, it was pointed out that some of the designs and prototypes had no simulation facilities and expertise in India and hence one had to depend on overseas consulting firms for checking and revalidation of the complex designs. Such costs were also not accounted for in the original feasibility study. Additional sanctions had to resort to, which were painful, slow and had an impact on costs.

The PM during the discussions agreed with the researcher that the concept of dynamic feasibility study may be a useful tool to handle such situations. This case study has further strengthened the concept which now will be published as a new reference framework for future reference by scholars and students.

Effective Communication with internal stakeholders project team and site personnel:

Effective communication is an important factor for the success of any project in the modern era. This point is already explained. One must note that as per one of the main surveys carried out about the failures of the projects, inadequate communication is one of the primary causes of the failure. The promoters of the project took a lot of care to ensure that the values/policies and plans of the organization were inculcated in the team members right from the beginning.

The senior management team ensured that the guidelines of the management were communicated as frequently as required to the working teams through small group meetings and briefings. This method was quite effective, supported by the internal methods and practices. Senior management took a lot of care to see that everyone was informed well in time about the plan and changes from time to time. This was critical for the success of the project at hand.

Attention to Quality Standards and Inspection to ensure that the project activities were carried out the first time. This activity had to be followed up even for the site work as a matter of standard of performance and expected quality norm for the entire project:

Many organizations boast about high-quality standards and the quality of services provided. However, quality standards are more talked about than implemented at the field level. The senior management was highly concerned about ensuring that the promised quality standards were maintained at every stage of execution. The senior management emphasized the expectations about quality standards at every stage of the project activities and generated adequate resources to supervise the activities and maintain required standards. This was accepted as the norm of working over a period and then became the standard of organizational working.

There is always a difference between talking about quality and implementing the same in all walks of life in an organization. This organization has achieved this difficult task by institutionalizing this mindset all over the organization. This is quite an achievement for such a large project:

This project team adopted the 'the first time right' approach to most activities (barring a few where modifications were done due to practical constraints), right from the start and management fully supported this method. The project is very successful and can be compared with similar efforts in international scenarios of projects. One can be rightfully proud of the wonderful work done by the Indian Engineers with the help of foreign experts.

Data management and analysis is another area which is expensive but essential for the project's success:

This has been an area that must receive due attention right from the beginning of the project. One can easily appreciate that this area is rather critical to manage the project successfully.

This area continues to be crucial to manage the project activities successfully. A lot of care was taken by the senior management team to ensure that all the data (and transaction details) were captured and analyzed for the project progress reviews and proactive actions. The organization ensured that the IT systems were made available to all the functionaries and site teams. It is difficult to carry out the activities in a smooth way without effective IT Systems. This was set up based on all the tools and methods available for the effective working of the organization.

Need for robust facilities planning and adequacy of QA / QC Testing facilities for such types of major projects:

For such a large project, it is necessary to develop adequate infrastructure for testing and a few other activities. This was not anticipated and provided for in the budgets. One can understand the reason for the same but at the same time not carrying out the required tests as per the guidelines is also not desirable. It is an important learning that for all such mega projects it is pertinent to plan for such facilities that will facilitate smooth working of the project teams.

Social issues that did affect the success of the project and caused unnecessary delays and escalated costs:

Any such an enormous size of project work generates a lot of social issues and bottlenecks for such a massive project. This project was no exception to this rule. At times political interference and social pressures can mar the speed and viability of the project due to many pressure groups operating in the society at large. This was known to the promoters, and they took all the care to ensure that such influences did not hamper the progress of work at any cost. However, this project also faced many challenges despite being a flagship project, sponsored by the Government of Maharashtra and the Mumbai Municipal Corporation. There were demands for local employment and pressure to pay compensations to fishermen for the loss of their livelihood for a few months. The project Manager was threatened and there were demonstrations and strikes against him and the project organization a few times. However good PR from the HO and PM helped save the situations from time to time.

Local municipality authorities initially were apprehensive, but they also supported the concept and participated in the clearance process:

The transparency in the basic approach and clean transactions helped get over the hurdles. The 'undeterred approach' of the leader helped win such battles. The senior management team went out of their way to enlist the support of the entire stakeholder community throughout the tenure of the project. Although local municipal authorities did cooperate, their 'red tape' factor led to a lot of delays and additional costs.

The organization had a very effective PR function and hence they were able to organize community meetings to propagate the need for such a new innovative bridge for Bandra-Worli Sea Link:

However, when everything appeared to be going smoothly a political party of significant influence decided to bring stay order to the entire project due to the dislocation of the current fishermen in the area where the proposed bridge was expected to be constructed. The political party looked at this as a chance to make prestige issues out of their demands to support the local population and generate prowess for the party in days to come. The project had to be stalled one day since there were slogan shouting and gherao for a few days followed by tool-down protests by the working crew members. This was a major setback and caused a lot of headaches and cash burden for the project.

Project Case:

Sr No	Project Characteristics	Comments
1	Size of the project:	230 million USD (INR 4000 crore in today's currency rates as Revenue Expenses based on initial capital expenses for the project.
2	Size of the project:	The core team of Senior managers included 20 core team members with more than 3500 workmen involved in the project.
3	Schedule:	The original plan was for 5 years, but in reality, it took more than 10 years for the total handover of the project. However as can be seen from the records, the concept of saving time for Mumbai commuters is a reality today and as such project has delivered the basic 'strategic intent' that gave birth to the project in the first place. The project was very well supported by society at large and many corporate organizations. This was possible only due to the flexible approach and untiring efforts of the initial team.
4	Classification of project:	This is a case of the 'Modern and Complex Engineering Marvel' project and is the first of its kind in the country. After the success of this project, the Government has now issued notification for such type of projects in the country with this project being declared as the 'model' project. This project will continue to remain a benchmark for many all over the country and all over the world in its class.
5	High-risk project:	There were many uncertainties/risks in the project. The project was undertaken in a very hazy and uncertain environment without clarity about the government guidelines. Additionally, it was difficult to enlist support for such a new initiative. The response from the bankers and financial institutes was 'Lukewarm' in the initial stages and this was also a big risk in the project. The size of the project itself was also one of the main risks. Similarly, there was every possibility of political and social interference in the project. Indeed, the project was full of risks. The project was indeed risky in many ways and 'hope' was the only resource based on which the project was undertaken by the group of 'experienced seniors.
6	Technology Choice / Maturity:	There was a plan to use state-of-the-art technology and modern methods for the project. The promoters had all the confidence in new technology, and they supported bold and unconventional methods in the project with the motto 'First time right'. This was indeed not at all a trivial issue to handle.

7	No. of suppliers/affiliates	The organization created a network of over 400-450 suppliers and over a period, treated them as partners in business rather than mere suppliers. This indeed was a difficult task.
8	Logistics/Clearances:	This was quite a challenge due to the time pressure to obtain appropriate 'Certifications / Registration / Licenses and permissions' were a challenge, as explained earlier. This was handled by assigning the tasks to various "task force groups" and their work was coordinated through the corporate office.
9	Location for co-ordination:	There were more than 6 locations in Mumbai, and 2 locations overseas, where work was being carried out. Coordination was a challenge since the project organization was attempting too many things at the same time.
10	Support from Sr. Mgt:	Senior management provided excellent and timely support in every aspect of the work cycle. Apart from conventional support, senior management also provided emotional and motivational support to all the workgroups, by conducting focused meetings and briefing sessions. Funding was a challenge in the initial period due to a shortage of funds. Similarly, there was no specific admin support in the beginning. Initially, Admin Support & Motivational Support was received from the senior management and main promoters. The teams were given complete freedom for action and expenditures based on allocated budgets and policy guidelines.
11	Involvement of Customer:	There was mixed support / hesitant support from the 'Corporate Organizations' but people were willing to listen and help. Over some time, they saw the quality of work and observed dedicated work done by the promoters and initial teams. This changed after experiencing initial progress. The customer teams were cooperative from certain stages onwards. They were willing to provide active support for the development of specifications and pilot studies at select locations. PM and the team had a difficult task to win over their minds in the initial stages. This made the situation quite complex for the project team.
12	Leader:	The program/Project Manager selected was a competent/committed professional with high values and integrity. His self-confidence and conviction about the practicality of the innovative concept were the main strengths of the organization.

Key positions in the team:

The team had to be manned with the following key positions:

- Project Director / Project Manager as 'Project Champions' (The founders of this project organization).
- Many Government / Semi-Government Officers (these personnel kept on changing causing problems at times).
- Engineering Director with a team of senior consultants for many aspects of engineering.
- Team of 'Core members' of the initial management team.
- Team of planners/architects and structural engineers from various countries.
- Suppliers of critical equipment and special services (local and Foreign).
- Module Leaders (4 initially and eventually over 12) for various critical aspects of the proposed project & modules.
- Training experts for soft skills and ethical behaviour and attitude-building exercises for the workgroups.
- Module / Field supervisors and site in charge.
- Treasurers managing financial issues/funding and auditors (advisors).
- Legal advisors and consultants.
- A panel of external consultants who were key members of the entire project 'Think Tank'.

Positives in the project environment:

- There was full support from promoters / senior management, however, there were too many agencies involved in the decision-making processes with different priorities and concerns.
- The focus of the team was very specific and worked toward a detailed implementation plan in cooperation with the vendors and suppliers.
- A continuous dialogue with Govt officials/Customer PM and local PM with resolve to address the issues immediately helped the team to complete the project in the required time. The senior managers from both sides attend project meetings monthly/quarterly to make decisions and move forward proactively. This was extremely useful for the team.
- Harmonious teamwork paved the path for a good quality/undisturbed work environment. This was crucial for the success of the project.
- Pre-dispatch inspection for every delivery involving local and customer QA/QC teams helped problem-free on-site implementation of the modules without delays and waiting periods.

- The team had full freedom for decision-making and commitment to expenses as per the decisions of the PM. This paved the path for smooth working for the team.

Project Success Criteria:

The project success criteria took into consideration customer expectations and organizational expectations:

- **Organizational expectations**
  - To complete the project in time without any compromise on quality of service.
  - To conform to stringent rules of Government and Semi-government authorities.
  - To achieve the project delivery for the targeted population as planned by the organization.
  - To develop project modules as a model project so that they can become reference projects for future activities.
  - To introduce state-of-the-art technology and innovations where possible throughout the project.
  - To maintain transparency and ethics in real sense of the terms in all activities.
  - To make vendors network as partners in business with long-term contracts.
  - To ensure that promises once made are honoured to all the stakeholders and 'no comebacks' on the promises.

- **Customer / User Expectations**
  - To ensure on-time delivery and implementation.
  - To achieve a committed target population and frequency of the project in the community service.
  - To achieve requisite accuracy & efficiency in operations that have a complex set of rules and changes.
  - To handle emotional and social issues effectively without interruptions.
  - To ensure the satisfaction of the team members Promoters/Volunteers/Staff and beneficiaries of the programs.
  - To ensure team satisfaction and development of new skills/domain expertise for the future.

Project Success Factors:

Based on the discussions with the leadership team members and their PM it becomes clear that the list of the following points would have been useful for them as CFSs for this project. However, it needs to be noted that this aspect was not necessarily thought about comprehensively before the project started.

- Clarity about the task at hand & clarity about scope and specifications.
- Commitment and participation by the customer teams in the development of the right ecosystem throughout the tenure of the project life cycle.
- Complete support from the senior management & freedom for actions for project module leaders.
- Competent Project Manager & trusted team members.
- Alert Risk Management especially in the form of timelines and scope/changes. This was done well but was not up to the mark at all times/stages.
- Control over project progress issues through impeccable communication and coordination/reviews.
- Excellent support from PMO personnel for ruthless tracking of issues and resolving them.
- Strong support from Audit teams and process control (support received due to strong and matured processes in the organization that have been developed over a period) through frequent reviews and communications in the small teams working on the modules.
- Exceptional teamwork and untiring support from the founding members in the initial period.
- Good support from Legal Experts and Admin teams as and when required.

Conclusion:

A highly successful project for society at large but not so successful from a project management process perspective. Users and common man on the street are very happy with the outcome of the project. Everyone saves at least 2 hrs of time every day and avoids road blockages. However, project management professionals are probably not comfortable since the results do not conform to the conventional norms.

The project was evaluated as a great success in the first 10 years. Although good work was done for the beneficiaries, the original team of founder members were very happy about the internal processes and internal efficiency. However, all of them expressed that they wanted to carry out more specific work with a high level of efficiency if they had the requisite freedom and authority right from the beginning.

They expressed that the project was a great success in the eyes of the common man on the street but from a project management processes point of view, it was not very successful.

Learning from the project:

- There are many learning opportunities from this project. However, the most significant aspect is that even very complex and intricate engineering projects can be handled in India based on detailed scope definition and understanding of the field situations and a detailed but flexible planning process that can be adapted to suit the dynamic changes in the field and process of execution. Large Infra-structure projects must adopt such an approach for the final success of the project.

- Such complex and long-period projects need a flexible and adaptive approach to planning with certain discretionary powers made available to the project teams. Additionally, there is a need to re-establish the feasibility all over again under specific conditions or constraints of the project. If in case one had to abandon the project the team should be empowered to stop the current activity. This concept has been now suggested for future projects under the new concept of 'Dynamic Feasibility System' which is specifically superior to many other approaches. Realize that if you face a problem that is tricky and difficult to solve and get caught in repetitive cycles it may be useful to cut off the cycle and start all over again. In a large project, you must be prepared for such changes in the world environment & order.

- For the overall success of a group of complex projects, it is a must to ensure that good quality enterprise-wide infrastructure and quality facilities are provided. One can see that such aspects are taken for granted in the overall scheme of things. Nobody is specifically assigned to tasks and at the same time expects that everything will also be available in time.

- One can learn from this study is a fact that if every stakeholder is running his list of goals, then the achievement of common goals will become impossible. The availability of adequately trained resources will matter the most for the final achievement of successful project delivery.

This project has given a boost to the image of Indian Engineers & Scientists who are capable of delivering 'world-class projects' in India. This is indeed very satisfying and deserves our salutes to all of them who have made pioneering contributions to the engineering marvel that has been constructed for the overall ease of transportation in Mumbai city.

Discussion Points:

Effective Project Management in Complex Engineering Projects:

- Emphasize the importance of detailed scope definition and understanding of field situations in managing complex engineering projects in India.

- Discuss how a flexible planning process that can adapt to dynamic changes in the field is crucial for success.

- Highlight the need for a comprehensive approach that considers the intricacies of the project from start to finish.

The Concept of 'Dynamic Feasibility System':

- Explore the idea of a 'Dynamic Feasibility System' and its benefits in handling complex and long-term projects.

- Discuss the importance of discretionary powers for project teams, allowing them to re-establish feasibility under specific conditions or constraints.

- Examine the advantage of empowering project teams to stop current activities if necessary and the potential impact on project success.

Enterprise-wide Infrastructure and Quality Facilities:

- Stress the necessity of providing good quality enterprise-wide infrastructure and facilities for the overall success of complex projects.

- Analyze how these aspects are often taken for granted and the importance of assigning specific responsibilities to ensure timely availability.

- Discuss the challenges that may arise if these factors are not adequately addressed in the overall scheme of project execution.

Stakeholder Alignment for Common Goals:

- Discuss the challenges posed by individual stakeholders pursuing their own goals, making it difficult to achieve common objectives.

- Emphasize the importance of aligning stakeholder interests and ensuring a shared vision for project success.

- Highlight the role of effective communication and collaboration in achieving a harmonized approach to project goals.

Human Resource Management and Training:

- Emphasize the critical role of adequately trained resources in the successful delivery of projects.

- Discuss the challenges associated with managing diverse teams and ensuring that all stakeholders are well-equipped for their roles.

- Explore strategies for enhancing training programs and developing skilled professionals to meet the demands of complex projects.

Global Recognition for Indian Engineers and Scientists:

- Celebrate the success of the project in boosting the image of Indian engineers and scientists on a global scale.

- Discuss the significance of delivering 'world-class projects' in India and the positive impact on the country's reputation.

- Acknowledge and salute the contributions of individuals who played a key role in the engineering marvel, recognizing their pioneering efforts.

Case No 19: Setting up a new Township for over 120,000 common citizens and over 50,000 visitors daily based on an innovative concept that has now become a role model in the country

Dr Jayasri Murali, Ms. Puja Gavande

Associate Professor, MBA@IICMR, Pune, Assistant Professor, MBA@IICMR, Pune

Extract:

Magarpatta City, a pioneering real estate venture, stands as an unprecedented project where 120 farmer families transformed their land into a holistic enterprise, spanning 400 acres. Led by Mr. Satish Magar, the chairman, and managing director, this initiative defied urbanization threats, turning farmers into proud stakeholders. Embracing a 'walk-to-school, walk-to-work concept,' Magarpatta City prioritizes convenience, greenery, and a stress-free life. Its state-of-the-art Cyber City IT parks house global giants. The project imparts invaluable learnings—emphasizing commitment, the influence of team quality, patience in the face of resistance, and adept handling of futuristic concepts. The senior management's resilience, patience, and maturity in overcoming opposition make Magarpatta City a role model in socio-political-economic matters. Kudos to the founding members and equity holders for fostering an innovative organization.

Introduction:

Magarpatta City is a township in the village of Hadapsar in Pune, India. Magarpatta City is built over 453 acres of land. It is home to a commercial zone, residential neighbourhoods, two schools, a multi-speciality hospital, a shopping mall, multiple restaurants, a gymkhana, and a large 25-acre serene park called Aditi Garden. It has eco-friendly development and green spaces that make up for 30 per cent of the area. It spans two postal zones: 411028 and 411013. It is indeed a city for the citizens of the 21st Century.

Magarpatta City is the first ever project in the history of real estate, where a group of about 120 farmer families converted their land into an enterprise, the first of its kind in the country. Spread over 400 acres of land, it includes a residential complex, hospital, shopping complex, school, restaurants as well as the top leading IT companies. About 10 years ago, this area was owned by farmers who were at risk of losing their land to urbanization. It was at this time that Mr Satish Magar, the chairman and managing director of Magarpatta city, who owned nearly 100 acres of the land, gathered all the families together, and convinced them to benefit from their land holdings. Now they are all the proud stakeholders, holding stakes directly proportionate to their land. Magarpatta city is a city which is not made by taking away the lands from the farmers, but it is made by the farmers.

Based on the 'walk-to-school, walk-to-work concept' Magarpatta City is an effort to ensure a convenient, enjoyable, and stress-free life for a family, providing all the basic amenities and facilities that a family would need. Children can walk to school thus reducing their travelling time. Special care is given to maintain the greenery, with about 120 acres of land being spared for gardens, trees, and various kinds of flora thus making it a pollution-free city and a beautiful place to live in.

Magarpatta has state-of-the-art Cyber city IT parks which enjoy the presence of leading global IT giants. Cyber city is blessed with international facilities. There are 12 towers and many other facilities which companies such as Amdocs, John Deere, Accenture, Mphasis, Avaya, WNS, EXL, and SYBASE. Refer to the link for a list of all the companies in Magarpatta City.

Based on the diamond analysis of the project classifications one can classify the project as specified below:

- Technology difficulty: T-4
- Complexity of design: C-5
- Novelty of the design: N-5
- Speed of implementation: S-4

Objectives of the project:

The objectives for the new organization set-up were as follows:

- To set up a new social initiative in Pune with the active participation of the original landowners to create a modern city with state-of-the-art infrastructure for the citizens of the 21st century.

- To create the futuristic infrastructure for the proposed city with all the facilities for the citizens of the new city being set up.

- To ensure that the farmers in the new organization become 'equity holders' and continue to earn income based on the growth and prosperity of the organization on a perpetual basis. This was a unique proposition and was being introduced in the history of the construction industry, and the country as such. There is no parallel project in the country that has promoted infrastructure projects by forming a commercial organization with the original landowners as shareholders of the company in proportion to the individual land holdings. This was a challenge indeed since there was neither a guideline nor any precedence in the matter in the entire country.

Mr Satish Magar (CMD) in a personal interview with the author said that "Keeping the trust of the equity holders in the new concept was a major challenge in all the sense of the term":

- To ensure that the proposed project makes use of the latest technologies and current innovations and ensure that the infrastructure can be maintained without any basic modifications for the next 50 years or more. This was also quite a challenge for the promoters/sponsors of this project.

- To generate a self-sustaining organization that will continue to generate profitable activities for the shareholders and keep them happy, supportive, and contended for days to come. (With this view in mind, the PM and promoters of the project formed an additional company that has been given responsibility for ensuring proper upkeep and housekeeping of the entire infrastructure and facilities planned in Phase 1 and Phase 2. This is a Herculean task because the complex is spread over 453 acres of land, with more than 400,000 square feet of commercial and housing complexes, over 150,000 citizens, and an additional 50,000, visitors daily. The subsidiary company manages security, housekeeping, maintenance and upkeep of all the equipment and facilities created in the project).

The key thought process behind the new concept for the project-pioneering work in India:

The core team under the leadership of Mr Satish Magar had a professional background in this industry and had seen all kinds of projects, infra projects (that were good/bad/ugly), and had seen the practical problems in the field. Since the promoters had their land & belonged to a traditional farming background, they had intimate knowledge about the issues and challenges the farming families faced in day-to-day life. They noticed that once the land is sold, the farmer's families spend a lot of money in the initial period and enjoy life. However, they have no proper plan as to how to utilize and invest the funds smartly. Hence, they again became bankrupt and lost what they had gained by selling their farming land. This is the typical story of every farming family that sold the land as a one-time sum and kept away from sensible, safe, and happy living. This was certainly not the best situation to be in for any farmer. Mr Satish Magar thought that all this should change for the better and hence he decided to work on a new model of the activity that could help change the fortunes of the farming families over a period.

The core team under the guidance of Mr Satish wanted to change this cycle to continue to make money for each farming family, in the regular monthly cycle. The journey was not pleasant, but untiring meetings and meaningful discussions with these families made it possible to change people's perceptions about the subject. Farmers and family members at this stage want to be part of the equity holders and would be glad to share the dividends based on the operations over the years. This adds to their wealth and continues to get returns on their basic investments in terms of the cost of land. This is a great advantage over the current arrangements and over a period local leaders from the villages and landowners accepted new schemes and methods.

This was indeed a great victory for the core group members and Mr. Satish Magar as the head of this newly conceived organization- the first of its kind in India.

The challenges of the project team:

The following points were noted based on the interaction with the project team members and Project Manager.

The author also had a detailed meeting with Mr. Satish Magar who is the main promoter of the newly formed organization and during the discussions, the author had a chance to ask him about the challenges faced during the project execution as such.

The key issues discussed are specified below for quick reference:

Internal issues and bottlenecks observed:

Some internal issues/aspects needed the attention of the project team, especially for the PM. Some of these issues are specified below:

- **Enlisting support and Commitment of the farmers and landowners as equity holders:**

This was one of the unique concepts in the Construction and Infrastructure Industry in the country and this was quite a challenge for the promoters of the proposed city project. Initially, the prospective shareholders and farmers had a lot of misgivings about the feasibility of the concept and thought that this was a ploy to acquire the lands at a very low price and the situation became very challenging for the founder's team.

The founder team decided to hold a series of meetings with the stakeholders and the families together with the entire team of promoters and explained to them endlessly the new concepts and the feasibility of the new project and shared with them the phase-wise plans and ways of financing the project till the phase 2. The older members had a completely negative attitude about the concept itself, but the younger members were willing to give this concept a try. Relentless efforts from the promoters helped people realize the new concept, its validity and practicality. Gradually the ice started melting and the people and village farmers saw light at the end of the tunnel. Patience on the part of the founding team paid results and there was an emergence of willingness to try the new concept.

The promoters also explained that they were investing their share in the form of their land in the project, and they would have the same rights as other shareholders, in proportion to their respective lands. This aspect was very convincing and hence all the members were willing to give it a try and were enlisted in the organization over a period. However, this 'new concept' in cooperation was the main hurdle in promoting this concept in the initial phase and took considerable time and effort on the part of the promoters. This effort took several years before the issues were sorted out to the complete satisfaction of the stakeholders, mainly the farmers who were willing to pool their lands for the project proposed.

Thanks to the founding members of the team, whose solid efforts over the years, have paid their contributions in many ways.

Permissions from Govt Authorities/Municipal Corporations/and other statutory authorities and completion of the other formalities:

The senior management of the newly formed company had decided from the beginning that they would complete all the formalities and certifications from the competent authorities in a clean and judicious manner and would refrain from cutting corners and making any adjustments.

Implementing such an approach posed few challenges in the beginning but was treated as the

way of working in the organization and the problems started melting away in favour of the newly formed organization.

One can easily appreciate that getting approval for such a huge and ambitious project is a herculean task and one has to face many impediments to obtain permissions. This is a tough task indeed. One of the major challenges was to obtain permission to set up such a modern city through a private enterprise. The Government authorities were also perplexed about such a new venture that was unprecedented in the history of the nation after independence in 1947. They were not at all convinced that such a project is feasible in terms of its practicality and acceptance (since there was no parallel in the recent history of the construction and infrastructure industry). The authorities involved in the approval process were not willing to put their career at stake for the approval since there was no history for this approach nor any guidelines. Issues were open and subject to different explanations.

Despite several visits and presentations made by the core team, the Government authorities, were reluctant to grant permissions and clearances from several ministries involved. Their basic problem with the proposal was that there were no guidelines, no rules, based on which the permission should be granted or refused. No senior authority was willing to approve the idea and sacrifice his career in the process. The situation was frustrating and confusing for them as well. Finally, after a lot of persuasion and repeated visits, the state decided to give it a try. Incidentally, during the tenure of the complete project, CMs changed 5 times, and part of the exercise had to be repeated again and again.

However, through untiring efforts and focus, the core team could obtain all the requisite permissions and certifications from the competent authorities. This however involved considerable delays and costs for the project organization. In the final analysis after the discussions with the project personnel, one can say that this was possible only due to transparency in all transactions, and a policy not to leverage anything additional from the current loopholes in the policies and regulations of the state Government. Someone may say that this was not the best way to obtain permission, but the promoters decided to stick to their values and principles despite many hurdles and finally succeeded in this endeavour. After numerous meetings and discussions/presentations, the permission was granted by the state.

Funding and bank finances was also a major challenge:

Like getting all the requisite permissions from the authorities, getting a nod from the banks and financial institutions was also a great challenge faced by the project team. The core team had to go through an agonizing period since the bankers were very reluctant to even look at the proposals submitted as they were more than convinced that such a project would not at all take off the ground. Additionally, the size of the fund's requirement was considerable and hence carried heavy risk in the transactions involved.

Nobody was willing to discuss even a basic feasibility report prepared and they thought that the idea itself was 'crazy' and had no chance of success in terms of practical reality. They thought that getting more than 1300 families and members to agree on the basic terms and equity-based activity was a 'no-no' case. This created a lot of frustration and anxiety for the promoters who had staked all their fortunes for the project. Approval was soon becoming a mirage for the team.

However, a breakthrough came when the CMD of the HDFC bank decided to look at the proposal and worked out several options for the funding needs of the project. Several business models and alternative modes of financing were worked out and finally, HDFC bank took a leadership position in supporting the project after carrying out due diligence for the project concept and the feasibility of this novel idea that was the first of its kind in the country. Once, one of the leading banks decided to support the project, other banks also decided to pitch in with the requisite funding. However, getting the right type of funding continued to be a challenge for the promoter team.

The challenge faced was the sheer 'size of the project':

This was the next challenge. One has to realize that the sheer volume/size and complexity of the project were enormous, and the issues involved had to be dealt with with due care and attention. Enthusiasm and dedication were not good enough to set up strong foundations for the success of the project. Very dedicated efforts and diligence were essential for ensuring proper planning and scheduling for the workmen and resources. **Proactive planning was the key aspect of the project's success.** The planning engineers involved in the project had to undergo proper training and orientation along with the change of conventional mindsets to handle such a challenging and voluminous project. One had to develop a helicopter view and an ability to deal with the details at the same time. This is not as easy as it may seem to be in the beginning. This was quite a challenge right from the beginning for the entire team. One can easily understand that the planning team had to keep the planning quite flexible but at the same time had to be reasonably accurate and realistic about the plans/schedules and estimates. Any wrong assumptions or mistakes would have significant implications on the costs and time schedules. This was quite a challenge for the planning team. However previous experience and dedicated efforts by a few of the core team members helped handle the situation well without any major hiccups or delays.

The complexity of the futuristic design and estimation efforts due to size/complexity & use of non-conventional approach to the entire project:

The complications increased further because the methods proposed for the project envisaged the use of state-of-the-art technologies. Some of the concepts proposed were never used in this type of infrastructure and construction activities. It was envisaged that the proposed township should not be required to undertake any structural modifications or new set-up for the next few decades (in fact for more than 50 years after the commissioning of the project). This was quite a challenge for the architects and engineers involved in the project at several locations and sub-projects. However, the good news is that the team has been able to cater to the needs of the stakeholders and will be able to stand their promises and honour their commitment.

The team of the promoters had to ensure that all the experts/architects and engineers in the project had the requisite skills/competencies and relevant experience before they were inducted into the team. Every new member in such teams was interviewed and short-listed personally by the CMD of the organization to ensure appropriate fit in terms of competencies/skills and the right attitude towards the challenges right from the beginning of the project.

Challenges related to Scope / Time and Costs (needs flexibility in approach):

Such projects of gigantic proportions undertaken by the PM render all the conventional methods and practices inadequate and insufficient. This is quite a challenge, as one can imagine since there is no precedence and standards for such innovative projects. The task at hand is quite challenging and highly onerous for the planning team. However, the good news is that for engineering tasks the standards are set and there is predictability for the technical and engineering tasks even for such gigantic tasks. Such a combination makes the drawing of the network diagrams a challenge and complex solutions need to emerge for such situations.

While discussing this point, Mr. Satish Magar the promoter explained that: "Under such an environment one had to adopt the completely flexible approach for planning and sometimes recast the scope/schedules and costs again and again without compromising the promise made to the citizens of the proposed city". This may sound against the basic approach and tenets of project management in the conventional sense, but keeping the basic direction the same, one had to make changes and sometimes significant changes to the scope of the proposed activity leading to a lot of changes for the projects. However, when the adoption of the best technologies and modern facilities are the critical success factors for the project, one needs to use flexibility in the approach to finalization of the scope (and hence schedules and costs). This was part of life at Magarpatta project, throughout the tenure of the project. One needs to understand that innovations and adoption of new approaches is a dynamic process in case of such projects and flexibility in our helps determine long-term success". However, flexibility also tends to increase costs and timelines for various project activities and tasks.

Getting a proper well-equipped office and basic infrastructure for running the new organization was not possible due to a lack of funds:

One can easily appreciate the difficulty faced by the PM in the initiating phases of such a project but very soon such facilities were created, and the PM insisted that the best modern facilities and tools were available to the team over a period. The funds were infused by the family members of the promoters right from the beginning. They were convinced about the success of the project and were willing to take risks. One must appreciate that giving empty promises is one thing but delivering all the commitments is not as simple, and the team has to ensure that someone is willing to take even such issues seriously and ensure conformance.

Setting up a flexible but effective organizational structure is one more challenge faced by the newly set up organization:

This is a perpetual challenge for any large project organization. Judicious choice of personnel and effective but flexible organization is the need for every large-sized project. Such a need demands able leadership and balance between 'people Vs tasks' issues for large project organizations.

Considerable efforts and discussions with experts led to the development of an organisational structure suitable for such a large project. However, getting the right fit of professionals with the right competencies/skills and experience was an additional challenge. However, this problem was personally handled by the CMD. He ensured that apart from technical skills due importance was given to candidates with the appropriate mindset for people to be inducted into the team. Although the problem was well managed, only the senior people had to spend the number of working days for every batch coming in.

Most of the operational management is done by site engineers. Without proper and well-oiled internal systems and control methods of work, it is difficult to carry out such a large project without problems. Futuristic engineering & Innovation:

One can appreciate that for any successful project, the core team members must be available for most of the key activities of the project continuously, at least in the initial few years. These organizations need very flexible but simple methods of work, and one cannot enforce corporate discipline in such voluntary organizations. Everything depends on personal priorities and the motivation of the individual members of the team of volunteers. This creates problems and impediments in the smooth working of many projects.

Considerable time and efforts were spent by the senior management personnel to ensure that the right type of systems and controls were developed in the newly formed organization to ensure proper work instructions, reviews of progress as per the plans and internal controls to ensure smooth working for the people at the site. The development of simple but effective systems paved the path for the success of the project. At this stage, it is pertinent to point out that planning had to be so deep and thorough that while planning for the pipes, pumps and control valves for water and other utilities, one had to plan for adequate sizes based on the next 50 years' needs and without additional costs. This aspect was seen physically by the author during the site visit. This is something which the country can be proud of.

Development of support infrastructure and support network of the vendors and sub-contractors was also a challenge for this project:

In the modern era, it is very important that any organization, public or private, must develop a good and reliable network of support organizations (in the form of resource providers, sub-contractors and vendors for specialized artefacts and services). In terms of modern project management practices, this aspect is seen as one of the CSFs for the success of any project.

PM and the core team decided that they would short-list the vendors judiciously and declared that for most of the services and supplies, they would develop and assign long-term relationships with the vendors, in fact as partners in the progress and spent a considerable amount of time and effort to develop such a network. The policy was to give the assured volume of workload on a long-term basis for all the partners in the group. The cost-plus base was chosen with the participation of the suppliers and the price formula was worked out on a long-term basis with most of the vendors. This policy and transparency in the transactions help the newly formed organization to generate an effective network of dependable vendors who would commit to required delivery times and maintain requisite standards of quality for the tenure of the project.

Effective Communication with internal stakeholders, project team and site personnel:

Effective communication is an important factor for the success of any project in the modern era. This point is already explained. One must note that as per one of the main surveys carried out about the failures of the projects, inadequate communication is one of the primary causes of the failure. The promoters of the project took a lot of care to ensure that the values/policies and plans of the organization were inculcated in the team members right from the beginning.

The senior management team ensured that the guidelines of the management were communicated as frequently as required to the working teams through small group meetings and briefings. This method was quite effective, supported by the internal methods and practices. Senior management took a lot of care to see that everyone was informed well in time about the plan and changes from time to time. This was critical for the success of the project at hand.

Winning customers (especially corporate customers as prospective buyers of the newly created complex):

This was an additional challenge for the promoters of the project. This was mainly because during the initial stages, everything was on paper only, and no real construction was ready. The customers had to commit large sums for the properties based on the trust and reputation of the promoters. Such reluctance reduced as the actual construction work began in full swing.

Attention to Quality Standards and Inspection to ensure that the project activities were carried out the first time:

Many organizations boast about high-quality standards and the quality of services provided. However, quality standards are more talked about than implemented at the field level. The senior management was highly concerned about ensuring that the promised quality standards were maintained at every stage of execution. The senior management emphasized the expectations about quality standards at every stage of the project activities and generated adequate resources to supervise the activities and maintain required standards. This was accepted as the norm of working over a period and then became the standard of organizational working. There is always a difference between talking about quality and implementing the same in all walks of life in an organization. This organization has achieved this difficult task by institutionalizing this mindset all over the organization. This is quite an achievement for such a large project.

Data management and analysis is another area which is expensive but essential for the project's success:

This has been an area that has received due attention right from the beginning of the project. One can easily appreciate that this area is rather critical to manage the project successfully.

This area continues to be crucial to manage the project activities successfully. A lot of care was taken by the senior management team to ensure that all the data (and transaction details) were captured and analyzed for the project progress reviews and proactive actions. The organization ensured that the IT systems were made available to all the functionaries and site teams. It is difficult to carry out the activities in a smooth way without effective IT Systems. This was set up based on all the tools and methods available for the effective working of the organization.

Social issues that could affect the success of the project:

- Any such an enormous size of project work generates a lot of social issues and bottlenecks for such a massive project. At times, political interference and social pressures can mar the speed and viability of the project due to many pressure groups operating in the society at large. This was known to the promoters, and they took all the care to ensure that such influences did not hamper the progress of work at any cost. Their contacts in society and network of well-wishers helped them avoid any such influences and complications.

- It was obvious that some of the self-appointed leaders would tend to misguide the farmers (shareholders in the new organization). These types of attempts were certainly made by such leaders and local influencers, but the organization stood the test of time. Such efforts were gradually nullified and everyone involved stood behind the promoters (realizing that the promoter also had a lot to lose if the project did not succeed). This is by no means a small achievement for the promoters.

- One peculiar issue for the project was to ensure that the sons and daughters of the shareholders should be given good jobs in the new complex. This was discussed and such persons were accommodated in many of the new jobs created in the new complex. This was highly appreciated by the family members and was a great morale booster in the process of enlisting their support for the overall welfare of the project. This also developed a permanent bond in the community.

- Local municipality authorities initially were apprehensive, but they also supported the concept and participated in the clearance process. The transparency in the basic approach and clean transactions helped get over the hurdles. The 'undeterred approach' of the leader helped win such battles. The senior management team went out of their way to enlist the support of the entire stakeholder community throughout the tenure of the project.

About the project:

Sr No	Project Characteristics	Comments
1	Size of the project:	615 million USD (INR 4000 crore in today's currency rates as Revenue Expenses based on initial capital expenses for the project).
2	People:	The core team of Senior managers included 6-8 core team members with more than 1236 families involved in the formation of the commercial enterprise who continue to be shareholders even now. It is amazing that even after so many years, not many families/farmers have divested their shareholdings to any other third party. The total workforce involved in the project activities was more than 10,000 workmen and supervisors apart from the vendors' personnel at their respective places of work. By and large, people expressed their satisfaction with being associated with this unique project.
3	Schedule:	The original plan was 7-8 years for phase 1 and an additional 5 years for the next phase and finishing work units at the 'Feasibility - Study'. It was estimated/expected that the pilot test would start right from the beginning and the speed of expansion would depend upon the response from the customers and support from various agencies. The approach was firm but flexible when required. However, as can be seen from the records, the concept was very well supported by society at large and many corporate organizations. This was possible only due to the flexible approach and untiring efforts of the initial team.
4	Classification of project:	This is a case of a new startup concept and the first of its kind in the country. After the success of this project, the government has now issued notification for such type of projects in the country, with this project being declared as the 'model' project.
5	High-risk project:	There were many uncertainties/risks in the project. The project was undertaken in a very hazy and uncertain environment without clarity about the government guidelines. Additionally, it was difficult to enlist the support of the stakeholders (more than 1600 as such) for such a new initiative and innovative concept. The response from the bankers and financial institutes was 'Luke-

		warm' in the initial stages and this was also a big risk in the project. The size of the project itself was also one of the main risks. Similarly, there was every possibility of political and social interference in the project. Indeed, the project was full of risks. The project was indeed risky in many ways, and 'hope' and detailed planning along with excellent communication, were the only mental & motivational resources based on which the project was undertaken by the group of 'experienced seniors'. Their faith in the concept produced excellent results.
6	Technology Choice / Maturity:	There was a specific thought-through plan to use state-of-the-art technology and modern methods for the project, as specified earlier. The promoters had all the confidence in new technology, and they supported bold and unconventional methods in the project with the motto 'First time right'. This was indeed not at all a trivial issue to handle. This conviction helped produce great results for such a huge project. There were many risks in this approach but with support from the senior management team, the project execution and design team handled the project to the satisfaction of the promoters and board members. This is credible by any standards for such a huge and complex infrastructure project.
7	No suppliers/ affiliates	The organization created a network of over 400-450 suppliers, and over a period treated them as partners in business, rather than mere suppliers. This indeed was a difficult task. However, the core members of critical suppliers were over 60 entities. These agencies were part of the regular formal communication, and their suggestion was analysed and acted upon during the project with due respect. Suppliers went out of their normal work to support the project in case of bottlenecks.
8	Logistics/ Clearances:	This was quite a challenge due to the time pressure to obtain appropriate 'Certifications / Registration / Licenses and permissions' were a challenge, as explained earlier. This was handled by assigning the tasks to various 'task force groups', and their work was coordinated through the corporate office.
9	Location for co-ordination:	More than 6 locations (Pune City has 4 locations & Work locations spread over a very large plot of land (> 453 acres) in site location in Magarpatta. Coordination was a challenge since the project organization was engaged in too many things at the same time.

10	Support from Sr. Mgt:	Senior management provided excellent and timely support in every aspect of the work cycle. Apart from conventional support, senior management also provided emotional and motivational support to all the workgroups by conducting focused meetings and briefing sessions. Funding was a challenge in the initial period due to a shortage of funds. Similarly, there was no specific admin support in the beginning. The promoters themselves were carrying out all the activities as and when possible. Initially, Admin Support & Motivational Support was received from the senior management and main promoters. The teams were given complete freedom for action and expenditures based on allocated budgets and policy guidelines. By and large, the teams were happy to work on the project.
11	Involvement of Customer:	There was mixed support / hesitant support from the 'Corporate Organizations and Banks, for such a novel project, but people were willing to listen and help. Over some time, they saw the quality of work and observed dedicated work done by the promoters and initial teams. This changed after experiencing initial progress. The customer teams were co-operative, from the funding stage onwards. They were willing to provide active support for the development of specifications and pilot studies at select locations. PM and the team had a difficult task to win over their minds in the initial stages. This made the situation quite complex for the project team.
12	Leader:	The program / Project Manager selected was a competent/committed person with high values and integrity. His self-confidence and conviction about the practicality of the innovative concept were the main strengths of the organization. This helped in the initial period. Her patience and professional approach to social work help solve many bottlenecks and impasse situations. The team of promoters was very supportive and took an active part in handling issues of teams and beneficiaries.

Key positions in the team:

The team had to be manned with the following key positions:

- Project Director / Project Manager as 'Project Champions' (The founders of this project organization).
- Team of 'Core members' of the initial management team.
- Team of town planners/architects and engineers from various functional disciplines.

- Module Leaders (4 initially and now over 12) for various critical aspects of the proposed project & modules.
- Training experts for soft skills and ethical behaviour and attitude-building exercises for the workgroups.
- Module / Field supervisors and site in charge.
- Treasurers managing financial issues/funding and auditors (advisors).
- Trustees' office for project tracking and liaison with customer teams and beneficiaries.
- Legal advisors and consultants.
- A panel of external consultants who were key members of the entire project 'Think Tank'.

Positives in the project environment:

- There was full support from promoters / senior management and families of the farmers who had ultimate trust in the leaders of this project concept.
- The focus of the team was very specific and worked toward a detailed implementation plan in cooperation with the vendors and suppliers.
- Continuous dialogue with Govt officials / Customer PM and local PM with resolve to address the issues immediately helped the team to complete the project in the required time. The senior managers from both sides attend project meetings monthly / quarterly to make decisions and move forward proactively. This was useful for the team.
- Harmonious teamwork paved the path for a good quality / undisturbed work environment. This was crucial for the success of the project.
- Pre-dispatch inspection for every delivery involving local and customer QA / QC teams helped hassle-free on-site implementation of the modules without delays and waiting periods.
- The team had full freedom for decision-making and commitment to expenses as per the decisions of the PM. This paved the path for smooth working for the team.

Project Success Criteria:

The project success criteria took into consideration customer expectations and organizational expectations:

- Organizational expectations
    - To complete the project in time without any compromise on quality of service.
    - To conform to stringent rules of Government and Semi-government authorities.
    - To achieve the project delivery for the targeted population as planned by the organization.

- To develop project modules as a model project so that they can become reference projects for future activities.
- Getting repeat requests from various communities where services were provided was an important organizational requirement.
- To introduce state-of-the-art technology and innovations where possible throughout the project.
- To maintain transparency and ethics in real sense of the terms in all activities.
- To make vendors network as partners in business with long-term contracts.
- To ensure that promises once made are honoured to all the stakeholders and 'no comebacks' on the promises.

- Customer / User Expectations
  - To ensure on-time delivery and implementation.
  - To achieve a committed target population and frequency of the project in the community service.
  - To achieve requisite accuracy & efficiency in operations that have a complex set of rules & changes.
  - To handle emotional and social issues effectively without interruptions.
  - To ensure the satisfaction of the team members Promoters / Volunteers / Staff and beneficiaries of the programs.
  - To ensure team satisfaction and development of new skills/domain expertise for the future.

Project Success Factors (as seen by the team members now):

Based on the discussions with the leadership team members and their PM it becomes clear that the list of the following points would have been useful for them as CFSs for this project. However, it should be noted that this aspect was not necessarily thought about comprehensively before the project started.

- Clarity about the task at hand & clarity about scope and specifications.
- Commitment and participation by the customer teams in the development of the right ecosystem throughout the tenure of the project life cycle.
- Complete support from the senior management & freedom for actions for project module leaders.
- Competent Project Manager & trusted team members.
- Alert Risk Management especially in the form of timelines and scope/changes. This was done well but was not up to the mark at all times/stages.

- Control over project progress issues through impeccable communication and coordination/reviews.
- Excellent support from PMO personnel for ruthless tracking of issues and resolving them.
- Strong support from Audit teams and process control (support received due to strong and matured processes in the organization that have been developed over a period) through frequent reviews and communications in the small teams working on the modules.
- Exceptional teamwork and untiring support from the founding members in the initial period.
- Good support from Legal Experts and Admin teams as and when required.

Conclusion: Highly successful project with few silver linings!

The project was evaluated as a great success in the first five years. Although good work was done for the beneficiaries, the original team of founder members were very happy about the internal processes and internal efficiency. They felt satisfied that true to their words they were in a position to deliver the promise to the farmer's families and ensured that all the stakeholders continued to benefit even now as shareholders of the organization and continue to prosper. The youth from these families have found themselves in lucrative jobs and future opportunities for growth. This is indeed a great achievement for the passionate promoters. The project has become a model for setting up such 'Smart Cities'. This project has won many prestigious awards in national and international forums. The organization has achieved a place of pride in the construction and infrastructure industry.

Learnings from the project:

- **The first learning is critical. When** committed and dedicated members once decide to take up a task on account of their conviction, 'difficult' starts becoming 'simple' and 'impossible' starts looking 'difficult'. This change is not possible without the direct involvement of the members and initial stakeholders. The Herculean efforts made by the senior founders' team and their mental/physical and financial patience paid rich dividends at the end of the project.
- It is very evident that the quality of the first team largely influences the nature of conviction about an idea and can pave a path for smooth progress if the team is of the requisite quality. This aspect, although may look so obvious, it needs to be implemented carefully in the project execution. This is crucial for the long-term success of the project endeavours. We know this but we tend to neglect it at times.
- Any new idea, even if it is good, will face resistance in the initial phase but patience alone is the solution for the same. The Socio-Political-Economic project under the review teaches us to be patient and show a lot of empathy for the issues raised by the stakeholders and their family members. Too much hurry or too much pressure may spoil the game plan right from the beginning. This is a great learning indeed.

- Making use of futuristic concepts and technologies poses additional challenges for the project team. This needs competencies such as visualization, innovation, and the ability to anticipate future needs. However, this project was handled by a team, committed to the cause and very competent in their respective fields, so that they could handle such needs and produce a futuristic project - a pride of the nation - from concept to reality. Kudos to such an endowed team.

- Managing effective communication and good image building with all important stakeholders is one more important aspect of such large projects. Constant dialogue and sharing of progress cards with all of them will create a long-lasting trusting relationship with them. This aspect has to be planned well and executed with ease and grace. This is not as simple as it may look and hence needs constant attention and time from the senior management. For the current project, this aspect was planned well and executed smoothly and effectively. For this project, critical stakeholders were farmers and family members, critical suppliers, bankers and funding agencies, various Government / Semi-Government authorities and offices, and society at large.

- Managing Funds Flows and seeking approvals from various statutory and local authorities was an onerous task for the project team. A lot of patience (Emotional, Political, Technical and Financial) was the essence of paving a path for future success. This aspect was handled by the project team in an exemplary way and managed very effectively. The financial aspect was very crucial and needed a lot of effort and patience but the breakthrough came when HDFC bank decided to support the new concept as explained earlier.

- One unique aspect of this case is the fact that the new concept / new ideas will always face opposition in real life. This is obvious, but your conviction and your focus on the new concept carry you through the period of opposition and difficulties. Your focus and your dedication to the cause will finally carry through although it may take a lot of time & effort. However, at the end of this gruelling period, it will make you successful. A lot of mental resilience and patience are required to see the end of the tunnel. The senior management, in this case, has shown such maturity and patience to finally get the case approved by authorities and bankers and have become winners in the process.

There is so much learning from such an important project that has now become a 'role model' for the professionals in the field of socio-political-economic subject matters Kudos to the founding members and the equity holders in the new concept-based modern, innovative organization.

Discussion Points:

The Importance of Initial Commitment and Conviction:

- How do the commitment and dedication of the initial team members impact the success of a project?
- Can you think of examples from other projects or initiatives where initial commitment played a crucial role?

Quality of the First Team and Long-term Project Success:

- In what ways does the quality of the initial team influence the success of a project in the long term?
- How can organizations ensure the careful implementation of assembling a high-quality team at the beginning of a project?

Handling Resistance to New Ideas:

- How can organizations effectively deal with resistance to new ideas, especially in the initial phases of a project?
- What are the consequences of being too hasty or applying too much pressure during the implementation of a new idea?

Challenges and Competencies in Implementing Futuristic Concepts:

- What competencies are essential when dealing with futuristic concepts and technologies in a project?
- How can teams foster a culture of innovation and visualization to anticipate future needs?

Effective Communication and Relationship Building:

- Why is effective communication crucial, especially in large projects with diverse stakeholders?
- Can you share examples of projects where effective communication positively influenced relationships with stakeholders?

Managing Funds Flows and Gaining Approvals:

- How do effective management of funds and seeking approvals contribute to the success of a project?
- What challenges can arise when dealing with financial aspects, and how can they be overcome?

Facing Opposition and Building Conviction:

- How can individuals or organizations maintain focus and conviction in the face of opposition and difficulties?
- Share examples from other industries or projects where resilience and patience led to eventual success.

Learning from Role Model Projects:

- What specific lessons can professionals in socio-political-economic fields learn from successful projects like the one mentioned?
- How can organizations adopt similar principles to become role models in their respective domains?

Balancing Patience and Urgency:

- Discuss the delicate balance between being patient and showing urgency in project management. How can this balance be achieved?

The Role of Senior Management in Project Success:

- How crucial is the role of senior management in steering a project through challenges?
- Share examples where senior management exhibited maturity and patience in overcoming obstacles.

These discussion points can serve as a foundation for exploring the various aspects of project management, leadership, and organizational success.

Case No 20: Development of a specialized software platform for 'Metallographic Inspection' (With the help from a foreign customer) for the first time in the world in a new startup software unit

Dr Jayasri Murali, Dr Vinod Bhelose

Associate Professor, MBA@IICMR, Pune, Assistant Professor, MBA@IICMR, Pune

Extract: Inaugurated by a fledgling 'Start-Up Software Company,' their pivotal debut project carried immense complexity and risk. The project's success was paramount, as its failure could spell closure for the entire organization. Partnering with a renowned client, a leading manufacturer of 'Metallographic Instruments' in Europe, specializing in high-precision applications for industries like Steel, Auto Parts, and Aeronautical Engineering, the challenge was formidable. The solution required a multidisciplinary approach, blending Physics, Optics, Mechanical and Metallurgical Engineering, Mathematics, Software, and QA/QC. Navigating uncharted territory, the project demanded a unique team of specialists, grappling with unforeseen setbacks and modifications, underscoring the intricate nature of pioneering technological advancements.

Introduction:

This was a project initiated by a new 'Start-Up Software Company' and the first project signed up by this organization was a very complex and challenging project. This project was indeed so important for the new start-up organization that if this failed the existence of the organization could lead to the closure of the Project and the Organization. The success of this project was certainly crucial for the organization.

The Client in this case had the reputation as the leading manufacturer of 'Metallographic Instruments' for QA / QC applications in Europe and the rest of the world with offices in the UK, Germany and a few other countries. The R&D units were operating out of UK & German labs. The customer organization had a high reputation for the quality & accuracy of their products. They supply a range of microscopes for high-quality control applications in Steelmaking, Auto Parts and Aeronautical Engineering applications. The basic application was in the form of use in 'Metallographic Usage' which demands a high level of accuracy and consistency for the analysis of metal additives and impurities in base metals. On many occasions, this method was also put to use to determine the metal compositions and the metal characteristics. The applications are very sensitive and demand a high level of products for such high-tech applications.

This organization was using certain rudimentary software along with the microscopic images and digital inputs available from the complex equipment that was used for completing part of the processes and for interpretation of some of the inputs available from the instruments. The project was set up after the start-up organization could complete many components successfully for the system and the customer was convinced about the competence of the Indian company.

The challenge at hand was significant and very complex. The proposed solution involved a multi-disciplinary approach and would involve multiple disciplines that included Physics, Optics, Mechanical Engineering, Metallurgical Engineering, Basic Geometry and Mathematics associated with, Software Discipline and QA / QC and finally integration of all these aspects to be built into the new platform being conceived. A challenge indeed by any standards!

The PM had a tough job of locating such experienced specialists and then enlisting the support of such Subject Matter Experts (SMEs) and other professionals. Such members had never worked together since this was the first of its kind development. The client was in the process of developing new equipment and this platform had to work seamlessly with the new system being developed. This complicated the project specifications further and generated several additional challenges as well. Due to the development phases of the new artifacts, there were many situations that the team encountered where they had to back to the drawing board and start all over again in case of a few situations. Such changes certainly affected the time and cost estimates and kept the entire team on tenterhooks throughout the tenure of the project.

Indeed, this was a challenging project. Based on the diamond analysis of the project classifications one can classify the project as specified below:

- Technology difficulty: T- 4
- Complexity of design: C- 5
- The novelty of the design: N- 5
- Speed of implementation: S- 4

The specifications for the proposed system were prepared by the powerful / technically astute group of consultants of repute in consultation with the client's technical committee. The proposed system and its variants were expected to be used in various high-tech environments and had very stringent technical specifications. It was specified that the system was designed and built in India.

About the project:

Sr No	Project Characteristics	Comments
1	Size of the project:	@ 0.54 million Pounds (INR 6.5 crore in today's currency rates)
2	People:	8 members in the core team with about 4 SMEs and 3 QA / QC experts (total strength of around 15-17 persons including support staff allocated)
3	Schedule:	Less than 20 months (when the original estimate was around 14 months). In reality, it took around 24 months. Still, this was an achievement.
4	Classification of project:	R&D project with field implementation (first of its kind in India if not in the world). This was a complex and difficult technical project and there are not many references of such kind and India.
5	High-risk project:	There were many uncertainties due to the new design and high-time "Pressure". Market prestige and organizational reputation were at stake hence there was no chance of failing. The pressure was too much. Some risks include financial risks / technical risks and the sheer fact that the solutions had to be out-of-the-box solutions.
6	Technology Choice / Maturity	This was the first of its kind effort and hence the approach was to develop this new application. Although some of the platforms and tools were known it was a new R&D effort and technology was not matured at all. Hence this was the main technology-based challenge for the project team.
7	No of suppliers:	Several consultants and SMEs were involved in the project and they had a significant role in the completion of the project. These persons acted as part of the team and provided active support. Such entities were about 6-8 for the entire tenure of the project.
8	Logistics / Clearances:	This was quite a challenge due to time pressure and the fact that trial and test platforms had to be imported into India and this was quite time-consuming and complex despite active support from the senior management. Import – Export procedures and documentation took a lot of effort. However, once the importance of this project was explained and understood by the authorities, they helped to clear the matters ASAP. This was possible only on account of effective PR work done by a few of the senior team.
9	Location for co-ordination:	More than 4 locations were manned with project team members. The coordination was tough but was managed very well by the PM and team members.

10	Support from Sr. Management:	Excellent support and timely funding/admin support & motivational Support. The team was given complete freedom for action and expenditures.
11	Involvement of Customer:	High involvement from customer personnel and keen participation due to the nature of the project and the impact on the organization. On many occasions, the technical experts from the partners abroad, visited India to clarify issues or to finalize the scope of some of the critical modules. This was indeed a great gesture from their side.
12	Project Director / Leader:	Very competent/committed R&D professional with a good Track record. He had worked with the Foreign Labs and worked there on complex R&D projects for international projects.

Key positions in the team:

The team had to be manned with the following key positions:

- Project Director / Manager.
- Manager (R&D) at HQ in foreign Labs.
- 3 Module Leaders (R&D) with support team members.
- Quality Leader / Site Quality Leader.
- Technical Manager with requisite engineering exposure in material sciences and software activities.
- Accounts Manager for the financial issues/funding and logistics support (logistics involved that was quite complex due nature of the complex and multi-location-based project).
- PMO office for project tracking and liaison with the customer team.
- SMEs (4) from various disciplines (especially metallurgy and materials sciences and optics and digitization with adequate model-building experience).
- Training in charge.

The challenges of the R&D team:

The main challenge for the R&D was the design & development of computerized/automated 'Metallography Inspection' with a digital data interface. One needs to note that such software was not available even to the customer and the new concept was being developed for the first time. It was difficult to estimate the time for completion of the task at hand. This is mainly because the output of the project was not known with certainty and this was indeed a challenge. The current software (which was rudimentary and was developed only for the old artefacts) was not adequate considering the development of new artefacts at European R&D Labs. Additionally, this was the first of its kind design and system integration effort with new technology components proposed by the customer team. Both the teams were in different phases of learning and this indeed was a challenge by itself.

The team members (15-16 persons) were highly qualified young professionals who had great trust in the competence & expertise of their leader. They were all willing to walk extra mile to ensure the success of the project at any cost. This was a major factor in favour of the project. The leader of the team was a committed competent professional who had an impeccable R&D record and contribution towards the success of the department in the past. The leader plus only 3 senior module leaders had requisite field experience with International projects. This was an additional constraint since many of the team members did not have the requisite exposure and experience with this type of project.

This was a high-risk project for the organization since failure would amount to possible displeasure and loss of face for both the organizations (Local partner and Foreign Principal). Failure of the project would lead to a loss of image and business / financial loss. This would be a fatal blow to the organizations involved. The concerned senior person (Project Director) had warned the Project Manager / Project Leads to spare no efforts for the project in the initial stages since he thought that the risk involved was too onerous. However, the team leader had full hope and confidence that his team could deliver the project on time and at the level of quality expected by the customer.

The proposed Lab indicated earlier was developing this system for the first time in India. The technology components, although worked upon by the principal labs abroad, it was being developed as an integrated system for the first time in India for an international group was a challenge indeed. The local lab, although good for conventional development, was not equipped for the proposed system testing. This compounded the difficulties faced by the team.

The foreign Design & Development lab was willing to provide all the necessary back-end support but they had no hands-on experience with this type of specific bespoke / customized design integrated system. They would supply a few of the important key components for the newly conceptualized system but had no field experience in integrating such components with the new design. This was also a challenge in the sense that the Indian R&D team had to depend on their knowledge and experience to complete the design and successfully implement the project.

The issues and challenges faced by the project team:

The issues and challenges can be summarized as follows:

- The first-of-its-kind design was being adopted by both organizations & hence a high-risk project with the use of new technology for the newly designed version of the 'Specialized Microscope'. The main challenge was the lack of adequate knowledge and experience in the specific aspects of technology. This was the main challenge and was handled through extensive training of all the team members involved and peer-to-peer testing methods before the actual engineering design was incorporated into the final solution. This helped the members to appreciate various issues before these were adopted in the final solution.

- The training was conducted based on the following methods:
  - Classroom training for every member and assignments carried out using CFTs for pilot mini projects (Brainstorming and learning together). This was very useful.
  - Continuous interaction between UK & German experts and the Indian Team with a lot of visits during the 'concept design and finalization stage'.
  - Participation of the experts from the UK & Germany at the Indian development centre during the finalization stages.
  - Hand-holding by foreign experts on the older version of the artefacts that were brought to India only to get hands-on experience (although on the old version).
  - Discussions and dialogue with Academicians in the initial phase.
  - The training efforts made in the initiation stages were very useful and helped the local team to start the work and reach some of the milestones in time.
- Tremendous time pressure on the entire team due to a shortage of time and new design changes leading to a series of re-engineering needs and rechecking of changes & impact (Engineering Changes) in the newly designed artifacts abroad in UK & German labs. The concurrent development of the new version of the artefact in UK & German Labs and the development of the software platform in India was quite complex and frustrating at times for the team. However, the customer team required patience and experience to support foreign teams. They were very understanding about time estimates and inherent delays involved in new dynamic product development situations. Foreign support & patience was critical for the local team to complete various tasks and recheck.
- Lack of detailed knowledge was one of the initial problems at the beginning of the project. The technology involved is not day-to-day usage-based activity and getting a few of the Subject Matter Experts (SMEs) on board was also a major challenge. However, once these experts were on board, they trained the entire team to understand the basic principles and issues involved in the approach adopted for this innovative project. This helped smooth the pressure and the team started understanding the nuances involved in the project.
- Risk management was carried out systematically and the 'risk status' was reviewed in every meeting. However constant changes in the designs and approach to development generated new possible risks and hence the 'risk analysis' had to be carried out on a dynamic basis. This was a challenge indeed since there was an eminent problem estimating the impact of changes on the overall project due to a lack of previous knowledge.
- Very high-risk project with uncertainty in many other respects apart from engineering challenges. The main challenge was project planning from two perspectives:
- Time estimates were fluid due to changes in the basic artefacts being developed and due to concurrent engineering involving HW and SW.

- Cost estimates for the efforts (need for a balanced approach to costing otherwise the project would not be viable).

- This problem was solved by using the 'Rolling Wave Planning' concept. The project was divided into three main phases:
  - Project initiation and its concept development and concept approval phase.
  - Execution and development phase.
  - Support and fine-tuning phase .

- The problem was handled partially by ensuring that the 'time' and 'costs' were finalized for each phase or part of the phase and this was taken as the budget for that phase or part of the phase. At the end of the phase, a meeting was conducted to forecast the remaining part of the phase and then budget for the next phase and this process was repeated with the rolling wave planning method. Every phase was quoted and finalized based on a fixed cost model and the same procedure was adopted throughout the tenure of the project.

- However, the team spirit and confidence to win were major factors that led to the success (partially for many features) of the project. The project manager during the discussions emphasized that without the requisite 'flexibility' in terms of scope /time and costs for the project, it would have been difficult to complete this type of project. Flexibility in scope, time, cost and approach was of the essence for the success of the project. This was very well understood by the senior management team and they supported the team through the tenure of the project.

- No previous experience even for the foreign R&D set up although they had good knowledge of the technology as such. Since the design was new even the foreign lab experts were also not too sure about the exact specifications for the modules to be developed in India. However, there was excellent understanding and cooperation between the Indian am of the development team and R&D personnel in the UK & Germany. The frequent visits from the foreign labs were very useful in clarifying doubts and developing a workaround.

- The Indian team had good young professionals but only three senior leaders who had exposure to the international standards and practices for such complex projects. However, the induction of the SMEs in the team was very welcome and together they were able to manage the completion of the task at hand.

- The main challenge was to get 'testing platforms' in India. In the absence of such facilities, it was very difficult to get a feel of the correctness of the modules being developed in India. Certain basic facilities were set up in India at the beginning but this was not complete and hence a lot of issues came up leading to delays.

- Set up for lab testing was not at all adequate in India and hence it was decided to carry out final testing at the site which was certainly risky. However, this was decided because there was no other go. The team made additional components and extra materials for changes at the site. This was a good move since some of the imported components and sub-systems did not work at the site and had to be altered at the site with an innovative approach.

- The SMEs inducted played a very crucial and supportive role and were available throughout the project tenure. They responded very well and supported the project because of the National prestige involved in the matter.

- Multi-location-based activities gave rise to many locations and co-coordination communication became difficult. However, with good support from senior management and the freedom to commit expenses for coordination, the problem was handled effectively. Flexibility for both scope and costs was the main factor that led to the partial success of the project.

Positives in the project environment:

- The scope of work and systems specifications were thoroughly discussed/refined and confirmed with the participation of customers and their consultants throughout the project period. The change management system was ruthlessly followed and immediate communication was sent to all the concerned for them to know about the changes. Feedback and confirmation about the same were meticulously followed by the team. This was one of the major cornerstones that laid the foundation for the success of the entire project.

- The customer team along with the consultants had carried out detailed analysis of the need and specifications for the proposed system. The Project Director / PM and key team members were also called for a detailed briefing on the project requirements and basic needs. The feasibility report was prepared with great details and the customer team was very confident that the proposed solution could be built in India although it was being produced for the first time in India.

- The PM had full authority to commit funds based on the project needs. Luckily finances and funds were not at all a constraint. This made life relatively simpler for the project team.

- There was full support from senior management and foreign partners and labs for such a complex project. The team was given the required flexibility for deciding 'scope/timelines/ costs' and that was very crucial for maintaining high spirits and motivation of the team. The team spirit was very high and people were willing to work extra time to complete their efforts to complete the project on time.

- Many innovative ideas were generated to simplify the design and avoid pitfalls. This was welcome and was supported by the pm and senior management.

- The process engineering part was handled well due to matured processes in the parent organization.

- Quality Assurance (QA) processes and QC activities were managed very well due to process maturity in the customer organization. The customer organization had provided for training QA / QC personnel at their labs to ensure consistency in test procedures.

- Communication and coordination were given high importance and were conducted well with due attention to detail.
- Risk Management was mainly in the form of specifications /changes & timelines. These were managed personally by the PM with the help of the PMO office and a trusted senior colleague who offered excellent support to the PM.
- The site task was made relatively easier by the active participation of the customer agencies and their consulting teams. They provided all the necessary help and logistical support at the site to ensure the proper conduct of testing activities at the site. This was indeed welcome and helped the project team.

Project Success Criteria:

As per the discussions with the team members and the PM the following aspects were pre-fixed as the success criteria for the project in consultation with the customers and their consultants:

- Timely delivery of the systems without any compromises to the technical aspects. Where required the changes in need specifications were discussed with market analysts. 100 % conformance to the specifications of the proposed systems was the essence of the project.
- Satisfaction of all the customers/consultants and senior management of the project.
- Satisfaction of the suppliers for the project with reasonable margins for them along with appreciation for their contributions to a nationally prestigious project.
- Satisfaction & appreciation of the project team.
- Satisfaction of the principal HQ and R&D personnel.

Project Success Factors:

Based on the discussions with the team members and their PM it becomes clear that the list of the following points would have been useful for them as CFSs for this project. However, it has to be noted that at the time of the project execution, such a list was not prepared formally. However, based on the experience of the team members and discussions with customer teams the list of important factors was prepared and kept track of during the tenure of the project.

The list of CSFs identified is specified below for reference:

- Need for reliable "Feasibility Study".
- Clarity about the task at hand & clarity about scope and specifications and the need for flexibility in the analysis of Scope / Time Lines / Costs .
- Commitment and participation by the customer teams .
- Complete support from the senior management .
- Competent Project Manager & trusted team along with active participation of SMEs involved .

- Alert Risk Management especially in the form of timelines and design/changes.
- Full support from the SMEs or the respective activities.
- Smart and timely support from the respective managers who worked very closely with the PM.
- Control over project progress issues through impeccable communication and coordination.
- Excellent support from PMO personnel for ruthless tracking of issues and resolving them.
- Strong support from QA / QC teams and process control engineers and support received due to strong and matured processes in the parent organization.
- Exceptional teamwork and untiring support from the task force members.

Conclusion: Very positive success:

The project was not an outstanding success considering the success criteria specified above but can be classified only as a partial success if we consider critical success factors (CFTs).

However, this project completion was highly appreciated project from all the stakeholders involved in the project situation. This is mainly because a new market visit was opened due to successful completion. Both the teams and labs were really happy since they had achieved something significant in terms of technical breakthroughs achieved by the researchers and engineers involved in the project. The inaugural launch of the first version was well received but internally everyone in senior management was not completely satisfied with the achievements.

The system developed by the R&D group in India was adopted as a standard system offering the world over by the parent organization and they also highly appreciated the efforts and untiring efforts made by the team for the overall success of this project. However, the PM and Project director, both rated the project as 'partial success' and not as complete success.

Learning from the project:

- The project at hand indicates that if there is good cooperation between the Customer and The Vendor it is quite possible to handle a complex and time-consuming issue that can be managed effectively. This is an important learning for both the Customer and the Supplier.
- It is yet again proven through this project that basic flexibility (in terms of scope and other basic parameters for the project) is essential for complex and technically difficult projects. It is also pertinent to notice that when many parameters change in an environment it may be useful to go back to the drawing board and re-establish the feasibility of the project concept all over again. This is called 'Dynamic Feasibility' and may be a very useful concept for very large and complex projects.

- It is evident that without the sterling contribution of Consultants and Subject Matter Experts (SME), the project would not have been successful. This case supports this observation in a significant way. One should realize that in technically complex projects taking help from SMEs and external experts is useful and critical. Senior Management Personnel must take the right lessons from this and learn to make good use of such experts despite the high costs associated with this.

- One unique aspect of this case is the fact that the new concept / new ideas will always face opposition in real life. This is obvious, but your conviction and your focus on the new concept carry you through the period of opposition and difficulties. Your focus and your dedication to the cause will finally carry through although it may take a lot of time & effort.

- In complex situations such as this case, it is essential to set up requisite test facilities for QA / QC purposes. This may look insignificant but it is the backbone based on which success can be achieved.

- This project required a 'multi-disciplinary approach' to define the scope of work and also the possible approach for building the final solution. Note that such an approach will work only if the team as such has excellent interpersonal relationships and harmony. It is therefore essential that such leaders who manage such projects must develop this skill. This is an important learning from this project. In the modern era, many projects are being handled that need such an approach hence this is important learning for project professionals.

- One can notice that the Project Manager –a senior professional was given all the authority and was allowed to make decisions in the best interest of the project. One can note that for such a complex project it is essential to give full authority to the PM and backup for his decisions is provided by the senior management. This is great learning from this case study.

- Logistics and Distribution of info also form an integral part of such a complex project where multi-location-based offices had to be in constant touch and had to share a lot of critical info about the project, especially scope and possible ways to provide solutions. In this case, the additional burden was to clear import-export consignments efficiently to avoid time delays. This aspect was handled effectively in this project.

- The importance of 'Excellent Communication' is one more critical aspect that needs constant attention from the senior management team to ensure the ongoing success of such projects. This aspect was very well handled in this project and helped generate efficient communication, sharing of critical information and a common understanding of the project status all across locations for the project.

Discussion Points:

The Significance of Customer-Vendor Cooperation:

- Discuss the importance of good cooperation between the customer and the vendor in handling complex and time-consuming projects.

- Share examples from other projects where effective collaboration between customer and vendor positively impacted project outcomes.

The Role of Flexibility in Complex Projects:

- Explore the concept of basic flexibility in project scope and parameters, especially in the context of complex and technically challenging projects.

- Discuss the idea of 'Dynamic Feasibility' and its relevance in re-evaluating project concepts when environmental parameters change.

The Contribution of Consultants and SMEs:

- Analyze the critical role played by consultants and subject matter experts (SMEs) in the success of technically complex projects.

- Discuss the challenges and benefits of integrating external experts into project teams and the importance of senior management's support.

Navigating Opposition and Challenges to New Ideas:

- Delve into the challenges faced when introducing new concepts and ideas, emphasizing the importance of conviction, focus, and dedication to overcome opposition.

- Share examples of other projects where perseverance in the face of opposition led to eventual success.

Establishing QA/QC Test Facilities in Complex Projects:

- Highlight the significance of setting up requisite test facilities for QA/QC purposes in complex projects.

- Discuss how seemingly insignificant aspects, like QA/QC facilities, can serve as the backbone for project success.

Importance of Interpersonal Relationships in Multi-disciplinary Approach:

- Explore the need for a multi-disciplinary approach in complex projects and the importance of excellent interpersonal relationships within the project team.

- Discuss how project leaders can develop interpersonal skills to foster harmony among team members.

Empowering Project Managers in Complex Projects:

- Discuss the critical role of empowering project managers with full authority and backing from senior management in complex projects.
- Share examples of successful projects where giving authority to the project manager proved instrumental in project success.

Effective Logistics and Distribution of Information:

- Examine the challenges and solutions related to logistics and distribution of information in multi-location projects.
- Discuss how efficient handling of import-export consignments can contribute to avoiding time delays in project execution.

Importance of Excellent Communication:

- Highlight the critical role of excellent communication in the ongoing success of complex projects.
- Discuss specific communication strategies employed in the mentioned project and their impact on information sharing and project understanding across locations.

These discussion points can foster conversations around key learnings and insights from the project, encouraging participants to share their experiences and perspectives on managing complex and challenging endeavours.

Case No 21: NM- Development of a specialized / customized IT platform for the National Stock Exchange (NSE) to ensure higher latency for the exchange (that is crucial for the efficient working of the National Stock Exchange (NSE)) for the first time in India

Dr Jayasri Murali, Dr Dipti Sharma

Associate Professor, MBA@IICMR, Pune, Assistant Professor, MBA@ IICMR, Pune

Extract: The National Stock Exchange (NSE) in India, a pioneering organization in stock exchange services, strategically invested in an IT trading platform to handle increased transaction volumes. Addressing challenges, the project emphasized meticulous planning and cautioned against unwarranted pressure from senior management. For complex ERP projects, dual-level planning, meticulous data compilation, and clarity on the scope of work were deemed essential. Cultural differences between customer and home office teams were resolved with patience. Training fostered a positive team atmosphere. A test facility, logistics support, and comprehensive technical documentation were crucial for success. The project successfully navigated the transition to a new system with effective communication and stakeholder engagement.

Introduction:

The National Stock Exchange (NSE) is one of the prestigious and pioneering organizations in India dedicated to providing stock exchange services to the investor and trading community in the country and thus serving the society at large. This organization has, strategically invested in building the IT trading platform, right from the inception to ensure efficient working of the exchange keeping in focus international benchmarks. The activities of the exchange have been successful over the years and the constant problem for them has been to improve the 'Latency' of their IT application considering the phenomenal increase in the volume of transactions (going from 10K per minute to around 50K transactions per second) the organization decided to undertake these project.

NSE: A cut above the rest: Special Features:

- The world's largest derivative exchange ahead of NYSE EURONEXT and NASDAQ.
- Over 14 million out of 30 million Indian taxpayers trade on NSE.
- Installed 2,00,000 trading terminals - the highest in the country.
- 45% of retail cash market turnover comes from Tier-III cities showing penetration.

NSE New Application: 'Nirvana' Status (as said by Mr Ravi Apte - CTO of NSE):

- Runs the world's largest electronic speed highways connecting 2,000 towns and cities.
- Implemented horizontal scalability to handle 10 times the current order flow.
- Trading at the speed of light, can handle two billion order messages per sec (the capacity or Latency).
- Has a co-location facility for over 200 racks.
- Each rack handles 2-3 servers, each server can trade for over Rs 200 crore worth of transactions.
- Among few exchanges doing real-time risk management.
- Facilitates tick-by-tick data feed, useful for high frequency or 'Algo' trading.
- Operates one of the country's largest private cloud 'NOW' with 36,000 daily log-ins.

Note the following from the interview of the CTO of NSE and the Program manager about this project and the results obtained:

"The country's premier stock exchange is no stranger to rosy adjectives, but even the ardent admirers of the National Stock Exchange (NSE) would not have thought of the one coined by Ravi Apte, its chief technology officer. NSE, according to Apte, has "attained nirvana" in technology.

"Trading speed on NSE is close to the speed of light. And this is the limit," he says. That's a significant competitive advantage in the exchange business where the name of the game is the pursuit of trading milliseconds ahead of the competition. So, if the London Stock Exchange (LSE) claims to have the fastest trading engine, executing orders in 124 microseconds, NSE's platform can trade at latency close to the speed of light. Latency is the time taken for order matching and confirmation of trade after a client's key the data. NSE has a Pan-India, high-speed network, which supported more than 200,000 terminals as of September 30, 2016.

Ravi Apte says "Since it's impossible to increase the speed further, the exchange is now focusing on horizontal scalability by increasing the count of its trading engines. Horizontal scalability is just like widening the lanes after building an express highway to handle more traffic. NSE stands out in this race as many exchanges (in the US and Europe) are still hung up on latency to win and keep their clients.

NSE has become the world's largest derivative trading platform for the number of contracts traded on its platform. It was ahead of NYSE EURONEXT and NASDAQ OMX of the US and the Korea and Shanghai exchanges. Data from the World Federation of Exchanges showed that more than 735 million contracts were traded on NSE from January to June (ref year 15-16).

Apart from the Nifty index, NSE's most tracked derivative index with an ecosystem comprising exchange-traded and index funds, the exchange offers trading in a wide basket of products. These include derivatives on the world's most tracked indices, like the S&P 500, Dow Jones Industrial Average and FTSE 100.

NSE currently operates with 10 trading engines and handles 450 million orders every day with 50,000 order messages per second for trading across asset classes. It can scale it to more than 200,000 messages and manage 10 times the current orders, retaining the round-trip latency in milliseconds, says Apte who has been with NSE for over six years now. Trading speed on BSE is less than 10 micro-seconds and the exchange's new trading system - BOLT - handles more than 20,000 orders per second and 100 million orders every day.

High-frequency trading in the US accounts for nearly 30 per cent of trades, but it started in India after NSE offered a co-location facility in 2010. Between 15-20 per cent of derivative volumes on the exchange are done through algorithmic trading. The exchange has sold rack space to more than 60 members while rivals have not managed to attract much attention. Exchanges host subscriber's server close to their trading engines through co-location to achieve speed. Brokers using it get a price feed every three milliseconds compared to the one in a remote place, which gets the same every 30 to 40 milliseconds.

NSE, however, is confident of holding on to the trading volumes. Apart from the head-start given by its secure trading highway, Apte says NSE is among a few to follow real-time risk management. This makes the trading highway among the most secure globally. "We have also installed several filters to check a flash crash like in the US," Apte says.

High-frequency trading has been under a regulatory cloud as algorithmic trading can play havoc while exchanges push for speed. But NSE says its systems check 300 million portfolios continuously during the day for any possible error and ensure that margin requirements of members are met at all points of time by analysing trends in price changes. Once the trading member limit has been utilised to the extent of 70, 80 and 90 per cent of their margin deposit, the exchange flashes a warning message and shuts trading terminals at 100 per cent margin utilisation. Other risk containment measures include monitoring member performance and track record.

Technology has helped in many other ways. Latest data show that investors from Tier-III cities contributed more than 45 per cent of the total cash market retail turnover in 2011- 12 on NSE, which has more than 2,00,000 trading terminals in over 2,000 towns and cities. Besides, these cities account for more than half the total retail investor base on NSE. No surprise that its trading terminal, NOW (Neat on Web), is among the largest private clouds in the country with more than 36,000 log-ins daily.

Project description as specified by the Project / Program Director:

The Problem: In just 4 years, the National Stock Exchange of India Limited (NSE) has had to deal with the tripling of transactions to handle, from 50 million messages to 150 million messages. The NSE had to design a new system that would be more effective than the current one, made in a new generation programming language, and capable of scaling its capacity to meet the current & future data demands of this fast-expanding trading network.

The Solution: A new system was designed that had a set of functionally independent sub-systems that could communicate with each other using a messaging framework that is low latency. The new system runs on an open-source Linux operating system, is implemented using a modern programming language and can run on commodity hardware instead of mainframes. A modern matching system was rolled out, which acts as the "heart" of the trading platform, implementing business rules and matching orders to each other.

The Result: The new system is handling 7 times the throughput of the old system, and has been able to bring down the latency by 40 times! Also, the new system has moved the NSE out of reliance on legacy infrastructure and propriety operating systems. Since a modern language has been used to implement the system, it is efficient, maintainable, and futuristic.

The Project Complexity and Challenges:

One can understand that with such out-of-the-world scope of work (complex and intricate projects) and expectations for a very high level of latency, the project was very challenging. The results expected out of this project were to achieve a specific level of latency based on international benchmarks. The organization could buy the solution from international vendors. **However, it was decided that the proposed solution would be developed in India and by the internal team of NSE. This was a very significant challenge indeed!**

The specifications for the proposed system were prepared by the powerful / technically astute group of consultants of repute in consultation with the client's technical committee consisting of professionals with international experience in similar development projects. The proposed system and its variants were expected to be used in various high-tech environments and had very stringent technical specifications. It has to be noticed/specified that the system was expected to be designed and built in India despite reservations from a few members of the senior management group and a few board members. However, the chairman of the company had a lot of faith in the technology team (CTO + Project director and his team) and decided to give the go-ahead to the internal team to undertake such a 'Herculean Challenge' based on the fact that it will lead to the development of international reputation for the organization and would result in the savings of significant proportion if it was carried out internally. The international price would have been around 500 Cr INR in comparison to an internal estimate of around 200 Cr INR. There was a big risk involved in this decision but the chairman decided to back up the internal team for this project.

The team had an onerous task at hand. The team decided to make a detailed plan for the project and developed confidence that the task at hand, although difficult based on the technical expertise of the internal team and some help from the international experts, could be handled effectively by the internal team. This confidence was crucial for the project team. A detailed project plan was prepared after the 'Feasibility' and 'Technical Compatibility' of the proposed solution was established by resorting to steps such as POC and pilots for the critical subsystems and routines. This step took over 6 months and the team was pleased with the results of the POC and Pilots for selective modules. After a rigorous review, the senior management gave final clearance for the final project with full support and requisite funding with flexibility. The team had developed detailed plans along with a fair amount of flexibility built into the plans considering various complex issues and time pressure.

Based on the experience and the insight developed the team decided on the project plan for the 36 months. Each step was worked out in detail (WBS + Resource allocations + Risk identification and mitigation). The team decided to work based on Basic Plan A along with Plan B and Plan C as backup plans right at the planning stage (considering the criticality and prestige involved in the project). This was crucial and the PM decided to start work on Plan A, Plan B and Plan C simultaneously considering the time pressure involved to complete in time. The team had confidence that at least one of the approaches would work well to the expectations of the sponsors.

The international experts were available but their willingness to work in India was a challenge. This was sorted out by the project team by convincing these experts to come to India for relatively longer periods of stay here. Once the experts were convinced, the project team made the following appeal to the Chairman and the Board of Directors about certain flexibility that the team desired in managing and executing the project of such gigantic proportion and impact (with eminent risk of failure):

- Complete autonomy, authority and flexibility to run the project as decided by the TMT for the project with fortnightly progress report to the chairman.

- Flexibility to make changes in scope if there was a dire need for the same subject to the approval from the committee of technical experts as specified earlier.

- An assurance that none of the team members will be transferred to any other assignment during the tenure of the project. This was important for the team. The senior management agreed with this since they understood the impact of changing personnel for such an assignment/project.

- A team of experts will simultaneously work on the acceptance standards and test data along with the development team. QA /QC functions were crucial for the project due to the sensitive application at hand (with stringent guidelines from the SEBI). Accordingly, a team of highly competent members was set up to ensure the QA/QC function for the entire project. This step was crucial considering the overall expanse of the project at hand.

- TMT asked for special sanctions for rewards and motivational schemes proposed by them considering the long tenure of the project at hand.

- Complete freedom and flexibility to set up test labs and simulation of the live environment and flexibility in terms of capital sanctions as required for this purpose.

- Freedom to engage the services of international experts (at due costs covered under the capital budget for this purpose).

- Complete flexibility to enlist support from the local experts and support organizations for the critical resources required for the entire project duration.

The project team had to go through tough scrutiny and due diligence for the above but finally won the battle and sought the approval and green signal for the proposed approach.

The PM had a tough job locating such experienced specialists and then enlisting the support of such Subject Matter Experts and other professionals. Such members had never worked together since this was the first of its kind development. The client was in the process of developing a new 'Concept' for the proposed new platform and this IT platform had to work seamlessly with the new system being developed. This complicated the project specifications further and generated several additional challenges as well. Due to the development phases of the new artefacts, there were many situations that the team encountered where they had to back to the drawing board and start all over again in case of a few situations. Such changes certainly affected the time and cost estimates and kept the entire team on tenterhooks throughout the tenure of the project.

Indeed, this was a challenging project. Based on the diamond analysis of the project classifications one can classify the project as specified below:

- Technology difficulty: T-5
- Complexity of design: C-5
- Novelty of the design: N-5
- Speed of implementation: S-4

About the project:

Sr No	Project Characteristics	Comments
1	Size of the project:	@ 50 M USD (INR 350 - 400) crore in today's currency rates effectively.
2	People:	10 members in the core team with about 4 SMEs and 3 QA / QC experts & module leaders. Total strength of around 65-75 persons including support staff allocated for the project, work during the tenure of the project.
3	Schedule:	Less than 36 months (when the original estimate was around 36 months, the team delivered in around 42 months).
4	Classification of project:	Complex R &D project with field implementation (first of its kind) although many team members had good working knowledge and nuances involved in running the stock exchanges.
5	High-risk project:	There were many uncertainties due to the new design and high-time 'Pressure'. Market prestige and organizational reputation were at stake hence there was no chance of failing. The pressure was too much on the team.
6	Technology Choice / Maturity	This was the first of its kind effort and hence the approach was to develop this new application. Although some of the platforms and tools were known it was a new R&D effort and technology was not matured at all. Due to the new design approach, the technical risks were significant and there was no one unique way to address all the issues in one go. One had to carry out small experiments and solve the bottlenecks one by one. This took a lot of effort and time.
7	No of suppliers:	Several consultants and SMEs were involved in the project and they had a significant role in the completion of the project. However, 4 specific consultants were critical (2 international experts and 2 local). These persons acted as part of the team and provided active support.
8	Logistics / Clearances:	This was quite a challenge due to time pressure and the fact setting up 'trial and test platforms had to be imported in a few cases. This was quite time-consuming and complex despite active support from the senior management and corporate logistics teams.

9	Location for co-ordination:	More than 4 locations were manned with project teams. The coordination was tough but was managed very well by the PM and team members.
10	Support from Sr. Management:	Excellent support and timely funding/admin support & motivational support. The team was given complete freedom for action and expenditures as per plans. However, even unplanned additions/modifications were also cleared ASAP.
11	Involvement of Customer:	High involvement from 'Technical Committee' members and keen participation from the seniors due to the nature of the project and the impact on the organization.
12	Project Director / Leader:	The TMT is comprised of very competent/committed R&D professionals (CTO + Project Director) with good track and relevant experience and unique leadership abilities. They had worked with the Foreign Labs and worked there on complex R&D projects for international projects.

Key positions in the team:

The team had to be manned with the following key positions:

- CTO.
- Project Director / Manager .
- Manager (R&D) at HQ.
- Module Leaders (R&D) with support team members.
- Quality Leader / Site Quality Leader.
- Technical Manager with requisite HW /SW and Networking expertise and exposure to similar activities.
- Accounts Manager for the financial issues/funding and logistics support (logistics involved that was quite complex due nature of the complex and multi-location-based project).
- PMO office for project tracking and liaison with 'Technical Committee'.
- SMEs (4 - 2 international experts + 2 local experts) with adequate model-building experience).
- Training in charge.

The challenges of the R&D team:

The main challenge for the R&D was the concept design & development of a computerized/automated application to improve latency (current needs + projected needs for the next 10 years) with a seamless interface with some of the currently running modules.

One must note that such software was not available even with the customer (internal) and the new concept was being developed for the first time. It was difficult to estimate the time for completion of the task at hand. This is mainly because the output of the project was not known with certainty and this was indeed a challenge. The current software (which was rendered inadequate due to the unprecedented increase in transaction volumes and was developed only for the old setup) was not adequate considering the new requirements and projected needs. Additionally, this was the first of its kind design and system integration effort with new technology components proposed by the customer team.

The key team members (15-16 persons) were highly qualified young professionals who had great trust in the competence & expertise of their leader. They were all willing to walk extra mile to ensure the success of the project at any cost. This was a major factor in favour of the project. The leader of the team was a committed competent professional who had an impeccable R&D record and contribution towards the success of the department in the past. The leader plus 6 senior module leaders had requisite field experience with International projects.

This was a high-risk project for the organization since failure would amount to possible displeasure and loss of face for the entire organization. The concerned senior person (Project Director) had warned the Project Manager / Project Leads to spare no efforts for the project in the initial stages since he thought that the risk involved was too onerous. However, the team leader had full hope and confidence that his team could deliver the project on time and at the level of quality expected by the customers/sponsors.

The proposed system as indicated earlier was being developed for the first time in India. The technology components, although known to the local team members, were being developed as an integrated system for the first time in India. This was a challenge indeed since their behaviour and response times were neither known nor predictable. The local lab, although good for conventional development, was not equipped for the proposed system testing. This compounded the difficulties faced by the team. However, with proper planning and some periods of hard work, the team managed to deliver excellent results with a lot of insight developed by a few key personnel in the NSE set-up. This has turned out to be a great boon for some of the people involved who could learn many new methodologies under the guidance of foreign experts.

The foreign experts, although willing to provide all the necessary back-end support, also had no hands-on experience with this type of specific bespoke /customized integrated system. They would supply a few of the important key concepts and ideas for the newly conceptualized system but had no field experience in integrating such components with the new design. This was also a challenge in the sense that the Indian R&D team had to depend on their knowledge, gut feelings possible innovations and actual trials/experience to complete the design and successfully implement the project.

In this trying situation, the idea of working on plan A, plan B, and plan C simultaneously was a great support. Although this concept jacked up the costs in the initial period, it worked well for the betterment of the project and for boosting the confidence of the team.

The issues and challenges:

The issues and challenges can be summarized as follows:

- The first of its kind design & hence high-risk project with the use of new technology for the newly designed version of the 'Specialized Platform'. The main challenge was a lack of adequate knowledge and experience in the specific aspects of technology, especially for a 'multi-fold' increase in latency. This was the main challenge and was handled through extensive training of all the team members involved and through active experimentation (and failures and setbacks).

- The training was conducted based on the following methods:

- Classroom training for every member and assignments carried out using CFTs for pilot mini projects (Brainstorming and learning together). This was very useful.

- Continuous interaction between local teams and foreign experts and the Indian Team with a lot of revisits during the 'concept design and finalization stage'.

- Participation of experts from foreign countries at the Indian Development Centre during the finalization stages.

- Hand-holding by foreign experts on a few occasions and for simulation of possible scenarios.

- Discussions and dialogue with Academicians in the initial phase.

- The training efforts made in the initiation stages were very useful and helped the local team to start the work and reach some of the milestones in time.

- Tremendous time pressure on the entire team due to a shortage of time and new design and a series of changes (Engineering Changes) in the newly designed artefacts and challenges during system integration (newly developed modules as well as currently running modules).

- The concurrent development of the new modules also posed some unique challenges (especially in the POC stage some of the modules were found to be inadequate or incomplete). This stage was quite complex and frustrating at times for the team. However, the QA / QC team required patience and experience to support and motivate design and development teams. They were very understanding about time estimates and inherent delays involved in new product developments.

- Lack of detailed knowledge was one of the initial problems at the beginning of the project. The technology involved is not day-to-day usage-based activity and getting a few of the Subject Matter Experts (SMEs) on board was also a major challenge.

- Risk management was carried out systematically and the 'risk status' was reviewed in every meeting. However constant changes in the designs and approach to development generated new possible risks and hence the 'risk analysis' had to be carried out on a dynamic basis.

- Very high-risk project with uncertainty in many respects. The main challenge was project planning from two perspectives:

- Time estimates were fluid due to changes in the basic artefacts being developed and due to concurrent engineering involving HW and SW.

- Cost estimates for the efforts (need for a balanced approach to costing otherwise the project would not be viable).

- This problem was solved by using the 'Rolling Wave Planning' concept. The project was divided into three main phases:

- Initiation concept development and concept approval phase.

- Execution and development phase.

- Testing / Pilots / Redesign & Developments and Support and fine-tuning phase.

The problem was handled partially by ensuring that the 'time' and 'costs' were finalized for each phase or part of the phase and this was taken as the budget for that phase or part of the phase. At the end of the phase, a meeting was conducted to forecast the remaining part of the phase and then budget for the next phase and this process was repeated with the rolling wave planning method. Every phase was estimated, reviewed with seniors and finalized based on a fixed cost model and the same procedure was adopted throughout the tenure of the project.

However, the team spirit and confidence to win were major factors that led to the success (partially for many features) of the project. The project manager during the discussions emphasized that without the requisite 'flexibility' in terms of scope /time and costs for the project; it would have been difficult to complete this type of project.

- No previous experience even for the foreign R&D experts (although their insight and previous experience was a great help and motivator for the entire team) although they had good knowledge of the technology as such. Since the design was new even the foreign experts were not too sure about the exact specifications for the modules to be developed in India. However, there was excellent understanding and cooperation between the Indian arm of the development team and R&D experts in support organizations. The frequent visits from the foreigners were very useful in clarifying doubts and developing a workaround.

- Indian team had good young professionals but only six senior leaders who had exposure the international standards and practices about such complex projects. However, the induction of the SMEs in the team was very welcome and together they were able to manage the completion of the task at hand. Some of the periods were highly frustrating for the teams and talking from the PM on such occasions to keep the hope alive was morale-boosting.

- The main challenge was to set up 'testing platforms' in India. In the absence of such facilities, it was very difficult to get a feel of the correctness of the modules being developed in India. Certain basic facilities were set up in India at the beginning but this was not complete and hence a lot of issues came up that led to delays.

- The setup for lab testing was not at all adequate and hence it was decided to carry out final testing at the site that was certainly risky. However, this was decided because there was no other go. The team made additional components and extra preparations for changes at the site. This was a good move since some of the sub-systems did not work at the site in the initial trials and had to be redesigned and developed with an innovative approach.

- The SMEs inducted played a very crucial and supportive role and were available throughout the project tenure. They responded very well and supported the project because of the National prestige involved in the matter.

- Multi-location-based activities gave rise to many locations and co-coordination communication became difficult. However, with good support from senior management and the freedom to commit expenses for coordination, the problem was handled effectively. Flexibility for both scope and costs was the main factor that led to the partial success of the project.

Positives in the project environment:

- The scope of work and systems specifications were thoroughly discussed/refined and confirmed with the participation of customers and their consultants throughout the project period. The change management system was ruthlessly followed and immediate communication was sent to all the concerned for them to know about the changes. Feedback and confirmation about the same were meticulously followed by the team. This was one of the major cornerstones that laid the foundation for the success of the entire project.

- The customer team along with the consultants had carried out a detailed analysis of the need and specifications for the proposed system. The Project Director / PM and key team members were also called for a detailed briefing on the project requirements and basic needs. The feasibility report was prepared with great details and the customer team was very confident that the proposed solution could be built in India although it was being produced for the first time in India.

- The PM had full authority to commit funds based on the project's needs. Luckily finances and funds were not at all a constraint. This made life relatively simpler for the project team.

- There was full support from senior management and foreign experts for such a complex project. The team was given the required flexibility for deciding 'scope/timelines/ costs' and that was very crucial for maintaining high spirits and motivation of the team. The team spirit was very high and people were willing to work the extra mile to complete their efforts to complete the project on time.

- Many innovative ideas were generated to simplify the design and avoid pitfalls. This was welcome and was supported by the PM and senior management.

- The process engineering part was handled well due to the matured processes in the parent organization.

- Quality Assurance (QA) processes and QC activities were managed very well due to process maturity in the organization. The organization had provided for training QA / QC personnel to ensure consistency in test procedures.

- Communication and coordination were given high importance and were conducted well with due attention to detail.

- Risk Management was mainly in the form of specifications /changes & timelines. These were managed personally by the PM with the help of the PMO office and a trusted senior colleague who offered excellent support to the PM.

- The site task was made relatively easier by the active participation of the customer agencies and their consulting teams. They provided all the necessary help and logistical support at the site to ensure the proper conduct of testing activities at the site. This was indeed welcome and helped the project team.

Project Success Criteria:

As per the discussions with the team members and the PM the following aspects were pre-fixed as the success criteria for the project in consultation with the customers and their consultants:

- Timely delivery of the systems without any compromises to the technical aspects. Where required the changes in need specifications were discussed with market analysts. 100 % conformance to the specifications of the proposed systems was the essence of the project.

- Satisfaction of all the customers/consultants and senior management of the project.

- Satisfaction of the suppliers for the project with reasonable margins for them along with appreciation of their contributions to the nationally prestigious project.

- Satisfaction & appreciation of the project team.

- Satisfaction of the HQ teams and the Board Members and external agencies / certifying agencies and international experts.

Project Success Factors (as seen by the team members now):

Based on the discussions with the team members and their PM it becomes clear that the list of the following points would have been useful for them as CFSs for this project. However, it has to be noted that at the time of the project execution, such a list was not prepared formally. However, based on the experience of the team members and discussions with customer teams the list of important factors was prepared and kept track of during the tenure of the project.

The list of CSFs identified is specified below for reference:

- Need for reliable "Feasibility Study" and willingness to start all over again when required.
- Clarity about the task at hand & clarity about scope and specifications and the need for flexibility in the analysis of Scope / Time Lines / Costs.
- Commitment and participation by the customer teams.
- Complete support from the senior management.
- Competent Project Manager & trusted team along with active participation of SMEs involved.
- Alert Risk Management especially in the form of timelines and design/changes.
- Full support from the SMEs or the respective activities.
- Smart and timely support from the respective managers who worked very closely with the PM.
- Control over project progress issues through impeccable communication and coordination.
- Excellent support from PMO personnel for ruthless tracking of issues and resolving them.
- Strong support from QA / QC teams and process control engineers and support received due to strong and matured processes in the parent organization.
- Exceptional teamwork and untiring support from the task force members.

Conclusion: Very positive success:

The project was an outstanding success (can be classified as an exceptional success because of the challenges and time pressure) and was a highly appreciated project by all the stakeholders involved in the project situation. The inaugural launch of the first version was well received and internally everyone in senior management, especially the chairman was completely satisfied with the achievements.

The Project Director said that "Clarity of specification along with Plan A and Plan B working simultaneously, innovative problem solving, consistent and transparent communication and complete trust in the team helped us to handle this Herculean task at hand". The senior Management was very happy and satisfied with the solution developed. They were supportive right from the beginning and this was one of the reasons for the grand success of such a complex and challenging project.

The system developed by the NSE technology group in India was adopted as standard system components offered the world over by the parent organization and they also highly appreciated the efforts and untiring efforts made by the team for the overall success of this project. This project has now become a landmark not only for the organization but for the country as well.

Learning from the project:

- **A matter of immense satisfaction and a sense of achievement, for the Indian Engineers and software professionals who dedicated themselves to the success of the project- new design / new approach for a time-bound, mission-critical project of national pride.** One can note that the team had no choice but to fail and had to produce a project that was right and appropriate 'the first time'. Kudos to the project director and his committed team that delivered the project to the complete satisfaction of the stakeholders and especially the national statutory agencies and authorities. This was an unprecedented challenge and the stakes were very high for the do-or-die situation for the organization, the team achieved the set goal based on a dedicated approach, good confidence in the technical competencies and unshakeable trust in the leadership team. This could be a great learning for the project management community in India.

- **Indeed, many times we as Indians, underestimate our capabilities and competencies. The internal team in this project, gave full confidence to senior management, hence the management could make a final decision in favour of carrying out the project internally.** They could such a decision despite the time and cost constraints but ultimately "Human feel' about whether we should go ahead with the project or not. It may not be prudent that you neglect the project's motivational aspects. One cannot make all the decisions only based on 'hard facts alone and should account for the 'gut level of feel' of critical players in the project. Based on this case one can learn about the human judgment that can play a crucial role in deciding the fate of the project.

- The sheer size of this project is overwhelming and one can sense that the larger the scope higher the possibility of bottlenecks and constraints. However, one can realize that good quality detailed planning, and flexible approach help the project teams achieve success. It is cardinally important that for such a large and technically complex project, the planning function must have both a 'helicopter view' and 'branch and leaves', balancing viewpoint while carrying out planning. Such skills are useful for such types of projects in general and this project in particular.

- For such complex and large projects, it is rather important to provide & manage basic infrastructure and basic facilities for the project to run smoothly. This is evident from this case. Managing good QA /QC and testing facilities is important for the overall success or otherwise for the project.

- Impeccable communication, smooth coordination and constant dialogue with team members go a long way in improving the probability of success for this type of project. This issue was handled very well in this case.

- Getting excellent support and good encouragement from the senior management group is critical for such kinds of projects. In this project, the senior management team was very supportive and they motivated the entire team with a lot of encouragement despite a few setbacks and difficult situations. This is a great learning indeed!

- Managing Risks is yet an additional challenge for projects. For complex and long-duration projects, risk management appears to take a back seat at times. Risk Management needs due attention from the team in the planning stage. Fundamentally any complex and long period-based project has many risky situations and hence needs attention. This aspect was paid its due attention in this case however, there were certain weak spots in the project.

- Training also has been an important part of the success story based on the project at hand. One can appreciate that when one is trying to use new technology and approaches, it is critical that all the members are brought on a common platform and everyone is oriented in the same direction. Training and technology participation that was carried out in the current project indicates the due importance given to this aspect to ensure the success of this project.

Discussion Points:

Team's Dedication and Achievement:

- Discuss the significance of the project as a mission-critical endeavour for national pride.
- Explore how the team's commitment and the leadership's trust played a pivotal role in meeting the project's goals.
- Consider the lessons that can be learned from the success of this project for the broader project management community in India.

Importance of Human Judgment:

- Analyze the role of internal team confidence in influencing senior management decisions.
- Discuss the value of considering both hard facts and gut feelings in decision-making, especially in mission-critical projects.
- Explore how understanding the human motivational aspects can impact project success.

Project Planning and Scope Management:

- Examine the challenges posed by the sheer size of the project and how detailed planning and a flexible approach helped overcome bottlenecks.
- Discuss the importance of having both a 'helicopter view' and a detailed view in the planning function for large and complex projects.
- Explore the general applicability of these planning skills to other large projects.

Infrastructure and Facilities Management:

- Discuss the role of basic infrastructure and facilities in ensuring the smooth running of complex projects.
- Examine the specific needs for managing QA/QC and testing facilities for overall project success.

Communication and Coordination:

- Explore the importance of impeccable communication, smooth coordination, and constant dialogue within project teams.
- Discuss how effective communication positively influenced the probability of success in this project.
- Explore best practices for maintaining effective communication in large-scale projects.

Senior Management Support:

- Analyze the critical role of senior management support in the success of complex projects.
- Discuss how encouragement and motivation from senior management contribute to team morale and project success.
- Explore ways to foster a supportive management culture in other project environments.

Risk Management Challenges:

- Discuss the challenges of managing risks in complex, long-duration projects.
- Explore the importance of giving due attention to risk management during the planning stage.
- Identify specific weak spots in the project's risk management and discuss potential improvements.

Training and Technology Adoption:

- Discuss the role of training in the success of the project, especially when introducing new technology and approaches.
- Explore how bringing all team members onto a common platform through training contributes to project success.
- Consider the broader implications for training in technology adoption within project environments.

Case No 22: Setting up new Steel Melting and Rolling shop for a 'Large Indian' Corporate Group in an economically backward area in Western India

Dr Jayasri Murali, Dr Dipti Sharma

Associate Professor, MBA@IICMR, Pune, Assistant Professor, MBA@IICMR, Pune

Extract: A major Indian Conglomerate aimed to establish a steel plant in an economically backward area, entailing significant capital investments and technical challenges. The vast scope involved developing marshy land, constructing a mini port for iron ore shipment, a 10-kilometre conveyor system, a township, a school, and a hospital. The greenfield project spanned 1200 acres, producing 1.2 million tonnes of steel annually, managed by a skilled team of 20 seniors and 50 juniors. Initial estimates of 800 Cr INR rose to 1200 Cr INR, with an 18-20% cost increase. Led by an experienced project manager, the venture aimed to revolutionize steel production, positioning the conglomerate strategically amid expansion plans. The ambitious timeline added to the project's inherent challenges.

Introduction:

There is a large Indian Conglomerate Group in India engaged in multi-faceted activities in the air and Steel Industries. This group wanted to set up a steel plant in an economically backward area to supply a certain quality of steel for a tube-making unit within the group (as a backward integration activity for the group). The task was onerous and involved large sums of capital investments (all the capital expenditure had to be committed right from the beginning & this was a challenge in itself).

It was proposed to set up the project in an economically backward area and this meant a lack of any infrastructure at the site. A certain portion of the proposed land to be acquired for the project had marshy land and hence right from developing the land till the plant was erected and operated was covered under the scope of the project. In a true sense, this was a green field project. Additionally, the steel-making process proposed for the plant was based on the use of natural gas as the basic source of power and hence there were many technical challenges as well.

One has to notice that the basic raw material (iron ore) was expected to arrive through ships and hence one had to plan for the construction of a mini port and warf for downloading the iron ore from the ships. The transportation from the wharf to the factory site was over 10 kilometres and one had to build the complete conveyor system as well as the transportation system before the plant could be operational. It was essential to also build a township, school and hospital at the proposed site since there were no other means of providing safe accommodation for the staff and workmen at the site location. The size of the proposed project was enormous and involved multiple engineering disciplines from a technical perspective.

The proposed project covered over 1200 acres of land and was being built to produce 1.2 million tonnes of steel every year. The core engineering team consisted of 20 seniors, 50 juniors and support staff and an overall employee strength of over 1400 workmen and helpers for various activities. The consultants appointed for the project were from Mumbai and they had over 50 site supervisors for the site work. The original estimate was around 800 Cr INR which was changed to over 1200 Cr INR as a revised estimation once the decision was to shift to the backward area. Finally, there was an 18-20 % deviation for the cost increase.

The proposed project manager was an individual who had very good knowledge and experience in the field of Steelmaking and had worked on similar projects in India and a few countries abroad. The group HQ selected/appointed this individual to manage the new company and appointed him in the parent organization to be the Project manager to set up the new organization. The project manager also had the responsibility to close the operations of the old unit due to technology obsolescence. The current note covers the project in the form of setting up a new project for the manufacture and application of steel using a new proposed technical design that was for the first time in India.

The project was novel in contemporary times and would be seen as a means to strengthen the position and image of the Group HQ in the country. This project was seen as very strategic in the group HQ due to their expansion plans for the group. The period in which this was expected to be delivered did not have mature systems working on these concepts. Indeed, this was a challenging project.

Based on the diamond analysis of the project classifications one can classify the project as specified below:

- Technology difficulty: T-4
- Complexity of design: C-4
- Novelty of the design: N-4
- Speed of implementation: S-3

Note the following aspects:

The scope of the project was enormous and included various modules and sub-systems. The volume of work involved was very large and the complexity of the tasks involved was significant. Added to this situation was the fact that the proposed technical solution for the plant was the first of its kind in the country (in fact the first of its kind in the world).

The original feasibility study was prepared based on setting up this project in the vicinity of Mumbai for the obvious availability of support facilities. However, considering the tax facilities and other concessions offered in the economically backward areas and the cost advantages in buying the land in this area, it was decided to shift to the backward areas. This decision had significant savings on one side but had the overhead of building other infrastructure and facilities such as housing complexes, schools and hospitals at the site location.

There was a need to re-establish the feasibility study all over again. It was noticed that in the backward areas, the availability of manpower was quite a challenge due to the non-availability of opportunities in this area. Similarly, many factors such as the need for the construction of a mini-port and warf and the conveyor belt to carry ore were not anticipated in the initial stages. This type of faulty understanding of the scope of work drastically affected the capital costs of the proposed project. Due to insistence from the co-promoter of the project and financial institutes, the site was shifted to an economically backward area. Although this was a good move in concept, in reality, this move posed a major challenge for the project team. One factor in favour of the shift was the availability of gas as fuel for the new technology that was proposed for the project.

Issues that need attention:

Additionally, a feasibility study was carried out without proper analysis of changing trends in the 'Steel Markets' the world over. There were dynamic changes in the steel market and there were unprecedented rate fluctuations in this industry. The analysis indicated that the project feasibility was sensitive to the following factors:

- Steel rate fluctuations in the international markets (+ / - 5 % changes were okay to be accommodated). However, if the rates fluctuate beyond this range then it can drastically affect the basic economy of the project. This aspect needs to be noted and incorporated into the basic working of economic feasibility.

- Rates of fuel and overall costs of power consumption also keep fluctuating and can affect feasibility with a significant impact.

- Timely availability and arrival of the basic raw materials 'iron ore' from various locations (captive mines were in the eastern part of India and this one had a lower % of iron in terms of the expected yield)

One can notice some of these factors are under control but few factors are outside the purview of the project environment and there is no control possible. However, precariously the feasibility is based on the combined impact of all these factors. This issue created problems for the project at later stages.

About the project:

Sr No	Project Characteristics	Comments
1	Size of the project:	@14 -15 million USD (INR 800-1000 crore in today's currency rates including Land / Building / Capital Expenses Capitalized / Other Equipment + Accessories and basic infrastructure).
2	People:	80 persons in Head Office / R&D group / (1500 people in all Including Site personnel + Support staff + workmen and casuals).
3	Schedule:	5 years was the planned project period as per the feasibility study. It was estimated/expected that the production would be started 48 months from the start of the project.
4	Classification of project:	New organizational set up as green field project (with certain actions required for the field trials and acceptance). This was the first of its kind activity in India at that stage and this meant that there were no such plants in India with specific experience of running such plants in India. Hence the project was full of uncertainties and risks.
5	High-risk project:	There were many uncertainties/risks due to the fact new site location, usage of the technology for the first time in India and fluctuations in steel markets the world over. There was a certain risk regarding the acceptance and suitability of the steel produced specifically in terms of resultant quality & prices in the market. The success of the project was dependent on this aspect. At a later stage due to the insistence of the co-promoter of the project, the location was shifted to an economically backward area. This aspect was not even thought about at the stage of the basic feasibility report. This posed new risks for the project. The details of this are explained in the sections below.
6	Technology Choice / Maturity:	The technology was evolving in this period. This new Technology gradually gained acceptance in the US & European Markets. However, this technology was completely new in India and was not particularly established in India. There was a shortage of knowledgeable people in the market about this technology and its applications.

7	No of suppliers:	The project's success was dependent on active support/participation from the principal consultants for the project. Additionally, several types of suppliers and vendors and sub-contractors (for materials, supplies and hardware items suppliers of raw materials, and various types of services for construction activities and erection) were critical parts of the project. Over 300 agencies were involved in the project activities. These suppliers provided good support to the project team.
8	Logistics / Clearances:	This was quite a challenge due to time pressure and the involvement of Financial institutes in the project. Several Government clearances/licences were essential to initiate overall project activities and hence logistics / legal matters were significantly important for the success of the project. Additionally, logistics and transportation support was required for a variety of items/equipment and materials.
9	Location for co-ordination:	More than 3 locations were manned with project team persons. Coordination was quite a challenge due to the non-availability of telecom services in the vicinity of the site location. Many things were dependent on manual transfer of communications and messages leading to delays in even routine matters. Transactions with financial institutes and various Govt / Semi-Govt agencies in the initial phase of the project were very complicated since they were located in cities and not willing to visit site locations.
10	Support from Sr. Management:	Excellent support and timely funding/admin support & motivational support. The team was given complete freedom for action and expenditures. However, at a later stage certain % of equity is taken up by a famous financial institute. This generated many constraints for the project team in particular.
11	Involvement of Customer:	There was no initial support from the customers in the project. However, some of the customers/end users had apprehensions about the use of these materials in current applications and this created certain constraints for the marketing team.
12	Team Leader:	The Project Manager who was selected for the post was a competent/committed person (expert in steel production processes with good expertise and experience in project management. He was trained in the UK & West Germany.

Key positions in the team:

The team had to be manned with the following key positions:

- Project Manager/
- Manager (R&D) at HQ / Factory Labs.
- A panel of expert consultants (Project Consultants and Steel Process Consultants).
- Quality Leader / Site Quality Leader.
- Production Manager with requisite engineering + production experience.
- Process Engineer / Process Engineer for exclusive support of key vendors.
- Procurement Engineer.
- Accounts Manager for the financial issues/funding.
- PPC / Logistics / Shipment Manager for managing imports and logistics involved that was quite complex due nature of complex and multi-location-based projects.
- Site manager with 2 site engineers for the plant erection and supervision.
- IT support services manager.
- Application Engineer for the introduction of composites at the customer end.
- PMO office for project tracking and liaison with the customer team.
- Legal expert & Liaison manager for managing relationships with all concerned including co-promoter.

The challenges of the project team:

The main challenge for the project team was the location of the site which was shifted from the city-based location to the economically backward area. Similarly, the priority shift in the technology (from conventional steel making to innovative process). These two factors created several challenges for the project team. Additionally, building a mini port and docking warf created new types of problems since no one in the team had an idea about the issues involved. Additionally, the acquisition of land from the local persons and getting environmental clearances was a major pain point for the project. These issues delayed the start of the project by several months. This aspect was covered very well in the initial feasibility submitted to the senior management. But in reality, the delays were beyond expectations.

The following points were noted based on the interaction with the project team members and Project Manager:

The issues and challenges: The issues and challenges can be summarized as follows:

- The proposed plant is the first of its kind plant in India and hence there was inadequate knowledge about plant design & engineering. However, the contractors and experts had an excellent technical team that provided adequate inputs to get over the Plant design & related inputs. However, the lack of knowledge about the new design approach and difficulties during the field execution continued to haunt the team during the tenure of the project.

- The relocation of the plant to an economically backward area raised unique challenges. Initially, it took enormous time to get the land allocated for the project. There was a refusal from the then commissioner who refused to allocate the land on the basis that this region does not need a high-tech plant. Additionally, the local people staged a "Dharana" agitation against the plant. Only after the Government of Maharashtra intervened the land was finally allocated with a counter promise that "a family member of the affected landowner will be given a job in the new plant". This entire process delayed the project efforts by 10 months. This delay was probably unwarranted and could have been avoided.

- The location of the plant in a backward area also gave rise to another problem in the form of the availability of trained manpower and lack of infrastructure for support services for the project. Selected qualified chemical & mechanical engineers with requisite experience refused to shift to the new location. This was quite a challenge and was solved by selecting a few students from several engineering colleges who were given special incentives to join the organization at the new plant location. Additionally, the project organization had to provide special accommodation for these young people at very concessional/subsidized rates.

- Tremendous time pressure on the entire team due to shortage of time and new designs/technology for steel making created bottlenecks. There were a lot of cases of trial & error. This amounted to extra time and costs.

- Very high-risk project with uncertainty in many respects. However, the team spirit and confidence to win were major factors that led to the success of the project. The team was willing to walk the extra mile for the success of the project. This was a welcome sign and helped the team to complete the work ASAP and also helped to manage the risks effectively.

- No previous experience led to a lack of knowledge of the technology such resulted in many delays for the entire project. The team had to solve some of the problems based on experiments and trial and error basis. However, with the help of the expert problems were resolved. This was a tedious process and consumed a lot of time for the Project Manager and his assistants. Set up for lab testing was not at all adequate in site lab and hence it was decided to carry out testing at other labs.

- Trying to set Indian team for this challenging assignment was a task & challenging task indeed. The team had good young qualified professionals but only three senior leaders who had exposure to the international standards and practices for such complex projects. This was quite a bottleneck for the entire project's progress. These senior experts had to guide the entire team about international standards & processes. This took a lot of time & effort on their part and hence there were many delays and hence higher costs. Again it was not very easy for local experts in this field with new technology experience.

- The suppliers' role in the project was crucial, especially for the erection and construction processes. Non-availability of trained workmen led to delays on many occasions.

- The initial project feasibility did not envisage investment in township plans. This was also a tedious activity. However, these issues were handled by the HO team and did not take too much time for the core project team. However personal contacts and good relationships with suppliers helped to solve this ticklish issue.

- Multi-location-based activities gave rise to many locations and co-coordination communication became difficult. This project faced many such situations.

The main challenges that rendered the overall project a failure despite successful project work:

The analysis indicated that the project feasibility was sensitive to the following factors: (as pointed out earlier).

1. Steel rate fluctuations in the international markets (+ / - 5 % changes were okay to be accommodated). The market became volatile and the project was derailed due to the unaffordable economics of the project output.

2. Rates of fuel and overall costs of the power consumption were again prohibitive and even the permission was not available in time to use this type of fuel. As pointed out the project feasibility was very sensitive to fuel pricing. The change in Govt regulations made the situation beyond correction.

3. Timely availability and arrival of the basic raw materials 'iron ore' from various locations (captive mines were in the eastern part of India and this one had a lower % of iron in terms of the expected yield)

One can notice some of these factors are under control but few factors are outside the purview of the project environment and there is no control possible. However, precariously the feasibility was based on the combined impact of all these factors. This issue created problems for the project at the feasibility stage as well as at later stages.

Unfortunately for this project, all three issues (stated above) were out of control and affected the project and even though the plant was ready it did not go to the stage of complete production cycles.

Positives in the project environment:

- **The project process performance was very satisfactory but the changes in the project environment killed the project as indicated below.** The processes and methodologies were okay but the rapidly changing business environment rendered all good things done, to an almost useless stage since the rate of change was random and too fast for the project team to respond to. Similarly, the remote location of the site itself brings severe constraints on the team to perform smoothly.

- **There was full support from senior management foreign partners and labs for this new project.** There was significant importance given by the Group HQ and as such the project team was supported and encouraged by the senior management and sponsors despite initial setbacks and delays.

- The PM had full authority and flexibility to make decisions and commitments for funds based on the project's needs. Luckily finances and funds were not at all a constraint. This made life relatively simpler for the project team.

- The team spirit was very high and people were willing to work extra time to complete the project in time. They had full confidence in the Project manager and senior team members. This faith ensured that there was no tension or apprehensions for the team members. The group although fairly young worked as a united team.

- Many innovative ideas were generated to simplify the design and avoid pitfalls in the implementation of the plant at the new site. This was welcome and was supported by the PM and senior management.

- The process engineering part was handled well due to matured processes in the parent organization & this helped the project team in a significant way.

- Quality Assurance (QA) processes and QC activities were managed very well due to process maturity in the organization. A leading technologist had joined the HO at Pune and he set up the entire R&D unit and QA / QC initiatives.

- Communication and coordination were given high importance and were conducted very regularly at all levels in the project organization.

- Risk Management was mainly in the form of specifications /changes & timelines. These were managed personally by the PM with the help of the PMO office and a trusted senior colleague who offered excellent support to the PM. However, this area could have been improved significantly if the feasibility study had been carried out judiciously in the first place and formal risk management practices had been followed up regularly.

- The site task was made relatively easier by the active participation of the HO team and their consulting teams. They provided all the necessary help and logistical support at the site to ensure the proper conduct of activities at the site. This was indeed welcome and helped the project team.

What happened and why did the project fail?

Many parameters and factors dynamically changed topsy turvy during this period which led to disaster and hence project failure. The main aspects that led to the failure of the overall project are specified below for quick reference:

- During this period there were major upheavals in the international steel markets prices reduced beyond expectations and the trends in price fluctuations also were drastic. This situation threw out of gear and generated financial pressure on the project. At this stage, it became clear that there was no point in pursuing the plans further because the new environment would never allow the project to go back to profit improvement possibilities. The senior management very reluctantly decided to close the project formally.

- An additional factor that led to major impediments in the form of promises made to family members in the area to give one job per family during the project implantation phase. Since financial feasibility went for a toss it was impossible to sustain this additional burden and this led to civil agitations against the organization and caused a lot of embarrassment for the organization and a lot of costs and delays.

- As pointed out earlier the logistics costs (transportation of RM from mines to site and handling of such quantities during the process and temporary stage of RM) were a significant part of operations and such costs became unsustainable for the project. This also led the senior management to make decisions in favour of the closure of the project.

- Additionally, it has been explained that the original feasibility plan did not anticipate the need for an independent Jetty & Quarry for downloading RM and a conveyor belt system that helped transport the RM from the Jetty to the plant. The capital costs for these systems increased the capital budget beyond control rendering the overall project feasibility to go down further.

- Considering all such factors the senior management had no other choice but to abandon the project and finally close the site. This means that the parent organization had to take the losses and close the activities.

It can be noticed from the above discussions that even if the project has many positives (especially in terms of technical aspects) the project had to be closed due to unprecedented changes in steel prices and increase and uncertainty of other costs, it destroyed the basic backbone of the project. It may be noted when basic assumptions and basic premises of the project environment change, it may be useful to go back to the drawing board and re-establish the feasibility all over again. This is called the **'Dynamic Feasibility' Study** for a few special occasions, this will help project organizations to judge if they should continue with the project or close the project.

Project Success Criteria:

As per the discussions with the team members and the PM the following aspects were conceptualized as the success criteria for the project in consultation with the senior management and sponsors:

- The main aspect of the project was to complete pilots and POC (Proof of Concept) for new processes and the quality of steel produced. The senior management was willing to support the entire project team during this crucial stage.
- Conformance to the specifications in the form of mechanical specifications and properties of the proposed trial batches was treated as specific success criteria for the project.
- Satisfaction of all the customers / technical consultants in the industry verticals was a major success criterion (as set based on the discussions with senior management of the project).
- Satisfaction of the suppliers for the project with reasonable margins for them along with appreciation of their contributions for new materials and new methods envisaged.
- Satisfaction & appreciation of the project team.
- Satisfaction of the principal HQ and R&D personnel at the project office.

Project Success Factors (as seen by the team members now):

Based on the discussions with the team members and their PM it becomes clear that the list of the following points would have been useful for them as CFSs for this project. However, it has to be noted that:

- Clarity about the task at hand (clarity about scope and specifications).
- Commitment and participation by the customer teams in the development of components using new SMC / DMC materials.
- Complete support from the senior management.
- Competent Project Manager & trusted team.
- Alert Risk Management especially in the form of timelines and design/changes for POC.
- Full support from the supplier network.
- Control over project progress issues through impeccable communication and coordination.
- Excellent support from PMO personnel for ruthless tracking of issues and resolving them.
- Strong support from QA / QC teams and process control engineers and support received due to strong and matured processes in the parent organization.
- Exceptional teamwork and untiring support from the task force members.
- Good support from Legal Experts and Admin teams.

From the notes and the discussions, it can be seen that many of the CSFs in the project team achieved success. However, the financial results were disastrous and the organization continued to report losses for the first four years. The cumulative loss for the first four years was around 15 crores and the fifth year achieved breakeven for the 5th year's operations.

Overall result assessment by the project team indicated that the project based on the results of the first five years was a failure. However, the group claimed that they could achieve few technical successes in this period. Successful Proof of concept (POC) trials in the fourth year and the fifth year were certification of the technical success in terms of the introduction of these new processes was seen as a success. **Conclusion: Failed project with few silver linings!**

The project failed in reality but senior management continued to support the same despite basic failure due to the strategic importance of this technology in the group. The project reported losses for the first 4 years and started showing a reversal of the sign in the fifth year.

However, unfavourable changes global steel market, non-availability of fuel due to changes in Govt policies and delays in receipt of raw materials in time led to the shutting down of the plant for over 2 years. At a later stage, staggering losses and unprecedented changes in the market conditions prompted the organization to sell the entire plant and subunits to some other group.

The Project Director said "We were very satisfied with the project performance but the overall project has failed due to the situation being out of our hands! It is like the operation was successful but the patient has died".

The project was not treated as a success story as can be seen from the rating specified by the Project manager in the response to the questionnaire specified above.

Learnings from this project:

- Many key learnings from this case would be useful for future project professionals. It can be seen that for long-term projects such as this, where long times are involved one needs to check the feasibility of the basic proposal from time to time. This is quite important that feasibility as such is revisited when there are changes in the assumptions made while establishing a feasibility study. This is called a 'Dynamic Feasibility Study'. This is important learning, especially for infrastructure projects / long-term projects where the project environment can change during the tenure resulting in throwing out of gear the original feasibility study. In such a case, at times it may be prudent to close the project rather than continue with the project.

- Such complex and difficult projects need qualitatively different approaches for planning of these projects. The flexibility required is in terms of:
  - Strategic Flexibility.
  - Financial and resource flexibility .
  - Technical & Operations flexibility.
  - Organizational structure .
  - Empowerment to make critical decisions at times by the Project Director.

  At times redesigning the project concept by going back to the drawing board if the original situation changes drastically.

- The second learning is that for any project, it is critical to concentrate on understanding the expanse of the 'Scope' of the work involved. In this specific case the significant part of the quarry, set up for docking of the ships and investment in the conveyor system, were completely forgotten right from the feasibility stage. Such a situation may not reflect the costs and hence the error will render the exercise completely redundant. Such Feasibility studies are useless and can cause harm to the cause to 'Vision / Mission' of the organization. This is certainly not desirable and project teams must learn to identify such issues before the Feasibility Study.

- Risk Identification and Management is a very important issue for the sustainable success of any large, long-term project. However, in many cases, this step is carried out mainly in the form of a ritual and not carried out as a professional step in the completion of the scope of the project. While addressing the issues regarding the 'Scope' of work one must assign the best from each type of talent pool. This has to be done effectively so that it does not fully draw the attention of too many people in the implementation cycle.

- Proper communication with all the stakeholders is quite crucial for the success of any large project in the infrastructure industry. Unless you manage this aspect for any project, it is difficult to become successful in the project endeavour. This is important for every project manager. This needs to be taken cognizance of for all types of projects in the world.

- It is indicated in the case that there is a need for 'flexibility in planning and scope definition for many types of projects, especially for the Engineering & Infrastructure industries. This is essential since there is a long period from project approval to project delivery. In this period many changes can occur in the environment. Some of the changes are supportive but others could be against the best interest of the project. To manage such changes and market dynamics, project scope and planning function must provide such flexibility to accommodate such changes. This aspect is important for infrastructure projects as well as projects with a long lead time for completion.

- Additionally, it may be noticed that for such long-term projects. It is pertinent that basic infrastructure and test facilities are planned well to ensure the success of the project at hand. This is specifically true in the Indian context since there is a predominant tendency to think that 'some of these problems will get solved by themselves (How? Miracles?).

- Such tendencies are noticed across all types of organizations and in reality, this is a dangerous path in actual practice. One has to guard against such tendencies. Based on the analysis it is recommended that such parameter is included in the list of CSFs for projects. Miracles do not happen in practice while executioner. However, taking things for granted growth and hence our plans and strategies should not be the practice adopted for projects based on various studies in such mindsets. Being practical and realistic should be the basis of planning the activities.

Discussion Points:

Dynamic Feasibility Study:

- Discuss the concept of a dynamic feasibility study for long-term projects, emphasizing the importance of revisiting feasibility when assumptions change.
- Explore instances where projects might need to be closed due to significant changes in the project environment.
- Consider the role of dynamic feasibility in mitigating risks and ensuring project viability over time.

Qualitatively Different Planning Approach:

- Examine the need for a qualitatively different planning approach for complex and challenging projects.
- Discuss the required flexibility in terms of strategic, financial, technical, operational aspects, and organizational structure.
- Explore the role of empowerment for the Project Director and the possibility of redesigning the project concept in response to drastic changes.

Comprehensive Scope Understanding:

- Analyze the critical importance of understanding the entire scope of work for any project.
- Discuss the consequences of neglecting key aspects of the scope, as seen in the example of the quarry, ship docking, and conveyor system.
- Explore strategies to identify and address scope-related issues during the feasibility study phase.

Risk Identification and Management:

- Examine the importance of risk identification and management as a professional and integral step in project completion.
- Discuss the need to assign the best talents to address scope-related issues.
- Explore how effective risk management contributes to sustainable project success.

Communication with Stakeholders:

- Discuss the crucial role of proper communication with all stakeholders in the success of large infrastructure projects.
- Explore the challenges and strategies associated with effective communication for project managers.

- Emphasize the universal applicability of this principle to all types of projects worldwide.

Flexibility in Planning and Scope Definition:

- Examine the need for flexibility in planning and scope definition, particularly for engineering and infrastructure industries.
- Discuss how long project timelines can introduce changes in the environment and market dynamics.
- Explore strategies to build flexibility into project scope and planning to accommodate changes effectively.

Basic Infrastructure and Test Facilities:

- Discuss the significance of planning basic infrastructure and test facilities for the success of long-term projects.
- Explore challenges specific to the Indian context and the importance of avoiding the assumption that problems will resolve themselves.
- Highlight the need to guard against complacency and the inclusion of such parameters in critical success factors (CSFs) for projects.

Practical and Realistic Planning:

- Discuss the recommendation of adopting a practical and realistic approach to planning activities.
- Explore the dangers of taking things for granted and relying on miracles in project execution.
- Emphasize the importance of being proactive and realistic in planning strategies based on various studies and practical experiences.

Case No 23: Case of up new Multi-Specialty Hospital set up by an NGO which was formed by young medical professionals at an early age to provide 'affordable medical services for the society at large, especially for the economically backward classes of society

Dr Jayasri Murali, Dr Swapnisha Khambayat

Associate Professor, MBA@IICMR, Pune, Assistant Professor, MBA@IICMR, Pune

Extract: A group of young doctors, driven by a shared commitment to societal welfare, established Dr Hedgewar Rugnalaya in Aurangabad under the Dr Babasaheb Ambedkar Medical Trust. The initiative aimed to provide affordable multi-speciality medical services, countering the prevalent high costs in India. Over 25 years, this dedicated team, childhood friends with diverse medical backgrounds, navigated challenges and sacrifices to build the hospital. Despite lacking formal project management, their selfless dedication and exemplary teamwork triumphed. The project, rooted in compassion for the downtrodden, defied societal norms. A renowned social worker's guidance and mass support ensured the success of their dream project, a role model for NGOs nationwide.

Introduction:

This project was set up under the name of Dr Babasaheb Ambedkar Medical Trust and the hospital was named Dr. Hedgewar Rugnalaya operating in Aurangabad.

The current state of medical facilities in India is far below the expected standards. Additionally, these services, especially advanced medical services are simply not affordable to every citizen due to the prohibitive costs associated with such hospitals. A group of young doctors motivated by the 'need to do something unique for the society at large' decided to set up a multi-speciality hospital for the needy in society at affordable costs' under the guidance of the social worker, in fact, a social reformer, in Aurangabad and today this has become one of the most reputed institutes in the Marathwada Region.

The group of young doctors who were childhood friends and had known each other for a long time throughout their formative years decided to get together and form a group. This helped them to come together (along with their spouses in a few cases who also belonged to medical fields from various disciplines and agreed to be part of this new group) and form trust under the active guidance of the renowned social worker. This happened almost 25 years back when the medical services profession was one of the most money-making professions in India (still known for this aspect).

However, this group of over 8 medical male doctors (belonging to various areas of functional medical disciplines) and 4 female doctors decided to set up a basic minimum set-up for the hospital and started the work with great enthusiasm. The young group of doctors were aware of the sacrifice they would have to make during the journey to develop such an institute of their dreams throughout their careers and life in general.

Due to unshakable faith in each member of the group and their resolve to make this project a great success they stuck together and started the basic facilities in a small rented location in Aurangabad and have today set up a multi-speciality hospital along with a few other initiatives for social transformation. Today they are role model for many in the country. This group of young professionals are together even today and work very hard to ensure the fulfilment of their 'Dream Project'. At present, they are busy setting up another hospital on similar lines in the Eastern Part of India.

This project is unique from many angles and various perspectives and indicates that despite not using formal project management methods and methodologies, only through selfless dedication, flexibility in approach and exemplary teamwork, projects can achieve outstanding success and satisfaction for all the stakeholders.

There are many things one can learn from this project, especially for NGO-like project situations. Despite many odds, the project team was able to complete the tough project (because of lack of funds) to set up such an ambitious project and generate historical landmarks in the region for such projects. The role of the philosopher, guide and active supporter of the project team made a difference between success and failure. His image, his contacts and his ability to influence the mass support helped the project team to set up the dream project successfully. The leader and initiator was one of the most renowned social workers of repute who decided to form this new initiative the project was the source of motivation. He was the problem solver/ decision maker for the young team of doctors who worked tirelessly to set up this hospital of repute in the country.

The following paragraphs indicate the spirit based on which the group of young medical professionals committed their careers to the development of a multi-speciality hospital of repute, a dream project:

"The year 1989 saw a group of young doctors coming together... to weave a dream... a dream of a 'NATION'... not merely a notion but a spirit that was to eventually become a reality. But back then, when they started their journey, they knew that this was a journey that was taken up rarely... a path rarely touched. Their dreams were unheard of in modern society. There was nothing strange really in the manner that these seven dreamers desired to serve society. Except that the route they had embarked upon was laced with compassion for the downtrodden, a path of charity, and that meant a life without the frills of 'materialism'.

Health includes physical, mental, social and spiritual well-being. 'Sarve Santu Niramayaha...' Let all be free from disease / let all be healthy, which was often used to express good wishes. Thus was formed a basic thought which manifested in the establishment of a Trust, 'Dr. Babasaheb Ambedkar Vaidyakiya Pratishthan'.

Every endeavour that is carried out finds its roots in this salutation to the father of the Indian Constitution. The hospital was born under the name of the thought-provoking, Dr. Hedgewar! Today, the hospital as it is known... Dr. Hedgewar Rugnalaya is the epicentre of all the endeavours of these young doctors, the finest human beings only to be joined by hundreds and thousands of people to make this an epic project of modern times!

Objectives of the project:

The main objective of the project was to provide excellent medical help for 'the needy' at an affordable cost and generate better hygiene and health awareness in society at large through the untiring efforts of dedicated volunteers and professionals in India. A noble aim indeed!!

The main objectives of the project are specified below for quick reference:

- To provide state-of-the-art multi-speciality medical facilities and expert medical services at an affordable cost to all 'the needy' and the society at large.

- To educate the masses about the importance of hygiene and health through various initiatives.

- To provide the necessary medicines and medical services free of charge to the people who are below the poverty line and hence cannot afford even basic medical aid in their lives.

- To set up state-of-the-art medical college / educational facilities for all the aspects of Health Care Disciplines (Medical education, nursing education, physiotherapy-based education) through setting up of an independent Educational Trust for this purpose.

- To set up a 'Social Awareness Programs Group' of volunteers to help underprivileged people continuously improve the quality of life they lead (financed through surplus funds from the hospital activities).

- To establish discussion forums for the villagers through their local leaders to ensure that the right and true perception about the project was shared by everyone. Similarly, there was a need to develop the right mindset for the villagers to sustain the efforts after the current project was complete.

- To initiate contacts with Corporate Organizations, Foreign agencies and HNIs (High Net Worth Individuals) to avail funds and support for conducting various medical and social initiatives indicated for activities specified above.

- To identify, select, counsel and induct volunteers for the proposed activities of the new organization. This activity is not as simple as it may appear to be. To enlist and nurture the development of 'young volunteers' who will provide such services on an ongoing basis continues to be a challenge even today.

The status of the hospital today!! The dream comes true!!

Dr Hedgewar Hospital, Aurangabad (Dr Hedgewar Rugnalaya) is a 300-bed Multi-Specialty Charitable Hospital, run by Dr Babasaheb Ambedkar Vaidyakiya Pratishthan. The Hospital is the 'epicentre' of a humongous social healthcare movement called "The Healing Touch". Now for more than 26 years, since its inception in 1989, the hospital has reached out to the poor and needy population of Aurangabad district in 9 Talukas, through the window of healthcare to offer holistic healing through innovative and customized projects.

The young Doctors who started this movement were very clear from the inception that they did not want to restrict themselves to operating from a building; rather reaching out to the masses was the prime goal. The 1st *'Slum Health Centre'*, catering to the migratory industrial population was kicked off within 6 months of the hospital launch. A doctor and his wife took a conscious call to relocate to the slums to dedicate their lives to the service of the population. One thing led to another, challenges arose, solutions were devised and today, after nearly 26 years there are 3 Slum Health centres and a Mobile Clinic visiting another 6 slums on the periphery of the city. Together they cater to a population of nearly forty thousand people. These Centres have now metamorphosed into a hub of activities offering multiple life-changing social-healthcare opportunities, transforming the entire landscape of the slum population.

The founder Doctors, who had just passed out of Medical College, started in a very small 100 sq. ft., 5-bed setup. All of them soon had to contribute towards creating a basic corpus to apply for a bank loan. Most of them borrowed money from their parents, while others had to take personal loans and thus began the journey. Very soon the local population began to take notice of these youngsters. Their commitment and passion to serve the poor and needy soon inspired individuals from the society to come forward and join hands in various capacities and thus began the movement. Challenges were plenty and still are, sometimes shaking the team to the core, but there was always light at the end of the tunnel. The founder Doctors were inspired by the philosophy of *"Service towards the nation"* and aptly guided & supported by veteran social activists. The guidance from these veterans was very valuable in the formative years of the hospital.

Very soon Medical teams from Dr Hedgewar Hospital started visiting the interior villages of Aurangabad district, around a periphery of 50kms, offering healthcare to people who were secluded from development. They were in such deep areas, which had no roads, no public transport and not even a single medical practitioner. Very soon after having experienced their first ray of hope, these villagers & farmers started opening up about their other challenges - unemployment, water shortage, loans, illiteracy, blanket youth migrations to cities, addictions, suicides etc.

Gradually with the help of experts, innovative programmes started to take shape to address these needs and provide a holistic and sustainable solution. As the workload grew from one village to another, from one project to five more, the need for a dedicated wing to monitor the social-healthcare projects arose and hence was born *"Savitribai Phule Mahila Ekatma Samaj Mandal (SPMESM)"*. As of today, SPMESM has 35 projects spread across 100 villages providing holistic development solutions to the villagers and farmers of the region. These initiatives are highly appreciated by the people in the villages and obviously, they started supporting these projects with a perception that these projects are helping society at large and people in remote villages in particular.

Things at the hospital also continued to grow at a brisk pace and then came the urgent need to have a dedicated blood bank to cater to the growing demand for blood. It was also decided that this blood bank would not refuse blood to anyone, irrespective of whether an individual could pay or not. The blood bank was named "*Dattaji Bhale Blood Bank*", and has grown immensely in size and stature. The Blood bank operates on a "No Loss - No Profit" basis and stands tall as one of the best blood banks in Asia and certified as the best in Maharashtra for two successive years. It is aggressive in the field of blood donation drives and conducts up to 400 blood donation camps around the year.

Over the last decade, the new multi-speciality, 300-bed building of the hospital has taken shape in 2 phases. The cornerstone of this modern infrastructure has been 'Mumbaikars'. Hundreds of well-wishers from the capital city have pledged their support to this unique project and contributed generously towards building a modern, state-of-the-art hospital with the latest technology and availability of dedicated medical professionals. The Hospital continues to attract Philanthropists & Corporate organizations alike from across the country and beyond to join hands and extend the noble work far and wide to many more who are still in need of basic healthcare. The seven Founder Doctors continue to lead the organization with the same vigour and enthusiasm and have now created a team of medical professionals who are not just employed with the hospital but have dedicated their lives to the service of the poor & needy population of the Aurangabad region.

The challenges faced by the core team of doctors/promotors:

The challenges were enormous but the need was genuine. If the project was to become a success in one place, there was a need to take the concept to other locations as well. Hence the project was strategic and the team was concerned about making this a great success at any cost.

The following points were noted based on the interaction with the project team members and Project Manager. The researcher had an opportunity to meet the founding members and it was great learning from them about the project management point of view. The key issues are specified below for quick reference:

Internal issues and bottlenecks observed:

Many internal issues/aspects needed the attention of the project team, especially for the PM. Some of these issues are specified below:

Enlisting the support and Commitment of the volunteers at the senior level including the initial teams that joined the project:

This was one of the main challenges for the founding team at the beginning of the project. This problem was partially solved by the use of a network of the founder trustees and their influence over some of the renowned social organizations. The challenge was mainly because the NGO had decided that none of the founders/trustees or volunteers would be paid market rate-based compensation and this was a great bottleneck right from the beginning. The problem was partially solved when a group of highly qualified volunteers and professionals (like-minded persons) decided to participate in the activities of the NGO. They committed that they would work with the senior members of the core team. One can note that their contribution was significant and note-worthy. At a personal level, they had to compromise a lot in the formative stages of the project. This was a challenge since the team was not confident about the project outcome in the beginning and had to go through considerable frustrations in the initial stages of the project. Smooth working at times becomes quite a challenge, especially for NGO organizations, in Indian conditions.

Lack of activity plans and required processes routines and standards for planning:

This was the next challenge. One has to realize that sheer enthusiasm and dedication do not result in the achievement of the organizational goals and the success of the projects at hand. Many NGOs face this type of challenge and it is not easy to organize such efforts into disciplined methods of working.

At times unavailability of various personnel for the decision-level meetings would result in delays and missed opportunities for NGOs. Additionally, the decisions are expected to be made democratically and conscientiously resulting in unprecedented challenges. One must realize that in NGOs, leaders cannot enforce the decisions down the line so easily and this continues a challenge for this NGO even now. These conditions in the method of work lead to compromised decisions and reduce the chance of success for the projects undertaken.

Challenges related to Scope / Time and Costs and overall project plans:

The projects undertaken by the NGOs are a challenge indeed for many types of NGOs. Such problems crop up because activities can be planned only after assurance of funding from the corporate CSR or HNIs. There are many supportive organizations (local and foreign) but their timing for approval is not fixed hence making definitive plans and time schedules is quite a challenge for the NGOs.

The plans and schedules need to be flexible and cut as per the availability of funds available. This is an inherent problem for all the NGOs even now. This is possible to be solved when the predictability of the cash flows can be established in advance. The current project plans also were affected on account of this difficulty. NGOs continue to face this type of challenge even now.

Challenge to enlist the support of the local people for the project:

Additionally, there was a peculiar problem in this case. It was rather critical to enlist the participation of the local citizens to support the project since was for their benefit in the long run. There were pressure groups in the local parts of the city and villages at various sites. This was quite a bottleneck and challenge that one had to get over. This was quite a difficult task and socially very complex & emotionally charged.

PM ensured that there was a dedicated group of volunteers who went to the site and stayed with the villagers for more than a few months so that the local group dynamics were well understood. After the group feedback, the PM set up a steering committee of the local personnel to decide amongst themselves about the priorities of the local villagers and other stakeholders. This was quite effective since it forced the local citizens to sort out their issues amongst themselves. Over some time, the local people developed confidence in the project team and they started to cooperate and participate in the activities. The effect was so positive that the local people collected over INR 20 lakhs as their contribution to the project funding. The patience shown by the PM and the project team finally paid rich dividends.

Getting technical personnel on board as volunteers was the next challenge:

The technical and engineering work required for the project was quite onerous and involved hard work in an environment without adequate facilities. This meant that getting qualified volunteers for the project was quite a challenge. However, due to the availability of a very strong network of volunteers through the parent NGO, it was possible to get a few highly qualified technical experts for the project. These people had adequate expertise and experience in similar projects. They agreed to make many site visits and helped the project team develop comprehensive plans and decide on technical specifications for the project. They also helped educate the citizens of the local villages about the details and advantages of the proposed methods over some time.

Co-ordination with many agencies was also an important task for the project's success that involved the following main groups of activities:

One can understand that many agencies are involved in the operations of any healthcare activity and require close coordination and monitoring for the project team and PM. The team had a lot of difficulties and problems while handling such activities. Soon after the initiation of the basic activities

Getting proper well-equipped hospital facilities and basic infrastructure for running the new organization was not easy due to the lack of adequate funds in the initial phase:

One can easily appreciate the difficulty faced by the NGO about the basic infrastructure due to acute shortages of funds. The funds are generated through operational activities (surplus available), and donations to start with. Realizing this difficulty, the founders requested one of their old colleagues to join them and carry out this aspect as his task. This person is very active and he spearheads such efforts even now.

Over the years the group has earned a position of repute and has been successful in managing help from all types of support groups such as Corporate organizations / High net-worth Individuals - HNIs (Local and international) and of course common man the street (who willing to contribute his bit in such a noble activity.

The volunteer base is at present strong but getting new volunteers is difficult:

This is a perpetual challenge for any NGO. They have to depend on personal contacts and carry out tireless efforts to enlist the interest of prospective volunteers who are willing to work for the NGOs without getting paid market rates for their time and contributions. These days many younger persons are willing to spend part of their free time on such efforts. This will continue to be a challenge for NGOs in general. Part-time volunteers, although useful, cannot depend on part-timers for serious and critical activities. The PM had to source volunteers from many sources and manage their time effectively.

Most of the operational management is done by volunteers, which may not be desirable in the long run:

One can appreciate that for any successful project, the core team members must be available for most of the key activities of the project continuously, at least in the initial few years. This is not so easy for NGO organizations. These organizations need very flexible methods of work and one cannot enforce corporate discipline in such voluntary organizations. Everything depends on personal priorities and the motivation of the individual members of the team of volunteers. This creates problems and impediments in the smooth working of many projects.

Professional finance services and legal matters are not affordable:

In the modern era, it is very important that any organization, public or private, has to conform to statutory norms and compliances. This task is not as easy as it seems. Such tasks need requisite professional expertise and experience to ensure that these tasks are handled judiciously and with due care. Such professionals are not necessarily willing to work without compensation and NGOs are not in a position to pay market rates for their services. However, the quality of accuracy and conformance to regulations cannot be compromised.

This poses quite a challenge for the NGOs and this project was no exception for the same. NGOs have to cut corners in many other aspects and conserve money to pay for professional services as explained above and this is certainly not easy. However, the parent NGO provided the requisite support where possible. This made the task relatively easy for the project team.

Communication among volunteers becomes sometimes difficult due to a lack of knowledge of computers, the internet/email:

This point is already explained above and was difficult to solve despite certain training courses conducted and canvassing carried out by the leaders. This issue continues to affect the operating efficiency of this organization even now. Corporate CSR organizations in a few cases are supportive to help in this aspect but lack of basic infrastructure and lack of trained staff continues to plague this aspect.

Permissions from corporations, formalities and paperwork for the Charity Commissioner's office are time-consuming and tedious and take a long time for approvals:

The procedural and statutory conformance routines are one of the most burdensome matters for NGO organizations that do not have any source except for donations-based funding. Many volunteers were naive and did not have adequate knowledge or personality to manage such affairs smoothly. This can cause many mental agonies and impediments in the smooth running of such projects. In addition to this many local authorities instead of helping such NGOs add to the miseries of the NGOs. Their lackadaisical attitudes cause a loss of effectiveness and a wastage of resources at times. This aspect is a real pain for many NGOs.

Lack of knowledge of actual field work causes difficulty in having a proper perspective of the work since volunteers do not necessarily have a social work background:

Getting motivated workers and volunteers has been a challenge as explained above. Additionally, even if one found willing volunteers to work free of charge, there was another difficulty faced by the NGO. This was in the form of a fact that these volunteers, however smart did not have adequate training and exposure to manage social projects that have very sensitive issues to be handled and managed with kid gloves. This is mainly because many stakeholder groups have different expectations and perceptions about the outcome. There are strong emotional stances and very vocal (many times unnecessary) explanations. The atmosphere in any project can be vitiated quickly by the slightest provocations. One must have requisite dexterity and judicious methods to handle such tricky situations. NGOs of any type can face many new challenges due to this type of project environment. Training and orientation of the volunteers can help address such issues but only in partial ways. The field supervisors have to spend a lot of effort and time in counselling sessions dedicated to solving such problems in the field and this is not easy.

NGOs did not have strong PR manpower and machinery to approach donors, keep follow up with past donors, and avail more funds:

For CSR funding also such machinery is necessary, but is non-existent. Presently fundraising happens due to records of running the projects well and also through personal contacts of volunteers. On many occasions, such efforts are far from satisfactory and result in unprecedented problems at the beginning or during the execution of the projects at hand. The senior professionals in PR areas are not willing to be part of such outfits due to lack of compensation and continue to drag such projects. This is a necessary hassle for NGOs but there is no easy solution for this type of problem.

Data management and analysis is another area which is expensive and not well looked after till now:

This has been an area that has not received due attention right from the beginning of the project and even now continues to be rather a weak area, despite few attempts to improve the same.

Such initiative is not yet observed, though there is some similar activity recently taken up, it is not carried out professionally since no one in the team has the expertise and experience to direct and manage such efforts. Professional help sought from outside also has not helped since the budgets are quite inadequate and not financed by CSR funding.

Social issues that affect the performance of various projects and initiatives:

Any social work involves a 'change in the mindset' of the main stakeholders and dedicated work by the 'pioneering teams' right from the beginning. Changes of this magnitude involve a lot of complex social /economic and emotional issues that cannot be addressed effectively without astute expertise, working knowledge and experience. This was evident in this project. Although basic social issues were known to many team members, they did not have the requisite experience and exposure to the nuances involved in this application. This was one of the main bottlenecks in the development and implementation cycles for the project. This did affect the growth in the initial phases but now is handled professionally with few professionals working in the organization.

- Strict control over on-site behaviour and conduct from the employees and committed volunteers is an area that needs attention. Since such resource persons do not have adequate experience and appropriate skill sets to handle the current environment and issues at the site. Training continuously was the main solution but was far from adequate on many project modules. The founder members had to spend a considerable amount of time gearing up the team of volunteers and trustees (to nurture & control the teams and individual members) to reach an acceptable level of performance. Misjudgments on the part of field-level personnel can create a lot of issues if the issues are not controlled in time. It is necessary to create proper mechanisms and review systems to avoid these problems.

- A strict process of reviews for project progress and change in plans was essential and was carried out meticulously by the founder members right from the beginning and now this become a norm in the organization. However, the flexibility in planning due to the source of funding and timing of funding continues to be a challenge for the organization even at this stage of activities.

- Interface with various other organizations for lateral cooperation for such social initiatives is essential to ensure the success of similar projects in the field as such. This is vital to ensure that the importance of such projects is communicated consistently and effectively from all the concerned NGOs in unison.

- Flexibility in plans and operations is essential to manage projects of such nature as described earlier. However, the funding agencies do not appreciate such an approach since it generates financial impact and this does not suit the corporate organizations. This can generate many issues and misunderstandings from time to time and can affect the delivery of the project at hand.

Based on the diamond analysis of the project classifications one can classify the project as specified below:

- Technology difficulty: T-4
- Complexity of design: C-3
- Novelty of the design: N-4
- Speed of implementation: S-3

About the project:

Sr No	Project Characteristics	Comments
1	Size of the project:	20 million USD (INR 50 crore in today's currency rates) as Revenue Expenses (in the initial period of first 5 years) based on donations from various sources in the society including manpower costs overheads + travel + incidental costs). However, this is not an issue any more due to the basic stability of the operations.

2	People:	The core team of 12 volunteers included 7 members in the founding team, consisting of reputed social workers, which has now expanded to around 12-14 members over the years. The total numbers were around 45 in the beginning and have now grown to 1500 including Medical experts / Employees and volunteers.
3	Schedule:	The original plan of 60 months was planned project period as per the 'Feasibility - Study'. It was estimated/expected that the pilot test would start right from the beginning and the speed of expansion will depend upon the response from the 'needy' and various funding agencies approached. This was possible only due to the flexible approach and untiring efforts of the initial team.
4	Classification of project:	This is a case of a new startup NGO. Although the basic concept was already tried out in other locations in the state, this was the first of its kind NGO in Aurangabad.
5	High-risk project:	There were many uncertainties/risks in the project. The project was undertaken in a very hazy and uncertain environment without the availability of enough team members at the beginning. This was indeed a challenge. Additionally, it was difficult to enlist senior volunteers since it was decided that there would be no compensation for such volunteers who would commit to work with less compensation in comparison to the market rates. The project was indeed a risky project in many ways and 'hope and hard work' was the only resource based on which the project was undertaken by the group of 'inexperienced young medical professionals.
6	Technology Choice / Maturity:	There is no specific technology as such recommended for such NGO Initiatives. However, the team consisted of highly qualified doctors who were experts in their field of activity. However, the core team faced many trying situations basically due to inadequate infrastructure and resources. Luckily for this project, there was a group of a highly experienced group of renowned social workers in the form of founder members who had the requisite confidence for successful project completion. The guidance from the mentors was crucial in the formative years. The mentors would provide sound advice and retain the motivation.

7	No suppliers/affiliates	For this project, there was a critical role for suppliers and vendors and they with a very positive attitude worked for low-margin contracts and helped the NGO efforts. There was a role for the funding /CSR funding partners as well in providing timely help. Additionally, partnerships and close associations in similar initiatives / social organizations were critical for initiating such an organization. Personal goodwill and the network of the founding members were very useful in the initial stage of the project.
8	Logistics / Clearances:	This was quite a challenge due to the time pressure to obtain appropriate 'Certifications / Registration / Licenses and permissions' were a challenge, as explained earlier. In many cases, NGO is a facade for other anti-social activities and hence getting proper clearance and certification from all the authorities was an important consideration before the activities could be launched. Initially getting the office space without rent was a challenge indeed. However, with kind help from one of the NGOs working for the 'old' people in the city, this problem was solved. Initial expenses for the newly set up organization were taken up by the 'core team members and their families and this was a great support.
9	Location for co-ordination:	More than 6 locations (Aurangabad City + 2 locations & Work Sites in the vicinity. Over the years this organization has set up the requisite facilities and as such the overall admin support is better. Additionally, a few of the initial 'Corporate' organizations have also provided active support during the implementation period in the first 5 years including providing office space and admin assistance at a few locations. But coordination continues to be a challenge.
10	Support from Sr. Mgt:	Senior management provided excellent support and timely however, funding was a challenge in the initial period due to a shortage of funds. Similarly, there was no specific admin support in the beginning. The trustees themselves were carrying out all the activities as and when possible. Initially, Admin Support & Motivational Support was received from the senior mentors as specified above.

11	Involvement of Customer:	There was mixed support / hesitant support from the village personnel in the beginning but people were willing to listen and help. Over some time they saw the quality of work and observed dedicated work done by the volunteers and they gave full support for the initiatives taken up. PM and the team had a difficult task of winning over their minds. This made the situation quite complex for the project team.
12	Leaders:	The project Manager selected was a competent/committed social worker of repute. This helped in the initial period. His dedication, basic values, mental patience and professional approach to social work helped solve many bottlenecks and impasse situations.

Key positions in the team:

The team had to be manned with the following key positions:

- Project Director / Project Manager as 'Project Champions' (The founders of this NGO).
- Team of social workers and technical experts with expertise in similar projects with social orientation.
- Tech Leaders / Discipline Leaders (5 initially and now over 16) for various critical aspects of the proposed project & modules.
- Training experts for soft skills and ethical behaviour and attitude-building exercises for the workgroups.
- Nursing Supervisors and volunteers in charge.
- Treasurers managing financial issues/funding and auditors (advisors).
- Trustees' office for project tracking and liaison with customer teams and beneficiaries.

Positives in the project environment:

- There was full support from senior management and corporate organizations.
- The focus of the team was very specific and worked toward a detailed implementation plan in cooperation with the mentor.
- Continuous dialogue with Govt officials / Customer PM and local PM with resolve to address the issues immediately helped the team to complete the project in the required time. Focused 'Project meetings were conducted regularly (monthly/quarterly) to make strategic and critical decisions and move forward proactively. This was useful for the team.

- A harmonious team paved the path for a good quality / undisturbed work environment. This was crucial for the success of the project.

- The initial resistance to the project from the local people was reduced after the 'Steering Committee' was formed and they were given the freedom to decide their priorities.

- The team had full freedom for decision-making and commitment to expenses as per the decisions of the Project Team (Founder Members). This paved the path for smooth working for the team.

Project Success Criteria:

The project success criteria took into consideration customer expectations and organizational expectations:

- **Organizational expectations**
  - To complete the project in time without any compromise on quality of service.
  - To conform to stringent rules of the Charity Commissioner's office for the NGO operations.
  - To achieve the project delivery for the targeted population as planned by the organization.
  - To develop project modules as a model project so that they can become reference projects for future activities.
  - Getting repeat requests from various communities where services were provided was an important organizational requirement.
  - To enlist the support and active participation of the local people in the project. This was done well.

- **Customer / User Expectations**
  - To ensure timely delivery of medical services (with proper diagnosis and medical care in every aspect of operational activities).
  - To achieve a committed target population and frequency of services provided with a level of quality and unshakeable ethics.
  - To achieve requisite accuracy & efficiency in operations that have a complex set of rules & challenges and medical rules and conformances to go by.
  - To handle emotional and social issues effectively in the core team and other participants).
  - To ensure the satisfaction of the team members Trustees / Volunteers / Staff and beneficiaries of the program 'the needy'.
  - To ensure team satisfaction and development of new skills/domain expertise for the future.

- To ensure the sustainability of the project for the future.

Project Success Factors (as seen by the team members now):

Based on the discussions with the team members and their PM it becomes clear that the list of the following points would have been useful for them as CFSs for this project. However, it has to be noted that this aspect was not necessarily thought about comprehensively before the project started.

- Clarity about the task at hand & clarity about scope and specifications.
- Commitment and participation by the core team members in the development of the right ecosystem throughout the tenure of the project life cycle.
- Complete support from the senior management & freedom for actions for project/module leaders.
- Competent Project Manager & trusted Medical Consultants and professional's / team members.
- Alert Risk Management especially in the form of timelines and scope/changes. This was done well but was not up to the mark at all times/stages.
- Control over project progress issues through impeccable communication and coordination/reviews.
- Excellent support from the mentor and strict tracking of issues and resolving them on time.
- Exceptional teamwork and untiring support from the founding members in the initial period.
- Good support from Legal Experts and Admin teams as and when required.

Conclusion: Highly successful project with few silver linings!

The project was evaluated as a partial success in the first five years. Although good work was done for the beneficiaries, the original team of founder members were very happy about the internal processes and internal efficiency but were continuously striving for perfection. Today they are proud trustees of the hospital that has become a 'Landmark' project in the country for a noble social cause.

The corporate CSR funding agencies were very happy. Above all, the recurring number of patients that are coming to the hospital for quality health and medical services, in ever increasing numbers to the hospital makes one proud of 'the dream project delivering great results'. Great success indeed!!

Lessons learnt from the case discussed:

Many aspects of this project are noteworthy, especially in the case of NGO organizations. Some of these leanings are specified below for quick reference:

- **It is noted that strong & clear convictions and unshakable passion for the project, drive the activities for a successful project, especially for NGO organizations like the case in point.** The case at hand points out that during the tenure of the project, a strong conviction about the goals and set priorities of the group helps you carry on despite hurdles and challenges faced by the group. This basic aspect, no doubt is also applicable to many commercial project situations helping lay strong foundations for the project.

- **A good project manager ensures through his communication skills, that such a strong message about the conviction & unshakable passion for the desired outcome of the project, is effectively communicated to the project team.** Such efforts are essential for the project to succeed through sharing such convictions & passion for the project that keeps the project team motivated and focused on the task.

- **In the field of medicine and healthcare, one develops a reputation for health care and the quality of services provided over the years. It is a process that is built carefully over the years.** There has to high conformance to QA / QC procedures in all activities of the organization. This care was taken in this project by the leadership team right from the beginning and these efforts have paid rich dividends to the organization. Kudos to all the leaders/experts and staff to have built such efforts towards 'quality of advice and quality of services' provided by an organization over the years. This aspect is quite critical for all types of NGO organizations to develop the right perspective and image of their organization over the years.

- **One can notice exceptional teamwork in this project team that started as college friends and has continued even after more than 40 years. Kudos to this team for their friendship and excellent tacit understanding among team members.** The trust amongst themselves was unshakable and this laid the basic foundation for long-term success. This element of trust and understanding appears to be a critical success factor for all types of projects, especially NGO projects.

- **Planning and that too Detailed Planning and Integrated View Planning being done simultaneously, appear to be the key success factors for many long-term projects, especially NGO projects.** For many large projects / long-duration projects, planning needs to be flexible (in terms of Strategy / Tactical / Scope /Time and Costs) and must be in line with the availability of cash -flows.

This is very tricky and challenging, however, it is essential for complex and long time frame projects. Similarly, at times there is a need for re-establishing a Feasibility study of the project as and when you hit a major road block for the project. This is very useful to establish if it is a good time before you close the project, based on the data presented to you. If you need to close a project, then it is better to do it straight away without spending additional money on the same. At times, it is seen that closing down the project is better than facing embarrassment and losing a lot of money and time/resources. This is an important Learning from this case study.

- **Admin & Management of any hospital involves fairly complex and intricate processes. Without well-defined & refined process routines, it will be almost impossible to run the Operations smoothly.** In this case, a lot of attention was paid to this aspect, after the size became complex and coordination across functions became essential. Now the hospital has well-defined routines and rather smooth working, integrated Hospital Management Software modules which are working effectively. It is well accepted across the organization and delivers desired results.

- **The basic theme of this newly created hospital is to provide cost-effective medical advice & services to society at large. This puts an onus on the senior team to keep a watch on the costs of running the establishment on an ongoing basis.** This aspect has been well-managed in this case. From the project manager's point of view, it is a good lesson to control costs at all times as a priority KRA for the hospital during the project phase and operating phase. The organization keeps developing new schemes to enhance the scope for providing a wide range of services to improve customer (Patient & Family Members) satisfaction.

- **Training & Development of skill sets of the employees and associates with other CSFs for the hospital.** This activity is elaborately planned and executed by this hospital. This aspect covers all levels - right from trainees to senior management team, courses and training inputs are provided to the team members and ensure that the organization is future-ready.

- **Risk Identification & Risk Management during this project was not seriously handled** in the initial but as the management team started getting more specifically aware about such matters, they started paying attention to the core issues involved. **The situation now is getting better and along with 'Hygiene & Safety' issues Risk Management matters also get duly addressed by the team during planning & execution cycles.**

- Considering the importance of **'Constant Communication & Dialogue' the senior management has developed a unique system to carry out communication in a very systematic way** and this scheme has paid rich dividends in terms of improvement in work cycles and employee satisfaction. This scheme is very practical and other organizations can make use of it effectively if implemented with due care. The scheme also helps to develop better work discipline and culture in an organization.

Discussion Points:

Convictions and Passion as Project Drivers:

- Discuss the role of strong convictions and unshakable passion in driving the activities of successful projects, particularly in NGO organizations.

- Explore how these fundamental aspects contribute to laying strong foundations, applicable even in commercial projects.

- Consider the challenges faced by project teams and the importance of unwavering commitment to project goals.

Effective Communication by Project Managers:

- Examine the significance of a good project manager in effectively communicating convictions and passion to the project team.
- Discuss the impact of communication skills in keeping the team motivated and focused on the project's desired outcomes.
- Explore best practices for project managers to convey strong messages to project teams.

Quality Assurance and Quality Control in Healthcare:

- Analyze the importance of maintaining high conformance to QA/QC procedures in healthcare organizations.
- Discuss how a focus on quality contributes to building a reputation for healthcare services over the years.
- Explore the critical role of quality in shaping the perspective and image of NGO organizations.

Exceptional Teamwork and Trust:

- Explore the exceptional teamwork demonstrated by the project team, starting as college friends and continuing for over 40 years.
- Discuss the importance of trust and tacit understanding among team members as critical success factors, particularly in NGO projects.
- Share insights into fostering trust and teamwork in various project environments.

Integrated View Planning and Flexibility:

- Discuss the key success factors for long-term projects, emphasizing integrated view planning and flexibility in strategy, tactics, scope, time, and costs.
- Explore the challenges and benefits of simultaneous detailed planning and flexibility in project management.
- Highlight the importance of re-establishing feasibility studies during major roadblocks.

Effective Administration and Management Processes:

- insights into successful implementations of Hospital Management Software modules.

Cost Control and Innovation in Healthcare:

- Examine the complexity of hospital administration and management processes.
- Discuss the importance of well-defined and refined process routines in ensuring smooth operations, especially in large and integrated healthcare organizations.
- Share Discuss the hospital's commitment to providing cost-effective medical advice and services to society at large.
- Explore the lessons learned from controlling costs during the project and operating phases.
- Share innovative approaches to developing new schemes for improving services and enhancing customer satisfaction.

Training and Development as Critical Success Factors:

- Analyze the significance of training and development for the employees and associates as critical success factors for the hospital.
- Discuss how the hospital plans and executes elaborate training programs covering all levels, ensuring the organization is future-ready.
- Share insights into building a skilled and competent workforce for long-term success.

Evolution of Risk Identification and Management:

- Discuss the evolution of risk identification and management during the project, initially not seriously handled but gaining attention over time.
- Explore how the management team improved its awareness of risk management issues.
- Share insights into how 'Hygiene & Safety' and risk management issues are addressed during planning and execution cycles.

Constant Communication and Dialogue Scheme:

- Discuss the unique system developed by the senior management for constant communication and dialogue.
- Explore how this scheme has contributed to improved work cycles and increased employee satisfaction.
- Share practical insights into implementing effective communication schemes to develop better work discipline and culture in organizations.

Case No 24: KGSN- Development of an innovative, comprehensive HR Database for the HR department of an Oil & Gas Industry interfacing with the existing ERP System in the Organization

Dr Jayasri Murali, Dr Rajendra Agawane

Associate Professor, MBA@IICMR, Pune, Assistant Professor, MBA@IICMR, Pune

Extract: One of India's leading software product and ERP application development organizations, with a turnover exceeding 25 crores and a workforce of over 200, ventured into the burgeoning African market, particularly Nigeria. Boasting prior experience and resources, the organization aimed to capitalize on Nigeria's growing economy, rich in natural resources. A prominent Nigerian Oil & Gas MNC sought a comprehensive HR database and bespoke application to align with existing ERP suites, prompted by regulatory changes. Despite the critical timeframe, the project's vast scope led to a phased approach. The complex task involved handling multi-division, multi-location, multi-currency, multi-country, and multi-frequency payroll, and leave and attendance modules across 27 individual modules. The Nigerian team embraced the challenge, ensuring a parametrically designed, platform-independent application.

Introduction:

One of the leading software product and ERP Application development organizations from India (with a turnover of over 25 crore and an employee base of over 200 people) decided to embark upon new market opportunities developing in African countries such as Nigeria. The organization had previous experience dealing with such systems and modules since they had developed similar applications for an Indian organization in the past over the previous 7 years using conventional platforms and development languages.

The organization had the requisite skill base and resources required to set up such activities in the African country- of Nigeria. Nigeria is an excellent country full of natural resources and has grown in terms of its economy and industrial activities over the last few decades. The country has enormous resources in the form of oil and gas and has organizations set up by many leading MNC Oil & Gas companies involved in the exploration/refining and distribution of oil and gas products. Additionally, many banks are set up in Nigeria and also have large textile mills and industrial manufacturing units involved in a range of FMCG and other activities. The economy is on the growth path and naturally needs better infrastructure for telecommunications and business software applications/modules. This gave rise to excellent opportunities for setting up new organizations for software development in that country.

One of the MNCs (Oil and Gas Company of repute in Nigeria) wanted to develop a comprehensive HR database and bespoke application for their complex organization. It was expected that the newly developed application should be interfaced seamlessly with the existing ERP application suite. This assignment was required to be completed as soon as possible since the old compensation system was rendered inadequate because there were modifications required due to changes in Government regulations. The design and structure of the existing system were inadequate to handle the new requirements. Since the change was inevitable, the senior management decided to improve and rationalize the complete HR suite of applications including the payroll modules. As mentioned earlier the schedule for the project was a very critical need for the project. However, the scope of the project was enormous and complex.

After a lot of discussions and re-estimation of the time schedules it was decided to split the project into 3 phases:

- Design phase (Phase 1) - 4 months.
- Payroll and related modules (phase 2) - 4 months.
- All remaining modules (phase 3) - 6 months.

The project was quite complex since it was expected to Handle.

- Multi-division
- Multi-location
- Multi-currency (payroll for ex-pats based on their country of origin).
- Multi-country (country of origin of the ex-patriot employees).
- Multi-frequency of payments (different categories to be paid at different frequencies).
- Multi-leave & attendance as per the

One can understand that producing well-developed code for such complex requirements was quite a task and the team from the newly formed Nigerian company took up the challenge. There were in all 27 individual modules and the application was expected to be Database Platform independent (Means either Oracle or MS SQL) and the design was expected to be parametric in design approach.

Based on the diamond analysis of the project classifications one can classify the project as specified below:

- Technology difficulty: T-4
- Complexity of design: C-4
- The novelty of the design: N-3
- Speed of implementation: S-3

About the project:

Sr No	Project Characteristics	Comments
1	Size of the project:	The size was around @.65 million USD (INR 4.25 crore) in today's currency rates including Manpower costs+ overheads + travel + incidental costs) The total period for the project was 1.5 years from the start of the project.
2	People:	There was a project team of around 8 persons(PM+2 module leaders +4 developers + 1 QA / QC).
3	Schedule:	The period for the overall delivery was around 18 months was the planned project period as per the feasibility study. It was decided that the pilot run for the 'Payroll' was 4 months and this schedule for the design & development was very tight.
4	Classification of project:	The project was classified as a 'New Application Development software project' with a novel design approach. For the newly formed Organization (without too much experience in the Nigerian environment) was quite a challenge and involved lots of risks. However, the team decided to undertake the project based on previous project track records in India.
5	High-risk project:	There were many uncertainties/risks due to the fact new concept / SW application was expected to be developed using a new database version and with the use of the new RADD tool. Additionally, it was difficult to source domain experts since the application was relatively unknown at this stage. There was considerable time pressure due to the proposed timelines especially since the region was completely new and one did not have any idea of the Nigerian market except for the scanty inputs received from the JV partners from Nigeria.

6	Technology Choice / Maturity:	The technology was evolving in this period. The application platform that was chosen for this application was very new and the local Nigerian team did not have any exposure to this new platform. There was eminent danger of the technology not working properly for the proposed application suits in Nigeria.
7	No of suppliers:	There was 'no role' for other suppliers for this project. The internal team from India was competent and they provided very good support from Pune.
8	Logistics / Clearances:	This was quite a challenge due to time pressure and the requirement of a lot of Visa clearances and travel logistics for additional members from India was a challenge. Some delays were due to their late arrival from India.
9	Location for co-ordination:	More than 3 locations (Lagos / Pune & Tel Aviv) were manned with project team persons. Coordination was not such a major challenge.
10	Support from Sr. Management:	Senior management provided excellent support and timely funding/admin support and motivation. Support was received from the senior management throughout the tenure of the project. The team was given complete freedom for action and expenditures. Additionally, the JV organization in Nigeria also provided excellent support in the operational and sales activities that helped the project to succeed.
11	Involvement of Customer:	There was excellent support from the customers in the project. The Customer team had carried out considerable homework before releasing the RFP for the project. This was a great help during the entire project period. However, some of the customer representatives had doubts about the abilities of Indian Software professionals' abilities to produce flawless software for this critical application. PM and the team had a difficult task to win over their minds. Over some time PM and his team won over the hearts of the customers and developed confidence in their minds.
12	Team Leader:	The Project Manager selected was a competent/committed software person. He was a professional, with good expertise in SW applications and good exposure to international projects. He had excellent team-building skills and good relationships with customer personnel. He was an expert in the Project Management Methodologies. This helped the project immensely.

Key positions in the team:

The team had to be manned with the following key positions:

- Project Manager.
- Business Analyst / Business Process Expert.
- Module Leaders (2) for various critical aspects of the proposed project & development team.
- Database Expert / Network expert.
- Quality Leader / Site Quality Leader.

The challenges of the project team:

The following points were noted based on the interaction with the project team members and Project Manager. The key issues are specified below for quick reference:

The issues and challenges:

- The proposed software development was for a very complex application for a relatively new segment of the market. The complexities were mainly revolving around business process sequences and rules and regulations applicable in various verticals in industrial markets. The mapping of the process routines and the logic for the calculations involved in certain routines was not easy for the current users since they did not have lucid communication abilities nor logical explanations for the routines for the last several years. However, to intimate involvement of customer professionals and the quality of the homework done by the teams helped the PM and his team members to handle the challenge effectively.

- One can easily appreciate that for implementation of any typical ERP system/module, it is essential to get basic data (Master Files / Databases / Constants and systems parameters along with system parameters as required) simply and cleanly ensuring authenticity/reliability of the data at the beginning of the project. It is however, a reality such is not the case in industries. No department in the old days was specifically responsible for this activity. This can lead to major hurdles and disastrous results and the outcome. One has to guard against this kind of episode.

The same was the condition in this project and one had to set up an independent group to gather/analyze and compile such data which was not the part of original specifications/scope of the project. However, it was prudent to guide a few members of the customer team along with a few from the supplier side to complete this task on priority. This saved the project as such from a possible disaster.

- Training & Development was an important aspect of this project since it was decided to use new technology and new development tools. The new RADD tool meant a completely new way to carry out work. The customer teams also had to be trained for this new tool and new approach. This was critical for the success of the project. Since both the teams were trained together it helped to generate common bonding and team development across the organizations for better communication and sharing of ideas throughout the tenure of the project.

- The time pressure for development was enormous. In the initial period, there was a lot of time that had to be invested to train and orient the members of the development to understand and grapple with the terminologies and processes routines. The main reason for the time pressure was that the existing supplier was not willing to support the application for more than 8 months from then due to the change of the owners of the existing supplier company.

- The team with the help of the customer had invested a lot of time in deciding ways to document in a standard way. This aspect was followed ruthlessly and helped the team enormously to stay on the correct path all the time. The minutes of the meeting and decisions were noted and documented well throughout the tenure of the project. The team members expressed that this aspect is the major cause that helped to sow the seeds of success for the project as such.

- There were cultural differences between customer teams and home office teams. This gave rise to many impediments and day-to-day difficulties. This had to be resolved gradually and with a lot of patience and care. This was carefully handled by the PM and key seniors in the team. The customer team was also supportive of this approach and things started falling in line after a few weeks.

- The communication with customer reps and within the team was carried out most efficiently and was well documented for everyone to refer to. The PM and his seniors helped carry out such frequent and clear communication with all the members (External + Internal) to help avoid confusion and misunderstandings. This step was critical from the project's perceive. Additionally, the team member had tacit trust in each other and their leadership which helped the PM to maintain harmony and establish a rhythm of working within the team despite difficulties faced in Nigeria.

- Due to the complexity of the application and domain environment "preparation of test data" was a major challenge. However good quality of homework carried out by the customer team was very useful in the matter. They provided all the support for trials at the home office and site.

- One more factor that had to be given due attention and time was 'Training & Technology skills development'. It is noticed that for many projects, this crucial aspect does not receive due attention leading to possible failure of the project at hand. However, due to nuances of technology and methods used, extensive training was conducted for the relevant topics and modules for the working teams and this was managed very effectively. This made the team members confident and their interdependence increased since they had to learn from each other. Training was welcomed by all including customer personnel who were involved in the overall development processes. Later these are the people who would run the show on their own.

- Planning for this particular project/module had to be flexible within certain boundaries but had to develop insight and appreciation from mechanical and electronic changes that had to be integrated into one simple–looking mechanism when everything integrated into one solution. The experience was awesome and worthwhile for every engineer in this field of technology.

Positives in the project environment:

- There was full support from senior management and foreign partners.
- The focus of the team was very specific and worked toward a detailed implementation plan in cooperation with the customer personnel.
- Continuous dialogue with the Customer PM and local PM with resolve to address the issues immediately helped the team to complete the project in the required time. Harmonious teamwork paved the path for a good quality / undisturbed work environment. This was crucial for the success of the project.
- Pre-dispatch inspection for every release involving local and customer QA / QC teams helped hassle-free on-site implementation of the software without delays and waiting periods.
- The team had full freedom for decision-making and commitment to expenses as per the decisions of the PM. This paved the path for smooth working for the team.

Project Success Criteria:

The project success criteria took into consideration customer expectations and organizational expectations:

- Organizational expectations
  - To complete the project in time without any compromise on quality.
  - To conform to stringent standards as specified for oil & gas and banking industry.
  - To achieve the project profitability a planned.
  - To develop this application as a model project so that it can become a reference project for future business.
  - To get repeat orders from the same customer.
- Customer / User Expectations
  - To ensure on-time delivery and implementation.
  - To achieve committed ROI from the project.
  - To provide good support and handholding services during implementation.
  - To provide good quality documentation & reduce time cycles for add-on modules.

- Satisfaction of the team members
    - To ensure team satisfaction.
    - To develop new skills/domain expertise for the future.

Project Success Factors (as seen by the team members now):

Based on the discussions with the team members and their PM it becomes clear that the list of the following points would have been useful for them as CFSs for this project. However, it has to be noted that this aspect was not thought of before the project started.

- Clarity about the task at hand & clarity about scope and specifications.
- Commitment and participation by the customer teams in the development of the system throughout the tenure of the project life cycle.
- Complete support from the senior management & freedom of action.
- Competent Project Manager & trusted team.
- Alert Risk Management especially in the form of timelines and design/changes for POC / UAT.
- Control over project progress issues through impeccable communication and coordination.
- Strong support from QA / QC teams and process control engineers (support received due to strong and matured processes in the parent organization).
- Exceptional teamwork and untiring support from the task force members.
- Good support from Legal Experts and Admin teams.

Conclusion: Highly successful project with few silver linings!

The project was evaluated as a complete success and the team was very proud of their performance. The customer and the senior management personnel were very happy about the project outcome. The project was finished in the requisite time and the quality of the project outcome was completely as per the expectation. The customers signed an AMC contract for the next 5 years. This project won an international award in 2001 for the MNC organization.

Lessons learnt from the case study:

Many new aspects and issues are observed in this case study and these will lead to useful learnings from this project. Some of the most useful aspects are specified below:

- Whenever there is too much time pressure in the project due to the commitment of the final date the scope of the project must be studied and documented very well and controlled thereafter. The changes are in any way part of the game, but if these are as minimal as possible due to quality homework carried out in advance by the development team, then the chance of delivery in time is achievable for the project. However, sometimes it is observed that the senior management team tries to generate 'pseudo-pressure' on the team then it may have a 'counterproductive' effect on the team. Such measures are not desirable in the long run. PM should protect his team from 'pseudo-pressure' situations.

- For complex & large ERP projects, it is pertinent to carry out planning at 2 levels- one at grass root level and the other at a helicopter view that is comprehensive and integrated. One can see that planning has to be integrated but implementation can be modular provided the PM ensures that at no stage do local deviations lead to inadequate integration. This looks easy in concept but is quite a challenge in the field where people seem to lose sight of the complete picture.

- Additionally, for ERP projects, it is important to work on the availability of basic data files and compile databases. One may like to know that even in professionally managed companies, the availability of such clean, complete and comprehensive data files and databases is not easily available. Delays in data availability tend to cause delays and hence additional commitment of resources and costs. Wrong data, at times, leads to wrong results and major frustration among team members. It is suggested that very focused attention is required for this data compilation and cleaning stage which gives good results. No attention may lead to even closure of the project which was otherwise developing satisfactorily.

- It is needless to emphasize the need for complete clarity about 'SOW' or 'Scope of Work' expected from the stakeholders and not only restricted to the IT department of the customer organization. End-user involvement right from the beginning is desirable so that there is a proper understanding of the real need and process sequences required for the completion of the tasks involved. This step should be carried out rigorously without shortcuts. This study takes time but it is better to spend this time in the beginning rather than waste a lot of time and costs during the implementation stages. In many organizations, it is noticed that such efforts or attention are missed out resulting in a lot of rework and rejection. This must be avoided at any cost to ensure the well-being of the project.

- There were cultural differences between customer teams and home office teams. This gave rise to many impediments and day-to-day difficulties between the two teams. This had to be resolved gradually and with a lot of patience and care. This was carefully handled by the PM and key seniors in the team from the project organization. The customer team was also supportive of this approach and things started falling in line after a few weeks.

- Training & Development of the Project Team (Internal + Customers Team) was essential for this project where new technical methods and new RADD tools were being introduced. The training sessions also helped to generate a friendly atmosphere and harmony between the teams and this was a very welcome outcome. Feeling together as a team also carry out the work in an efficient way which was indeed a great positive contribution. Such harmonious relationship also helps improve interpersonal as well as intergroup communication and dialogues. This was appreciated by all the stakeholders.

- For such a complex system, where mathematical algorithms and speed were essential, it was equally important to provide a test facility for the checking of the fully ready system. Without such a system the team would have been impossible to simulate conditions and test the program. However due to the presence of few senior personnel, such a facility was planned right from the beginning. It is important to provide test facilities and test harnesses based on the specific customised tools for the sake of the project.

- Logistics and admin support are also equally important where locations for actions are across multiple countries. Such support was provided by the customer office in a very effective way and this helped manage smooth operations for the teams between different locations. Procedures for Visa and Travel permits were managed well and that was very useful.

- One can appreciate that when you change from a current home-grown system to a new & sophisticated system, it is necessary to orient & educate people about the same. Without such initiatives the reality of challenges and the solutions it will bring to the organization. Such dialogues and sharing of genuine information to all the stakeholders. All stakeholders have their agendas to push but such efforts do not help the organization at large. This was handled well in this project. Getting everybody on board with such a unified notion is not an easy task. It takes a lot of effort to manage such a change of mindset. This is a critical factor to watch for such a sensitive project.

- Additionally, one may notice that an ERP project will demand proper technical documentation including systems documentation. This is very crucial for the project both in terms of short-term and long-term time spans involved. This works like the Bible for the entire project team and is very useful while the implementation stage is being completed. This aspect was well handled in the current project by the home team which was very useful during the tenure of the project.

Discussion Points:

Effective Scope Management:

- Importance of studying and documenting the project scope under time pressure.

- Quality homework in advance to minimize changes and ensure timely delivery.

- Caution against senior management creating 'pseudo-pressure' and its counterproductive effects.

- PM's role in protecting the team from unnecessary pressure situations.

Strategic Planning for ERP Projects:

- Planning at both grassroots and helicopter views for complex ERP projects.
- Integration of planning while allowing modular implementation.
- Challenges of maintaining a comprehensive view in the face of local deviations.
- The balance between integrated planning and modular implementation.

Data Compilation and Cleaning:

- Significance of clean, complete, and comprehensive data files for ERP projects.
- Delays and additional costs associated with data availability issues.
- The impact of wrong data on project outcomes and team frustration.
- The a need for focused attention during the data compilation and cleaning stage.

Clear Understanding of Scope of Work (SOW):

- Emphasis on complete clarity about the Scope of Work (SOW) from stakeholders.
- Involvement of end-users from the beginning to understand real needs and process sequences.
- Rigorous steps are required for a thorough SOW understanding to avoid rework and rejection.
- Balancing the time spent in the beginning against potential time and cost waste during implementation.

Managing Cultural Differences:

- Identification and resolution of cultural differences between customer teams and home office teams.
- The role of the Project Manager and key team members in handling cultural conflicts.
- The importance of patience and care in resolving day-to-day difficulties between teams.

Training and Development:

- The necessity of training for the internal and customer project teams.
- The positive impact of training on creating a friendly atmosphere and team harmony.
- Improved interpersonal and intergroup communication resulting from harmonious relationships.

Test Facilities and Tools:

- The importance of providing test facilities and test harnesses for complex systems.
- The role of senior personnel in planning a test facility from the project's inception.
- The necessity of simulating conditions and testing the program before implementation.

Logistics and Admin Support:

- The equal importance of logistics and admin support, especially in multi-country projects.
- Effective support from the customer office in managing smooth operations between different locations.
- The significance of well-managed procedures for visas and travel permits.

Change Management and Stakeholder Education:

- The necessity of orienting and educating people when transitioning from a home-grown to a sophisticated system.
- Challenges in managing change of mind-space and getting stakeholders on board.
- Handling agendas of different stakeholders for the benefit of the organization.

Technical Documentation for ERP Projects:

- The demand for proper technical documentation, including systems documentation.
- The critical role of documentation during both short-term and long-term phases of the project.
- The documentation is important as a guide for the entire project team, especially during implementation.

Case No 25: Setting up a new railway track of strategic importance in Jammu & Kashmir for the Government of India in difficult terrain and an aggressive environment

Dr Jayasri Murali, Ms Pooja Nalawade

Associate Professor, MBA@IICMR, Pune, Assistant Professor, MBA@IICMR, Pune

Extract: India's ambitious Udhampur Banihal Railway Link (USBRL) project, initiated in 1999-2000, aimed to connect the challenging terrain of Jammu & Kashmir, demonstrating strategic and national importance. The government entrusted Konkan Railways with the contract due to its experience, yet challenges arose in project management. The Ministry of Railways split responsibilities, with Member Engineering overseeing design and management, and Konkan Railways handling construction. The project faced setbacks early on, with the Member Engineering's decision causing internal conflicts. The challenging terrain, including mountain ranges and river beds, led to unforeseen difficulties. Original estimates proved inaccurate, as initial feasibility studies lacked comprehensive surveys, impacting the project's feasibility, cost, and time. Militancy in the region, unexpected security concerns, local resistance, and labour shortages added further complications. The need for local employment led to training programs, extending timelines and costs. Change only occurred after a change in government and a new Member of Engineering's intervention. After six months of reevaluation, the revised project plan was accepted, providing additional funds and allowing real work to commence. The Project Director, upon taking charge, emphasized the need for a re-feasibility study, uncovering critical oversights and proposing solutions. The project now progressing in its third phase, aiming for completion within an additional two years. The USBRL project exemplifies the intricate challenges and adaptations required when executing major infrastructure projects in complex terrains, underscoring the importance of meticulous planning and adaptability.

Introduction:

India is a large country and in fact, is like a sub-continent and has large national boundaries. There is ever-increasing pressure for better transportation and roadways/railways to take care of the needs of the society at large and in a few locations strategic ease for military movements. The state of Jammu & Kashmir has difficult terrain and so far is not connected in terms of railway tracks all over the state. The government of India in the nineties decided to set up such railway-tracks in a select part of the state. This initiative was taken up way back in 1999-2000 by PM A B Bajpayee and accordingly after scrutiny of the proposals the Government of India decided to award the contract to Kokan Railways because Konkan Railways had the requisite experience. However, it was decided to manage this project under the control of the Ministry of Railway considering the Strategic and National importance of the project proposed.

The project was titled 'USBRL' - Udhampur Batra Banihal Railway Link and the initially sanctioned budget (as per the approval given for the concept note) was INR 3000 Cr for the overall railway track of 72 Km. The project was expected to be completed in around 6-7 years from the beginning. As indicated earlier the proposed project was managed by the Ministry of Railways (Member Engineering from the Board was in charge of this project) and the Construction work was supposed to be contracted to Konkan Railways.

The members of the Konkan Railways team pointed out right from the beginning that the Current Design, Organization Structure & Engineering Approach' are not suitable for such a gigantic project. This aspect was followed by several meetings to sort out this issue. The team pointed out that such a dichotomy (Overall ownership with Min of Railways) and work responsibility with Konkan Railways. This split responsibility and authority would mar the interest of the overall project considering the strategic importance and nature of complexity involved in the project environment. They also pointed out that no further transfer of officers from various railway departments should be on the condition that during the tenure of the project such personnel will not be transferred to any other post outside the project (this was based on their experience for Konkan Railway Project under the able leadership of the CMD of Konkan Railways at that time). They had learnt that the transfer of such officials during the project tenure causes lots of problems and delays in the project's progress since there is a loss of continuity in many departments and activities. They proposed that the project be handled from 'unified command and one agency should be allowed to handle the complete project with full responsibility and authority for the project success and timely completion'. However, due to insistence from the Ministry of Railways, the project was assigned with double charge   Project Design & Project Management to be handled by the Member-Engineering and Construction responsibility with the Konkan Railways Team) was very disturbed about such an approach, which he thought, was bound to fail. According to the Project Director from Konkan Railways (who was at the site for many years, and directly responsible for the project said that "the first seeds for failure (not completing in time and budget) were sown apparently in this wrong decision and the project (as proven over some time) suffered heavy setbacks due to insistence by the member Engineering at that time to control the project. Member Engineering and his sitting in Delhi were not in a position to visualize and understand the nuances in the field and hence would arrive at ad hoc or incomplete analysis and info. This was indeed disturbing.

Another significant factor in this project was the fact that the terrain for the construction was very challenging, difficult and aggressive from all points of view. The track of 72 Km was through many mountain ranges and river beds with very wide river beds in few places but very narrow and steep ravines in few places. It was necessary to build bridges in such locations. This was a very hard and onerous task for the project teams and proved to be a very difficult job throughout the tenure of the entire project (which was still not complete at the time of the interview and detailed interaction with the Project Director). The gradient considered for the railway link was starting around 1700 feet above the ground level and going up to 7500 feet above the ground level. On re-evaluation of the estimates made by the project team, it was apparent that the budgetary estimate for the project was completely out of sync with the actual design scope and ground realities.

When the work started, it was noticed that the original feasibility was carried out based on estimates/estimates (Contour Maps were not prepared based on surveys that were not a comprehensive survey). Some of the locations. It was noticed that there was a need to undertake the construction of tunnels instead of bridges which were in a way very difficult tasks. Konkan Railways after visiting the completing the aerial Survey and physical inspection of the critical locations, proposed a new approach that was based on revisiting the project scope. This was not agreeable to the Member Engineering (since he was the approver of the initial feasibility study). This generated a situation of confrontation between the two organizations. This was again pointed to the Member Engineering of the railway board who did not pay attention to the suggestion in the initial stages. The stalemate was resolved based on the basis interventions from the Ministry of Railways. This started the work but key members from the Konkan Railway team resigned and went away since they were not happy with the decision taken by the Member Engineering from the railway ministry. This was a major setback for the project.

At this stage, there was a change in the central Government and the old Member Engineering was reassigned to a new position and another person was appointed. He took over 6 months to review the entire situation and asked all the parties concerned to revisit the project concept and asked all the parties to make presentations and suggestions for the prestigious project at hand.

However, the good news after 6 months was that the new Member Engineering agreed with suggestions made by the Konkan Railway engineers and sanctioned additional funds for the project and for the first time real work started at the site camp.

When the Project Director took official charge of the project he felt that the project estimates were not sensible and he insisted on carrying out a re-feasibility study of the project all over again. The findings were astonishing. It was established that the following issues were not at all addressed in the initial feasibility study:

- There was no detailed survey of the terrain that covers 72 Km of the proposed railway track was carried out and many fine aspects which are significant for the project were missed out. One such example was the need to build roads to reach the location for some of the excavations and piling where vehicles could not reach due to the 67% gradient on some of the roads. It was estimated that in many locations for 10 Km worth of railway tracks 150 Km of winding road would have to be built before any equipment could be carried out to that location. This was a big surprise to everyone in the entire project stakeholder community. Such aspect would affect the feasibility and the exercise had to be redone all over again. There was no provision not even mention of these items in the budget proposal. This was very embarrassing for the leaders and Railway Ministry officials. Such situations increased the cost and time elements and Budgets had to be enhanced for all such issues. Lots of waste of time which was avoidable.

- The area was full of militants and terrorists and one such camp was looted by the terrorists on a day and they took away all the food items and essentials from the camp site. They made it mandatory for the project team to provide security to all the personnel at the project site. This was certainly not provided for in the original budget and one had to obtain a special sanction for the same and the waiting period for this sanction was over 3 months. Every such episode naturally resulted in increased costs & time. And in reality, there were many such episodes.

- The local population in the meantime decided that they would not allow the site team to fill water in regular water supply locations (they had sent armed local 'goondas' to manage this part) unless the project promised to keep at least one person per family in that area some job at the site. This was another surprise when the work started. This was sorted out by the Project Director with the help of local seniors and Sarpanch from the villages around the campsite.

- Now another unprecedented thing happened the labour suppliers' personnel (from other states) fled the camp site never to return to the site. They refused to work under such conditions in addition to the hardships faced by them at the site. The project environment, the field conditions and the ambience were not human populations and this was also a challenge. This was another jolt to the project team as such. Again there was a stalemate situation at the camp. It was further decided that they would train local labourers and diploma engineers for the work on the projects and project modules. This also meant 2 months of training for the labourers and 6 months of training for the supervisors and engineers. This meant an additional few months of activities and delays and increased costs for the project.

- The area was not at all used to industrial activities and such local support for any of the ancillary activities. The logistics were quite complex and getting approval from the seniors was the most time-consuming and tedious activity.

- There were many technical firsts for the project undertaken and these aspects have been summarized in the sections below for quick reference. Many such technical snags were identified and corrected which increases time & costs.

The current progress indicates that 2 basic project phases are now completed and 3rd may take an additional 2 years for the final handing over of the project to the Ministry of Railways for daily operations.

Objectives of the project:

The objectives for the new project organization set-up were as follows:

- To build a railway track in a challenging, aggressive and difficult mountain range of the Himalayas in Jammu & Kashmir bridge with a strategic location (that is critical for strategic and defence perspective) when no other nation has built a railway track at the highest altitude in the world. This project is also known as USBRL.

- To ensure that international quality standards right from the stages of concept design to final delivery (EPC standards) even though the state of the art technology is used in this project.

- To ensure that this project is completed within the stipulated time of 84 months (estimated at the initial stages of project approval) considering the strategic importance of the project (in reality it took over 12 years and the project is only 60% complete due to various constraints).

- To ensure that the design and architecture are modern and styling should be such that it becomes a landmark project without any compromising in Engineering Standards and Specifications.

- To ensure that the design is such that it will achieve the requisite standards of safety and sustainability as per the international standards – for now and for the future.

- Ensure that the design and engineering construction incorporate safety and security measures and provide uninterrupted power supplies for the ultra-modern equipment and facilities provided in the design.

- To incorporate "Energy and Environmental" friendly construction and make use of natural (non-fossil based energy sources) as far as possible.

- To ensure the safety and security of the railway link, working personnel and society at large during and after construction of the railway link.

The challenges of the project team:

The following points were noted based on the interaction with the project team members and Project Manager. The key issues are specified below for quick reference:

Internal issues and bottlenecks observed:

Many internal issues/aspects needed attention from the project team, especially for the PM. Some of these issues are specified below:

The challenges of the project team:

The following points were noted based on the interaction with the project team members and Project Director.

The researcher had a chance to meet him personally (who has now retired from Konkan Railways and is in consulting activities now) and during the discussions, the author had a chance to ask him about the challenges faced during the project execution as such. The key issues discussed are specified below for quick reference:

Internal issues and bottlenecks observed:

Many internal issues/aspects needed attention from the project team, especially for the PM. Some of these issues are specified below:

Too many agencies were involved in the decision-making and approval process (at times no one knew who was responsible and accountable for the decisions and the impact of the decisions) which led to delayed decisions and resulted in additional costs for the project (that could have been avoided).

Although the project organization had defined lines of reporting and well-defined authority structures, these at times were rendered ineffective on account of interventions by the agencies specified above. Many times there were pressures from various ministries and senior officials from Delhi. This was very disturbing & difficult for the team members including Project Director and Project Managers.

This was one of the unique challenges for such a complex project. The coordination among the agencies was a nightmare for the project team. All these agencies in concept were focused on the project objectives, they had their viewpoints, approach to work, internal processes and priorities for the work. This made life very miserable for the project teams. The team had a tough time due to this aspect. Better cooperation amongst the agencies would have helped avoid delays, cost overruns stress for the project coordinators and frustrations for the working teams. As luck would have it during the tenure of the project, there were 3 different members of engineering knowledge on the Railway Board and all of them had their 'own' viewpoints and needed to show superiority of their judgment over the others. Such politics and pressure tactics from seniors were an issue of great concern for everybody involved in the project for long periods.

The project is an 'Engineering Marvel' and very complex in terms of Railway Engineering Design and Construction, Structural Engineering Designs and Confirmations and Concept Testing Site Work Challenges.

The design of the track layout in different segments was unique and full of engineering challenges, No local experience was available for the Indian Teams at different locations. At certain points there were tunnels and at other several locations bridges were pre-modelled. Each location had unique issues and they had to be installed as per QA guidelines and achieve milestones as per the schedules planned. Completion of the task on time is a matter of pride for the team when they can manage on time.

Additionally, there were many bridges in very difficult terrain that could not be handled with current Indian know-how and available technical competencies, equipment and available resources. The firms in Hong Kong and the Netherlands were enlisted to support the project in terms of Engineering & Structural Designs and Field Supervisory help at the site since they had similar (not exactly similar) experiences and this was welcome. But again such costs were not provided for in the initial budgets and this caused many confrontation issues with multiple authorities and delays in the process for approval for additional funds.

In addition to the main aspects of the challenges specified above, while talking to the Project Manager the following major Design & Engineering issues/challenges were identified (from a Technical / Engineering angle) that are specified below:

- Engineering Design / Construction / Technology Choice and associated Technical Challenges. (Complexities increased due to the enormous size of the project compounded by aggressive project environmental conditions, working in the Mountains and Rivers that have very fast currents and unpredictable changes from time to time).

- Meeting challenges of complex site conditions in the Himalayas conditions without adequate type of equipment and personnel with previous relevant experience. In one of the locations, the entire road roller had to be dismantled and part by part had to be pulled up the hill and re-assembled. This is not an easy task. There are considerable challenges even lifting the mass at higher levels. Additionally, there was no workshop facility at the site (not easy to manage without basic infrastructure).

- Ground Stabilization (this was a tough challenge and was compounded on account of unpredictable weather conditions & seasonal fluctuations).

- Piling installation in hard rock without overburden at such enormous height.

- Initial Erection of Trusses in peculiar weather conditions / Relocation of Trusses.

- Construction of cable-stayed bridges where required.

- Stringent precision levels are to be achieved during the construction of bridges.

- Complex conditions for Tunnels and construction work at high altitudes where it was difficult to navigate vehicles, dumpers and other earth-moving equipment and excavators.

- Construction of Bridge structure & Geometry control without the availability of the right equipment at such locations.

- Working during all the seasons with aggressive conditions and with minimal equipment and safety devices for the site workers.

- Erection of Pier table segments.

- Logistics in site locations.

- Link bridges (Design & Construction) which had to be done based on site conditions & locations.

- Stringent requirements towards conformance to engineering standards.

- Innovations at every stage of work and one had to observe strict engineering guidelines for the innovations as well. Every workday came up with a new challenge.

- The psychological conditioning of the people who followed without 'chalata hai' attitude was also a big challenge they were not at all used to working to such standards and engineering accuracies and methods of work.

- Facing the wrath of the local population, terrorists and workmen (ever-boiling and emotion-filled work environments).

One can easily understand that with such conditions, where everything that can change the basic design/concept and the respective impact these issues can drive the project personnel crazy at times, especially when the changes are significant. Since the project was the first of its kind in India, there were not many people to consult within India. For everything one had to depend on foreign experts and their approval was crucial before anything could change site.

For the construction of one of the complex bridges, there was a need to build a model for the bridge and before the design could be approved, it had to be tested based on a simulator that was available in the Netherlands. This was planned in the presence of the design and engineering team from India along with a group of senior consultants from 5 countries. The simulation proved that the current design was far adequate and hence the entire design had to be changed based on the advice from the Netherlands Engineering Team. Every such design change had a spiralling effect on the activities leading to delays and cost escalations.

Such situations, drove the design and engineering teams at the site crazy affecting the morale of the team. The PM had to play a significant role in managing the mindset conditioning of the team. A very difficult task indeed!

Budgets and Permissions / Approvals from Govt Authorities / Railway Board and other statutory authorities and completion of the other formalities:

The senior management of the newly formed division of the company (for this project) had decided from the beginning that they would complete all the formalities and certifications from the competent authorities cleanly and judiciously and would refrain from cutting corners and making adjustments. This was made possible since this was a Government project monitored by the PMO office and hence there were no hiccups. However, the sanction for the new plans and Budgets and approval from various authorities was a big challenge for the project team.

One can easily appreciate that getting approval for such a huge & ambitious project is a Herculean task and one has to face many impediments to obtain permissions & approvals. This is a tough task indeed. One of the major challenges was to obtain permission to set up such a modern Rail Link where the scope was undergoing lots of changes. The Government authorities were also perplexed about such a new venture that was unprecedented in history. There were too many unknowns and anxiety to approve itself was a challenge at times for the officials. They were not at all convinced that such a project is feasible in terms of its practicality and acceptance (since there was no parallel in the recent history of the construction and infrastructure industry).

Despite several visits and presentations made by the core team, the Government authorities were reluctant to grant permissions immediately and the project team had to make several presentations and dialogues with the authorities when the scope was changed due to the need for additional funding. On many occasions, intervention from the Minister of Railways / Defense and the involvement of PMO, did the problems got resolved.

It appeared at times that the project team at the site and the Ministry of Railways were at loggerheads and this further complicated the situation. Konkan Railway team did not want to spoil their hard-earned position of pride for only financial reasons and delays. This, however, such efforts resulted in considerable delays and avoidable costs for the project organization. Unfortunately, such confrontations were faced on many occasions than desired for such a critical project. Governmental procedure to more important than engineering needs. Such was the reality of efforts that frustrated PM & others.

Funding and bank finances was also a major challenge:

Similar to getting all the requisite permissions from the authorities, getting a nod from the Finance Ministry was also a great challenge faced by the project team. The core team had to go through an agonizing period since the officials were very reluctant to even look at the proposals submitted since they were more than convinced that such a project would not at all take off the ground. Additionally, the size of the funds requirement was considerable and there was a pile of losses over and above the original budgets hence carrying heavy risk in the transactions involved. This delayed the entire project and the motivation of the entire team.

This created a lot of frustration and anxiety for the promoters who had staked all their fortunes for the project. Approval was soon becoming a mirage for the team. However, through the intervention by the PMO secretary (he was a great supporter of the project idea) and some of the Senior Officials of the Government, the issues were resolved. However, getting the right type of funding continued to be a challenge for the promoter team.

The challenge faced was the sheer 'size of the project' under consideration:

This issue- the sheer size of the project was the next challenge. One has to realize that the sheer volume/size and complexity of the project was enormous and the issues involved had to be dealt with due care and attention. Enthusiasm and dedication were not good enough to set up strong foundations for the success of the project was not good enough in the initial stages. This aspect was noticed by the seniors and their astute attention to the issues paved the path for 'sure success'. Very dedicated efforts and diligence had to be put to use to ensure proper designs, structure analysis, site planning, infrastructure availability and detailed project planning and scheduling for the workmen and resources. Along with this, it was essential to provide reliable drawings and reliable work instructions. This helped the project to be set right on the path and one could see considerable progress in various activities of the project.

Proactive planning was the key aspect of the project's success. The planning engineers involved in the project had to undergo proper training and orientation along with the change of conventional mindsets to handle such a challenging and voluminous project. One had to develop a helicopter view and an ability to deal with the details at the same time. This is not as easy as it may seem to be in the beginning. The sheer size of the project had an impact on the design & engineering and planning teams throughout the tenure of the project. The senior management team had to keep track of such issues and ensure that activities were kept under control.

In a particular instance, the project needed a typical bridge at a specific location. It was decided to simulate the conditions at the site through the help of a Consultancy from the Netherlands. When the experiment was carried out the current design was not suitable for this location since within 10 minutes from the start the bridge would collapse in the field. This meant a complete redesign (or relocating the bridge), This resulted in delays and additional costs. There are many such episodes during the tenure of the project. Such aspects were not easy to comprehend and adopt at the engineering design stage even for the experienced design engineers in the beginning and hence on many occasions the organization had to bank on foreign expertise and this certainly escalated time & costs for the project.

The complexity of the design and estimation efforts due to size/complexity & use of a non-conventional approach to the entire project.

The complications increased further because the methods proposed for the project envisaged the use of state-of-the-art technologies for the project. Some of the concepts, designs and methods of construction, proposed were never used in this type of infrastructure and construction industry in India. Additionally, the type of project equipment envisaged for the project was not normally used in India. Some of this equipment was not even considered while preparing the basic feasibility study and had an impact on the project plans and budgets. Such items (especially capital equipment on lease or hire) can drastically affect the costs of the project since they throw out-of-gar current assumptions. There were many such shocks from these aspects which were identified and had to be corrected during the tenure of this project. One can learn from this situation that for large infrastructure projects, 'infrastructure &facilities planning needs a lot of assumptions.

Konkan Railway had to ensure that all types of engineering experts (Design Experts / Architects, Construction Site Engineers with relevant experience) were inducted into the project. Induction should include both Technical & Soft issues and should help the individuals to develop intrinsic strengths that will help that individuals to achieve their own goals. Cross-functional teams (CFTs) help in many such areas where things are being explored for the first time. Here one can see the classic dispute between technical issues of the projects vs commercial & financial issues of the problem situations. This particular project has seen many such situations resulting in delays and higher costs.

Challenges related to Scope / Time and Costs (needs flexibility in approach):

Such projects of gigantic proportions undertaken by the PMO render all the conventional methods and practices inadequate and insufficient. This is quite a challenge, as one can imagine since there is no precedence and standards for such innovative projects. The task at hand is quite challenging and highly onerous for the planning team.

While discussing this point, the Project Director explained that:

"Under such an environment one had to adopt a completely flexible approach for planning and sometimes recast the scope/schedules and costs again and again without compromising the promise made to the promoters of the project. This may sound against the basic approach and tenets of project management in the conventional sense, but keeping the basic direction the same, one had to make changes and sometimes significant changes to the scope of the proposed activity leading to a lot of changes for the project parameters. However, when adoption of the best technologies and modern facilities are the critical success factors for the project, one needs to use flexibility in the approach to finalization of the scope (and hence impact on schedules and costs)". One can easily appreciate that without 'Flexibility' in approach and methods of work (hence in scope/time and costs) it would have been impossible to achieve the desired success.

However, 'flexibility' certainly does not mean a 'carte blanche' approach to the project team. Every new suggestion and proposal for new methods/type of equipment was analyzed and scrutinized before clearances for the same. This was an essential management control mechanism without which the project could have gone haywire.

Setting up a flexible but effective organizational set up one more challenge faced by the newly set up organization:

This is a perpetual challenge for any large project organization. Judicious choice of personnel and effective but flexible organisational structure are the basic needs for every large-sized project. Such a need demands able leadership and balance between 'People Vs tasks' issues for large project organizations. Against all the theories of organization structure design, such projects need a quick and flexible approach to respond to the changing needs of the project at a specific time and situation. Additionally, despite the requisite skills it was essential to assess the fit of the person in the team and his mindset for unstructured situations was also a challenge for the selection of the core team. This had to be undertaken with due care and attention by the HR team.

However, this problem was handled by the HO HR team supervised by the CMD. He ensured that apart from technical skills due importance was given to candidates with appropriate mindsets for people to be inducted into the team. Despite such efforts, there were casualties and few key personnel from Konkan Railways felt the job was in critical stages. Finding their replacement within the team was not an easy task for the CMD & PM.

Most of the operational management is done by site engineers. Without proper and well-oiled internal systems and control methods of work, it is difficult to carry out such a large project without problems:

One can appreciate that for any successful project, the core team members must be available for most of the key activities of the project continuously, at least in the initial few years. This is not so easy for dynamic project organization. These organizations need very flexible methods of work and one cannot enforce corporate discipline in such organizations. This creates problems and impediments in the smooth working of many projects. This project was no exception and it continued to face such challenges during the entire tenure of the project. However, due to experience in previous projects, the PM ensured that such procedures/methods and processes were well documented for effective use by all the field workers & supervisors.

Considerable time and effort were sent by the senior management personnel to ensure that the right type of systems controls and communication are developed in the newly formed organization to ensure proper work instructions, reviews of progress as per the plans and internal controls to ensure smooth working for the people at the site. The development of simple but effective systems paved the path for the success of the project. This activity was judiciously carried out throughout the tenure of the project and even now.

Development of support infrastructure and support network of the vendors and sub-contractors was also a challenge for this project:

In the modern era, it is very important that any organization, public or private, has developed a good and reliable network of support organizations (in the form of resource providers, sub-contractors and vendors for specialized artefacts and engineering services). In terms of modern project management practices, this aspect is seen as one of the CSFs for the success of any project.

However, this aspect could not be well handled in the initial phases of this project due to the peculiar location of the activities in the mountains where the normal day-to-day environment is not very smooth and friendly. One of the challenges for this PM was that the 'Feasibility Study' was not carried out with due attention and some of the support services were simply not included in the basic assumptions made for the estimates (hence not provided for in the Budget). Similarly, contractors and vendors from other states were not willing to work on this project due to the obvious fear of terrorists operating where work was being carried out. This was resolved in a way by training and deploying local gangs of workers who were in good sync with local conditions and even with terrorists at times (since they knew some of the gangs personally). However, this workaround did cost lots of additional funding for the project.

Additionally, it was pointed out that some of the designs and prototypes had no simulation facilities and expertise in India and hence one had to depend on overseas consulting firms for the checking and revalidation of the complex designs. Such costs were also not accounted for in the original feasibility study. Additional sanctions had to be resorted to that were painful, slow and had an impact on costs.

The PM during the discussions agreed with the researcher that the concept of dynamic feasibility study may be a useful tool to handle such situations.

Effective Communication among internal stakeholders project team and site personnel:

Effective communication is an important factor for the success of any project in the modern era. This point is already explained. One must note that as per one of the main surveys carried out about the failures of the projects, inadequate communication is one of the primary causes of the failure. The promoters of the project took a lot of care to ensure that the values/policies and plans of the organization were inculcated in the team members right from the beginning.

The senior management team ensured that the guidelines of the management were communicated as frequently as required to the working teams through small group meetings and briefings. This method was quite effective supported by the internal methods and practices. Senior management took a lot of care to see that everyone was informed well in time about the plan and changes from time to time. This was critical for the success of the project at hand.

Attention to Quality Standards and Inspection to ensure that the project activities were carried out the First Time Right.

Many organizations boast about high-quality standards and the quality of services provided. However, quality standards are more talked about than implemented at the field level. The senior management of this organization was highly concerned about ensuring that the promised quality standards were maintained at every stage of execution. The senior management emphasized the expectations about quality standards at every stage of the project activities and generated adequate resources to supervise the activities and maintain required standards. This was accepted as the norm of working over some time and then became the standard of organizational working. The learning at the Konkan railway project was very useful in managing quality at the site due to the matured processes deployed at Konkan Railways. Considering the need for the 'Railway' usage the project personnel had to conform to standard quality norms while carrying out activities at the project sites and offices. This was critical for the success of this project.

The project is very successful from the engineering standpoint (that what is achieved at the site in terms of quality conforms to international standards) although the overall project using conventional parameters appears to be a great failure.

Data management and analysis is another area which is expensive but essential for the project's success.

This has been an area that has to have received due attention right from the beginning of the project. One can easily appreciate that this area is rather critical to manage the project successfully.

This area continues to be crucial to manage the project activities successfully. A lot of care was taken by the senior management team to ensure that all the data (and transaction details) were captured and analyzed for the project progress reviews and proactive actions. The organization ensured that the IT systems were made available to all the functionaries and site teams. It is difficult to carry out the activities in a smooth way without effective IT Systems. This was set up based on all the tools and methods available for the effective working of the organization. Here again, the deployment of matured processes at Konkan Railway was useful and supportive for the team.

Social issues that could affect the success of the project:

- Any such an enormous size of project work generates a lot of social issues and bottlenecks for such a massive project. This project was no exception to this rule. At times political interference and social pressures can mar the speed and viability of the project due to many pressure groups operating in the society at large. This was known to the promoters and they took all the care to ensure that such influences do not hamper the progress of work at any cost. During the tenure of this project, including several extensions on the dates, the Central Government changed a few times and the Member Technical changed more than 5 times. One can imagine the delays and turmoils this project faced during the period. Today the project is still not 100% complete but will be completed soon. This project being strategically important was continued and financed by the Government due to the National Commitment and its defence implications.

- Added to this was fear of attack from the terrorists and local gangs. This was systematically resolved by making fixed arrangements with these agencies and afterwards, they started taking care of project personnel safety themselves.

- Additionally, the project environment and the ambience around this region were very aggressive and only a few types of people in the region could work in this fierce environment. It was not very easy to find such people. In fact, at times local people were inducted and trained on the project to carry out certain types of tasks.

- Senior management had to keep constant vigil to retain their people at the site. The impact was enormous and there was a heavy penalty the project had to take in terms of additional costs and delays.

About the project:

Sr No	Project Characteristics	Comments
1	Size of the project:	800 million USD (INR 5600 crore in today's currency rates was the planned Revenue as per the original budget has gone to over 15000 Crs INR and the project is still not fully commissioned).
2	People:	The core team of Senior managers included 20 core team members with more than 6500 workmen involved in the project from time to time.
3	Schedule:	The original plan was for 5 years but in reality, it took more than 14 years for the first phase and will take a few more years for the handover of the project.

		However, as can be seen from the 'Strategic Intent' of the project one can conclude that the Govt Authorities will keep supporting this unique venture in terms of the National Priority for the Project. The project was very well supported by society at large and many corporate organizations. This was possible only due to the flexible approach and untiring efforts of the initial team.
4	Classification of project:	This is a case of the 'Modern and Complex Engineering Marvel' project and is the first of its kind in the country. This project will continue to remain a benchmark for many all over the country and all over the world in its class despite a failure from the project management process angle.
5	High-risk project:	There were many uncertainties/risks in the project. The project was undertaken in a very hazy and uncertain environment without clarity about the government guidelines. Additionally, it was difficult to enlist the support of support for such a new initiative. Similarly, there was every possibility of political and social interference in the project. Indeed, the project was full of risks. The project was indeed risky in many ways and 'hope' was the only resource based on which the project was undertaken by the group of 'experienced seniors'.
6	Technology Choice / Maturity:	There was a plan to use state-of-the-art technology and modern methods for the project. The promoters had all the confidence in new technology and they supported bold and unconventional methods in the project with a motto 'First time right'. This was indeed not at all a trivial issue to handle.
7	No suppliers/affiliates	The organization created a network of over 400-450 suppliers and over some time treated them as partners in business rather than mere suppliers. This indeed was a difficult task. However, with dedicated efforts from the team, it was accomplished.
8	Logistics / Clearances:	This was quite a challenge due to the time pressure to obtain appropriate 'Certifications / Registration / Licenses and permissions' were a challenge, as explained earlier. This was handled by assigning the tasks to various 'task force groups' and their work was coordinated through the corporate office.
9	Location for co-ordination:	More than 3 locations in Delhi, the HQ of Konkan Railways in Mumbai and 3 active locations at the site where work was being carried out. Coordination was a challenge since the project organization was attempting too many things at the same time.

10	Support from Sr. Mgt:	Senior management provided excellent and timely in every aspect of the work cycles. Apart from conventional support senior management also provided emotional and motivational support to all the workgroups by conducting focused meetings and briefing sessions. Funding was a challenge in the initial period due to a shortage of funds. Similarly, there was no specific admin support in the beginning. Initially, Admin Support & Motivational Support was received from the senior management and main promoters.
11	Involvement of Customer:	There was mixed support / hesitant support from the 'Local people' but people were willing to listen and help. Over some time, they saw the quality of work and observed dedicated work done by the promoters and initial teams. PM and the team had a difficult task to win over their minds in the initial stages. This made the situation quite complex for the project team.
12	Leader:	The Program Director / Project Manager selected was a competent/committed professional with high values and integrity. His self-confidence &conviction about the innovative concept were the main strengths of the organization.

Key positions in the team:

The team had to be manned with the following key positions:

- Project Director / Project Manager as 'Project Champions' (The founders of this project organization).
- Many Government /Semi-Government Officers (these personnel kept on changing causing problems at times).
- Engineering Director with a team of senior consultants for many aspects of engineering.
- Team of 'Core members' of the initial management team.
- Team of planners/architects and structural engineers from various countries.
- Suppliers of critical equipment and special services (local and Foreign).
- Module Leaders (4 initially and now over 12) for various critical aspects of the proposed project & modules.
- Training experts for soft skills and ethical behaviour and attitude-building exercises for the workgroups.
- Module / Field supervisors and site in charge.
- Treasurers managing financial issues/funding and auditors (advisors).

- Legal advisors and consultants.
- A panel of external consultants who were key members of the entire project 'Think Tank'.
- Security & Safety Team.

Positives in the project environment:

- There was full support from promoters / senior management, however, there were too many agencies involved in the decision-making processes with different priorities and concerns. This was handled well by Pragmatic and Smart Leadership on the ground, they handled the localized politics and ministry-level politics effectively.

- The focus of the team was very specific and worked toward a detailed implementation plan in cooperation with the vendors and suppliers.

- Continuous dialogue with Govt officials / Railway Ministry, Project Director and local PM (at each of the sites) with resolve to address the issues immediately helped the team to complete the project in the required time. The senior managers from both sides attend project meetings monthly / quarterly to make decisions and move forward proactively. This was useful for the team but delays still occurred due to diagonally different viewpoints, egos and personal preferences even for such a large project.

- A harmonious team paved the path for a good quality / undisturbed work environment. This was crucial for the success of the project.

- Pre-dispatch inspection for every material delivery involving local and customer QA / QC teams helped hassle-free on-site implementation of the modules without delays and waiting periods.

- The team had full freedom for decision-making and commitment to expenses as per the decisions of the PM. This paved the path for smooth working for the team.

Project Success Criteria:

The project success criteria took into consideration customer expectations and organizational expectations:

- Organizational expectations
  - To complete the project in time without any compromise on quality of service.
  - To conform to stringent rules of Government and Semi-government authorities.
  - To achieve the project delivery for the targeted population as planned by the organization.
  - To develop project modules as a model project so that they can become reference projects for future activities.

- To introduce the state of the art technology and innovations where possible throughout the project.
- To maintain transparency and ethics in real sense of the terms in all activities.
- To make vendors network as partners in business with long-term contracts.
- To ensure that promises once made are honoured to all the stakeholders and 'no comebacks' on the promises.

- Customer / User Expectations
  - To ensure on-time delivery and implementation.
  - To achieve a committed target population and frequency of the project in the community service.
  - To achieve requisite accuracy & efficiency in operations that have a complex set of rules & changes.
  - To handle emotional and social issues effectively without interruptions.
  - To ensure the satisfaction of the team members Promoters / Volunteers / Staff and beneficiaries of the programs.
  - To ensure team satisfaction and development of new skills/domain expertise for the future.

Project Success Factors (as seen by the team members now):

Based on the discussions with the leadership team members and their PM it becomes clear that the list of the following points would have been useful for them as CFSs for this project. However, it has to be noted that this aspect was not necessarily thought about comprehensively before the project started.

- Clarity about the task at hand & clarity about scope and specifications.
- Commitment and participation by the customer teams in the development of the right ecosystem throughout the tenure of the project life cycle.
- Complete support from the senior management & freedom for actions for project module leaders.
- Competent Project Manager & trusted team members.
- Alert Risk Management especially in the form of timelines and scope/changes. This was done well but was not up to the mark at all times/stages.
- Control over project progress issues through impeccable communication and coordination/reviews.
- Excellent support from PMO personnel for ruthless tracking of issues and resolving them.

- Strong support from Audit teams and process control (support received due to strong and matured processes in the organization that have been developed over some time) through frequent reviews and communications in the small teams working on the modules.
- Exceptional teamwork and untiring support from the founding members in the initial period.
- Good support from Legal Experts and Admin teams as and when required.

Conclusion:

A failed project but given national priorities the project is still live and will be finished soon. However, the Engineering Success of the project cannot be denied and hats off to such engineers and experts who made this possible.

They expressed that the project was a great success in the eyes of the common man on the street but from a project management processes point of view, it was not very successful, in fact, a severe failure as one can assess it from a third-party point of view.

Lessons learnt from this case study:

- One has to take care to see that everything is done only after establishing 'Feasibility – Technical / Commercial / Financial' with due diligence. If there is any basic change in the project environment, it may be worthwhile to recast the feasibility all over again. This may appear to be tedious but it will save a lot of future embarrassments and costs through 'Dynamic Feasibility Study'. Not paying attention to such possible situations, organizations may land spending money - that is too large sums- that will be just a waste. The organization may end up making a fatal impact on the project. DFS a step for diagnostic gives pre-waring to Project Sponsors and PM. This method has to be used judiciously as the situation demands. The conditions for DFS can be documented after the discussions about the nature of the project and environmental conditions.

- It can be noted from this case study that a project of this criticality/size and capital budget needs far more preparation and planning. 'Ad hocism' in the form of decision-making, will not work for this kind of project in any case. Rolling wave planning, Flexible and Adoptive Planning mode is the essence of Planning for this kind of project. This mode of planning (along with the Feasibility & Dynamic Feasibility System) is one of the Critical Success Factors (CSFs) for this type of project. One has to learn to make plans that point to the direction and overall goals and not to pin them down by dates and amounts when the basic situation is fluid. This does not mean everything is flexible and open to all. This is a difficult skill but will be required for large-scale infrastructure projects, especially for senior teams and planning groups.

- Organizational structure is yet another important aspect that one needs to understand in the context of large and long-duration projects such as Infrastructure Projects in India. Contrary to normal management science practices, this type of project, needs an evolving and adoptable organization structure. This means one should have the required dexterity

- In addition to the Organization structure, there is another critical issue for the project success for such types of mega projects. In the initial period (at least 5 years), the original team of senior members must remain with the project. If this is not paid attention the project may gradually lead to a path of disasters and failures. One has to realize that the assumptions and constraints under which such a core team arrives at decisions, they have adequate background & knowledge about why such a thing was decided in a specific way, may be lost if the core team leaves. This could be a great loss for the project. One needs to pay attention to this aspect for sure.

- One can see from the ongoing discussions about the case study, one would notice that there are too many Government and semi-government bodies and entities involved in this type of infrastructure project. Every entity has its stance, viewpoint and ego. Managing these agencies and their egos becomes a hassle for the PM and other personnel in the project. However, there is no choice and hence right from the beginning, it may be prudent to develop the right communication and effective PR initiatives to manage these entities becomes an important issue for the project organization. This must be done with due diligence. Failure to manage this may have a fatal impact on the overall project as such. In this case study lot of time and attention had to be given to managing these relationships.

- Selecting & retaining team members for site work is the next challenge faced by such projects, especially senior managers & HR functionaries. It can be noticed that the work environment for projects at the site, is not very conducive and is very harsh & aggressive. It is normally, not so say easy & convenient to stay at the site. Added to this there was the presence of terrorists and tribal presence and they would come and attack the campsite very often. This also makes safety a key concern for the participants. This aspect was well understood and managed very well by for the case of this project. There were many situations concerning people issues (which are very sensitive & volatile) where senior personnel had to observe restraints and controls before taking actions or sending communications (if not controlled well these could have been bitter confrontations).

- Such mega infrastructure projects also need support from Admin & PR teams to ensure conformance to local laws and conditions and adherence to basic project policy guidelines, as an ongoing service to the Project Team. This is very critical for the possible success of the project at hand. Such teams also handle the logistics issues (concerning people and other routine activities) which is welcome for the project teams.

- Constant Communication/Feedback and interactions with all stakeholders, especially employees and contract labour, are crucial for this type of project. This aspect was very well handled in this project.

- Finally paying a lot of attention to Training & Development activities plays an important role in the success or failure of such projects.

and flexibility to adopt a suitable form based on the need of the project at a given point in time.

Discussion points:

Feasibility Studies and Dynamic Feasibility System:

- The importance of establishing Technical, Commercial, and Financial feasibility.
- Advocacy for dynamic feasibility studies in case of changes in the project environment.
- The role of Dynamic Feasibility Studies (DFS) in providing pre-warning to Project Sponsors and Project Managers.

Advance Planning and Critical Success Factors (CSFs):

- Need for extensive preparation and planning in critical infrastructure projects.
- Emphasis on avoiding ad hoc decision-making and adopting rolling wave planning.
- Flexible and adaptive planning as a Critical Success Factor (CSF) for large-scale projects.

Evolutionary Organization Structure:

- Understanding the need for an evolving and adaptable organization structure for mega projects.
- The importance of flexibility to adopt a suitable organizational form based on project needs.

Retention of Senior Team Members:

- The criticality of retaining the original team of senior members in the initial project period.
- The potential loss of background knowledge and assumptions if the core team changes.

Managing Government and Semi-Government Entities:

- Challenges posed by the involvement of multiple government and semi-government bodies.
- The necessity for effective communication and PR initiatives to manage relationships.
- Potential fatal impacts on projects if relationships are not managed properly.

Selecting and Retaining Team Members for Site Work:

- Challenges in selecting and retaining team members, especially in harsh and aggressive work environments.
- The presence of external threats, such as terrorists and tribal activities, requires safety measures.

- Sensitivity and restraint are needed in dealing with people's issues to avoid confrontations.

Support from Admin & PR Teams:

- The critical role of Admin and PR teams in ensuring compliance with local laws and project policy guidelines.
- Handling logistics issues and providing ongoing services to the Project Team.

Constant Communications and Stakeholder Interactions:

- The crucial nature of constant communication, feedback, and interactions with all stakeholders.
- Effective handling of communication with employees and contract labour.

Training & Development Activities:

- The importance of paying attention to Training & Development activities for project success.
- Enhancing skills and preparedness for the challenges posed by mega infrastructure projects.

Case No 26: Setting up of manufacturing unit for production of Decanters in India for global requirements

Dr Jayasri Murali, Mr Harshal Patil

Associate Professor, MBA@IICMR, Pune, Assistant Professor, MBA@IICMR, Pune

Extract: As part of a renowned Fortune 50 MNC with over 150 years of global recognition, the organization prioritizes excellence, adhering to strict QA/QC norms. Specializing in designing and manufacturing products for food processing and industrial use, the MNC faced challenges in the Decanter market. Subsidizing Decanter costs for the olive oil market became unsustainable. To address this, a dedicated manufacturing unit for Decanters was established in India after a thorough feasibility study. To achieve a Group Manufacturing Unit (GMU) status, the project aimed for world-class production, 30% cost reduction, global quality, reliable local networks, stakeholder satisfaction, and strict adherence to MNC standards.

Introduction:

This organization is part of a world-famous MNC that is among the Fortune 50 companies in India. This MNC organization is more than 150 years old and has earned a name of pride across the globe for its Products, Projects and Services. This organization has developed a passion for excellence and they take care to ensure that what they produce observes strict QA / QC norms and practices in every endeavour. This organization is engaged in designing & Manufacturing a variety of products & systems for food processing & industrial applications.

MNC was producing Decanters at their factory in Denmark to cater to the world market. All was well till the competition was less and MNCs were dominating the market. Decanters for the olive oil market were becoming costly, day by day and MNCs had to subsidize the product cost to enable selling it in the market. It was not possible to continue like that in the long run.

Simultaneously, here in India, an Indian company was exploring the market for Decanters for different applications. There was a market but good enough to justify investment!

Considering the need for cost reduction in product cost for the world market and to make the investment viable for the Indian market, it was decided to set up a new dedicated manufacturing unit for 'Decanters' in India which will cater to the world market as well as the Indian market. Accordingly, the project was started after undertaking a feasibility study and subsequent due diligence for the world market needs. After a lot of deliberations and analysis of alternate countries, the MNC Management gave a green signal for the project. It was proposed that after considering engineering standards, consistency of quality and cost- cost-competitiveness over the years, the new unit will be recognized as 'Group Manufacturing Unit' (GMU).

The local management and PM aimed to see that finally this new unit was declared as GMU as soon as possible.

Objectives of the project:

The main objectives of the project were set as specified below:

- To set up a state-of-the-art world-class manufacturing unit which will deliver 80% of its production to the world market and the remaining to the domestic market. (It was expected to have a 30% cost reduction compared to that of the Denmark factory as a reference.)
- To achieve the same quality level as in Denmark so that it will have a brand of MNC having global quality. In addition to Quality, it was expected that the consistency of the supplies is in line with set norms.
- To develop a reliable network of local suppliers/vendors and sub-contractors in India (same quality but very competitive costs and willing to adopt your norms for manufacturing).
- To ensure total satisfaction for all the stakeholders involved over a long period (>5 years).
- To ensure 100% alignment with the processes and admin routines specified by the MNC.

Scope:

When the project was given a clearance it was specified that some of the Technical / Engineering specifications should be met by the unit being created. A few examples are specified below for reference.

The following types of products were decided to be produced in India

- Olive oil machines
- Environmental application machines.
- Local specifications meeting market expectations in India.

Challenges to the project team: Internal - Setting up the core Project Team:

There were several challenges for the project and this project was no exception. Some of the challenges are specified below for the reference.

One may realize that setting up a new manufacturing unit for a complex and intricate product for any organization. The stringent specific expectation added to this makes the new project (setting up GMU) even more challenging.

The initial challenge was to select a capable and experienced Project Manager for the project who had adequate technical competence along with intimate knowledge about the culture of this MNC group along with standards for processes and cost control. After a lot of discussions & searches, a few candidates were short-listed and the senior management members of the Indian arm made their final decision in favour of a competent and gusty member who was declared as the Project Manager formally. It was identified that he was the one who could provide the desired results as explained above. PM was given the freedom to pick his first team for this project and finally, the team was officially assigned to the project.

In addition to the PM and core team, it was important to select & assign a good design expert and an experienced cost accountant, as key additions to the team. These requirements are very specific and dictated by the project objective by themselves. Additionally, it was important to induct an effective Vendor Development & Procurement Manager in the team to ensure conformance to cost reduction and quality conformance issues that are the main requirements of the project (as expected by the HQ team in the MNC).

Out of all the challenges, keeping costs (Indian Costs < than Denmark Costs) less than the reference point was the most challenging of all. Additionally, it was also mandated that the quality of Indian products should match that of those produced in India. Apart from modern techniques such as Value Engineering, Rationalization & Optimization and Design thinking, one will have to depend a lot on a reliable vendor network that can handle & manage the quality standards. One certainly cannot afford to neglect the development of a Vendor Network.

The competent project team under the strong leadership of the PM of the project. Although there were certain hiccups and bottlenecks, the team could achieve the requisite performance standards and the organizational unit, newly created, was accepted as 'GMU for the HQ' in Europe.

There were many other challenges in the tenure of the project that are specified below:

Internal:

Some internal issues/aspects needed the attention of the project team, especially for setting up of manufacturing unit in India. This project demanded a new specific approach to ensure the desired outcome, that was successfully deployed. The key aspects are as specified below:

Specific Approach for this Project:

- A dedicated team with project managers from Europe and India decided to work with an MS Project Plan sheet with time-bound tasks to meet milestones. A capable PM with leadership qualities and adequate technical and managerial expertise was given charge and authority to make non-conventional decisions.

- A dedicated Team leader from India was head of "Purchase and Vendor Development'. This person also had very thorough shop experience as well.

- 7 selected competent members were transferred to new projects (Technical, Design & Engineering, Manufacturing & Procurement).

- The first few machines were produced by using SKDs to ensure that the process sequences and fine-tuning were well understood & followed as per the standards & guidelines).

- Blue collars were trained for critical operations like balancing bows and conveyors. This was done for all blue-collar employees along with a few from vendor locations for critical components.

- The first few critical parts were produced by the CNC shop for other products till volumes were built gradually.

- It was decided to send the products to a factory in Denmark for thorough checking before they go to end customers. This process continued till confidence was developed about the quality of products coming from India. This would be a major achieve achievement.

- Proving the products to MNC specs and standards was focused on the initial rather than worrying about costs at the beginning to make technically correct products. Later the focus was shifted to costs and consistent quality and supplies.

- Suppliers were taken into confidence to ensure timely deliveries of purchase parts. Their contribution to the process was evaluated and appreciated for good suggestions and support. This approach helped develop confidence which was further boosted when the Indian Organization provided them better tooling on their own.

- Above all cultivating a 'First time right' approach in the organization is welcome for improving the success factor of the project. This is at times well said but very difficult to practice.

Planning for the Project:

Considering the importance given by the HQ in Europe, it was pertinent that the PM had to plan for 2 different levels for this project:

- Helicopter view of Planning for overall directions, scope involved and overall capital Budget required for the project along with comprehensive Feasibility (updates/changes etc.)

- Ground Level Planning (weekly/monthly reviews and addressing bottlenecks with a lot of details describing activities.

Additionally, with many things not clear and available, planning modules had to make use of assumptions and situations. It is not very easy to plan so efficiently with such constraints. However, there was no escape from the burden of planning to ensure that the PM and team could make gross-level plans for Budgets and push for certain activities (that may change).

Vendor development for effective quality & costs as per the norms specified by MNC HQ:

Vendor development was one of the most critical aspects of this project due to the obvious reasons explained above. There were a lot of issues with the challenges posed by the project team. Some are specified below:

- Lack of consistency in available suitable standard raw materials in the Indian market suitable for international standards.
- Lack of infrastructure at the vendor end & lack of willingness to invest in better capital equipment and facilities only for a specific company unless volumes are large and spread over the years.
- Lack of adequate technical skills at the vendor end.
- Lack of quality standards and processes that can match international expectations.
- Lack of financial ability to invest in tooling/jigs and fixtures for vendors.

The assigned for vendor development was trained and they resolved these issues with the help of senior management and experts at MNC HQ.

Time cost and quality:

It was expected that the product would be developed in India within a year and the cost target of reduction by 30% would be achieved within 2 years which was a challenge. This challenge was resolved with help from the vendor network over some time. However, this required a lot of patience and skill to make vendors accept your terms and needs.

The product was entirely new and selecting project team selected to work hard to meet the above goal.

a. Overall quality level in India was not up to the mark to meet global expectations.
b. Blue-collar selection to training was a time-consuming process.
c. There was a need to involve experts from the parent company right from the start which was done.
d. A lot of fabricated items were required to be developed and special-purpose machines were to be procured.
e. Long lead time, CNC machines were to be procured to process machined components.

Management pressure:

Making Decanters in the Indian Unit was a priority for MNC HQ as well as for the Indian Senior Management obviously on account of international markets opening up for this product and its applications. However, just generating pressure and too much pressure, may become counterproductive. One has to guard against this type of situation.

- Management was keen that the project would fly as soon as possible.

- The subsidy for olive oil Decanters was a direct loss for the company –MNC HQ. They would not appreciate delays nor would like to lose advantages as first movers in the market. The pressure was a lot and the PM Team had to face the same. This issue was handled very well by PM with active help from the local management.

- There was a lot of pressure on team members to meet both objectives forcing them to burn the midnight oil. The team worked very hard and focused and finally accomplished the task to the satisfaction of the MNC HQ (Local + International).

Domain of expertise:

For the unit to become, GMU for the MNC, it was obvious that the unit had to develop their expertise for the technology and intimate specifications for the customer needs, required processes and quality standards. It was pertinent that without active help from the MNC HQ experts coming to India along with visits of Indian Engineers getting trained in Europe was critical. Luckily this was well planned right from the beginning and it paid very rich dividends this could be accomplished within 16-18 months for the initial stages and was continued forever as an ongoing improvement program for the project activity. This established confidence amongst working members on both sides and this was effective. Over some time MNC HQ personnel have developed full trust in the Indian unit and that was a big one for local engineering & procurement teams.

- The product was a proven product for years, so there were no design issues. However, this was not the case with the local team. Many of these members trained in European units. The results were very encouraging.

- All the manufacturing processes were well established and available to be transferred to India. The parameters for manufacturing had to be fine-tuned to ensure suitability for the Indian set-up.

- Experts from Europe were sent to India to guide the Indian team. Their contributions in terms of technology issues/design issues and production setups were brought to par with sharing basic ideas and then supporting them in the beginning, helping ramp up facilities in India at a good speed.

- For initial production, critical parts were imported from the parent company.

- A project manager from Europe was involved to guide the Indian project manager and used to visit periodically. Personalized communication helped both sides to ensure smooth responses & contributions.

- Some original work had to be carried out by India for such applications of the product that was specifically developed for the Indian market. After the initial period of learning this was also accomplished to the satisfaction of the foreign team. PM took personal initiative in this and made it a success.

Availability of infrastructure:

In the initiation stages, this was a major challenge since the current capital investments in the existing plant were not all compatible with the requirements for the new range of products. One had to depend on a lot of outsourced facilities and integration under the same roof was quite a challenge.

- A factory shade was spared for this project from the existing factory after a lot of discussions and arguments. However, the issue was finally resolved with the help of senior management of the Indian Unit.
- The budget for expenditure was worked on and reworked several times and finally was approved quickly. This was good.
- Manufacturing processes were copy-pasted from the parent company, with fine-tuning where required.
- Team members were trained in Europe and also in India about various aspects of engineering practices, standards and quality norms. This was important.
- Help from other units in the local factory was available without an additional cost burden for the project.
- Team members were spared by different departments for at least a two-year minimum period. This helped the core team a lot.

Development of components:

- With the help of technical experts, and suppliers the components were available / made possible.
- With a few imported parts and a balance of locally produced parts, the product could be assembled.
- Balancing machines were made available along with the required software.

Technical:

- Technical documents were made available & queries were properly addressed and answered by the HQ team. This was welcome.
- Bills of materials of products to be produced were transferred, cross-checked and fine-tuned by the Indian office. Later it was synchronized by the team in both locations to avoid any confusion or miscommunications. This helped a lot.

- A technical expert from the parent factory was stationed in India and Indian Engineers were trained and oriented abroad. This helped communications & co-operations to improve.

- Welding experts for critical components & systems were made available from the existing fabrication shop and were very useful.

- Special tooling was imported from the parent company in the initial stages while indigenous activity was further developed in India – internally as well as with a few select vendors.

External:

- It was difficult to digest the idea of MNC HQ experts that the products would come from India being well aware of the practical difficulty faced by Indian Companies. However, since this project was within the group they were willing to try it out.

- India's image was not good enough to sell "Made in India" products in the world market.

- There was a threat from external customers for a price reduction for products coming from India and competitors taking advantage of their own 'Made in Europe products' v/s 'India made products' There was an eminent danger of losing market share and generating a bad image. Both were not acceptable to anybody in the company.

- Even within the group company, there were reservations from colleagues in Europe about getting quality products from India at competitive prices and consistent quality.

- The products coming from India were looked into with a "Big lens" for defects, especially by lobbyists against India.

- Delivery on Time was a relatively new concept for the Indian environment and many people were apprehensive about it including a few team members.

About the Project:

Sr No	Project Characteristics	Comments
1	Size of the project:	Investment phase I was 12 Crore. Investment for phase II was 10 Crore. Capacity of production 200 nos. Markets served: Olive oil, environmental and Oil and gas.
2	Manpower:	10 White Collar and 25 Blue collar
3	Period:	Phase I was 2 years but completed in 16 months. Phase II was 1 year and was successfully done.

4	Classification of project:	A New Division set up by MNC
5	High-risk project:	Many uncertainties but well supported by the MNC hence risks, pressure and unknowns were reduced considerably.
6	Technology Choice /Maturity:	Technology was established in Europe and hence fewer problems. Indigenization posed many challenges, especially the selection of materials available in India.
7	suppliers/affiliates	No suppliers were 24 – both Global and in India.
8	Logistics / Clearances:	Many issues with logistics for importing critical materials and components Suppliers spread over India in many states Logistics was set up by assigning a shipping company for all exports. Packing contractors were identified and trained for export packing requirements.
9	Location for co-ordination:	Denmark, India, Sweden and many locations in India Coordination was well managed due to modern facilities
10	Support from Sr. Mgt:	Senior management gave all necessary support and encouragement to the team members and appreciated their efforts and individual contributions to the project.
11	Involvement of Customer:	Few preferred customers were taken into confidence to conduct on-field trials of Indian products.
12	Leader:	The project Manager selected was a 'competent/committed Mechanical Engineer' (with good expertise in purchasing and having leadership qualities).

Key Positions in the team:

- Project manager: From Denmark.
- Project manager: From India.
- Engineering manager from India.
- Purchase manager India.
- Quality manager India.
- R and D manager from Denmark.
- IMPEX manager India.
- Production manager India.
- Finance and Accounts & Costing Manager in India.

Conclusion: This highly successful project is envied the world over in the MNC Group!

This was a highly successful project due to proactive planning, dedicated efforts and focused attention from the leaders & all team members and due to active guidance from Denmark (Project Manager from Denmark). Today, after 22 years, it has become the biggest and the best Decanter factory in the world producing over 800 machines consistently. It is the biggest factory within MNC India having its own factory building and dedicated team of over 175 employees. It has a significant share in the global business of MNCs. This project has now become a role model for the MNC, the world over, in the MNC Group.

Lessons learnt from this project:

The urgency to take to the market the new product ASAP along with cost-benefit advantage, technically 100% compatible with international market needs without compromise to Engineering specifications and standards of performance in the shortest possible time, from a new country and new location. This multi-parameter-based challenge is quite a challenge since it rolled all in one. This makes the case unique from a learning point of view. The main aspects of learning are specified below for reference:

- Any complex activity that has to be carried out in a real environment, needs a smart and practical plan. Focus on the results, Flexible Planning approach- long term and short term, Excellent Technical Knowledge & Experience, Control over Operations & Quality (paying attention to details of the activities) and Effective Procurement, will lead to success. Above all, it is also critical to ensure the 'first-time-right' approach in all endeavours & activities is the 'Mantra' for possible success. This is a great guideline, for all future projects that involve the development of new 'Product Ranges in different regions'.

- Selection of the critical core team, as explained earlier was the essence of the paving path for success of the project at hand. This has to be learnt again and again for future Project Managers in the world. This was taken up in the right spirit in this project and one can see that this has paid rich dividends.

- Developing adequate technical & application knowledge and hands-on experience with 3 considerations of (Scope / Time & Costs). For the development of new products and hence new markets & new applications, the team needs expertise & exposure to technology and manufacturing along with engineering abilities to develop & support new applications for the emerging market segments. This takes a lot of planning & systematic efforts to acquire such skills & expertise.

- For this specific project, it was very important to develop a technically competent and commercially cooperative support structure of vendors / sub-contractors for various components of the organizational needs. This was a must for this project to succeed and give complete satisfaction to the MNC HQ and local management. This is a very useful lesson for future project managers the world over especially in the context of product development activity for the world market.

- Clarity of the task at hand (Scope), Effective team spirit and excellent internal Communication go a long way in establishing basic strong foundations for the project. In this project, this aspect was managed very well by the PMs (Europe + India) along with respective senior management personnel. Additionally, one can note that sending the team leads to each other's locations helps in the jellying of minds forms a strong bond of friendship and helps better communication and coordination,

- Additionally, good documentation (with good update support helps improve project performance. This is a good approach and should help all future endeavours. Future project managers keep in mind about projects related to 'Product Development', that documentation and technical repositories are very important for the overall success of the project at hand.

Discussion Points:

Smart and Practical Planning:

- The necessity of smart and practical planning for complex activities in real environments.
- Emphasis on a flexible planning approach, considering long-term and short-term goals.
- The role of excellent technical knowledge, experience, and attention to detail in achieving success.
- The importance of effective procurement strategies for project success.

'First Time Right' Approach:

- The critical importance of ensuring a 'first time right' approach in all project endeavours.
- Guideline for future projects, especially those involving the development of new product ranges in different regions.

Selection of the Core Team:

- The essence of selecting a critical core team for the success of the project.
- The impact of a well-chosen core team on project outcomes.
- The importance of this lesson for future Project Managers worldwide.

Technical Knowledge and Application Expertise:

- The necessity of developing adequate technical and application knowledge along with hands-on experience.
- Considerations of scope, time, and costs in acquiring expertise for new product development and market entry.

Vendor and Sub-contractor Support Structure:

- The significance of developing a technically competent and commercially cooperative support structure with vendors and sub-contractors.
- The essential role of this support structure is to ensure project success and satisfaction for both local and HQ management.

Clarity, Team Spirit, and Internal Communication:

- The importance of clarity in understanding the project scope.
- The role of effective team spirit and internal communication in establishing strong project foundations.
- The benefits of sending team leads to each other's locations for better communication and coordination.

Documentation and Technical Repositories:

- The role of good documentation and update support in improving project performance.
- The significance of documentation and technical repositories in the context of product development projects.
- A reminder for future project managers to prioritize documentation for overall project success.

Case No 27: Setting up of a new greenfield project for the design and manufacture of 'Sports garments' set by a team of young highly qualified engineers

Dr Jayasri Murali, Ms. Dipti Bajpai

Associate Professor, MBA@IICMR, Pune, Assistant Professor, MBA@IICMR, Pune

Extract: 'Apace,' founded in 2012-13 in Pune, India, is a rapidly growing sports apparel brand born out of the passion of two highly qualified engineers and sports enthusiasts. Recognizing the lack of affordable and well-designed sports garments in India, Mihir and Aditya embarked on a journey to fill this gap. Specializing in performance apparel for running, cycling, and triathlon, Apace has garnered a reputation for its purpose-made fabrics, customized colour palette, and functionality-centric design. With an expanding range and a dedicated in-house team, Apace aims to provide high-quality performance wear accessible to both elite athletes and weekend warriors.

Introduction:

Many startup projects are not necessarily based on business considerations but based on the 'passion' of the individual entrepreneurs. Once the idea is born then the entrepreneurs work on the business plans and tend to justify the (idea originally based on passion and gut feel) need for the new business venture. Generally, this is the situation for most 'Start-up Organizations.

This was a project initiated by a young team of highly qualified engineers (two of them). These individuals belong to highly qualified families and both of them completed their Engineering graduation and then went abroad for their post-graduation (One of them went to the UK and the other to the USA) and worked for MNCs for a few years. After coming back to India these two young persons worked for a few days with reputed organizations.

Right from childhood these persons were sports enthusiasts (one played tennis and participated in other sports activities and over the next few years became a tennis coach (in one of the popular gymkhanas) while the other was an athlete and concentrated on marathon, half marathons, cycling and triathlons. Since they worked earlier in the Western world they found that the sports facilities and sports equipment available in India were very costly and not easily available for the sportsmen in India. Realizing this they decided to study this aspect in more specific detail and realized that the same was the case for sports garments (one problem was the costs involved and the second was that these garments were not properly designed for the ease of use considering physical needs of different sports and the individuals involved in sports). The details were discussed and an idea was born in their minds. After consulting a few of the textile experts and a few garment designers and manufacturers of repute they decided to set up their new venture for the design and manufacture of sports garments, especially 'performance sports garments'.

Founded in 2012-13 in Pune, India, 'Apace' is a fast-growing sports apparel brand specializing in performance apparel for Running, Cycling and Triathlon. Today a team of young entrepreneurs are in the process of scaling up their activities for customized design garments for a few other sports' needs. With an in-house design team, purpose-made fabrics, a customized colour palette, and a wide range of products, apace offers performance wear that does not break the bank. Functionality is the key to good performance apparel, and Apace design revolves around functionality. The well-designed and purpose-made apparel will satisfy the elite athlete, as well as the weekend warriors.

Mihir, an avid sports fan, has been playing tennis since his school days. Mihir is a certified Level 1 ITF coach and a Level 4 AITA coach with a total coaching experience of 15 years. He has also been a coach (LTA certified) at the Watford Club, London, UK during his Master's studies at Middlesex University. Currently, he coaches tennis beginners at the PYC Hindu Gymkhana, Pune. Aditya Kelkar: Aditya is a Mechanical Engineer with a Master's degree in Industrial Engineering from the State University of New York at Buffalo, USA. He worked in enterprise software for close to 10 years, handling product design/development, implementations, and customer support. Also, a sports fan, Aditya has been a football player and trekker during his school days, apart from dabbling in badminton, and tennis. He started running in 2005 and has completed 7 full marathons and numerous half marathons. He is also a cyclist, and a triathlete, with a couple of Olympic distance and half-iron distance triathlons under his belt. Today Apace has achieved a name of repute in the sporting community in India as well as in a few countries overseas.

Based on the diamond analysis of the project classifications one can classify the project as specified below:

- Technology difficulty: T-4
- Complexity of design: C-3
- Novelty of the design: N-4
- Speed of implementation: S-3

The specifications, for the performance sports garments, are very stringent (apart from the fitment specs for the elite athletes) and this aspect is highly technical if one has to design & produce garments of very high standards. This aspect is not understood by many in the current industry (since they do not have personal experience in the sports arena). This was a 'gap' noticed by the market team and their theme for the project was based on providing solutions (customized garments with design flexibility and dexterity) for fulfilling this gap. The designs are discussed and are run through athletes of repute (who try out initially designed artefacts and based on the feedback the designs are tweaked for better specifications and higher batch quantities) and a few experts from the textile industry. The sports garments are designed for men and women and hence have many variants in terms of design specifications.

The proposed system and its variants were expected to be used in about 7 different sports and have very stringent technical specifications. The specification standards are based on the needs of mainly Indian need and built in India. This was a challenge indeed. The general classification would say that the project was certainly: Technically Challenging / Very Complex / Time Critical / Quite Novel in Approach, especially considering conventional approach in the Indian Markets. It may be pointed out here that the market size in this segment is over INR 1000 Crore per year and is growing at least at a CAGR of 11-12 %. This site needs better-engineered garments for high-profile athletes.

About the project:

Sr No	Project Characteristics	Comments
1	Size of the project:	@ 0.4 million USD (INR18-20 crore in today's currency rates)
2	People:	2 persons in R&D group / 15 people in all including shop personnel
3	Schedule:	15 months (when the normal period could be 24 months). Hence there was considerable time pressure.
4	Classification of project:	New startup project with field implementation by a group of engineers without any experience in Textiles or garments.
5	High-risk project	There were many uncertainties due to the new design and new approach to customized performance garments. Additionally, the promoters had no background or exposure to this industry. The organization's reputation and the careers of two youngsters were at stake hence there was no chance to fail. The pressure was too much for the young team. The project was full of risks - some known & some unknown.
6	Technology Choice	There is no specific technology but there are various issues concerning the design and processing of basic cloth varieties and making standard patterns for the sizes/styles. Knowledge of Textile fibres (natural & manmade) and manufacturing processes is very useful & critical for the success of this venture. In addition to technology, intimate knowledge & judgement about costing is a must to ensure success.

7	No of suppliers:	Several suppliers, but 3 were critical suppliers who had refused to help since they had no credibility in the industry circuit. Suppliers went out of their way to support the R&D team after the pilot lots were accepted in the market. Later stage the unit made plans to bring all the skills under one roof when volumes would justify the same.
8	Logistics / Clearances:	This was quite a challenge due to time pressure. Good admin support was provided by family members and a few friends at the start. However, the team had to invest time and cash to build this skill and expertise and this has been done well training a few internal members during the initial period.
9	Location for co-ordination:	More than 4 locations were manned with project team members. The coordination was tough but was managed very well by the PM and team members.
10	Support from Sr. Management:	Excellent support and timely funding/admin support & motivational support from senior family members. The team was given complete freedom for action and expenditures.
11	Involvement of Customer:	High involvement from customer personnel and keen participation of a few athletes from the beginning for trials and pilots.
12	Team Leader: Two-leader team with complementary skills.	One person in the team is a very competent and committed person with an innovative design and production approach. The other person is an excellent marketing person and hence as a team, they are quite effective. The other person provides sales and production expertise to ensure smooth operations.

Key positions in the team:

The team had to be manned with the following key positions:

- Project Managers.
- Manager (R&D) and Sales Manager.
- 2 Module Leaders (R&D) with good exposure and training in garment production.
- Quality Leader / Production Supervisor.
- Accounts Manager for the financial issues/funding.
- PPC / Logistics / Shipment supervisor.
- Senior Consultant with textile industry experience.

The challenges of the new team:

Lack of experience in the Textile and Garment industry for the Promoters of the project:

The main challenge for the new startup team was the lack of exposure to the textile and garment industry in which they were nurturing the ambition to set up the new unit. This task was onerous and would decide the success or failure of the project at hand. R&D was about the design & development of 'performance sports garments'. This aspect is a very involved activity and would need a lot of experience and fine design acumen to be able to produce the artefacts and other accessories to the expected standards and acceptance of the lead athletes in the country, especially in western India. The team worked for over 8 months and discussed the issues and challenges with many persons and made several prototypes for a series of garments (different design patterns, types of base cloth and different methods of production) at hand was not adequate considering the time pressure. Additionally, this was the first of its kind design and production since the promise was to make such garments as per the customized requirements. This was a great challenge and the team handled the same by untiring efforts and many experiments before they finalized the list of designs and artifacts to be included in their business plan. Since both the promoters are engineers, the design & development concepts & methods were learned & mastered by them in a reasonable time. Learning never stops but for a startup unit, this step was crucial and deciding the success of the new unit. Continued contact with a few of the elite athletes and industry professionals helps the team to finalize the Game Plan / Business Plan. These people gave unbiased and direct feedback to the promoters and this helped the team to catch up with current trends in designs and styling. This was very useful for the young team.

The team members (15 persons) were highly committed young persons and they were willing to support the promoters right from the word go. This helped the core team to carry out the first year's activities with great enthusiasm (they had great trust in the competence & expertise of their leaders). They were all willing to walk the extra mile to ensure the success of the project at any cost. This was a major factor in favour of the project. The leaders of the team were committed competent professionals who had a good 'R&D attitude' and this was a major contribution towards the success of the projects.

Lack of support from the vendors and suppliers in the initial phase:

In the initial period, the team found a lot of issues with the key suppliers since the creditworthiness of the newly formed organization, was not established. This raised a lot of issues & problems for the young team.

This problem was necessarily about the payments or the confidence in the success of the new venture. They were concerned about the company doing garments business without their manufacturing unit. The concept promoted by the new organization was unique and they did not plan for their manufacturing unit to start with and this was an area of doubt in the minds of the suppliers. This was sorted out based on the dedication and sincerity displayed by the core team over some time. Over the years these suppliers have become an important part of the organization and the relations with them are positive and supportive for the project. The promoters of the project worked hard to gain the confidence of the suppliers & associates by raising funds to finance working capital as well as keeping promises made to them. Together they gathered momentum and the team had far better response from the supplier network.

Development of creditability through association with elite athletes and renowned sports personalities:

This was seen as a challenge by the team to start with but due to their sports background and track record, they were in a position to manage this aspect well. The initial support from these persons was very valuable. These persons were very supportive and went out of their way to support the newly designed garments and helped to promote the sportswear so designed for customized use. Such personalities were very happy that qualified engineers were promoters & were working very hard to promote the activities of the new unit. Some of them went out of the way to support the new team and this help was very useful & pioneering.

Lack of image and positioning in the marketplace from (tough time) initial marketing perspectives:

In the initial period convincing the customers was a difficult problem for the new unit. However, they sponsored some of the athletic events of repute where they gave concessional gifts to some of the teams participating in the event and by word of mouth the people started taking their designs and products very seriously. This gave relief to the team and boosted their confidence to launch their goods on a larger scale. Currently, they book orders through various channels (such as displays in malls and retail shops, contact with corporate organizations for the sports club needs and also through the marketing website. Currently corporate organization market is a significant market size for them and there are many walk-in customers based on the word of mouth publicity. Due to personal contacts in corporate organizations, the team was able to generate many breakthroughs and booked decent sales of orders which helped initial growth and establish themselves as a significant player in the 'served market'.

The lack of self-generated funds was a constraint in the initial phase:

It is obvious that there was a problem due to a shortage of funds in the initial stages (as is the case for many startups) and the team was forced to implement their plans in a phased-out manner (the retail market issue was addressed only during the 3rd / 4th year and web-based sales was implemented now). However, the core team worked very diligently and started reporting profits right from the first year and this was seen as a big and significant achievement by the team as well as financial experts in the business environment.

Conservative approach to increase the team size in the first two years:

Although this was a challenge in the initial period, it came as a blessing in disguise for the team. Initially, the two promoters used to carry out all the work themselves. This made them aware of all the aspects of the business personally. This learning was welcome. Initially, promoters managed with a core team of only 4 persons. But this forced the promoters to do everything by themselves and this indeed was a great learning for them. Now the team is over 12 persons and they plan to expand the activities.

The issues and challenges:

The issues and challenges can be summarized as follows:

- No exposure to the market & technology for the prompters and hence everything, in some sense was vulnerable & risky for the proposed project. Additionally, sportswear is a competitive market. This made the basic proposition very questionable, especially the bankers & financial institutes. This meant that the young team had to garner a lot of funds of their own in the initial phase of the. This was quite a challenge for the new start-up unit.

- The first of its kind design & hence high-risk project with the use of new technology and approach.

- Tremendous time pressure on the entire team due to shortage of time, funds and new design complexities to suit & excel customers' needs. Tracking all things together was the greatest challenge for the newly created organization.

- Very high-risk project with uncertainty in many respects. However, the team spirit and confidence to win were major factors that led to the success of the project.

- No previous experience even for the R&D set up although they had good knowledge of the technology as such. However, for the unique position of the unit, generating a specific USP was critical. At this stage, it was possible through better / innovative designs and engineering approaches. Hence, generating an internal design & engineering approach was a priority for the young team. This was done with a lot of effort & attention to the project by the team of promoters themselves. This was welcome and has pioneered the USP and growth for the entire unit over the years, by innovative designs and better engineering of products based on the field feedback from expert athletes. This was very crucial for the sustained growth of the organization.

- The suppliers had to work for very small quantities with new design features but due to good relations and timely payments, they responded very well and supported the project. This was possible only on account of good relations developed by the promoters with suppliers over some time.

- The response time from suppliers was critical but was complicated due to small batch sizes and small margins for the orders. This was made more complex because of many changes in components due to continuous modifications to improve the field performance of the products supplied by the new unit. This has proven to be very effective and is still carried out as part of the working strategy & operations for a range of products.

- Multi-location-based activities (production at supplier locations) gave rise to many locations and co-coordination communication became difficult. However, the young team managed this part well with initial hiccups.

Positives in the project environment:

- The scope of work and systems specifications were thoroughly discussed/refined and confirmed with the participation of customers and their consultants throughout the project period. The change management system was ruthlessly followed and immediate communication was sent to all the concerned for them to know. Feedback and confirmation about the same were meticulously followed by the team. This was one of the major cornerstones that laid the foundation for the success of the entire project.

- The PM had full authority to commit funds based on the project's needs. Luckily finances and funds were not at all a constraint. This made life relatively simpler for the project team.

- There was full support from senior family members.

- The team spirit was very high and people were willing to work extra time to complete their efforts to complete the project on time.

- Many innovative ideas were generated to simplify the design and avoid pitfalls. This was welcome and was supported by the PM and senior management.

- The process engineering part was handled well due to past working experience for the promoters.

- Quality Assurance (QA) processes and QC activities were managed very well.

- Communication and coordination were given high importance and were conducted well.

- Risk Management was mainly in the form of specifications/changes & timelines. These were managed personally by the PM.

Project Success Criteria:

As per the discussions with the team members and the pm the following aspects were pre-fixed as the success criteria for the project in consultation with the customers and their consultants:

- Timely and simultaneous delivery of the custom-based orders was critical in the beginning.

- 100 % conformance to the specifications of the proposed design and standards for the International Sports event.

- Satisfaction of all the customers/consultants and senior management of the project.

- Satisfaction of the suppliers for the project with reasonable margins for them along with appreciation for their contributions to a nationally prestigious project.

- Satisfaction & appreciation of the project team.

- Satisfaction of the family members.

Project Success Factors (as seen by the team members now):

Based on the discussions with the team members and their PM it becomes clear that the list of the following points would have been useful for them as CFSs for this project. However, it has to be noted that at the time of the project execution, such a list was not prepared formally. However, based on the experience of the team members and discussions with customer teams the list of important factors was prepared and kept track of during the tenure of the project.

The list of CSFs identified is specified below for reference:

- Need for reliable "Feasibility Study".
- Clarity about the task at hand & clarity about scope and specifications.
- Commitment and participation by the customer teams.
- Complete support from the family members.
- Competent Project Manager & trusted team.
- Alert Risk Management especially in the form of timelines and design/changes.
- Full support from the supplier network.
- Control over project progress issues through impeccable communication and coordination.
- Strong support from QA / QC teams process control engineers and suppliers.
- Exceptional teamwork and untiring support from the task force members.

Conclusion: Very positive success:

The project has been a significant success and a highly appreciated project from all the stakeholders involved in the project situation. The unit is now running with concrete plans for growth and expansion. They have rationalized their product range and decided to concentrate on specific niche markets and this has given them a lot of success. Additionally, they have made a detailed study of the cost structure underlying the product line and have streamlined the production facility based on the impact on costs + overhead for the operations. This has given them complete flexibility for production capacity as well as for end-user pricing. The emphasis on web-based marketing, the spread of retail stores across the regions, and sponsoring major teams in sports events, have helped them improve reach and increase in volumes. This organization is now on a growth path and based on the confidence gained, they have invested a larger amount of funds to support working capital & marketing efforts. These moves have made them scale up quickly and the team is hopeful of growth in volumes and profitability. Their unique products have a good draw in the select markets for the products developed.

Lessons learnt from this case study:

- For start-up organizations, it is futile to get into a new domain without a detailed study of the market size, market dynamics and competition analysis (short & long Term). One must carefully understand & analyze what is the specific customer need and what is the specific 'gap' (in reality or perception) that one is trying to fulfil before one gets into the activity with full gusto. Just a 'gut level' feeling may not be prudent to bank on before you commit to the project as the new start-up unit. This is a crucial learning that may help future entrepreneurs and project managers.

- One can notice that every domain in the marketplace has its technology, processes and methods of work. One needs to understand very clearly these aspects of the domain before one decides to embark on the same. It is cardinally important that the team of promoters have to grapple with and gain mastery over these aspects before they can set up full-fledged operations irrespective of the product range or services in the segment.

In this particular case, both the promoters were very aware of this and they carried out a lot of homework & field knowledge acquisition before they plunged into this activity. This hame work was very effective in laying out proper & firm foundations for the entire project and ensured that risks & vulnerabilities were reduced as much as possible. Every new start-up organization can learn a valuable lesson from this and not rush in the operations with blindfolds. Such reckless action may be a disaster for the project and the venture at hand.

- Selecting the core working team and assigning responsibilities to the individuals was the next key bottleneck that had to be overcome. The promoters did a fairly good job of this and collected a group (all levels inclusive) before they embarked on the operations. They also spent considerable time with the key vendors and invested valuable time and goodwill to build strong relationships with them. These steps were crucial for the future success of the unit. The promoters decided as a policy that they would not compromise on technical & personal soft skills before getting a new person on board. This policy has paid great dividends for the unit.

- The next issue for one to address is the realistic cost estimates for product conversion costs (or conversion costs with overhead allocations) or contribution analysis. Over the first 2 years the promoters understood that without a firm grip on the costs, they would not be able to get to choice of product range and the right pricing for the market. Every product cost along with the Overhead allocation mechanism had to be rationalized and fine-tuned before they could get back to the right pricing and right margins for each of the market segments. They decided to undertake such a study with a lot of attention and then finalized the method of overhead allocations and margins for each product in each segment. This was quite a task but they have done this successfully and seen positive results based on intended growth and profit margins for the subsequent few years. This has now given them full confidence and also announced attractive schemes for the customers.

Leaders of start-up units may learn a great lesson from this and ensure a good understanding of costs and overhead allocation. This input has made the recast business plans and fine-tune their ambitions in each of the segment addresses.

- The important learning is about the channels for promotion & distribution. In modern times, one has a lot of options to go to the market. However, selecting the right channel for the unit was a challenge. The classic distribution model, self-employed sales personnel & web-based approach were possible methods of work for this unit. After many trials and errors, they finalized the judicious combination of these methods, they decided action plan. Now with this approach, their visibility, reach and volumes of business have improved. For pure promotion, they continue to sponsor teams for major sports events and key influencers have gone a long way in putting the organization on a growth path. Aggressive pricing along with these approaches has helped them pick up better market share and improve profitability.

- The unit has plans to bring all the activities under a single roof. But they have been waiting for the volumes to pick up and then only they will take the necessary steps. The current volumes are well managed with dependence on key suppliers.

- Communication and clarity of goal have been emphasized again and again and this is true of this unit as well. The promoters carefully manage all communications and share goals with the team again & again to maintain high motivation levels.

Discussion Points:

Market Study and Customer Needs:

- Start-ups should conduct thorough market research, analyzing size, dynamics, and competition before venturing into a new domain.
- Understanding specific customer needs and addressing real or perceived gaps is crucial, emphasizing the limitations of relying solely on gut feelings.

Mastery of Domain-Specific Aspects:

- Acknowledge that each market domain has its technologies, processes, and methods, and gaining mastery over these is essential for successful operations.
- Highlight the importance of extensive homework and knowledge acquisition before entering a new domain to establish a solid foundation and minimize risks.

Team Selection and Vendor Relationships:

- Emphasize the significance of selecting a competent core team and assigning responsibilities to individuals.
- Building strong relationships with key vendors by investing time and goodwill is crucial for long-term success.

Realistic Cost Estimates and Pricing Strategy:

- Stress the importance of realistic cost estimates and contribution analysis to determine product conversion costs and pricing strategies.
- Highlight the need for a firm grip on costs, overhead allocations, and rationalizing product pricing based on market segments.

Effective Promotion and Distribution Channels:

- Discuss the challenge of selecting the right channels for promotion and distribution.
- Highlight the benefits of a judicious combination of classic distribution models, self-employed sales personnel, and web-based approaches.
- Mention the success of sponsoring sports events and engaging key influencers for effective promotion.

Growth Plans and Communication:

- Address the unit's plans to centralize activities under a single roof, contingent on volume growth.
- Emphasize the importance of clear communication and goal-sharing with the team to maintain high motivation levels.

Case No 28: Case of setting up 'Food Products' startup unit in an economically backward area of Maharashtra as a startup initiative by an existing corporate organization

Dr Jayasri Murali, Ms Puja Gavande

Associate Professor, MBA@IICMR, Pune, Assistant Professor, MBA@IICMR, Pune

Extract: A renowned player in the food industry ventured into a successful startup, establishing an additional dairy plant near Khopoli for processing milk into specialized milk sachets targeting the airlines and hospitality sector. Backed by a thorough feasibility study led by a competent consultant, the CMD approved the project despite concerns about location and capital expenses. With an initial investment of over 85 Cr INR, the plant, now operational, employs 110 individuals, achieving a turnover of approximately 300 Cr INR. The ongoing expansion aims to meet market demand. The project's success is attributed much to the pivotal role of the technical consultant, acting as a mentor from concept to delivery, ensuring both project outcome and management process success.

Introduction:

One of the most successful groups involved in the Food industry markets decided to set up a new startup unit for making and distributing these products to various segments of the food industry. The proposed project was expected to be set up in a village near Khopoli with a Head Office in Mumbai.

This organization had previous experience of successful such initiatives in the past. The current project was being discussed to set up an additional Dairy Plant for the processing of milk to a standard product (milk sachets) for use in the airline and Hospitality Industry. The proposed product was 'Milk Sachets' to be used as a special product (conceptualized based on the requirements of a few international customers) in the chosen market segment, with an emphasis on exports. This product line appeared to be very potent in terms of size and profitability. There was no significant competition (at the time of analysis) and the prospects for this line appeared healthy and strong. This situation prompted the CMD of the organization to set up a study group with the inclusion of a consultant who had the technical and commercial background to lead the group.

The existing organization is a successful organization of repute with good standing in the Dairy and Food market industry. They have a nationwide network of dealers and retailers for marketing their products as well few foreign brands. They have excellent contacts in the hospitality industry, tourism and airline industries. Based on the market survey and detailed analysis of the market demand presented by the group as specified above, the CMD gave a nod to the project. He decided that the project be taken up for serious evaluation. This was completed in the next few months, under the able leadership of the consultant appointed for this work. The feasibility report was prepared with due care and judicious data analysis (including specific market projections for the next few years). After discussing the report in the close group, the CMD gave a clearance for the project. However, he was still concerned about the location and overall capital expenses involved in the project. Although the CMD was very confident about marketing the products of the proposed new venture, he was concerned about the basic R&D involved in the product development and reaching international standards for the pot of the proposed project and continued to hound the CMD. Despite these doubts, he decided to take the risk and decided to go ahead with the project.

After a lot of research and analysis of the options available, a plot of land in the Khopoli area was selected for the proposed project. The total capital outlay for the project was over 85 Cr INR at present rates.

The plant is now running very successfully employing over 110 persons and a turnover of around 300 Cr INR. This was a great success indeed! The plant is currently under the expansion stage to increase the capacity of the plant and to accommodate the proposed new product range that has good demand in the marketplace. This is very good indeed! While talking to the project personnel it was clear that the technical consultant played a major role in the project -right from the concept to delivery. His advice and good support played a significant role in ensuring the success of the overall project. He was a real mentor for the project as such and this helped the team towards assured success.

The project is seen as a successful project from the 'Project Outcome' as well as 'Project Management Process' success and the details of this aspect are covered in the paragraphs below in the respective sections.

Objectives of the project:

The main objective of the project was to initiate the 'Manufacture of internationally approved 'Milk Products' that conform to the international standards of hygiene and aseptic milk packaging' project in Khopoli near Khandala and to ensure that the project generates sustainable growth and profitability for the future.

The main objectives of the project are specified below for quick reference:

- To set up the proposed new plant in the required time and cost without compromising the engineering and hygiene standards to be approved by the international FDA audit agencies to ensure acceptance by the local and international customers.

- To set up an effective Marketing & Sales network across the country and key international locations.

- To set up an R&D team with the active participation of industry experts and dairy engineers to ensure the development of proposed products as per the international standards for the product & packaging.

- To set up the state-of-the-art manufacturing facility with a view to expand and scale up the facility in the future. This activity is not as simple as it may appear to be.

- To set up good relationships with the people in the surrounding areas to provide the raw milk supply in the requisite quantities at the right and affordable costs with a fair margin for the suppliers and enlist their commitment and support on a long-term basis.

- To enlist and nurture the development of 'technical skills in the young persons' who will participate in smooth operations and intended growth of the proposed new division on a long-term basis.

The Project Director:

The Project Director - who initiated this task was a veteran food and milk industry professional with many years of versatile experience in his career. He was a forward-looking person with ambitious plans for the continuous growth of the organization. He had adequate experience and skills to manage such initiatives. His hands-on approach and quick mindset to size the proposed action plans to handle the task were major positives for the project to start. His speed of decision-making and organizing the activities was noteworthy. His charismatic personality and down-to-earth approach helped the project teams respond to the unstructured needs of the new project. His attitude, to achieve 'perfection' in every walk of the activities acted as the source of inspiration for the project team throughout the project period (as confirmed by the team members).

The basic capital was provided by the parent organization and later the financial proposal was processed and approved by the bankers. By and large, there was no pressing problem due to a shortage of funds during the entire tenure of the project.

Another critical issue for the Project Director was to enlist the confidence, support and participation of the seniors from the nearby villages in the project for the proposed project since the plant operations were dependent in terms of raw milk supply from the villages in the vicinity of the plant site. This aspect was managed very well. Frequent visits and discussion forums help the team to enlist their active support. Management also plans to conduct visits to villages and listen to citizens' problems about dairy issues and plans to provide technical guidance for solving problems. Such efforts go a long way in establishing good relationships.

The challenges of the project team:

The following points were noted based on the interaction with the project team members and Project Manager. The researcher had an opportunity to meet the founding members and it was great learning from a project management point of view. The key issues are specified below for quick reference:

Internal issues and bottlenecks observed:

Many internal issues/aspects needed attention from the project team, especially for the PM.

Some of these issues are specified below:

- The main challenge came up while the construction of the plant started. The soil condition in the plot of land was far more 'loose' and the foundations of the proposed building required very firm ground. The estimates, prepared by the architect and civil engineers were far away from the ground reality. This posed a major bottleneck for the project and resulted in additional capital expenses and delays in the initial stages of the project.

- The complete layout, (which had challenges due to the site conditions), had to be redesigned going back to the drawing board. The estimates also had to undergo changes and changes had to be made in the sizes of the equipment (forced due to the changes as explained above) due to available space after the new layouts were changed. This change also led to preparing the feasibility study all over again since the changes were significant and resulted in higher capital expenses. This was a major setback for the project right in the beginning. However, the support from the CMD helped overcome the bottleneck and impasse-like situation. CMD decided to take an additional burden and gave a green signal.

- Additionally, there were many issues concerning the sizing of the plant equipment. This was mainly accounted for by two factors. The first one was that the original plant design was specifically 'oversized' considering future growth plans and the corresponding expansion of the plant capacity. It is often seen that although some of the processes are akin to scalability, some of the equipment (for example, boiler it is better to install a higher size boiler right from the beginning rather than put an additional boiler later on) had to be selected available items in the market. These may not fit your exact specifications but you have no choice.

As explained earlier, unprecedented problems with the layout also created the need to reassess and carry out resizing the entire list of equipment. This created confusion and also resulted in the delay & additional capital costs.

- Another important challenge for the project during the initial phase was to find suitable R&D personnel for work on developing the new product that was proposed to the main line of business for the proposed new project. As mentioned earlier, the 'product' had to be in conformance with stringent international and FDA norms and standards. This was not at all an easy task. This was a pivotal point based on which the viability of the entire project would be decided. The main issue was the fact that no one else had been able to produce a product with such stringent specifications in India so far. Hence nobody in the professional circuit had the exposure and experience to undertake the development of such a range of products. This is the period during which the help from the experienced professional consultant was very handy. He helped to locate a person of repute in the field and he decided to give his dedicated time for the development of such complex products.

- An additional challenge concerning product development was the fact that there was a need for an appropriate lab for use by the R&D team. This also proved to be a significant challenge since some of the essential equipment requisitioned by the new R&D manager was not available in India. Make-shift arrangements had to be resorted to till the imported equipment was made available to the team. Obviously, at the time no one had anticipated importing the equipment for the lab and hence adequate provision was not made in the original budget for this purpose. Again the CMD had to intervene and help solve the problem.

In addition to the above, there was another issue cropped up during the pilot studies some of the specifications of the proposed control systems had to be changed due to the experience gained during the trials and pilot studies. This again meant additional expenses and delays. Some of the project personnel were very anxious and decided to leave the organization during this period and this also was a setback to the project's progress. But there was no way in which one could make the effort at this stage.

The main issue was that no one in the main / core team was trained in the 'Design and Manufacturing processes required for Dairy and Food Processing'.

However, this knowledge was critical considering the sensitivities of the manufacturing challenges likely to be faced in the plant. This could have been a major bottleneck for the project to take off. However, the expertise & experience of the senior consultant helped to resolve this issue.

This problem was tackled by enlisting the support of a food technologist and the mentor /consultant who had a working knowledge of all such processes and insight into technology proposed to be used for the project, in the past. This was very handy and this team trained more than 60 people (Engineers / Supervisors and workmen) before the plant was operational. Such training has now become an ongoing activity in the organization.

The main and urgent challenge was to generate activity plans and give a ray of hope to the affected villagers.

Along with the above aim the leader made activity plans to enlist the support of the villagers. This was mainly important because they supported better availability of milk at competitive rates. This was done well by the PR team and the plant manager in the initial phase.

However, the path was not very smooth since at a later stage, the local politicians got involved in the matter and they called for the strike and kept the plant closed for a few days before the issue was settled amicably (by paying additional sums to the leaders and higher wages for the workers). This was certainly not anticipated while preparing the budgets and business plans. Here again, CMD supported the project and resolved the issue for the time being.

Enlisting the support from the locals was a great challenge in the initial phase of the project

Around the same time, the chairman-Sarpanch from the village gave his land as a gift to the project for starting the plant. However, he also had his agenda. At a later stage, many people claimed ownership of the land and they went to court to resolve the problem. This became a major headache for the PD / PM. Based on untiring efforts from the Project Director such issues were finally sorted out but the project had to take an additional cost burden for such an event.

Lack of activity plans and lack of requisite processes, routines and standards for planning:

This was the next challenge. One has to realize that sheer enthusiasm and dedication do not result in the achievement of the organizational goals and the success of the projects at hand. Many organizations face this type of challenge and it is not easy to organize such efforts into disciplined methods of working.

In the case of such a project, where everything was dynamic and urgent, making detailed plans was a difficult task. Similarly, there were too many changes in the plant layout and the entire team was frustrated hence the basic plans that were prepared were of no value now. Reworking everything was onerous on their mind. Not many members of the team were willing to take up such a task due to sheer frustration.

However, on account of the vast experience of the CMD and Project Director and his alert monitoring of the situation this issue was addressed. Although the basic plan for the activities was prepared by the team during the initial period, one had to play by the ear to progress. Actions had to be planned based on careful planning, communicating with locals to enlist their support and the funds available for the next step. Such events in any project are very critical and flexibility in approach is the essential CSF for such social projects. Without flexibility in the approach, working becomes almost impossible in the field.

Challenges related to Scope / Time and Costs and overall project plans and costs:

As explained earlier there were too many changes in the plans, and this was not a pleasant experience for many in the team. All the changes certainly affected the morale of the team and also had a major effect on the capital costs and the schedules for the project.

Additionally, there were changes required to be made based on the field trials and fine-tuning of some of the parameters. Such feedback also led to some changes in the specifications of some of the already selected capital equipment. The fine-tuning of the parameters is needed for any food product plant. Such problems crop up because activities can be changed based on changes in live situations and need to be handled in flexible ways / innovative ways. However, it may be pointed out that day-to-day monitoring based on current live info is essential even for such extreme projects.

The plans and schedules need to be flexible and need to be planned per the availability of funds and resources available. This is an inherent problem for all the NGOs even now. This is possible to be solved when the predictability of the cash flows can be established in advance. The current project plans also were affected on account of this difficulty.

Getting technical personnel on board was the next challenge:

The technical and engineering work required for the project was quite onerous and involved hard work in an adverse environment (lack of workshop facilities, difficulty in transport, lack of communication facilities, hot weather conditions, lack of water and electricity supply for long hours) without adequate facilities. This meant that getting qualified personnel for the project was quite a challenge. However, the availability of good people continued to haunt the project forever.

Communication among engineers becomes sometimes difficult due to lack of knowledge of computers, internet/email.

This point is already explained above and was difficult to solve despite certain training courses conducted and canvassing carried out by the leaders. This issue continues to affect the operating efficiency of this organization even now.

Permissions from Govt authorities, corporations, (formalities and paperwork) offices are time-consuming and tedious and take a long time for approvals.

The procedural and statutory conformance routines are one of the most burdensome matters for any new organization. This project also had to face such challenges but was sorted out over some time.

Data management and analysis is another area which is expensive and not well looked after till now.

This has been an area that has not received due attention right from the beginning of the project and even now continues to be rather a weak area, despite few attempts to improve the same. Such initiative is not yet stabilized, though there is some activity recently taken up, it is not carried out professionally since no one in the team has the expertise and experience to direct and manage such efforts. Professional help sought from outside also has not helped since the budgets are quite inadequate. Currently, effort is being made to correct this aspect. However, the unit continued to hold review meetings and the exchange of information was more informal than formal.

Based on the diamond analysis of the project classifications one can classify the project as specified below:

- Technology difficulty: T-4
- Complexity of design: C-3
- Novelty of the design: N-4
- Speed of implementation: S-3

About the project:

Sr No	Project Characteristics	Comments
1	Size of the project:	10 million USD (INR 60-65 Crore in today's currency rates) as Capital Expenses in the initial period of the first 5 years). This aspect was well managed and the team did not face any challenges about this.
2	People:	The core team of 15 (12 + 2 project managers + R&D Manager + Senior Consultant) carried out all the activities of the project. This expanded to around 110 people by the end of year 1 of the operations.
3	Schedule:	The original plan of 18 months was planned project period as per the Original plans but it took much longer time due to various difficulties faced by the project teams. The project was closed after 36 months.
4	Classification of project:	This is a case of a new startup by an existing organization. Although the basic concept was already tried out in other locations in the state (UP / HP), this was the first of its kind in the country.
5	High-risk project:	There were many uncertainties/risks in the project. The project was undertaken in a very hazy, aggressive and uncertain environment without the availability of enough team members at the beginning. This was indeed a challenge.
6	Technology Choice	This was a major challenge as explained earlier. The project organization did not have adequate experience, no skill sets, and no financial bandwidth to handle this project.
7	No of suppliers:	For this project, there was a critical role for suppliers and vendors. They worked with very positive attitudes worked for low-margin contracts and helped the organizational efforts. However, in the 2nd year, there was a strike and pressure on the project due to intervention by the local leaders.
8	Logistics / Clearances:	This was quite a challenge due to the time pressure to complete the basic facilities to be built in time. The project team managed this aspect well barring initial hiccups due to changes in the plant layout.
9	Location for co-ordination:	More than 3 locations (Mumbai / Pune / Khopoli). Coordination was initially difficult but was smooth over the years.
10	Support from Sr. Management:	Senior management provided excellent support and timely however, funding was a challenge in the initial period due to a

		shortage of funds. Similarly, there was no specific admin support in the beginning. The team members themselves were carrying out all the activities as and when possible. Initially, Admin Support & Motivational Support was received from the senior mentors as specified above. CMD was supportive right from the word go.
11	Involvement of Customer:	There was mixed support/hesitation from the customer personnel in the beginning but people were willing to listen and help. Over some time they saw the quality of work and observed dedicated work done by the project organization and they gave full support for the initiatives taken up. PM and the team had a difficult task to win over their minds.
12	Team Leader:	Project Director (Engineer) & R&D Manager (Food Technologist) was a competent/committed professional. This helped in the initial period. However, the major support was provided very valuable guidance and support for the project.

Key positions in the team:

The team had to be manned with the following key positions:

- CMD of the parent organization.
- Project Director / Project Manager as 'Project Champions'.
- R&D Manager.
- Team of dairy engineers and technical experts with expertise in similar projects.
- Tech Leaders / Discipline Leaders (2 initially and later over 4) for various critical aspects of the proposed project & modules.
- Technical experts / Consultants (Civil Engineering, Agriculturists, Architects, Technicians, Food Industry Experts and Workshop Managers, Non-conventional Power experts).
- Treasurers managing financial issues/funding and auditors (advisors).
- Trustees' office for project tracking and liaison with volunteers, teams and beneficiaries.

Positives in the project environment:

- There was full support from senior management and corporate organizational units.
- The focus of the team was very specific and worked toward a detailed implementation plan in cooperation with the mentor CMD).

- The contribution by the senior consultant was noteworthy. His expertise & experience were a great help in handling & managing many situations.

- Continuous dialogue with Govt officials / Customer PM and local PM with resolve to address the issues immediately helped the team to complete the project in the required time.

- Focused 'Project meetings were conducted regularly (monthly/quarterly) to make strategic and critical decisions and move forward proactively. This was useful for the team.

- Harmonious teamwork paved the path for a good undisturbed work environment. This was crucial for the success of the project but did not bear fruit.

- The initial resistance to the project from the local people was reduced after the 'Steering Committee' was formed and they were given the freedom to decide their priorities.

- The team had full freedom for decision-making and commitment to expenses as per the decisions of the Project Team (Founder Members). This paved the path for smooth working for the team.

Project Success Criteria:

The project success criteria took into consideration customer expectations and organizational expectations:

- **Organizational expectations**
  - To complete the project in time without any compromise on quality of service.
  - To conform to stringent rules of FDA and other International authorities.
  - To achieve the project delivery based on the business.
  - To develop project modules as a model project so that they can become reference projects for future activities.
  - To get repeat requests from various customers.
  - To enlist the support and active participation of the local people in the project. This was done well.

- **Customer / User Expectations**
  - To ensure timely delivery of product (with proper hygiene and aseptic standards).
  - To handle emotional and social issues effectively in the core team and other participants).
  - To ensure team satisfaction and development of new skills/domain expertise for the future.
  - To ensure the sustainability of the project for the future.

Project Success Factors (as seen by the team members now):

Based on the discussions with the team members and their PM / PD it becomes clear that the list of the following points would have been useful for them as CFSs for this project. However, it has to be noted that this aspect was not necessarily thought about comprehensively before the project started.

- Clarity about the task at hand & clarity about scope and specifications with a flexible approach to work in the environment explained above (The director took the risky decision despite the warnings) that led to disasters.
- Commitment and participation by the core team members in the development of the right ecosystem throughout the tenure of the project life cycle.
- Complete support from the senior management & freedom for actions for project/module leaders.
- Competent Project Manager & trusted Consultants and professionals/team members.
- Alert Risk Management especially in the form of timelines and scope/changes. This was done well but was not up to the mark at all times/stages.
- Control over project progress issues through good communication and coordination/reviews.
- Exceptional teamwork and untiring support from the founding members in the initial period.
- Good support from Legal Experts and Admin teams as and when required.

Conclusion: Successful project:

The project was evaluated as great a success with few hiccups in the initial period. Currently, the organization is on a growth path that indicates continued success!! The financial support & funding given by the CMD was critical in completing this project, although late & over the Budget. However, in the end, the team was able to tie all the loose ends and make a success. The current situation indicates the new venture is on a growth path with improved profitability.

Although there was a delay and cost escalation, the project was a great commercial success!

Lessons learnt from this project:

Many important aspects must draw the attention of future project managers & practising professionals. The main issues that need attention are as follows:

- The first thing to notice is that the scope finalization and feasibility study based on the changing assumptions must be revisited, whenever there is significant change in the project situation or changes due to practical considerations. This means whenever such changes are seen as inevitable, the feasibility must be revisited and re-established. The approach has to be flexible and accommodate such changes that are inevitable for the start-up projects.

- Planning has to be flexible and must have ways to accommodate changes in the initial period (flexibility in terms of scope/timelines & costs leading to changes in CAPEX & OPEX). This is an important learning.

- Providing adequate R&D resources and budgets is equally critical without which complex technical projects will not take off and will pose many impediments, leading to delays and cost escalations.

- Adopting international standards & norms is not very easy and needs expertise and experience in the team. Such expert resources are, at times, difficult to acquire and adequate budgets have to be provided for the same.

- For new product development activities, it is essential to build a competent R&D team and also develop the requisite infrastructure & facilities for the new venture. In the case of this project, it is seen that this aspect was not planned and it became an additional burden for CAPEX adding a substantial part.

- For a project in the backward area, a lot of attention must be paid to developing good working relationships and constant dialogue with the surrounding villagers and their leaders. If this aspect is not well planned it can hit the project at the wrong time and pose a major challenge for the project's progress.

- For export-quality product development, it is pertinent to adopt and practice international norms for QA/QC. Generally, people do not have adequate exposure to such practices, especially in India. Such orientation also has to be given to all the critical suppliers and associates to improve awareness about such QA / QC practices in specifics.

- Training & development as an ongoing activity is a must for the start-up unit as one can easily understand.

- Effective dialogue and frequent communication help share many aspects of the project's progress with all the stakeholders, especially employees and the contract workforce. Such efforts help generate focus and harmony in operations.

Discussion Points:

Feasibility Study and Changing Assumptions:

- Revisit and establish feasibility when significant changes occur in the project situation or due to practical considerations.
- Adopt a flexible approach to accommodate inevitable changes in startup projects.

Flexibility in Planning:

- Emphasize flexibility in planning, allowing adjustments in scope, timelines, and costs during the initial period, impacting CAPEX and OPEX.

R&D Resources and Budgets:

- Allocate adequate resources and budgets for research and development, crucial for the initiation and success of complex technical projects.

Adoption of International Standards:

- Recognize the challenges in adopting international standards and norms, requiring expertise and experience within the team.

Competent R&D Team and Infrastructure:

- Establish a competent R&D team and develop the necessary infrastructure for new product development to avoid additional CAPEX burdens.

Community Relations in Backward Areas:

- Pay significant attention to building positive relationships and constant dialogue with villagers and leaders in backward areas to prevent challenges in project progress.

International QA/QC Practices:

- Implement international quality assurance and quality control (QA/QC) practices for export-quality product development, ensuring alignment with global standards.

Training and Development:

- Prioritize ongoing training and development activities as essential components for the success of a startup unit.

Effective Communication:

- Foster effective dialogue and frequent communication with all stakeholders, especially employees and contract workers, to enhance focus and harmony in project operations.

Case No 29: Development of an innovative, comprehensive Communication for the new International Airport of Pride

Dr Jayasri Murali, Ms Puja Gavande

Associate Professor, MBA@IICMR, Pune, Assistant Professor, MBA@IICMR, Pune

Extract: In the early days of the Indian telecom boom, a significant project unfolded to establish a cutting-edge 'Communication Platform' for a newly constructed international airport. Acting as the subcontractor for a major EPC company, a prominent Indian organization, part of an MNC Group, undertook the challenge. Despite unprecedented technological advancements in the telecom domain, the organization navigated tight schedules and evolving customer preferences. The fixed-price bid added complexity, yet the organization continued for national prestige. With objectives to initiate a "Comprehensive Internal Communication Services Backbone Network," the project involved two data centres, over 950 active devices, 120 hubs, and 28,000 nodes. Meeting >99.00% network uptime and ensuring security complexities, the team completed this prestigious project.

Introduction:

This is the era when the telecom boom was getting introduced in India. The use of the Internet for improving overall communication infrastructure is being set up in the country. This is a case of the project was setting up the state of the art 'Communication Platform', for the internal needs of a newly built international airport. The principal contractor for the project was a large EPC company and the reputed International Project Organization under discussion acted as the sub-contractor for this organization. The project was challenging and the organization decided to take up the challenge for the sheer challenge and size of the project.

The project was taken up by a large Indian Organization (Part of MNC Group) well known for its position of pride and contribution to the upliftment of basic communication infrastructure in the country. The group was already involved in setting up Telecom Infrastructure projects and was in a position to provide a wide range of services in this important segment of the market. The outlay for the phase 1 was around 50 Crore INR and was completed satisfactorily. Other phases were in the initial planning stages.

It is worthwhile to point out at this stage that during the same period, there was unprecedented advancement in terms of technology in the Telecom Domain. It was essential to keep track of such developments and the latest advancements had to be incorporated in the proposed architecture of the proposed network due to market needs and expectations. Trying to match the features of the network with international standards was the requirement of the proposed project and this was an onerous task indeed. This unprecedented technical advancement posed many challenges for the project organization.

However, the schedule for the project was very tight and during the same period the end customer made changes in the choice of the technology proposed as per their RFP (although the new technology choice was better than the original). Since it was a fixed-price project bid and hence there was no additional compensation for the project organization. However, the organization decided to continue with the project considering the national prestige for the project.

Objectives of the project:

The organization decided to take this opportunity to initiate the "Comprehensive Internal Communication Services Backbone Network" for international services. The Project Director and Senior Program Manager (Head of Technology) were appointed and they set up a team of over 40 personnel to undertake this prestigious project. The following table indicates the enormous size of the project undertaken.

- 2 Data Centers
- \> 950 Active devices
- 120 hubs
- \> 28000 nodes (12000 fiber based + 16000 Copper based)

Looking at the vastness of the installation one can imagine the complexity of the communication platform envisaged in the project. Additionally, it was important to ensure > 99.00 % uptime of the network. Added to this complexity, was an eminent need to take care of network security and data security. This made the project a great challenge and the team responded very well and completed the project successfully.

The main objectives of the project are specified below:

- To set up a state-of-the-art high-speed network compatible with international standards to provide a range of Telecom services for the newly set up International Airport in India in partnership with one of the world leaders in this segment to ensure technical superiority over possible competition.

- To develop a Telecom Backbone Network with high speeds that will not only cater to the needs of retail customers but will provide specialized services for Corporate & Institutionalized customers as well (with close conformance to DOT norms and guidelines).

- They develop an excellent support services network for providing 24x7 support to the active customers (with low maintenance and modification needs and easy for interfaces and easy scaling up possibilities).

- To develop special service packages and applications for the customers to ensure that the special features of the proposed network are used efficiently in the country.

- To ensure that the design/architecture of the proposed Network is scalable and can connect to various International Networks seamlessly.

- To ensure that the proposed architecture of the new application is capable of inter-location connectivity & setting up of private secure networks.

- To ensure the Network 24x7 service support group is in line with proposed SLAs and to set up an efficient system to handle/address customer complaints and escalation schemes.

The challenges of the project team:

The following points were noted based on the interaction with the project team members and the Program/Project Manager. The key issues are specified below for quick reference:

Internal Challenges:

Many internal issues/aspects needed attention from the project team, especially for the PM. Some of these issues are specified below:

Time, Cost and Quality:

The main challenge for the team was to conform to the conventional project success factors and complete the project in less than 24 months. This was a challenge because the project required the requisite permissions and licences from DOT (Government of India) for the proposed architecture and required lines for the network.

This was one of the main hurdles for the Project Director and the PM handling this critical and complex project. The main issue was there were too many agencies involved in the decision-making. Although there was a lot of follow-up done by the team members there was a lot of delay in clearance of the licences and various permissions required at different offices. This was one of the main hurdles in the project schedule since it resulted in a delay of more than 12 months. Such a delay resulted in an escalation of the Budget by more than 15 % of the costs and over 25 % in terms of schedule.

A major change in specifications due to technological advances:

As indicated earlier the specifications of the required platform were changed after the project was initiated. This could have been a major bottleneck but the organization took the risk and made appropriate changes in the configurations and managed the change quite well. However, this affected the profitability since the project was awarded in 'fixed price mode'. Later through a lot of follow additional funds were sanctioned due to this change that was made at the request of the end-user. However, the change did put the team under pressure due to cost escalation & time pressure along with technical nuances involved in the redesigned architecture of the proposed solution.

Management pressure:

The management of many Telecom companies saw unprecedented opportunity in this sector at this stage and hence competition was getting intense and early entry was essential for the overall success of the proposed project. Hence naturally there was a lot of pressure on the project team to complete the basic infrastructure as soon as possible. This developed a lot of excitement and urgency in the team to launch such services and complex applications as soon as possible.

This naturally resulted in generating too much pressure on the engineering / development and site teams. However, one must realize that at times, excessive pressure results in slip shod ways of working and compromised decision making due to time pressure. This project was no exception to this situation.

Domain expertise for the new team was not adequate:

Many Telecom personnel / people knew about the existing systems and processes but did not have judgment about how to adopt the proposed changes and their implications on working systems using new technologies. This was obviously a great problem. The main challenge for the project team was to understand and adopt new specifications with a view to provide efficient services to the market. This was an area of great concern & pain for the project team. Additionally, the problem was compounded on account of a fact that few very senior personnel left the organization and this obviously had a great strain on the entire and PM.

Addition, deletion and changes of technical staff and 'security clearance for the new members':

The Telecom & IT industry has traditionally faced the problem of high employee attrition rates and this project was no exception for this project. The project manager had the freedom to choose the team of his choice but he had to spent considerable amount of time to ensure that his team members do not leave in between. However, in reality this problem continued throughout the tenure of the project.

Additionally, it was important to obtain 'security clearance' for every new member joining the team at site. The process involved was quite complex and hence there were additional time pressure and delays caused due to the same. This necessitated need for the back at HO. Obviously increasing overall costs for the project, delays and lot of headache for the PM.

Availability of Telecom infrastructure for 'In-house simulation & testing' for such an important and technically critical project:

Fortunately, the senior management of the company was very proactive and supportive for the project and provided adequate funds for the Development Labs for the engineering & development team. However, the project team had to spent considerable amount of time and efforts to ensure to procurements of the requisite equipment in the organizational set up of due to involved approval processes and sequences. Such efforts were onerous and people had to be patient with the requisite procedures for QA / QC.

Developing requisite interfaces / Integration of various components for the communication network along with regional hubs for the same:

One of the challenges for the project was developing requisite interfaces for an assortment of various devices / modules involved in the proposed solution. This was an enormous challenge since the basic modules were from different sources / technologies & countries and the protocols used were not necessarily compatible and the development team had to carry out certain amount of work before one could integrate the complete solution.

Development of application software for customer management and usage tracking along with billing modules:

Such a complex solution will also need an adequate smart system application to handle all the administrative and customer management modules for efficient handling of such an application. Due to the ever-changing configuration and complexity of the task at hand, such development was also quite challenging and the entire team had to work hard to complete this aspect in time under heavy time pressure

Technical Challenges:

Technology changes of this magnitude involve lot of complex technical issues that cannot be addressed effectively without astute technical knowledge and experience. This was clearly evident in this project. Although basic technology issues were known to many team members, they did not have the requisite experience and exposure to the nuances involved in this application. This was one of the main bottlenecks in the development and implementation cycles for the project.

Lack of expertise on the customer side for such a complex project:

The basic RFP was worked out by a team of experts form a consulting company and the level of expertise in the internal team was not adequate. This caused delays and confusion in the initiation phase. Additionally, the concerns of the certifying agencies were based on the old technology and they did not have adequate exposure to the finally selected new technology. This led to lot of rework only to satisfy their concerns. Such confusion and delays could have been avoided if there was no need to press for the advanced version based on the new technical approach. One can say that such issues are part & parcel of any technically advanced field and cannot be avoided completely.

Strict control over product design and database design:

The size of the application, considering the various modules and routines involved, called for effective and smart architecture for the proposed applications. The enormity of the application software posed many challenges for the team. The designs had to be fine-tuned for better performance during QA / QC cycles and at times one had to go back to the drawing board for redesign efforts.

Strict process for change control through "Engineering Change Control Notice" and judicious evaluation of such requests:

This aspect required lot of attention from the PM in view of its importance for the success of the project. The team had to allocate senior resources from the team to ensure proper control throughout the tenure of the project.

Flexibility/parameterization and its impact on design complexity:

Flexibility in design and parameterization is an important aspect while finalizing the design architecture and database designs. However, one can appreciate that too much of flexibility and too much parameterization renders the system top heavy and can affect response times for various process routines for such a large system. One has to achieve optimum balance between these functions for good performance of the system.

Additionally, there was design overhead due to the expectation that this had to be developed as a "Standard Product" and not a bespoke application for a particular bank. This generated several challenges and issues for the team during the design and implementation stages.

External Challenges:

Several external factors were identified as eternal factors that could affect the probability of success of the project.

One of the main hurdles in the project was the 'Issues concerning Licenses and requisite permissions from the Telecom Authorities of the Government of India'. There were multiple types of challenges as specified below:

- The resistance from the authorities to be willing to change over to new paradigms due to lack of understanding and acceptance of the new technology and resistance to change with hardened attitudes. Such resistance was mainly from the seniors who did not feel comfortable with the onslaught of new technologies.

- Slow decision making at various offices with endless queries and loads of documentation, was a challenge in itself. This affected the speed of development for the entire project. Continued untiring efforts from the team members helped to resolve these issues.

- Co-operation from the regional offices at various locations during implementation phase was suspect in the initial stage and gradually improved after series of discussions with key members and engineering personnel and senior management from the DOT. Too much of time was continuously wasted in these non-value adding activities.

- Export/import obligations were time-consuming and again non-value-adding activities. A lot of time could have been saved.

- Size and site readiness was one more concern and coordinating with customer agencies was a nightmare for the project team. A senior member was assigned only for this task to avoid delays.

Approach:

A dedicated team headed by a project manager was assigned to this project. The project manager was supported by a team of over 5 professionals. Some of the critical issues are specified below for quick reference:

Product Design team to handle and control product design aspects:

The size of the project as indicated earlier was enormous and at times unmanageable. Hence controlling the design and ensuring compatibility of the filed data at every stage was critical aspect for the design control team.

Domain experts had to rationalize and standardize the process routines:

This was indeed a challenging task and had to be carried out by some experienced professionals who had adequate knowledge about the operations of a Telecom Networks. One had to pay lot of attention and at every stage estimate the impact on finalized designs and routines. This aspect was driving the entire team on the edge and there were moments of frustration for all the members of the project team.

Technical writers for creating documentation and operating instructions:

Any Complex system under development needs good quality documentation. Additionally, the myriad of rules & regulations applicable also required documentation and updates from time to time. One may be aware that in IT industry there are not many professionals who have flair for proper documentation and write ups. This was hence a bottleneck for the project team. The project team involved Telecom Professionals and formed a task force to complete this difficult task.

Educating customer IT departments and seeking co-operation from all of them was also a challenge due to new concepts and technologies being introduced.

In the period, in which this system was developed, the country did not have mature systems working on these concepts. The application concept developed was completely new for the Indian Telecom sector and naturally, there was resistance from the existing employees and especially from the old Government Departments and indeed this was a challenging project.

Based on the diamond analysis of the project classifications one can classify the project as specified below:

- Technology difficulty: T-4
- Complexity of design: C-5
- Novelty of the design: N-4
- Speed of implementation: S-3

About the project:

Sr No	Project Characteristics	Comments
1	Size of the project:	The size of the project was around @ 6.5 million USD (INR 56-60 crore in today's currency rates including manpower costs+ overheads + travel + incidental costs).
2	People:	The number of developers and other staff involved in Mumbai / Pune and at site locations was 30 as core team members and around 120 contract personnel working at the site from time to time.
3	Schedule:	The original time schedule was 24 months that was later changed to 30 months & to 36 months due to basic changes made in the specifications. However, on account of various licensing issues the time schedule was derailed and actually it took additional 6 months for completion & handover.
4	Classification of project:	A New Project team was set up for the existing organization considering the prestige and security issues that were involved in the project. This was the first of its kind activity in India at that stage and this meant that there was no such product available at that time in India. This was indeed a challenge for the project team. The team handled the challenge very well and completed the project to the complete satisfaction of the end users.

5	High-risk project:	There were many uncertainties / risks due to the use of proposed new Paradigm, technology & new software applications. Additionally, it was difficult to source domain experts since the application was relatively new in India.
6	Technology Choice	The technology was evolving in this period. This new application, although was well developed in USA / Europe, it was being developed for the first time as a standard service / product. There was obviously shortage of knowledgeable people in the market about this technology and domain applications.
7	No of suppliers:	For this project there was not much of critical role for suppliers but there was a role for the technology partners and associates. Their role & active participation was critical for the success of the project. Additionally, site contractors played a significant role in the activities.
8	Logistics / Clearances:	This was quite a challenge due to the time pressure to obtain appropriate licenses and permissions as explained earlier. Additionally, there was a need for many Government clearances at each of the locations. However, there was very good support from the HO and senior management for the same. They helped with expertise for completing the paperwork required. Additionally, there was a need for 'security clearance' for new members. The HO provided active support for this activity.
9	Location for co-ordination:	More than 4 locations (Mumbai / Pune & Customer sites at 3 branch locations) were manned with project team members. Coordination was not such a major challenge since all the offices had excellent communications and infrastructure facilities.
10	Support from Sr. Management:	Senior management provided excellent support and timely funding / admin support & motivational support throughout the tenure of the project. The team was given complete freedom for action and expenditures.
11	Involvement of Customer:	There was mixed support / hesitant support from the department's personnel / professionals. However, some of the customer representative had doubts about the abilities of Indian Telecom / Software professionals' abilities to produce flawless software for this critical application in the first attempt. PM and the team had difficult task to win over their minds. This made situation quite complex for the project team.
12	Team Leader:	The project Manager selected was a 'competent/committed telecom Engineer' (with good domain expertise & excellent exposure to Software applications). He also had some exposure to International projects and telecom standards.

Key positions in the team:

The team had to be manned with the following key positions:

- Project Director / Project Manager as 'Project Champion'.
- Business Analyst/Business Process Expert with expertise in the Telecom sector (especially about new concepts and technologies/operations).
- Module Leaders (4) for various critical aspects of the proposed project & modules.
- Database Expert/Networking Expert and group of consultants.
- Quality Leader/Site Quality Leader/Site manager with 2 site engineers for implementation at branches.
- Delivery Manager for the project (one of the senior module leaders played this role). In the overall success of the project, this role played a critical role and ensured proper instructions and accurate deliveries at various stages of the project.
- Accounts Manager for the financial issues/funding.
- PMO office for project tracking and liaison with customer team for progress tracking and resolving issues.

Positives in the project environment:

- There was full support from senior management and foreign partners.
- The focus of the team was very specific and worked toward a detailed implementation plan in cooperation with the customer personnel.
- Continuous dialogue with Govt officials / Customer PM and local PM with resolve to address the issues immediately helped the team to complete the project in the required time. The senior managers from both sides attend project meetings monthly / quarterly to make decisions and move forward proactively. This was useful for the team.
- A harmonious team paved the path for a good quality / undisturbed work environment. This was crucial for the success of the project.
- Pre-dispatch inspection for every release involving local and customer QA/QC teams helped hassle-free on-site implementation of the modules without delays and waiting periods.
- The team had full freedom for decision-making and commitment to expenses as per the decisions of the PM. This paved the path for smooth working for the team.

Project Success Criteria:

The project success criteria took into consideration customer expectations and organizational expectations:

- Organizational expectations
    - To complete the project in time without any compromise on quality.
    - To conform to stringent rules of DOT for the Telecom sector operations and security standards.
    - To achieve the project profitability as planned for the organization (This was a challenge due to the fixed price contract).
    - To develop this application as a model project so that it can become a reference project for future business in the Telecom segment.
    - To get repeat orders from the same customer was an important organizational requirement.
- Customer / User Expectations
    - To ensure on-time delivery and implementation.
    - To achieve committed ROI from the project.
    - To achieve requisite accuracy & efficiency in operations that have complex sets of rules & changes.
- Satisfaction of the team members
    - To ensure team satisfaction and development of new skills/domain expertise for the future.

Project Success Factors (as seen by the team members now):

Based on the discussions with the team members and their PM it becomes clear that the list of the following points would have been useful for them as CFSs for this project. However, it has to be noted that this aspect was not necessarily thought about comprehensively before the project started.

- Clarity about the task at hand & clarity about scope and specifications.
- Commitment and participation by the customer teams in the development of the system throughout the tenure of the project life cycle.
- Complete support from the senior management & freedom of action.
- Competent Project Manager & trusted team.
- Alert Risk Management especially in the form of timelines and design/changes for POC / UAT. This was done well but was not up to the mark at all times/stages.

- Control over project progress issues through impeccable communication and coordination.
- Excellent support from PMO personnel for ruthless tracking of issues and resolving them.
- Strong support from QA / QC teams and process control engineers (support received due to strong and matured processes in the parent organization).
- Exceptional teamwork and untiring support from the task force members.
- Good support from Legal Experts and Admin teams.

Conclusion: Highly successful project with few silver linings!

The project was evaluated as a comprehensive & complete success and the team was very proud of their performance. The customer and the senior management personnel were very happy about the project outcome. The project was not finished in the requisite time due to several licensing and permissions delays but the quality of the project outcome was completely as per the expectation. The customer signed an AMC contract for the next 5 years.

The senior management was very pleased and decided to constitute additional teams to handle Telecom sector applications. This division is still in existence and is doing good business every year. Due to quality of the work carried out in this project, additional customer accounts from various Corporate Organizations in addition to retails services in the next 5 years. This made a big impact on the growth of the organization and ensured continued profitability.

The project manager was promoted as "SBU Head" handling this business independently. The product of the project has been further refined and is now one of the flag sheep product of the organization.

Lessons learnt from the case study:

- The most important learning from this case study is, that one must have flexibility in terms of scope, time and costs for such infrastructure projects. One will have to keep an open open-minded approach to planning activities for such situations. One should not be bullheaded trying to freeze all specifications & scope at the beginning of the project. This is important learning for future project managers & young professionals.

- One can also appreciate that if there are drastic changes in terms of specifications, upgrades to new technologies and changes in the business environment, one will have to go back to the drawing board and re-establish the 'feasibility' again. If this aspect is not looked at astutely then there is a high risk that the project will lead towards failure.

- In this particular case, there were too many Government / Semi-Government authorities and outside agencies involved. In such cases managing 'Stakeholder' expectations becomes quite a challenge. Each of the entities has its agenda and expectations (coupled with the egos of the authorities involved. This makes the entire project environment murky and hence quite a challenge to handle for the project team. Strong PR efforts & skilful handling of each of them become a priority. In this case, the MNC organization could manage this aspect quite well due to their contacts and ways of managing such situations over the years. However, for future PMs and young professionals, it is important to note this aspect and hone their skills for managing 'stakeholders' in a non-controversial way.

- Considering the criticality of the application & stringent service conditions / SLAs (Service Level Agreements) planning had to ensure considerable buffers and additional equipment & components for the entire project. The contract drawn between the customer had to be very specific and realistic and had to be approved by many agencies. This was quite a headache since many lawyers (who had no clue of the technical nuances had to be convinced) were involved in the process and this was a painful task. However, the experienced team of lawyers at the HQ helped the project team handle such a task without too many hiccups.

- Yet another difficulty was to generate appropriate testing facilities at the site. This problem was partially due to active support from the customer's technical team that provided many facilities & equipment required for this purpose.

- Eminently, for such infrastructure projects, there are many inherent risks and hence appropriate provisions to manage such occasions need to be provided right from the stage of initial estimates. Failure to do so will pose difficult and embarrassing situations during the implementation stage that can be very time-consuming and very costly. This is important learning for future Project managers.

- There was a very peculiar situation for this project on the technical front. The customer requested to adopt the new technology (since it had very useful new features) after the project was initiated and planning was done based on the old technology. This meant that one had to go back to the drawing board and redo almost every design, new cost estimates, new time estimates and resource allocations including a new feasibility study. This task was onerous for the team and vulnerable from the point view that it introduced an element of uncertainty (due to lack of detailed knowledge & grip over the new approach) and of course many types of risks. One had to be careful to manage changes and also to keep the team motivated all the time. Quite a challenge for the PM.

The PM, on account of his experience and skills, could handle the changes smoothly. However, a lot of time was lost and the customer as usual was not willing to pay for the changes even though the changes were made due to their request. However, the HQ personnel and CMD had to get involved and settle the matter amicably through senior officials in the ministry and other statutory authorities. Additionally, a lot of effort & time was lost in seeking approvals for the new designs/engineering (even for the authorities the new technology was not known).

- Training & re-orientation of the entire team had to be organized with a lot of care and attention since there was a major change in the technology due to the adoption of the new technology, midway through the project. This activity was well planned and conducted effectively with the help of technical experts & consultants working with the team. This paved a smooth path for the solid foundation for the success of the project.

- Additionally, due to national security reasons managing permissions for the new team members to work at the site was quite a challenge. Too many agencies were involved in the process and the PM decided to keep one resource to manage only such permissions. Apart from this, whenever any of the team members left the organization same procedure had to be followed even to cancel the permission. However, with active help from PR managers at the HQ, such processes were handled effectively.

- The project involved a lot of documentation and follow-up. A dedicated 2-member team was assigned the responsibility to manage logistics & transportation and they carried out such tasks very effectively. This otherwise could have become a very major bottleneck for the project at hand.

- For a mega project like this, clarity of purpose (scope of work that satisfies the strategic intent' at the customer end) is a must for the project manager & the team to manage all the activities. For this, it is pertinent that effective communication channels are established to monitor and control two-way communications all the time. Effective communication ensures smooth operations and paves a path for the final success of the project. Professional project managers should take cognizance of the all and keep focus on quality communications.

- Developing excellent Management Control & Operations Control modules is an important aspect of running a successful project. The project organization, being part of the MNC group, had a strong background in this aspect. This helped them to develop & operate an effective control mechanism that was useful for reviewing and controlling the project's progress. This is an important aspect that future project managers need to learn and use in their future endeavours.

Discussion Points:

Flexibility in Project Planning:

- Emphasizes the importance of flexibility in scope, time, and costs for infrastructure projects.

- Advises against rigidly fixing specifications at the project outset, urging an open-minded approach.

Feasibility Reassessment:

- Highlights the need to revisit feasibility when there are significant changes in specifications, technology upgrades, or shifts in the business environment.

- Stresses the risk of project failure if feasibility is not carefully reconsidered under evolving circumstances.

Stakeholder Management:

- Discusses the challenges of handling numerous government and semi-government authorities and external agencies.
- Encourages future project managers to focus on honing stakeholder management skills, emphasizing the importance of public relations efforts.

Legal Challenges in Contracts:

- Describes the complexities of creating specific and realistic contracts, especially when dealing with multiple lawyers lacking technical expertise.
- Recognizes the role of experienced legal teams in navigating legal challenges during the project.

Testing Facilities and Risks:

- Highlights difficulties in setting up testing facilities on-site.
- Stresses the importance of providing provisions to manage inherent risks in infrastructure projects from the initial estimating stage.

Adapting to New Technology:

- Discusses challenges when the customer requests a shift to new technology mid-project.
- Emphasizes the need for careful management of changes, motivation of the team, and resolution of issues with stakeholders and authorities.

Team Training and National Security:

- Describes the careful organization of training and reorientation due to a major change in technology adoption.
- Discusses challenges in obtaining permissions for team members due to national security reasons, highlighting the involvement of multiple agencies.

Document Management and Logistics:

- Acknowledges the importance of a dedicated team for documentation, logistics, and transportation to prevent major bottlenecks.

Clarity of Purpose and Effective Communication:

- Emphasizes the necessity of clarity in project purpose and the establishment of effective communication channels.
- Advocates for professional project managers to prioritize quality communications for project success.

Management and Operations Control:

- Highlights the significance of developing excellent management control and operations control modules.
- Discusses the advantage of leveraging a strong background in these aspects for effective project review and control.

Case No 30: Case of setting up 'The Khandsary Sugar Project in an economically backward area of Maharashtra as a startup initiative by Renowned NGO

Dr Jayasri Murali, Dr Sarita Samson

Associate Professor, MBA@IICMR, Pune, Assistant Professor, MBA@IICMR, Pune

Extract: Renowned NGO, based in Pune, aimed to drive entrepreneurship in economically backward areas. Their project to establish a Khandsary sugar production unit faced scepticism within the organization. The project was initiated to provide local employment, create a market for sugarcane crops, and enhance overall prosperity in the region. The decision, however, lacked a comprehensive feasibility study and market understanding. Predictably, challenges arose, including political and market complexities, impacting the project's success. Lessons from this endeavour include the importance of thorough feasibility studies, understanding market dynamics, and anticipating external influences. The NGO's commitment to local initiatives remains evident through tasks like setting up market alternatives, social awareness programs, and engaging local leaders. Despite the setbacks, the project underlines the significance of holistic community involvement in sustainable development.

Introduction:

One of the aims of a Renowned NGO of international repute, in Pune, is to ensure that entrepreneurship-based initiatives are taken up in the economically backward areas in the country. This is with the hope of giving local employment to the youth in those areas and ensuring that the new venture becomes an economically self-sustainable model and the local population takes over the project in due course of time. Founded in 1962 with the motto "Motivating Intelligence for Social Change", its work now has grown into multiple directions &

platforms of social work. The main purpose of this organization is to develop leaders who can serve the nation by tackling & solving various problems being faced by India. Renowned NGO, headquartered in Pune, aims at the development of physical, mental, intellectual and spiritual qualities of people in general and of the youth in particular. This development should lead to leadership qualities, motivation building, and attitude forming leading to help solve the problems of India. This organization had previous experience of making a success of a few such initiatives in the past. The current project was being discussed to set up a Khandsary Sugar production unit at a location near Sinhgad Fort in an economically backward area.

The basic reason for such a project in this area is the fact that this area is full of sugarcane crops and many small farmers grow this crop as a regular item in their small farms and have small quantities of production. They had to spend a lot of money on transportation if they had to sell these small quantities to commercially managed sugar mills in the region. Hence these community leaders approached the director of a Renowned NGO to take up their cause and start a Khandsary sugar production in the nearby village. One of the rich farmers in this area was willing to give his plot of land at a very concessional rate to the NGO for this project. They said that the capital investment was very small (about INR 1.5 Crs). The Director immediately asked someone to study the proposal and without any feasibility study and due diligence decided to set up this project. However, there were many persons in the governing body of the NGO warned him that it was not prudent to invest in this project for the following reasons:

- Renowned NGOs did not have a specific sales organization with good market development experience at this stage of the organization and did not have sufficient funds to bear the loss in case of probable failure.

- The Sugar Business in Maharashtra is specifically controlled by the political lobby and it was impossible that the lobby would allow an outsider to enter this space in Western Maharashtra and would not allow any other enterprise to put forward their produce in the territory and succeed without their hold on the unit.

- The selling price of sugar was completely dependent on the Government panel's decision and not based on the open market pricing principle and there was no scope for a Renowned NGO to influence such decisions in the favour of the farmers from the small community.

- Additionally, the yield of sugar as such in the Khandsary sugar production is lower due to the inherent production process and the cost of fuel per kg of sugar is likely to fluctuate based on the sugar content of the basic crop. This means there will be a lot of pressure on the cost of production for such a unit.

Such arguments had very specific logic and strong arguments against the new project and many members pleaded with the director not to undertake the project based on taking the capital expenses and responsibility for the local production of the proposed Khandsary sugar. The director had his ideas about promoting the village-based enterprises for a larger social cause and hence decided to set up the project (and did sow the seeds for the failure of the project). Based on the sketchy and incomplete feasibility study and committed the funds for the project based on his gut feeling that the project will 'somehow' succeed.

The actual result was that in the next 3 years draining complete reserve funds of the NGO, the project had to be closed down with the loss of goodwill and a lot of money spent on the dream project.

Objectives of the project:

The main objective of the project was to initiate the 'Khandsary Sugar' project near Pune with the help of local people and ensure that the project generates sustainable growth and profitability for the village-based activity.

The main objectives of the project are specified below for quick reference:

- To set up a Khandsary sugar production unit in an economically backward area. This was intended to provide local employment for the youth and provide a local market for the sugarcane crop for the farmers nearby and help them prosper over the years and sustain growth for all.

- To set up a task team with the active participation of the locals to quickly alternate markets for their crop of sugarcane. This would save them the cost of transportation and provide solace to their anxieties every year.

- To set up a 'Social Awareness Programs Group' of local volunteers to help underprivileged people from the community. This was done well with the help and active participation of the seniors and youth from the local population.

- To establish discussion forums for the villagers through their local leaders to ensure that the right and true perception about the project was shared by everyone. It was expected that this would ensure their participation in the project.

- To initiate contacts with Corporate Organizations, Foreign agencies and HNIs (High Net Worth Individuals) to avail funds and support for conducting various initiatives in the area with the Khandsary sugar project as the base for all such initiatives.

- To identify, select, counsel and induct volunteers for the proposed activities of the new organization. This activity is not as simple as it may appear to be.

- To enlist and nurture the development of 'young volunteers' who will provide such services on an ongoing basis from the nearby villages.

The Project Director:

The Project Director- who initiated this task was a veteran social reformer and committed project manager. He had adequate experience and skills to manage such initiatives. His hands-on approach and quick mindset to size the proposed action plans to handle the task were major positives for the project to start. His speed of decision-making and organizing the activities was noteworthy. His charismatic personality and down-to-earth approach helped pacify the village people right from the beginning. He was able to mobilize a group of more than 40 volunteers within the next few months to work with him on this project.

The financial aid provided by the Head Quarter along with a group of additional volunteers was very useful to start work. One must mention that most of the volunteers were current and past students from Pune and Sholapur. They were groomed in a highly disciplined work culture and selfless dedication to work. This helped the Project Director to quickly form the requisite modules/work groups and each module was assigned a specific task for the project.

Another critical issue for the Project Director was to enlist confidence, support and participation of the seniors from the nearby villages in the project for the proposed project and this was done very well.

The challenges of the project team:

The following points were noted based on the interaction with the project team members and Project Manager. The researcher had an opportunity to meet the founding members and it was great learning from a project management point of view. The key issues are specified below for quick reference:

Internal issues and bottlenecks observed:

Many internal issues/aspects needed attention from the project team, especially for the PM. Some of these issues are specified below:

The main issue was that no one in the main / core team was trained in the 'Process and Design' of the Khandsary production unit. This was the main bottleneck for the project to take off.

This problem was tackled by enlisting the support of a sugar technologist in the team from the outside. Additionally, a two-member team was sent to attend the specialized sugar technology module for 2 months. This was useful but none of them could claim expertise at this stage of the project. The sugar technology in the meantime had prepared technical requirements documentation for the proposed project (layout with flow diagrams, schematic drawings and basic need for the capital equipment for the project). Such data was required for the proposal to be made to the bankers and this was completed in a hurry to catch up with the next sugar season. However, the core team had no working knowledge of the Khandsary Plant operations or what are the critical factors based on which the plant performance could be controlled. It was very evident that this aspect was going to make or mar the overall success of the project.

The main and urgent challenge was to generate activity plans and give a ray of hope to the affected villagers.

Along with the above project initiation plans, the leader made activity plans to enlist the support of the villagers. This was mainly important because their support for better cultivation of sugar cane crops with modern methods was essential for the input of raw materials (required quantity and quality during the main season). Along with this, it was also important to price the raw materials at affordable prices in the unit. This was a major challenge since the sugar selling prices were controlled by the Government authorities in a very turbulent socio-economic-political environment which was by no means any simple task to anticipate & handle effectively. The Project Director had to involve himself in this entire activity. The balancing act of 'better rates for the farmers and cost of input RMs' for the plant, was a tricky task. This issue continued to haunt the project for the entire tenure of the project. This aspect also led to the final debacle and failure of the project.

Enlisting the support from the locals was a great challenge in the initial phase of the project.

Around the same time, the Chairman-Sarpanch from the village gave his land as a gift to the project for starting the plant. However, he also had his agenda. At a later stage, many people claimed ownership of the land and they went to court to resolve the problem. This became a major headache for the PD. Based on untiring efforts from the Project Director such issues were finally sorted out but the NGO had to take an additional cost burden for such an event. This also resulted in unprecedented delays for the project and generated unnecessary tensions among the stakeholders, especially in the initial phase causing emotional imbalances within the members of the community.

Generating adequate finances through donations from Corporate Organizations / HNIs / other NGOs and the common man on the street.

One can easily understand that any such a complex and long-term project would require backing through financial aid. The parent body at Pune and Sholapur helped generate such funds within the first few weeks and this was the main bloodline for keeping the activity live (hence the project alive and active). At a later stage contacts with NRIs and Foreign Social organizations helped to keep the flow of money for the next few years and helped the organization to invest in capital costs. However, the parent body had a lot of hardships in providing such funds for the capital funds required. The cash trap continued for the entire tenure of the project. It must be pointed out at this stage that due to a lack of experience and exposure to the project management methodology, Risk Management was not carried out with due attention and this was the beginning of generating a cash trap for the entire project.

Enlisting support and Commitment of the volunteers at the senior level including the initial teams that joined the project:

This was one of the main challenges for the founding team at the beginning of the project. This problem was partially solved by the use of a network of the NGO and their past students. The problem was partially solved when a group of highly qualified volunteers and professionals (like-minded persons) decided to participate in the activities of the NGO. They committed that they would work with the senior members of the core team. However, they were not willing to shift their residence to the site where there were no facilities like cities at all. In such an environment PD himself decided to shift residence at the site. This was quite a step in his age group to shift his residence to the village. However, such a bold step at least resulted in initiating many activities and starting a proper site office for the project.

Lack of Project Master Plan / Activity plans and required processes routines and standards for planning:

This was the next challenge. One has to realize that sheer enthusiasm and dedication do not result in the achievement of the organizational goals and the success of the projects at hand. Many NGOs face this type of challenge and it is not easy to organize such efforts into disciplined methods of working. This is obviously due to a lack of training/knowledge and experience in the modern methods of project management.

In the case of such a project, where everything was dynamic and urgent, making detailed plans was a difficult task. However, on account of the vast experience of the Project Director and his alert monitoring of the situation this issue was addressed. Although the basic plan for the activities was prepared by the team during the initial period, one had to play by the ear to progress. Actions had to be planned based on careful planning, communicating with locals to enlist their support and the funds available for the next step. Such events in any project are very critical and flexibility in approach is the essential CSF for such social projects. One main difficulty due to the lack of a proper plan, is every activity tends to be critical and this is certainly not desirable and easy to handle. NGOs, by and large, are not well prepared to handle such aspects professionally, barring very few exceptions in the field.

Challenges related to Scope / Time and Costs and overall project plans:

The projects undertaken by the NGOs are a challenge indeed for many types of NGOs. Detailed planning and use of elaborate project planning and monitoring routes and methods cannot be deployed in such fluid situations. This situation gets further compounded due to the lack of ability to invest large sums of money upfront which is not possible for the NGOs. This project also suffered on account of such inability. NGOs are completely dependent upon donations from all over and the timing is unpredictable.

Such problems crop up because activities can be changed based on changes in live situations and need to be handled in flexible ways / innovative ways. However, it may be pointed out that day-to-day monitoring based on current live info is essential even for such extreme projects.

The plans and schedules need to be flexible and need to be planned per the availability of funds and resources available. This is an inherent problem for all the NGOs even now. This is possible to be solved when the predictability of the cash flows can be established in advance. The current project plans also were affected on account of this difficulty.

Challenge to set up the production unit:

This was a real problem for the unit since the day the project was kicked off and started as pointed out earlier. The project team realized that buying the entire plant was unaffordable and hence they decided to subcontract some of the modules (based on homemade drawings and specifications). This way forward was completely far from desired and was riddled with many shortcuts & slipshod methods. Due to a lack of expertise and shortage of funds, there were many compromises made in the technical aspects. This idea in concept appeared to be sensible but was proven to be a disaster right from the beginning. No one had hands-on expertise in 'Sugar Making' and hence the sizing and manufacturing issues were handled in an amateurish way and good money was spent after bad money. This should have alarmed many including the Chief and this was the best time to stop the project. However, due to insistence from the Director of the NGO efforts were still carried on.

Getting technical personnel on board as volunteers was the next challenge:

The technical and engineering work required for the project was quite onerous and involved hard work in an adverse environment (lack of workshop facilities, difficulty in transport, lack of communication facilities, hot weather conditions, lack of water and electricity supply for long hours) without adequate facilities. This meant that getting qualified volunteers for the project was quite a challenge.

However, due to the availability of a very strong network of volunteers through the parent NGO, it was possible to get a few highly qualified technical experts for the project. These people had adequate expertise and experience in similar projects. They agreed to make many site visits and helped the project team develop comprehensive plans and decide technical specifications for the project. However, the availability of good people continued to haunt the project forever.

Co-ordination with many agencies was also an important task for the project's success that involved the following main groups of activities:

One can understand that many agencies are involved in the operations of any such project activity and require close coordination and monitoring for the project team and PD / PM. The team had a lot of difficulties and problems while handling such activities. Such agencies involved many Government Authorities, Local & Professional Bodies, Municipalities Gram Panchayats and local village bodies. Due to diverse expectations from such entities co-ordination was quite a challenge. Soon after the initiation of the basic activities and availability of funds the pressure was reduced. It may be pointed out that all the government agencies and semi-government agencies (local and state level) were very considerate and provided all the necessary support. Without their active support completion of the project would have been very difficult but there was a lot of unnecessary effort for the project team to manage Public Relations with such agencies.

The volunteer base is at the beginning was good at the beginning but continued to be a problem:

This is a perpetual challenge for any NGO. They have to depend on personal contacts and carry out tireless efforts to enlist the interest of prospective volunteers who are willing to work for the NGOs without getting paid market rates for their time and contributions. These days many younger persons are willing to spend part of their free time on such efforts. This will continue to be a challenge for NGOs in general. Part-time volunteers, although useful, cannot depend on part-timers for serious and critical activities.

Most of the operational management was a disaster right from the first year:

One can appreciate that for any successful project, the core team members must be available for most of the key activities of the project continuously, at least in the initial few years. This is not so easy for NGO organizations. These organizations need very flexible methods of work and one cannot enforce corporate discipline in such voluntary organizations.

As explained earlier the plant operations started with great gusto but in the pilot run the yield of sugar was far below the industry standard in Khandsary Industry. Again experts were invited to solve the problems through trial and error methods which meant a lot of additional expenses. They opined that some of the production equipment was substandard and these had to be replaced. Again this meant a lot of additional equipment expenses (which were not budgeted). The fund shortage led to delays and hence regular production was postponed.

The problems were partially solved but then a major catastrophe struck the project. The Government regulations were changed and the cost advantage based on which the project was torpedoed. This was a major shock for the Director of Renowned NGO and he called an emergency meeting of the Board and it was decided to close down the project with immediate effect.

Although the intentions behind this project were noble it did not pass the test of 'Financial & Technical Feasibility' right from the beginning (as explained earlier) the project was a complete failure.

Professional finance services and legal matters are not affordable:

In the modern era, it is very important that any organization, public or private, has to conform to statutory norms and compliances. This task is not as easy as it seems. Such tasks need requisite professional expertise and experience to ensure that these tasks are handled judiciously and with due care. Such professionals are not necessarily willing to work without compensation and NGOs are not in a position to pay market rates for their services. However, the quality of accuracy and conformance to regulations cannot be compromised. This poses quite a challenge for the NGOs and this project was no exception for the same. It was becoming obvious that the NGO was attempting to undertake a task that was certainly beyond their innate strengths and financial abilities. This was proven right since the project was a complete failure despite time warnings against the idea right from the beginning.

Communication among volunteers becomes sometimes difficult due to a lack of knowledge of computers, the internet/email.

This point is already explained above and was difficult to solve despite certain training courses conducted and canvassing carried out by the leaders. This issue continues to affect operating efficiency for many such organizations even now.

Permissions from corporations, formalities and paperwork for the Charity Commissioner's office are time-consuming and tedious and take a long time for approvals.

The procedural and statutory conformance routines are one of the most burdensome matters for NGO organizations that do not have any source except for donations-based funding. Many volunteers are naive and do not have adequate knowledge or personality to manage such affairs smoothly. This can cause many mental agonies and impediments in the smooth running of such projects. In addition to this many local authorities instead of helping such NGOs add to the miseries of the NGOs. Their lackadaisical attitudes cause a loss of effectiveness and a wastage of resources at times. This aspect is a real pain for many NGOs.

NGOs did not have strong PR manpower and machinery to approach donors, keep follow up with past donors, and avail more funds:

For CSR funding also such machinery is necessary, but is non-existent. Presently fundraising happens due to the record of running the projects well and also through personal contacts of volunteers. On many occasions, such efforts are far from satisfactory and result in unprecedented problems at the beginning or during the execution of the projects at hand.

However, this problem was not faced by the current project because the HQ team had adequate experience in such matters and they supported the project teams from Pune and Solapur offices.

Data management and analysis is another area which is expensive and not well looked after till now.

This has been an area that has not received due attention right from the beginning of the project and even now continues to be rather a weak area, despite few attempts to improve the same. Such initiative is not yet stabilized, though there is some similar activity recently taken up, it is not carried out professionally since no one in the team has the expertise and experience to direct and manage such efforts. Professional help sought from outside also has not helped since the budgets are quite inadequate and not financed by CSR funding.

Based on the diamond analysis of the project classifications one can classify the project as specified below:

- Technology difficulty: T-2
- Complexity of design: C-2
- Novelty of the design: N-2
- Speed of implementation: S-2

About the project:

Sr No	Project Characteristics	Comments
1	Size of the project:	0.35 Million USD (INR 2.0 crore in today's currency rates) as Revenue +Capital Expenses (in the initial period of the first 5 years) based on donations from various sources in the society including manpower costs+ overheads + travel + incidental costs).

2	People:	The core team of 12 volunteers included 7 members in the founding team, consisting of reputed social workers, which expanded to around 12-14 members over the years. The total number was around 25 in the beginning and remained the same during the tenure
3	Schedule:	The original plan of 18 months was planned project period as per the Original plans but it took much longer time due to various difficulties faced by the project teams. The project was closed after 36 – 40 months.
4	Classification of project:	This is a case of a new startup by an NGO. Although the basic concept was already tried out in other locations in the state (UP / HP), this was the first of its kind NGO in the Khed Shivapur site. There were lots of risks involved in the concept itself.
5	High-risk project:	There were many uncertainties/risks in the project. The project was undertaken in a very hazy, aggressive and uncertain environment without the availability of enough know-how/expertise based only on hope and gut feel. Even NGO organizations need not be foolhardy about such projects. This was indeed a challenge. The project was risky in many ways.
6	Technology Choice	This was a major challenge as explained earlier. NGO did not have adequate technical experience, requisite business skills or financial bandwidth to handle this project.
7	No of suppliers:	For this project, there was a critical role for suppliers and vendors. They worked with a very positive attitude worked for low-margin contracts and helped the NGO efforts. However, they were also frustrated in the end.
8	Logistics / Clearances:	This was quite a challenge due to the time pressure to complete the basic facilities in time. The efforts were amateurish and the project faced many problems due to delays in this.
9	Location for co-ordination:	More than 3 locations (Pune / Khed Shivapur and project site). Coordination was difficult.
10	Support from Sr. Management:	Senior management provided excellent support. However, funding was a challenge in the initial period due to a shortage of funds. Similarly, there was no specific admin support in the beginning. The volunteers themselves were carrying out all the activities as and when possible. Initially, Admin Support & Motivational Support was received from the senior mentors as specified above.

11	Involvement of Customer:	There was mixed support / hesitant support from the village personnel in the beginning but people were willing to listen and help. Over some time they saw the quality of work and observed dedicated work done by the volunteers and they gave full support for the initiatives taken up. PM and the team had a difficult task of winning over their minds. This made the situation quite complex for the project team in the initial period.
12	Team Leader:	The Project Director / Manager selected was a competent/committed social worker of repute. This helped in the initial period. His patience and professional approach to social work helped solve many bottlenecks and impasse situations.

Key positions in the team:

The team had to be manned with the following key positions:

- Project Director / Project Manager as 'Project Champions' (The founders of this NGO).
- Team of social workers and technical experts with expertise in similar projects with social orientation.
- Tech Leaders / Discipline Leaders (2 initially and later over 4) for various critical aspects of the proposed project & modules.
- Technical experts / Consultants (Civil Engineering, Agriculturists, Architects, Technicians, Food Industry Experts and Workshop Managers, Non-conventional Power experts)
- Treasurers managing financial issues/funding and auditors (advisors).
- Trustees' office for project tracking and liaison with volunteers, teams and beneficiaries.

Positives in the project environment:

- There was full support from senior management and corporate organizations but the project concept itself was on loose footing leading to disaster in 3 years.
- The focus of the team was very specific and worked toward a detailed implementation plan in cooperation with the mentor. But the efforts failed and the project also failed.
- Continuous dialogue with Govt officials / Customer PM and local PM with resolve to address the issues immediately helped the team to complete the project in the required time. Focused 'Project meetings were conducted regularly (monthly/quarterly) to make strategic and critical decisions and move forward proactively. This was useful for the team.

- Harmonious teamwork paved the path for a good undisturbed work environment. This was crucial for the success of the project but did not bear fruit.

- The initial resistance to the project from the local people was reduced after the 'Steering Committee' was formed and they were given the freedom to decide their priorities.

- The team had full freedom for decision-making and commitment to expenses as per the decisions of the Project Team (Founder Members). This paved the path for smooth working for the team.

Project Success Criteria:

The project success criteria took into consideration customer expectations and organizational expectations:

- **Organizational expectations**

    - To complete the project in time without any compromise on quality of service.

    - To conform to stringent rules of the Charity Commissioner's office for the NGO operations.

    - To achieve the project delivery for the targeted population as planned by the organization.

    - To develop project modules as a model project so that they can become reference projects for future activities.

    - Getting repeat requests from various communities where services were provided was an important organizational requirement.

    - To enlist the support and active participation of the local people in the project. This was done well.

- **Customer / User Expectations**

    - To ensure timely delivery of the product (with proper diagnosis and medical care in every aspect of operational activities).

    - To achieve a committed target population and frequency of services provided with a level of quality and unshakeable ethics.

    - To handle emotional and social issues effectively in the core team and other participants).

    - To ensure the satisfaction of the team members Trustees / Volunteers / Staff and beneficiaries of the program 'the needy'.

    - To ensure team satisfaction and development of new skills/domain expertise for the future.

    - To ensure the sustainability of the project for the future.

Project Success Factors (as seen by the team members now):

Based on the discussions with the team members and their PM / PD it becomes clear that the list of the following points would have been useful for them as CFSs for this project. However, it has to be noted that this aspect was not necessarily thought about comprehensively before the project started.

- Clarity about the task at hand & clarity about scope and specifications with a flexible approach to work in the environment explained above (The director took the risky decision despite the warnings) that led to disasters.

- Commitment and participation by the core team members in the development of the right ecosystem throughout the tenure of the project life cycle.

- Complete support from the senior management & freedom for actions for project/module leaders (This was a question mark). Competent Project Manager & trusted Consultants and professionals/team members.

- Alert Risk Management especially in the form of timelines and scope/changes. This was done well but was not up to the mark at all times/stages. (This was not done well otherwise the project should not have been initiated).

- Control over project progress issues through good communication and coordination/reviews.

- Exceptional teamwork and untiring support from the founding members in the initial period.

- Good support from Legal Experts and Admin teams as and when required.

Conclusion: Complete failure of the project!

The project was evaluated as a great failure and the parent organization had to suffer a setback for the other activities in 3 years. It took them a lot of time to recover from the shock. The original concept itself had a lot of risks and inadequacies. Feasibility was not well established y and the project was taken up only on hope and gutfeel which was disastrous at the end. The Founder Director of the NGO Organization should have listened to the advisors who spoke against the project idea right from the beginning. NGO had to pay a heavy price for the failure of this project.

Key learning from the Case Study:

However, there can be great learnings from this project, in general, but for NGOs in particular in terms of what factors lead to failure and which are the obvious traps for NGO projects that must be avoided at any cost. A few of these aspects are specified below for quick reference:

- Any commercial project undertaken by an NGO has to be carried out on a professional basis (this is tough for many NGOs). However, if this is not the case the project becomes vulnerable and the chances of failure are very high. NGOs need to guard against such

- possibilities. Additionally 'Feasibility Studies' need to be carried out with due diligence and care. Failure to do this may lead to disastrous results.

- In modern times, initiating a project only based on gut feeling and a sense of commitment to the social cause is not the best step forward even for NGO organizations. Very effective 'Feasibility Analysis' is a must for NGO projects as well. If during the tenure of the project, some of the assumptions or factors in the environment change it may be prudent to re-evaluate the feasibility all over again before one may decide to continue the ongoing efforts. It is futile to run after the mirage and hope that somehow things will fall in line. The business world is not kind to anyone not even to the NGOs.

- It is also pertinent to note that there is a lot of confusion in NGO organizations, where competencies / technical skills are taken for granted based on dedication & hard work on behalf of the senior volunteers and promoters of such NGOs. This is a complete misconception and certainly not sensible for any modern project organization. This project has also suffered from such tendencies.

- When NGOs run commercially oriented projects it is important to establish the basics of the project feasibility and align required technical, business and commercial expertise before the project is initiated. Taking things for granted based on wishful thinking is not going to be effective in any case.

- Slipshod decision-making and hopeful thinking on the part of NGOs are not going to help successfully deliver even Socially Oriented projects. NGO Leaders need to learn from such disastrous episodes.

- Without a very rigorous feasibility study & realistic business plan, it is futile to initiate a new project in modern times. Gut feel, although important, is not good enough input based on which one may take the risk of starting a new unit. This approach has a lot of risks involved and chances of failure are higher for the new business unit. One does not have to rush into new business before proper assessment (short term & long term).

- One cannot take technical skills for granted in a sense any volunteer can pick up skills only based on dedication & hard work. Such thinking is not suitable in modern times and must be avoided. Developing & nurturing such skill sets with the help of experienced consultants is a must for technical projects, even for NGO Organizations. This is an important learning.

Additionally, the selection of the 'Core Team' has to be made based on a detailed analysis of the expertise, skill sets and attitude of the individual concerned. Failure in this aspect may lead the project towards disastrous results and failure. This case study indicates that such an effort was not done and this posed many problems for the project.

Discussion Points:

Professional Approach in NGO Projects:

- Commercial projects by NGOs must adhere to professional standards to avoid vulnerability and failure.
- Feasibility studies are crucial, demanding diligence and care. Neglecting this can result in disastrous outcomes.

Feasibility Analysis for NGO Projects:

- Relying solely on gut feeling and commitment to a social cause is inadequate; effective feasibility analysis is essential.
- Changing assumptions or environmental factors during the project should prompt a re-evaluation of feasibility, avoiding blind optimism.

Competencies in NGO Organizations:

- Competencies and technical skills in NGOs shouldn't be assumed but need to be established with expertise, especially in commercial projects.

Establishing Basics Before Project Initiation:

- For commercially oriented NGO projects, establishing project feasibility and aligning technical, business, and commercial expertise before initiation is crucial.

Learning from Disastrous Episodes:

- Slipshod decision-making and wishful thinking in NGOs, even for socially oriented projects, lead to failure. Lessons must be learned from such episodes.

Rigorous Feasibility Study & Business Plan:

- A rigorous feasibility study and a realistic business plan are prerequisites for initiating new projects; relying on gut feeling alone poses high risks.

Avoiding Assumptions about Technical Skills:

- Technical skills cannot be taken for granted; developing and nurturing these skills with experienced consultants is crucial, even for NGOs.

Importance of Core Team Selection:

- Selection of the core team must be based on a detailed analysis of expertise, skill sets, and attitude to avoid project problems and failure.